# More praise for
## *The Improvement Guide*

"We have used the work of these authors since 1994 to successfully operate, improve, and build a customer-focused and employee-oriented company. We owe them a great debt of gratitude. The improvements made to this edition, specifically about the role of leadership in improvement, make it a great resource for businesses of all sizes."

—**O. Joseph Balthazor,** president and
CEO, Hallmark Building Supplies, Inc.

"*The Improvement Guide* has opened my eyes regarding the science of improvement. In my role as a healthcare leader, I use the methods of systems understanding on a daily basis. The methods presented in the book have resulted in better outcomes and more integrated care for our patients."

—**Mats Bojestig, M.D., Ph.D.,** chief medical officer,
Jönköping County Council (Sweden)

"If you're frustrated by significant investments in improvement not adding up to better sustained performance of your business, you'll find *The Improvement Guide* to be of enormous help."

—**Ian Bradbury,** president and
CEO, Peaker Services, Inc.

"The methods described in *The Improvement Guide* have been instrumental to our efforts to continually improve quality and productivity. The second edition is a must-study for any organization wanting to sustain profitability in a challenging business environment."

—**A. Kim Brittingham,** site manager,
Lewes DE Plant, SPI Pharma

"If you are in a fast-moving and rapidly changing sector, whether not-for-profit or commercial, the technology taught in this book is organizationally transforming. It includes but goes far beyond 'lean.' We've incorporated these methods into our health insurance business and created a network of 'collaborations' with our doctor, clinical, and hospital partners to mutually transform a broken medical system together. Our experience found that these methods were enthusiastically accepted: the impact is profound and rapid. This book and the sets of methods taught here are robust and foundational to tactically and strategically being a rapid, continuously adapting, world class firm."

—**David Ford,** CEO, CareOregon

"The authors have successfully turned Dr. W. E. Deming's 'what to do' into 'how to do' in a simple yet effective and pragmatic way. We have used *The Improvement Guide*'s Model for Improvement at Unicard since 2001. Besides the results, the organization's great new ability to mobilize and transform itself has greatly impressed me. These characteristics bring a built-to-last capability to the company and renew our expectations regarding future results."

**—Carlos R. Formigari,** general director,
Unicard Unibanco (Brazil)

"Health care is a values-based system and must be part of a continuing learning process. The Model for Improvement provides ways for articulating, agreeing on, and inculcating values that focus on the patient, and it creates methods that have energy, so that we can be refueled in our own efforts."

**—Göran Henricks,** director of
development, Jönköping (Sweden)

"*The Improvement Guide* was instrumental in helping Armstrong World Industries win the Malcolm Baldrige National Quality Award and in helping HP reach industry-leading levels of customer satisfaction and loyalty. Combined with the expertise API provides in teaching and guiding, this has proven to be a very powerful approach to achieving performance excellence."

**—Bo McBee,** vice president of total customer
experience and quality, Hewlett-Packard

"Dr. W. Edwards Deming provided a timeless theory for management and transformation through the application of his system of profound knowledge. The authors have masterfully answered the question, 'How do I apply the lens of profound knowledge in my business or organization?' We have used the methods and tools from *The Improvement Guide* to make improvement part of every employee's job, with terrific results."

**—Roger B. Quayle,** senior vice president,
CH2M HILL OMI; Malcolm Baldrige
National Quality Award Recipient, 2000

# THE IMPROVEMENT GUIDE

## A Practical Approach to Enhancing Organizational Performance

## Second Edition

Gerald J. Langley

Ronald D. Moen

Kevin M. Nolan

Thomas W. Nolan

Clifford L. Norman

Lloyd P. Provost

JOSSEY-BASS
A Wiley Imprint
www.josseybass.com

Published by Jossey-Bass
A Wiley Imprint
989 Market Street, San Francisco, CA 94103-1741—www.josseybass.com

Jossey-Bass books and products are available through most bookstores. To contact Jossey-Bass directly call our Customer Care Department within the U.S. at 800-956-7739, outside the U.S. at 317-572-3986, or fax 317-572-4002.

Jossey-Bass also publishes its books in a variety of electronic formats. Some content that appears in print may not be available in electronic books.

**Library of Congress Cataloging-in-Publication Data**

The improvement guide : a practical approach to enhancing organizational performance / Gerald Langley . . . [et al.]. — 2nd editon.
    p. cm.
Includes bibliographical references and index.
ISBN 978-0-470-19241-2 (cloth)

  1. Organizational effectiveness.   2. Organizational change.   3. Quality control.   I. Langley, Gerald J., 1950-

  HD58.9.I467 2009

  658.4'063—dc22

                                         2008055670

Printed in the United States of America
SECOND EDITION
HB Printing        10  9  8  7  6  5  4  3  2  1

# CONTENTS

---

**APPENDIXES   355**

# FOREWORD

I am not sure what makes a "classic," but I am sure this book is one. It is, overall, the most useful text I know for the student of the modern approach to system improvement—accessible, sensible, systematic, and remarkably complete.

My journey into the world of quality improvement began in the mid-1980s. I was responsible for reporting on the quality of health care in the largest health maintenance organization in New England, the Harvard Community Health Plan. I was classically trained as a physician and as a health services researcher and was teaching both pediatrics and health care evaluation (statistics, decision theory, cost-effectiveness analysis, and such) at Harvard Medical School and the Harvard School of Public Health. I thought that I understood quality in health care, that I knew how to assess it, and that I knew how to improve it. I was wrong on every count.

Like most people with my training, I actually knew far more about fragments than about the whole; my understanding of approaches to quality of care came from what health care experts called "quality assurance," and what W. Edwards Deming would have called (as I would soon thereafter find out) "reliance on inspection to improve." The foundational sciences of modern quality management outside health care, such as systems theory, analytical studies and the study of variation, human psychology in production systems, and the epistemology of cycles of change and learning (especially *local* cycles), were not well understood or highly honored in the world of health care. Few of us were systems thinkers and fewer still had any theoretically grounded approach to the improvement of care beyond inspection and accountability. Health care leaders generally assumed that the growth of subject-matter expertise and scientific knowledge were sufficient for the growth of systemic capability.

Serendipity brought me under the wing of generous improvement scholars patient enough to teach me. My friend Paul Batalden started me on the path. Paul, so far as I know, was the first medical leader who really came to understand and value what Deming had to teach. Deming's four-day seminar followed (at Paul's suggestion), along with visits to world-class corporations outside health care. Most crucially for me, I formed what has since become a deep professional tie with A. Blanton Godfrey, who, when I met him, was the head of Quality Systems and Theory at AT&T Bell Laboratories. Soon thereafter he became Joseph Juran's hand-picked choice to lead the Juran Institute. In 1986, with a small grant from the John A. Hartford Foundation, Blan Godfrey and I started a National Demonstration Project on Quality Improvement in Health Care, and NDP remained for four more years the generative center of my own personal learning about improvement. I also served between 1989 and 1991 as a member of the panel of judges of the then-new Malcolm Baldrige National Quality Award, a cat-bird seat if ever there was one from which to study the best of the best in detail, in the company of some of the most capable improvement scholars and practitioners in the world.

As my network of mentors and my shelf of books grew, the field of quality management became, for me, first a country and then a continent. To this day, I remain excited by the vastness of the field and by its endlessly challenging intellectual texture. Deming's formulation of the four areas of "profound knowledge" (knowledge of systems, knowledge of variation, knowledge of psychology, and knowledge of how knowledge grows) is deceptively efficient, for it encodes more topics and more sciences than any reasonable human being is likely to master in a lifetime.

The problem is that managing quality is not just an intellectual endeavor; it is a pragmatic one. The point is not just to know what makes things better or worse; it is to make things *actually better*. In the world of manufacturing or service industries, it is organizational survival, jobs, and the fate of the consumer that all hang in the balance. In health care, it is all of that plus (sometimes) life and death. Modern quality management stands in the same relationship to the scientific disciplines of "profound knowledge" as modern medical care does to biomedical science. It is an applied field tethered to strong, formal science. Practitioners who lose touch with the science run aground; scientists who lose touch with applications fly off into irrelevance.

Moving from theory to application is so difficult that it tempts one to reach for what Deming called "instant pudding," by which I think he meant the quick and memorable formula that makes deep thought unnecessary and that takes uncertainty out of the picture. Countless consultants and airport-bookstore authors make a good living on instant pudding. It is attractive because it is easier than thinking. It is also, usually, unhelpful, at least for the long haul.

Finding the alternative to instant pudding is a daunting task: to build a bridge from the sciences of improvement to the practice of improvement without either claiming too much or collapsing too much. I wish that system improvement were simple, but it is not. Getting around is more like navigating Paris than like flying from Boston to Los Angeles.

Enter *The Improvement Guide*. I don't know how the authors did it, but they managed in this book to make proper improvement methods accessible without robbing them of their needed depth. They have neither oversimplified nor given way to the arcane. They put tools in our hands without claiming that the tools are magic.

The best of the tools is the Model for Improvement. With humility, the authors share their premise that the three questions ("What are we trying to accomplish?" "How will we know that a change is an improvement?" and "What change can we make that will result in improvement?") linked to learning through testing—the "Plan-Do-Study-Act" cycle—embed a significant proportion of the pragmatic tasks that can link system knowledge to effective redesign. This model is not magic, but it is probably the most useful single framework I have encountered in twenty years of my own work on quality improvement. It can guide teams, support reflection, and provide an outline for oversight and review; it is thoroughly portable, applying usefully in myriad contexts. The model gets even more traction with the use of the rich family of change concepts these authors have harvested from their collective experience, and that they summarize in their stunningly helpful Appendix A.

For more than a decade, I have had the privilege of working hand-in-hand with the authors of this book. They have become, and they remain, my teachers and my guides. No day in the year gives me as much professional satisfaction as a day spent with them individually or as a group, delving together into new problems at new frontiers, or, even better (when I muster the self-restraint), just standing aside quietly and watching them at their work. Encountering novices, they are patient and nurturing with the first steps of discovery; encountering journeymen, they coach with respect and joy; encountering experts, they remain ever open to the real dialogue that marks true scholars; and when they are meeting somewhere off on their own they share the thrill and camaraderie of the best of expeditions into the uncharted. The authors are not into catechisms; they are learners, and they have never met a doctrine that they weren't willing to question every single day.

This second edition of the book is a gift to anyone in the journey to the practice and leadership of improvement. It is the mainstay text for my own teaching, and its usefulness and clarity speak to the commitment to knowledge and to open-minded inquiry that its authors model for us all.

*February 2009*

*Donald M. Berwick, MD, MPP*
President and CEO, Institute for Healthcare Improvement
Cambridge, Massachusetts

# PREFACE

This book is for people who want to make improvements—or more specifically, those who realize that making effective changes in how businesses are run is a matter of survival. Change is occurring so rapidly in our society that we have no choice but to embrace it and make it work in our favor. We all have a choice to make: to accept passively the changes that are thrown at us, or to use our resources to create our own changes resulting in improvement. This book should be viewed as a survival guide for people who realize the importance improvement plays in keeping an enterprise viable. It is our hope that the ideas and methods presented in this book will guide you in increasing the rate and effectiveness of your improvement efforts.

As statisticians involved in improvement since the early 1980s, we have seen many tools, methods, and techniques presented as the one best way to achieve results. Many of these approaches indeed have merit. The overall effect, however, has lacked integration. Results have been mixed. In this book we hope to provide a fundamental approach to improvement that promotes integrated improvement activities that deliver more substantial results in less time.

Since the dawn of the twentieth century, a science of improvement has emerged. The intellectual foundation for this science was recognized by W. Edwards Deming and articulated in his "System of Profound Knowledge." Practical, pragmatic examples of the application of this science have been seen in industries throughout the world. Dramatic results have been obtained. However, this science has been applied in only a small fraction of the circumstances in which it is applicable. The purpose of this book is to describe a system of improvement based on this science that will increase substantially the number of successful applications.

In preparation for the first edition of this book, we studied the needs of people who were attempting to make improvements in quality and productivity in many diverse settings in the United States and abroad. They included manufacturing plants (for computers, food, and pharmaceuticals), hospitals, clinics, trucking firms, construction companies, law offices, government agencies, landscape architecture and maintenance firms, schools, and industry associations. As we observed or participated in these improvement efforts, we asked ourselves what methods would help increase the effectiveness and results of these efforts.

Given this context, we eagerly absorbed, enhanced when we were able, and integrated a variety of methods and approaches. In the United States, many of these approaches were introduced with much fanfare and in a way that implied the method replaced what had come before. For example, in the early 1980s the emphasis was on continuous improvement of processes throughout the organization. The idea was that everyone should have a chance to improve his or her work. This was a positive approach. The emphasis had two weaknesses, however: major subsystems—in particular, business subsystems—were not improved holistically, and the changes that were made were relatively small and produced only incremental improvement. When reengineering (major innovation in large subsystems) was introduced, it addressed those weaknesses. But it came to be seen as replacing the incremental approach to improving process rather than as supplementing it. Our approach integrates these ideas, and other worthwhile approaches, into a complete system.

## Second Edition

Since the release of the first edition, we have continued to work with our customers to research the crossroads of the theory underlying improvement and the pragmatic application of fundamental improvement methods. They are the ones who kept us grounded, who helped us take a pragmatic approach to improvement. They learned and we learned. With this second edition of the book, although the underlying concepts have not changed, we feel that we have presented a much more complete and effective set of methodologies for guiding improvement efforts.

We made the following changes to the second edition on the basis of many ideas for improving the book from readers of the first edition and reviewers of the manuscript: strengthened the focus on business operations (throughout the book); laid a foundation for the science of improvement in developing, testing, and implementing changes (Part Two); added chapters on spreading changes and improving large systems (Part Two); expanded the concepts for working with people in improvement (Parts Two and Three); provided more insight into the role and methods for leadership of improvement (Part Three); redesigned Appendix A (Change Concepts) to be more user-friendly; and added an appendix on improvement tools (Appendix B) and one for other improvement approaches (Appendix C).

# ACKNOWLEDGMENTS

Many people have helped us with this work or inspired new ideas. We wish to acknowledge our clients who have shown the applicability of the ideas and methods described in this book. Their willingness to test new methods contributed greatly to the material.

Noriaki Kano first introduced us to the ideas that led to the three categories of improvement covered in Part Three. Edward de Bono's work on methods for creativity provoked some new ideas that eventually led to the list of change concepts. We were also influenced by Brian Joiner's book *Fourth Generation Management* to use stories and examples to convey substantive concepts and methods.

Ultimately, it was Deming who, in the 1980s and early 1990s, gave the world the theoretical foundation for a science of improvement with his development of the System of Profound Knowledge and who inspired us to write this book. To him we owe our deepest debt, and to his memory we once again dedicate this second edition of the *Improvement Guide*.

Finally, we heartily express our appreciation to our families for their sacrifices, which allowed us time to do our research and to write the many drafts of both editions of the book.

*February 2009*

*Gerald J. Langley*
El Dorado Hills, California
*Ronald D. Moen*
Clarkston, Michigan
*Kevin M. Nolan*
Silver Spring, Maryland
*Thomas W. Nolan*
Silver Spring, Maryland
*Clifford L. Norman*
Georgetown, Texas
*Lloyd P. Provost*
Austin, Texas

# THE AUTHORS

All of the authors are part of a unique professional collaboration called Associates in Process Improvement (API). The aim of the collaboration is to develop and apply methods for the improvement of quality and value. The collaboration within API has benefitted individual organizations on six continents, in many industries, and the field of quality improvement in general. The collaboration has resulted in four books, numerous articles, and thousands of presentations. Three of API's current or former clients have been recipients of the Malcolm Baldrige National Quality Award. API's roots are in the theory and philosophy of W. Edwards Deming. Members of API assisted Deming at his pioneering and influential Four Day Seminar from 1980 to 1993. API's Model for Improvement is based on Deming's body of work.

*Gerald J. Langley* is a statistician, author, and consultant whose main focus in both his consulting work and his research is helping organizations make improvements more rapidly and effectively. His expertise with data and computers plays a key role in this work. As a Senior Fellow of the Institute for Healthcare Improvement (IHI), Langley has served on the faculty of numerous improvement initiatives in areas such as improving medication safety, innovations in planned care, and improving service in health care, but much of his work has been focused on helping reduce health disparities in underserved populations. He earned his BS degree (1973) in mathematics at the University of Texas at Austin and his MS degree (1975) in statistics at North Carolina State University. He has published articles on sampling and survey design, modeling, and fundamental improvement methods.

*Ronald D. Moen* is a statistician, consultant, and teacher to industry, government, health care, and education. He has MS degrees in mathematics and statistics and has given over eighty presentations and technical papers throughout the United States, Canada, Mexico, Europe, Africa, and Asia over the last thirty-five years. He is coauthor of the book *Quality Improvement Through Planned Experimentation,* 2nd edition (McGraw-Hill, 1998) and *Quality Measurement: A Practical Guide for the ICU* (HCPro, 2003). He is the 2002 recipient of the Deming Medal.

*Kevin M. Nolan* is a statistician and consultant with API. He earned a BS degree in mechanical engineering from the Catholic University of America and MA degrees in measurement and in statistics from the University of Maryland. Nolan has assisted manufacturing, service, and health care organizations to accelerate their rate of improvement. As a Senior Fellow of the Institute for Healthcare Improvement (IHI), he has served on the faculty of numerous improvement initiatives, including improving hospitalwide patient flow and improving performance in emergency departments. He has also supported a number of large-scale spread projects. He is the co-editor of the book *Spreading Improvement Across Your Healthcare Organization* (Joint Commission Resources, 2007).

*Thomas W. Nolan* is a statistician, author, and consultant. Over the past twenty years, he has assisted organizations in many industries in the United States, Canada, and Europe, including chemical and automotive manufacturing, distribution, health care, and social services. Among his clients is a recipient of the Malcolm Baldrige National Quality Award. Nolan holds a doctorate in statistics from George Washington University. He has published articles in a variety of peer-reviewed journals as diverse as the *Noise Control Engineering Journal* and the *British Medical Journal.* He was the year 2000 recipient of the Deming Medal awarded by the American Society for Quality.

*Clifford L. Norman,* an author and international consultant with API, earned both his BS degree (1975) in police science and business administration and MA (2002) in behavioral science from California State University. He has held management positions for more than fifteen years in manufacturing and quality positions with Norris Industries, McDonnell Douglas, and Halliburton. Since 1986, Norman has worked internationally in computer, health care, and manufacturing industries using improvement as a business strategy while developing internal consultants for these organizations. Norman helps organizations build productive relationships while viewing the organization as a system, and helps to develop their use and understanding of analytic statistical methods following the Model for Improvement. As an improvement advisor and faculty member for the Institute for Healthcare Improvement (IHI), Norman has been instrumental in developing and supporting the IHI improvement and advisor course. He is a member of the American Society for Quality and an ASQ Certified Quality Engineer (CQE).

*Lloyd P. Provost* is a statistician, advisor, teacher, and author who helps organizations make improvements and foster continuous learning and improvement. His experience includes consulting in planning, management systems, planned experimentation, measurement, and other methods for improvement of quality and productivity. He has consulted with clients worldwide in a variety of industries, including health care, chemical, manufacturing, engineering, construction, automotive, electronics, food, transportation, professional services, retail, education, and government. Much of his current work is focused on health care improvement in developing countries. He has a BS in statistics from the University of Tennessee and an MS in statistics from the University of Florida. He is the author of several papers relating to improvement and coauthor of *Quality Improvement Through Planned Experimentation*, 2nd edition (McGraw-Hill, 1998). He was awarded the American Society for Quality's Deming Medal in 2003.

# THE IMPROVEMENT GUIDE, SECOND EDITION

Because of interest in creating better continuity between patients and providers, a rural health care organization held a meeting to explore ways to increase continuity. (*Continuity* here means the percentage of times that a patient sees his or her own doctor, as opposed to another provider.) The organization had a small hospital with an emergency room (ER), a drop-in urgent care (UC), and an appointment-based day clinic. The organization for many years used a system of rotating providers through all four services (hospital, ER, UC, and three day-clinics).

At the meeting, one of the new doctors asked if it would be possible to not rotate providers through all four services, but rather have assigned providers for each service type. The idea was not well received by the leadership at the meeting: "We will lose providers if we do that. They all want the diverse experience. Patients are better served by well-rounded providers. It would not be fair for those assigned to the ER, because of the on-call nature of that work and the long weekend hours. This burden should be shared by all."

Someone else at the meeting said, "Didn't Dr. Shear quit last year because he wanted to be a full-time ER doc?" The new doctor followed that with, "My patients cannot get in to see me in the clinic because my schedule fills up so fast. I'm only in clinic four days per month. Instead, many of my patients try to see me at urgent care on the days I'm there, even though the wait is usually many hours. They do this because they know they can see me there. To get a scheduled appointment at the clinic, they normally have to accept an appointment with another provider."

Leadership responded: "We should be able to improve the situation by telling the schedulers to focus more on putting patients with their assigned providers when an appointment at the clinic is being scheduled. Also, we can send a notification to all patients encouraging them to schedule appointments in advance so that they can see their provider."

Much discussion ensued, and it became obvious that the issues could not be fully resolved at the meeting. So, when the medical director suggested that they try the idea in a very small trial, everyone agreed. They decided to ask for two providers to volunteer to be assigned full-time to one of the three clinics for one month. In addition, it was decided to survey all the providers to see if they had a preference for rotating versus not, and if not, which of the four service areas they would prefer.

At the end of the month, they held another meeting and discussed the results. They had collected data on several important aspects of the clinic: continuity, no-show rate, patient reaction/satisfaction, staff satisfaction, and several clinical measures, among them screening rates for depression, smoking status, follow-up on referrals and so on. Although the time period was short at just one month, the results were already overwhelmingly positive. It was clear that for the two providers in the test fewer of their patients went to urgent care during the month and their patients commented that they were able to get appointments in the clinic that were convenient for them and with their provider.

How can you make changes that will lead you in a new direction? With the small hospital in this case, the desired change was patients being able to see their primary care provider in the day clinics, so that patients could have better continuity with their provider. All improvement requires change, but not all change will result in improvement. The application of the concepts and methods described in this book is meant to increase the chance that a change will actually result in sustained improvement from the viewpoint of those affected by the change. Because of the central role of change in improvement, it is useful to contemplate what is meant by change and how it comes about.

People use the word *change* all the time, but it can mean many things. We change our clothes. We change a tire on our car when we have a flat, and the oil in the engine when it is dirty. We change a light bulb after it burns out. All of these changes are really reactions to things wearing out or breaking, reactions to problems. It is important to react to special situations when they happen, but this is not usually a source of improvement.

The provider scheduling case illustrates some common reactions to problems. The leadership's first reaction was to defend the status quo. The system is running the best it can, given the external limitations that are present. They were sure a change would make the situation worse.

The leadership's second reaction was to simply exhort the schedulers and patients to do better. They hoped for improvement without real change. Somehow, the situation would just get better on its own. One can easily imagine the undesirable consequences had they continued this behavior. Bad situations left unchanged usually do not stay the same; they get worse.

Despite these reactions, an idea was finally developed and tested that resulted in a very successful change to the provider scheduling. The characteristics of this development illustrate some of the more useful ways of making improvements:

- The change was innovative (relative to the current system); it fundamentally changed the system for the better.
- The idea was tested first on a small scale for one month to increase the degree of belief among the participants that the change would be an improvement.
- The change did not require undue restrictions on providers, staff, or patients; nor did it add any requirements or resources.
- The change actually resulted in a simpler scheduling system, to the benefit of the organization and patients; it did not add additional complexity.

This book is primarily concerned with improvements in business and other work settings. The objective embraced by many organizations can be stated succinctly: make changes that result in improvement from the viewpoint of the customer. In nonbusiness settings, "customer" could be replaced with "beneficiary," "organization's purpose," "family," or "individual." What is so difficult about accomplishing this objective? Why the need for this book, and others about improvement? These are some of the difficulties that arise in putting this objective into practice:

- Taking the time to meet the objective—time that may currently be devoted to carrying out the day-to-day business and solving pressing problems.
- Thinking of a change that anyone would predict is an improvement. When trying to develop a change, people often have difficulty imagining how tasks could be done or results be accomplished differently from the way things are currently done.
- Motivating participation in change. Even when an innovative change is suggested and shows promise, it is difficult to get others to try the change and adapt themselves to the new situation.
- Recognizing when a change is an improvement. The goal of this book is not change for the sake of change. The goal is improvement. No matter how long you ponder a change and plan for its implementation, you cannot be absolutely

sure that improvement will result. Changes must be tested, preferably on a small scale, and even well-designed tests do not guarantee certainty.

• Satisfying diverse or changing viewpoints. Customers may have varying viewpoints about what constitutes an improvement. Customers are free to change their mind whenever they choose. What is desirable today may be undesirable tomorrow because of advances in competitors' products or services.

You can no doubt add to this list, and despair at the thought of trying to make significant progress. While these difficulties are real, they can be overcome. Helping people surmount these difficulties is a primary focus of this book.

## Why Take the Initiative?

Why should you bother with making changes? Why not simply deal with problems as they arise and try to maintain the status quo? The theme of this book is making changes that (1) will not happen unless someone takes the initiative, and (2) will have a significant long-term positive impact. Change is happening all around us, in all aspects of our lives. Information is moving faster than ever. The skills needed to earn a living are rapidly changing. Many of the concerns that were important in our lives and businesses ten years ago have been replaced with new concerns. What are our choices, in light of all this change?

In business, there is only one choice: change faster and more effectively than your competitors, or you are gone. As the U.S. automobile industry found out in the seventies and eighties, being the biggest on the block does not ensure success. Japanese auto manufacturers developed better cars more quickly than Detroit thought possible. The U.S. automakers had to learn how to make improvements. They are still learning.

Ultimately, the answer to the question "Why change?" is "You do not have a choice." Change is going to happen. The choice you have is to let the change happen to you, or be more proactive and make the changes. Once you have made this decision, the methods and skills described in this book will help make your efforts more successful.

## How Is This Book Different?

Some practical, pragmatic approaches to the improvement of quality and productivity that rely heavily on the elements of knowledge in Deming's framework have been developed in Japanese and U.S. industries and in other countries throughout the world. Kauro Ishikawa, Joseph Juran, and Deming have been instrumental in documenting these approaches since the 1950s.

For an organization to be successful at improvement, it needs the will to improve, ideas for improvement, and the skills to execute the changes. This book focuses on the development of ideas for improvement and the skills and methods to execute change. Although our experience has shown that the act of making changes that result in improvement can also build will in an organization for change and improvement, the main responsibility for building the will for change belongs to the leadership of the organization. In Part Three of this second edition of the book, we have added material for leadership and building will.

The theory underlying the science of improvement (Chapter Four of Part Two) is interesting in itself. But improvement comes from action: from developing, testing, and implementing changes. These basic components of a system of improvement are dealt with in detail in this book. A brief introduction to the issues that will be addressed is given here.

## Model for Improvement

The foundation of this system is a framework that we call the Model for Improvement. The model is based on three fundamental questions:

- What are we trying to accomplish?
- How will we know that a change is an improvement?
- What changes can we make that will result in improvement?

The questions define the endpoint. Any effort to improve something should result in answers to these questions. The answers could be obtained in a variety of ways depending on the complexity of the situation and the inclinations of those doing the work. These three questions are combined with the Plan-Do-Study-Act (PDSA) Cycle to form the basis of the model. We designed the model to be flexible and comprehensive, because we observed some of the inhibiting aspects of the rigid, step-by-step approaches to improvement that have been in use.

## Change Concepts

Another aspect of our approach that makes this book different from others is our focus on change. Much of the book is concerned with developing, testing, implementing, and spreading changes. We recognized some time ago the fundamental relationship between improvement and change. By this we mean specific, identifiable changes, not broad or vague organizational or cultural change. The rate and extent of improvement is directly related to the nature of the changes that are developed and implemented. It is through this focus on developing substantive change that the *art* of improvement is combined with the *science* of improvement.

Developing changes that are new, by definition, requires a creative effort. Just for clarification, we want to point out that in most cases the use of the singular word *change* could be replaced with the plural *changes*. This is because in almost every situation change is not a simple switching of only one characteristic but rather of a grouping of changed characteristics (expanded in Chapter Seven of Part Two). However, for the sake of simplicity we have attempted to use the singular *change* except in cases where the plural is needed to indicate discrete efforts.

To assist people in making changes, we have suggested a variety of methods. Particularly noteworthy is our list of seventy-two change concepts contained in Appendix A. Three examples of change concepts are smoothing the flow of work, scheduling into multiple processes rather than one, and building in consequences to foster accountability. This catalogue of change concepts, along with real-life examples, is a major contribution to the science and art of improvement. This list allows beginners to have at their disposal concepts of change that would, up to this point, only have been found in the heads of some of the world's most experienced practitioners in improvement.

## Developing a Change

Some common approaches to developing a change, which are well intentioned but misguided, are making changes only in response to problems, developing changes that are "more of the same," and trying to develop the perfect change. The old saying, "If it ain't broke, don't fix it" is not a recipe for improvement. In a dynamic world, making changes only in reaction to problems leads to decline. To counteract or take advantage of forces in the market or changes in society, individuals and organizations must continuously look for different and better ways to accomplish their goals. Organizations that are averse to change are often slow to recognize a problem, and they may not recognize it until it is too late. Their inclination to avoid change, and their lack of practice in making real change, can cause them to deny the need for change even as a crisis approaches.

Many people who are unskilled in improvement react to the need for change by advocating more of the same: more people, more time, more money, more equipment. If crime increases, build more prisons. If sales decline, spend more on advertising. If profits decrease, work longer hours. If test scores decline, lengthen the school year. Though recognizing that increased effort or time may be appropriate in some situations, more of the same is very limited as a long-term strategy for improvement.

An inhibitor of real change is the search for the perfect change. It is believed that continued analysis and debate will eventually find it. The job will then be to implement the perfect change with a sufficiently well-thought-out plan. Because unanticipated side effects are always possible and objections to any change can usually be articulated, the search for perfection can continue endlessly. One result of this approach is an attempt to make very broad changes by relying on planning rather than on testing the proposed changes. Another possible result is a reduction in the magnitude of the change because of fear of unanticipated side effects. It appears that large organizations, both private and public, are particularly susceptible to this pitfall.

Alternatives exist to these three approaches to developing changes. This book emphasizes the development of changes that fundamentally alter the system to achieve better performance. The changes can be developed in one of two ways: (1) by examining the current system using, pictures, flow diagrams, or data, and—on the basis of learning and common understanding—identifying possible changes to aspects of the current system (in other words, by redesigning an existing system); or (2) by inventing a new idea, without recourse to the way things are presently done (that is, by designing a new system). Obviously, technology may play a part. Both of these approaches to developing change are discussed extensively in this book.

## Testing a Change

One reason for advocating "If it ain't broke, don't fix it" is that a change can make matters worse. What sounds like an improvement in the conference room may turn out in practice not to be an improvement. Systems often have delays built into them, so a change may even appear to be an improvement at first but result in serious negative consequences some time later.

The approach to improvement described in this book is based on trial and learning. Develop a change, find a way to test it on a small scale to minimize risks, and observe how the system reacts to the change over time. The change may be fine as is, or it may need to be modified or discarded. Whatever the outcome, something will be learned and the next test or trial will be better informed than the previous one. The pursuit of improvement relies on cycles of learning.

For some people, testing a change implies a large and exhaustive study of the type that might be conducted in a research and development facility or at a university. Such large experiments certainly are one means of testing a change, but this book will usually refer to less sophisticated approaches. In many organizations, changes and decisions are made without any reflection on the result. Our objective is to improve that situation. We offer methods for people to make a change on a small scale and study the result of that change using data acquired in the course of their daily work. The data may be as unsophisticated as collecting subjective impressions of people affected by the change at a meeting a month after the test has begun.

Some people fear that emphasizing testing will slow progress and give people a means to resist change. If a test fails—that is, if it is determined the change will not result in improvement—people should learn from it and develop the next change from a higher level of knowledge. Testing is not meant to facilitate a decision about whether to keep the current system as it is, but rather to promote continuous change and improvement in the system. Our standard for moving from testing to implementing is "satisfactory prediction of the results of tests conducted over a wide range of conditions."

## Implementing a Change

It is not enough simply to show in a test that a change is an improvement. The change must be fully integrated into the system. This takes some planning, and usually some additional learning. It is easy at this stage to assume that implementation is simply a matter of planning and careful execution of the physical change itself.

People who were not part of developing the change must accept it and help to sustain it. A balance must be struck between dictating the change and delaying progress until a full consensus has been reached. Some people will resist any change. It is difficult to know whether the objections are reasonable and the specific change must be adjusted or whether the objections are emotional and the process of change must be addressed.

This book supplies some methods to help with implementing changes so that they are sustainable. The methods will address both the physical and the emotional aspects of change.

## Spreading Improvement

In most situations, once a change has been successfully tested and implemented at a specific area or location within an organization, there will be a need to spread the change to other areas or locations. Although spreading improvement (change) to other locations relies on skills and methods similar to testing and implementing, it makes sense that the spread of change should be faster and perhaps more effective than in the original testing and implementing.

To achieve this desired increase in effectiveness and speed of change, five important areas should be considered and addressed:

- Strong leadership to ensure that the spread initiative is viewed as a strategic effort
- Better ideas with examples of change ideas have been tested and implemented successfully
- A spread plan, including a communication plan, a measurement plan, and a work plan are put into place
- The social system is considered in the communication of both awareness to attract adopters and technical content needed to guide the change
- Measurement, feedback, and knowledge management are used to monitor and guide the spread work

## Working with People

Although the topic of working with people in improvement efforts does not have its own chapter, it is a topic of equal importance to testing or implementing or spreading change. The reason it does not have its own chapter is because it is important in all of these activities. We have chosen to weave this critical aspect of being successful with improvement efforts into chapters on the activities and methods themselves. For example, in Chapter Seven on testing a change, a number of the ideas around testing a change on a small scale give guidance on how to work with people to make the testing successful. Similarly, in Chapter Eight on implementing a change, which has to do with making a change permanent, the people issues of motivating others to embrace the change are addressed. Chapter Fourteen in Part Three describes the people issues and methods for developing improvement capacity in an organization.

## Leadership for Improvement

Part Three is devoted to leadership issues and is meant to offer managers and executives methods for improving the value of their organization's product or service and thus improving their competitive position. Specifically, methods for connecting the improvement to the business planning are covered in detail.

## Structure of the Book

The book is structured in three parts plus several appendixes. Part One, "Introduction to Improvement," introduces the fundamental principles for making changes that result in improvement, including the Model for Improvement. Also, some of the basic skills needed to be most effective at improvement are described. The reader does not need to have any prior experience with formal improvement methods to be able to read and understand this part. Those with some experience in improvement methods should find this part a good review and will appreciate the fundamental nature of the principles and the simplicity and flexibility of the model. The book as a whole is aimed at audiences who desire to make improvements in businesses or other work settings.

Part Two, "Methods for Improvement," is concerned with the core of the science and art of improvement: developing, testing, and implementing changes. This part delves into the business applications of improvement at a more advanced level than Part One, including integrating methods for the improvement of value and a systems view of improving value.

Part Three, "Improving Value as a Business Strategy," discusses the implications for leaders of improvement. Change is organized into two aspects of leadership for improvement: connecting improvement to business planning and developing improvement capability.

Appendix A contains a rich collection of ideas for improvement (called change concepts) and examples of their application. To develop the appendix, we reviewed hundreds of improvements in which we have been involved or with which we had some familiarity. For each improvement we identified the specific change and the basic concept behind the change. For example, a hospital organized services around the needs of patients. By combining patients with similar needs on the same unit, they were able to locate the most frequently used diagnostic tests on the unit. This eliminated the work and delays associated with transporting the patient to a central testing area. The change was organizing patients and equipment by health care needs. The more general concept underlying the change was to "move steps in the process closer together." Seventy-two of these more general change concepts as well as several examples of the application of each are contained in the appendix.

Appendix B describes a broad set of tools that can be used within the methods described within the book. For each tool in the appendix, five aspects are described:

- What is this tool?
- Why would someone choose to use this tool?
- What are important considerations when planning to use this tool?
- What other tools might be useful in conjunction with this tool?
- What are the basic mechanics of using this tool?

Appendix C contains an overview of a number of other frameworks or roadmaps that have been used to guide improvement projects.

To make the book more readable, we chose not to break up the text with footnotes or reference indicators. Instead, the references are placed in a single location in the back of the book. You will notice that a reference contains information as to what page of the main text the reference applies to. In addition, we often put an explanation with a reference to help place the reference material in context. We did not isolate the referencing to discount the wealth of material that helped us in writing the book, but solely to make the book more readable.

## How to Read the Book

A relative novice to formal improvement methods could improve his or her ability to make effective changes by a combination of reading and applying the methods. The reader could start with Part One and begin applying the Model for Improvement to some aspect of work. Another approach is to read Part One and some parts of Appendix A to gather some ideas about the types of changes that others have found useful. As skill is increased or particular problems are encountered, the reader may want to read specific sections of Parts Two or Three. Appendix B can serve as a guide to tools that the novice may wish to learn about and apply in honing improvement skills.

The more experienced reader could quickly read Part One as a review of the fundamental principles of improvement methods and skills to support improvement. Part Two will give a firm grounding in the Model for Improvement that provides the framework for the methods discussed in the book. Even readers experienced in improvement will find in Part Two new ideas and approaches to making improvements. Those skilled in improvement will no doubt find in Appendix A many of the ideas they have applied in their efforts to make improvements. Nonetheless, we believe that they will be intrigued by the comprehensive list of change concepts and examples. We hope that this collection will motivate readers to add to the list and customize it to their own industry or profession. Appendix B can be used by the experienced improver as a reference for tools to support improvement methods. Appendix C will help the experienced reader understand alternative frameworks or roadmaps for improvement.

Although Part Three is aimed specifically at leaders in organizations, we advise them to read Parts One and Two as well.

Throughout the book, we have attempted to include substantive content that describes the essence of what improvement is about and how to accomplish it. We have also strived to make the reading pleasant and interesting by including many stories and examples to illustrate the concepts.

## PART ONE

# INTRODUCTION TO IMPROVEMENT

The chapters in this part of the book present a foundation for improvement by introducing the basic concepts of improvement along with a framework for all improvement efforts called the Model for Improvement (Chapter One) and some of the basic skills needed to become efficient and effective at improvement (Chapter Two). Examples of improvement efforts are in Chapter Three.

The reader need not have any prior experience with formal improvement methods to be able to read and understand this part of the book. Those readers who have some experience with improvement methods should find Part One to be a good review and will appreciate the simplicity and flexibility of the concepts and the framework.

## CHAPTER ONE

# CHANGES THAT RESULT IN IMPROVEMENT

Most people at one time or another have thought about trying to do something better. It might be at home or at work, in recreation or business, for friends or customers. Thinking about doing something better is often easy; actually making a change usually is not. What is the best way to approach trying to make a change that results in improvement?

## Principles of Improvement

Fundamental to the success of any improvement effort is the understanding that improvement requires that change occur. Unfortunately, not all changes result in improvement. It is this focus on change and an understanding of basic principles of improvement that leads to efficient and effective improvement efforts. In this chapter, we explore these two basic areas:

- What is a change? More specifically, what is a change that will result in improvement?
- What are the fundamental principles of improvement?

What is a change that results in improvement? Is fixing a burnt-out light bulb a change? Is fixing a flat tire a change? Yes, of course these are changes, but they are not the type of change that leads to improvement beyond what has been seen before. These types of changes simply reset things back to where they were. A broader definition of a change that results in improvement is needed. Think of a situation you have experienced recently where improvement occurred. Were you able to recognize the change that led to the improvement? Could you describe it? Could you "see" what was different? How did you know the change resulted in improvement?

What is meant by the term *improvement*? Improvement has meaning only in terms of observation based on given criteria. In other words, improvement is a useful concept when it is defined by characteristics such as faster, easier, more efficient, more effective, less expensive, safer, cleaner, and so on. Sometimes it is enough to observe the impact of a change on these characteristics, but usually it is best to document the impact (collect data).

Because the concepts of improvement and change are tied together so strongly, it is more useful to define them together. Fundamental changes that result in improvement:

- Alter how work or activity is done or the makeup of a product
- Produce visible, positive differences in results relative to historical norms
- Have a lasting impact

An example of an improvement effort helps explore these concepts and the fundamental principles for successful improvement.

> CanDew Cleaning Services, a company devoted to cleaning homes and small businesses, was started by two sisters six years ago. In that time, the company has grown from the two of them cleaning eight to twelve houses per week to an organization with four "crews" of workers cleaning approximately sixty houses and fifteen small business offices per week. Six months ago, just after bringing on their third and fourth crews, the sisters began to hear complaints from customers. In addition, two of their long-term customers stopped using their service. When they looked into the complaints, they found a number of problems, but poor cleaning of restrooms seemed to be a repeating issue.

The first two central principles of improvement are (1) knowing why you need to improve and (2) having a way to get feedback to let you know if improvement is happening. The first is sometimes referred to as the aim or purpose of the improvement effort. The improvement aim of CanDew Cleaning Services was clear; they first needed to make changes to how their crews were cleaning the restrooms to deal with customer complaints. Unfortunately, their only feedback loop was from customer complaints. Waiting to hear about quality problems from your customers will typically cost you customers.

The sisters turned their attention to developing specific changes that would address customer issues and produce better results. They knew, from customer complaints, there were problems with the cleaning of restrooms. However, they did not have enough information to know the origin of the perceived problems. The sisters decided to select one cleaning job from each of the four crews to inspect and photograph the restrooms. What they saw surprised them. Despite the initial training they had given to all of the crews, the cleaning of restrooms varied from crew to crew in significant ways (variation in order of steps or tasks, different supplies, level of completeness, and so on). The photographs allowed them to "see" the resulting differences in outcomes.

The sisters realized that their knowledge of the apparent quality problems was based solely on customer complaints. They needed a better way to see the quality their services were delivering. By picking a small sample of restrooms to observe, they were able to add to their knowledge about the quality problems. They saw specific areas where changes were needed.

Now that they had some feedback, the sisters were faced with the critical question: What changes could they make that would result in improvement? Of course, they had some ideas, such as getting all the crews to use the same, effective cleaning process and to use the same cleaning supplies. However, because they did not know why that was not already happening, they chose to have a meeting on the following Friday, at the end of the work day, with the four crews to discuss ideas for changes. More surprises were in store for them at the meeting. They found out that their original training of the crews had left many of the workers unclear about the work—for example, which cleaning materials to use on which surfaces or the order of the cleaning steps. They found that one crew had purchased some cheaper cleaning supplies to save money.

One crew member asked for a checklist for the cleaning steps, with all the steps in the "standard" order. This struck the sisters as a specific idea that they could develop and test very quickly. After the meeting, the sisters drafted a list of specific steps for cleaning a restroom, on the basis of their experience and knowledge.

The third central principle of improvement is (3) developing a change that you think will result in improvement. The sisters used the meeting with the four crews to generate ideas. The ideas for change have to be specific enough so they can be described and planned for.

Having a specific idea for a change is not enough. The change must actually be made and sustained. However, as was said at the beginning of this chapter, not all changes result in improvement. There is a tendency in all of us to jump straight from an idea for change (for improvement) directly to implementation. This is normally not a good approach. In fact, it can be said that for most changes going directly to implementation (that is, making the change permanent) without first testing the change idea in some way usually leads to making things worse.

The fourth central principle of improvement is (4) testing a change before any attempts to implement. Testing is a way to find out if the change is really a good idea or not. Testing, if done well, offers a way to learn about the impact of the change without risking uncalled-for damage to the system. Can you imagine the types of damage that might occur to their business if the sisters simply decided that everyone would start using checklists for everything starting on Monday? Here are a few questions they might learn the answers to by testing:

- Will the use of checklists lead to better-quality cleaning?
- For which operations do we need checklists?
- How detailed should checklists be?
- Will the use of checklists slow down the cleaning work?

Through testing you can learn about aspects of the change, so when you are ready to implement, the change is understood well enough to be implemented correctly and sustained. The first step to test a change is to *plan the test*. Planning should include the who, where, when, what, and how of the test and should include the collection of information during the test to let you know what happened.

> The sisters needed a plan for testing the use of the checklist. They decided to keep the test very small and use only one crew for one day. The plan included using the last half hour of the day for a review of the test results with the crew. They created the test checklist so that it fit on one piece of paper, with a place to write the time (hour and minute) each step was started and stopped. To begin the actual test, on Monday morning they met with the crew to explain the form and how to use it. Questions arose during the Monday morning meeting about the specifics of some of the steps in the checklist. They gave some guidance during the meeting, but they also noted the questions so they could deal with them more thoroughly later (and with all the crews). Several workers thought the checklist would slow them down. The sisters reminded the workers that data concerning time would be collected on the checklists.

The second step of testing a change is to actually *run the test*. This, of course, means putting the plan into action. A key to successfully running a test is to be ready to learn from the unexpected results of the test, as well as the planned ones.

> On Monday evening, they met with the test crew as planned. The workers shared this information:

The checklist form was hard to use in a number of ways:

- Got wet from being placed on damp counter.
- Took too long to fill out, with all of the times that had to be entered.
- Hard to write on some surfaces (for example, tile).
- Had to stop several times to find a writing utensil.
- Several steps did not apply to the specific job (for example, steps for cleaning a shower or bathtub did not apply to the one business job they had that day).

It helped to have the list; nothing was forgotten and rework due to wrong order was eliminated (for example, cleaning the counter top before the mirror resulted in cleaning liquid being spilled on the counter while the mirror was being cleaned, which meant the counter had to be wiped down a second time)

Two customers were impressed by the use of the checklist form

The third step of testing a change is to take time after the test to review and *summarize what was learned.* In this way, the actions that follow the test (especially the implementation of the change) will be based on knowledge maximized from the test.

The sisters talked about the meeting Monday evening and summarized things they had learned about the use of a checklist:

- The workers would need a better way to handle the checklist, to keep it dry and protected.
- A writing utensil and the checklist had to become inseparable.
- It did not make sense to collect the beginning and ending time for every step.
- The checklist needed more instructions to make it more self-explanatory during use.

The fourth step of testing a change is to decide *what action is warranted,* on the basis of the learning from the test. The action might be to implement the change, it might be to refine the change and test again, or it might be to abandon this particular change and look for others. In this case, the sisters decide to refine the checklist and the process for using it, and to test the refined checklist. The next few paragraphs describe their experiences through their second test of the use of the checklist (all four steps for testing a change are employed: planning, running the test, summarizing what the test taught them, and then deciding on the next action).

The sisters were pleased with the knowledge they gained from the test of the checklist, but they were concerned that there were too many problems during the test to begin using it with all jobs. They decided to refine the form and test it again. The changes they chose to test were to:

- Give every crew a clipboard for the checklist with a pen attached
- Group the steps into sections, so that only the beginning and ending times for each section were required
- Use simple checkboxes for all the steps (instead of beginning and ending times)
- Include some instructions in the form about skipping certain steps if they did not apply (such as no shower or bathtub)

They decided to test the new form on Wednesday with all four crews. Again, they had an early morning meeting to explain the use of the checklist and hand out the clipboards and forms. Many people at the meeting thought the use of the checklist would cause the cleaning to take more time, but most agreed it would be useful. Crews were scheduled so that they could meet for thirty minutes at the end of the day.

At the Wednesday evening meeting, this is what they learned:

- The crew who had used the earlier checklist on Monday said that the new system (clipboard and pen attached) and checklist form were better than what they had used on Monday.
- Again, several customers were impressed with the checklist.
- Contrary to predictions, the crews felt the restroom cleaning actually took less time using the checklist than when they did not use the form.
- Workers suggested several refinements to the checklist (clarifying two steps and adding one new step).
- The sisters were surprised by the positive attitude and reaction of their crews to the use of the checklist. They decided to implement this change for all cleaning jobs. Also they realized they should expand this idea to other cleaning areas.

The fifth central principle of improvement is (5) implementing a change. Implementation is different in that the questions being asked and hopefully answered during implementation are no longer about the goodness or appropriateness of the change, but rather about how to make the change permanent. The biggest risk with implementation is that the change will not stick.

To implement the checklist, they:

1. Edited the form to incorporate the suggestions made by the workers in the Wednesday evening meeting.
2. Had the checklist form polished up by a friend who is a technical editor and good with computers.

3. Had a supply of the checklists printed up (and purchased some backup clipboards).

4. Had a formal kickoff meeting the following Monday morning, where the final checklist form was explained and discussed. The process for using and filling out the checklist, as well as the sisters' plans for using the data from the checklists (times and items not checked), were presented.

5. Added a discussion of the use of and results from the checklists to their weekly Friday meeting with all crews.

6. Developed a short training program for new employees on the use of the checklist.

The implementation of the use of the checklist went well until a problem arose three weeks later. Three customers called and complained about the cleaning at their homes. The complaints were all from jobs done by the same crew. In fact, this crew had been considered the most reliable! On investigation, it turned out one of the crew members (the most experienced worker from all the crews) was sick that day. When the sisters asked about the use of the checklist, it turns out the crew had not really adopted the use of it but rather had relied on the knowledge of the experienced worker.

The sisters learned that making changes resulting in improvement is not a mechanical process. People are involved, and therefore people's motivations for improvement have to be considered. As part of testing and implementing a change, the reason for the improvement effort should be made clear to everyone involved. People need an opportunity to participate in the development and testing of the changes. After implementation, activities are needed to prevent the change from lapsing.

The sisters met with the crew having the experienced worker and talked about the importance of maintaining a standard of service that could be followed no matter who was working with whom. They also explained that they had larger plans for the checklists, whereby the checklists would become the pricing and bidding tool for new work, and that they would need this worker's help in testing these new ideas. The experienced worker was excited about this opportunity and assured the sisters that his crew would be using the checklists from now on.

Once people get a taste of successful improvement, they want more. It can be exhilarating to consciously and purposefully change something toward a particular aim. This is a good thing. The only danger is that the improvement effort may outgrow the original aim and feedback loops. Revisiting the aim and feedback loops may result in expanding them (as we will see, the sisters did this for the scope of improvement they wanted), or it may result in abandoning the specifics of one aim and creating a brand new one.

The sisters decided they needed to focus their attention on a more general approach to improving their company's services. To begin with, they formulated an aim for the improvement effort. They hoped that this would ensure consistency and communicate their intentions to their employees and customers. Here is the original statement of their improvement aim:

"In order to become the best cleaning service, CanDew Cleaning Services will continuously work to improve their services. We will do this by working to match our cleaning services to the needs of our customers. Our focus will be on cleanliness and reliability. We want our customers to know that they can rely on our services."

They went on to state several goals:

- "Our customers will be satisfied with the cleanliness of their house or business when we finish a job, and
- We will arrive on time and
- We will finish on time."

To support their improvement efforts, they started regularly collecting data from their customers. After each job, the customer was given a short survey to fill out. The survey was put on a self-stamped postcard, which the customer could easily put into the mail.

The Survey Postcard:

---

Date: _____ Location:_____

Did the cleaning crew arrive on time?

Were the floors and surfaces cleaned to your satisfaction?

Were the restrooms cleaned to a sanitary level?

Were your things left in an appropriate way (where you wanted them, in good condition, etc.)?

Did the crew communicate with you about any issues that needed discussion?

Was the job done on time?

---

The sisters went on to adopt quality improvement as a theme for their company. It was clear to all their employees and to all of their customers that change was a constant focus, but that the change always had a specific aim: improved quality of their cleaning services.

What if the sisters want to expand their services to include basic household repairs and handyman work? What if they want to add twenty new crews in two cities? Clearly they will need to adopt a more formal approach to their improvement efforts. Later in this book, we present methods that furnish this structure and formality, as needed. For example, there is a chapter each on the topics of testing a change, implementing a change, and spreading a change.

This chapter introduced principles of improvement that have been shown to maximize the results of improvement efforts:

Document an aim for your improvement effort, one that is clear enough to guide the effort over unknown territory and yet grand enough to excite the participants.

Make sure you have (or create) a feedback loop that can let you know if the improvement effort is actually moving results toward your aim.

Develop a change that you have reason to believe will result in improvement. The change has to be specific enough so that tests of the change can be conducted quickly.

Test the change(s) before you implement. Testing a change has four parts:

- Plan the test
- Run the test
- Summarize the learning from the test
- Take action that is based on the learning from the test

Implement the change(s).

In most business-related improvement efforts, there is a need to use a common framework for the improvement work. A common approach promotes increased effectiveness and efficiency in both the impact of the changes and the learning (for the individuals and the organization). The framework, called the Model for Improvement, imparts a structure for the five principles of improvement presented in this chapter.

## The Model for Improvement

The Model for Improvement is made up of a set of fundamental questions that drive all improvement and the Plan-Do-Study-Act (PDSA) Cycle. Although the term *PDSA Cycle* may be familiar to many people, it is, unfortunately, widely misunderstood

## FIGURE 1.1. THE MODEL FOR IMPROVEMENT.

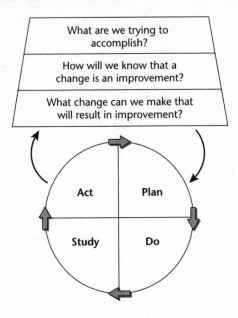

and misused. In Part Two of this book, the misconceptions and appropriate use are addressed. Combined, the three questions and the PDSA Cycle are the framework called the Model for Improvement (see Figure 1.1).

The three fundamental questions, the answers to which form the basis of improvement, are:

- What are we trying to accomplish?
- How will we know that a change is an improvement?
- What changes can we make that will result in improvement?

These three questions parallel the first three principles of improvement introduced in this chapter. For ease of reference, the three questions will at times be referred to as the first, second, and third improvement questions. In practice, the questions can be answered in any order. Although the chapters in Part Two focus on using these questions to guide improvement efforts, it is worth pointing out that many people have also found these questions useful in performing their day-to-day work. For example, managers often give their employees assignments that are not clearly defined. The manager assumes that the employee understands the aim and the expected results. Giving or receiving assignments by supplying answers or partial answers to the three questions would improve managerial processes.

To help people develop tests and implement changes, we suggest the use of the PDSA (Plan, Do, Study, Act) Cycle as the framework for an efficient trial-and-learning methodology. The cycle begins with a plan and ends with action according to the learning gained from the Plan, Do, and Study phases of the cycle. As demonstrated by the improvement work of the CanDew Cleaning Service, multiple PDSA cycles are often needed to make successful changes.

The use of the word *study* in the third phase of the cycle emphasizes that the purpose of this phase is to build new knowledge. It is not enough to determine that a change resulted in improvement during a particular test. As you build your knowledge, you will need to predict whether a change will result in improvement under the diverse conditions you will face in the future.

The model is an improvement framework, both widely applicable and easy to learn and use. As an introduction to a framework for improvement, the Model for Improvement has been found to support improvement efforts in the full range from the very informal (for example, the sisters working together to improve their cleaning business) to the most complex ( introduction of a new product line or service for a major organization). Efforts may differ with the complexity of the product or process to be improved, in terms of whether the effort is focused on a new design or on a redesign, on the basis of the depth of knowledge possessed by those people closest to the process or product, or because of the number of people involved in the improvement effort.

To support these potential differences in improvement efforts, applying the Model for Improvement will vary in terms of the formality of the approach. A more formal approach might increase the amount of documentation of the process, the complexity of the tools used, the amount of time spent, the extent of measurement, the degree of group interaction, and so on. Part Two of this book (specifically Chapters Five through Nine) discusses how the application of the model can accommodate these diverse activities.

## Key Points from Chapter One

- Improvement comes from the application of knowledge.
- These are the five fundamental principles of improvement:
  1. Knowing why you need to improve
  2. Having a feedback mechanism to tell you if the improvement is happening
  3. Developing an effective change that will result in improvement
  4. Testing a change before attempting to implement
  5. Knowing when and how to make the change permanent (implement the change)
- The Model for Improvement is a framework for applying the five fundamental principles of improvement.

CHAPTER TWO

# SKILLS TO SUPPORT IMPROVEMENT

As pointed out in Chapter One, making improvements requires change. For people to be better able to make a change that results in improvement, they could increase their knowledge of specific subject matter—for example, the science behind a chemical reaction, new methods to do surgery, or techniques to grow flowers. Knowledge of subject matter is essential to make changes that result in improvement, but there is also another very useful body of knowledge. It focuses on six skills to support improvements. These skills are described here and explored further in the sections that follow.

Supporting change with data: What is meant by the term *data*? How can we use data to guide actions for improvement?

Developing a change: Where do ideas for change come from? What should we consider when trying to develop change aimed at a long-term positive impact?

Testing a change: Why should we test a change? Can we increase the possibility a change will result in improvement?

Implementing a change: What is the difference between implementing a change and testing a change? What can we do to sustain the positive impact of a change?

Spreading improvements: How can we get wider impact from successful change? How do we attract others to make the change?

The human side of change: How will the change affect people? How do we obtain the cooperation necessary to make and sustain improvements?

## Supporting Change with Data

To make effective changes we have to be observant. Observation is an important source of learning while trying to improve. There are, however, some weaknesses associated with relying on observation alone:

- Our mind filters observations. We often observe only what we want to or expect to observe. We may not notice certain actions of friends but will notice those actions in strangers.
- Our present observations are affected by our past observations, especially those in the immediate past. A temperature of 50 degrees Fahrenheit will feel warm if the previous week's temperatures were in the twenties, and quite cold if the previous temperatures were in the eighties or nineties.

We would have a difficult time agreeing what the temperature is if we used only observation. It is useful, then, to turn observations into data. *We define data as documented observations, including those that result from a measurement process.* We can agree on the temperature because there is a standard process to measure it.

### Collecting and Displaying Data

There are many types of data helpful in making changes that result in improvement. Documented observation could include a video of a manufacturing process, an entry in a journal, or a written complaint or compliment. In the CanDew Cleaning Service example in Chapter One, the owners photographed the restrooms to understand the source of customer complaints.

Five types of data have been found to be useful in supporting improvement efforts: continuous measurements, counts of observations, documentation of what people think and feel, rating, and ranking. Examples for these types of data are shown in Table 2.1.

No matter what type of data you are collecting, the collection of data should start with a plan. Include in the plan:

- What data will be collected
- How they will be collected

## TABLE 2.1. TYPES OF DATA TO SUPPORT IMPROVEMENT EFFORTS.

| Type of Data | Examples |
| --- | --- |
| Continuous measurements | Temperature |
| | Weight |
| | Time to complete a task |
| Counts of observations | Number of people in a waiting room |
| | Number of scratches on a tile |
| | Number of patients admitted to a hospital between noon and 4:00 P.M. |
| | Number of complaints received |
| What people think; how they feel about something | Responses to the question, "Is this format for the newsletter easier to read than the current one?" |
| Ratings | A user rating a new procedure or a piece of equipment on its ease of use, on a scale of poor, fair, good, very good, excellent |
| | A patient rating on a scale from strongly agree to strongly disagree with the statement "I received care in a timely fashion" |
| Rankings | People being asked to place a one beside the item in a list they think is most important, a two beside the next most important item, and so on |

- Who will collect them
- When and where they will be collected

You can decide what data to collect from the questions you are trying to answer. Developing, testing, implementing, and spreading changes all lead to a natural set of questions. Some of those questions might be:

- Developing a change: What are the sources of problems in a work activity? At what time of day do problems occur? What do customers want?
- Testing a change: Has a change affected performance?
- Implementing a change: Is performance being sustained after a change?
- Spreading improvements: How many other sites have adopted the change?

The data you collect will help you answer these and other questions that arise in your improvement efforts.

A supervisor at the state's department of motor vehicles wanted to know what problems a new employee at the help desk was experiencing with his job. The supervisor and the employee decided to collect some data to answer that question. They believed the data would help develop changes to improve the

### TABLE 2.2. COUNT DATA COLLECTED TO HELP EMPLOYEE UNDERSTAND PROBLEMS WITH A NEW JOB.

| Things That Went Wrong | How Many Times |
| --- | --- |
| Interruptions | X X |
| Computer lockup | X X X X X X X X X |
| Did not know answer | X X |
| Bad phone line | X X X |
| Multiple calls on hold | X |

employee's productivity and job satisfaction. Together they constructed a form to collect and display data on problems as they arose. The employee collected data for one week. Both the employee and supervisor could see from review of the data, shown in Table 2.2, that the computer system was causing the employee problems. Further data collection resulted in learning that lockups occurred when the employee was accessing files from the network. The Information Systems (IS) Department was then able to make a fix they believed would eliminate computer downtime.

There are many tools that can be used to display data, and some are explored in this book. In this example, after the IS department made the fix the supervisor and new employee could collect data on the number of computer lockups to learn whether the fix had any impact. They could display the data on lockups each week on a run chart, as shown in Figure 2.1.

## Learning from Data

The employee and the supervisor at the state department of motor vehicles used data to answer an important question about problems experienced with accomplishing work. They developed a plan—who, what, where, and when—for the data collection and constructed a simple data collection form. They also set aside time to review the data. They believed they had learned enough after a week to begin to take action to relieve the problem with accessing files. They continued to collect data to determine if the changes made a difference, but they did not get caught in endless data collection before moving to test changes.

Learning often comes from understanding the themes and patterns in the data. Themes can be gathered from documented observations such as complaints from customers. For example, people who shop at a supermarket could register

## FIGURE 2.1.  RUN CHART ON COMPUTER LOCKUPS EACH WEEK.

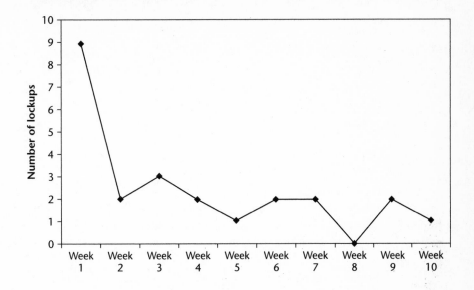

complaints about the parking, the checkout lines, or the selection of food. The manager of the supermarket might ask, "What types of complaints are we getting?" and collect data to answer this question so she could develop some changes to increase the satisfaction of customers. Patterns in data also arise in using the different types of data shown in Table 2.2. When dealing with continuous measurements or counts of observations, patterns are often easier to recognize when the data are plotted over time, as in Figure 2.1.

> Sharyn recorded the time she spent on homework each day for a month. She could see from a chart of her time spent studying that the reason she always complained on Sunday night about all the homework she had to do was that she did no studying on Friday and Saturday. Sharyn decided to find an hour to study on Friday (right after school) or early Saturday morning. After making this change, Sharyn no longer had to spend two hours or more studying on Sunday night.

Figure 2.2 shows the data that Sharyn collected. Plotting data over time maximizes the learning from data. It allows the information to unfold as it happens and eventually display a pattern. The pattern may show improvement if you are testing a change (as with data on computer lockups) or an opportunity for improvement (as with the data displayed in Figure 2.2 for Sharyn).

## FIGURE 2.2. MINUTES PER DAY SPENT STUDYING.

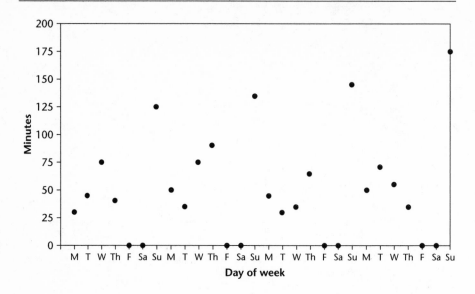

Our ability to understand variation in data helps us learn from patterns. We encounter variation constantly and make decisions based in part on our interpretations of that variation. Is revenue increasing? Is it time to have the car tuned up? Is crime increasing in my community? In the early twentieth century, Walter Shewhart developed the concept that variation in data should be viewed in one of two ways: either as variation that indicates something has changed or as random variation. Data that varies randomly exhibits patterns similar to those seen in the past. That is, the values are predictable within certain limits.

> Bill had been on his new diet for two weeks, but the scale said he weighed two more pounds than he had the day before. Bill knew it would take a while to *lose* weight, but he didn't think he should be *gaining* weight. He decided to give up on his diet.

Figure 2.3 is a chart of Bill's weight taken every morning for one month. The weights vary, but the variation appears to be predictable within a range of 164 to 168. Although Bill was not yet losing weight, the chart indicates he was not gaining weight either. If Bill had used such a chart, he might have decided to stick to his diet. A key idea behind Shewhart's concepts is that one should not react to each observation. One should plot data over time and observe the patterns.

## FIGURE 2.3. DAILY WEIGHT READINGS.

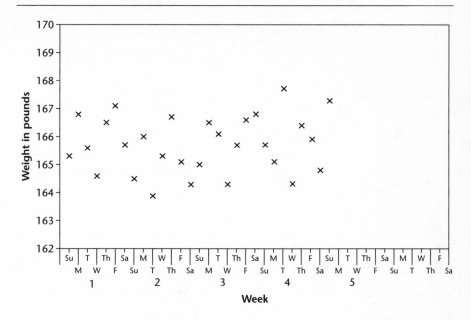

The administrators of the hospital were worried. The total number of patient beds being used was down. Some of the administrators said it had been going down for a while, others thought the drop was more recent. But the real argument started when they discussed why it was down and what they were going to do about it. They decided to plot patient bed use for the previous five years [see Figure 2.4]. The variation in the data indicated the biggest drop had occurred two years before, at about the time a group of local physicians started an emergency clinic.

If data are available from both before and after a planned change, a plot of data over time can be used to see if the change resulted in improvement. If the data depicts a random pattern within a predictable range, we should not infer that a change in performance has occurred. Shewhart's concept of variation can also be used to help develop a change—that is, help to answer the fundamental question of the Model for Improvement, "What changes can we make that will result in improvement?" Plotting data over time can reveal when the variation in the data no longer follows a predictable pattern. The chart may show an isolated observation or two that are outside the predictable range, or show a new trend. If the random variation in the data is disturbed by some specific circumstance,

## FIGURE 2.4. FIVE YEARS OF MONTHLY DATA ON PATIENT BEDS.

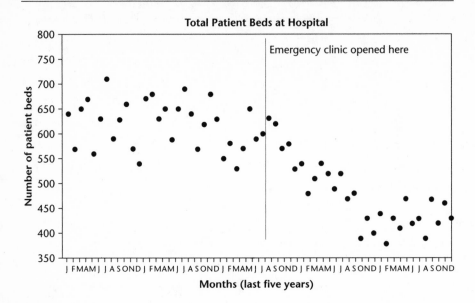

as shown in Figure 2.4, improvements can be developed by understanding what these special causes are. People can make changes to remove or overcome these causes if performance is worse, or continue them if performance is better.

The data plotted in Figure 2.5 were readings taken by a young man who was trying to learn to deal with his asthma. The readings were made to test for lung capacity using a Wright Peak Flow Meter. The man took readings twice a day for ten days and then one reading per day thereafter. On the thirty-first reading, it was obvious his lung capacity was reduced. He started his medication on that day. Collecting and plotting data helped this young man reduce the frequency and severity of his asthma attacks by allowing him to react quickly to special circumstances.

If the pattern of variation seen in the data is random within a predictable range, more fundamental changes are usually needed to bring about an improvement. Bill's weight in Figure 2.3 exhibits such a pattern. Bill made the change of going on a diet. He shouldn't overreact after two weeks to the random variation he sees in his daily weight. If, however, after a few more weeks his weight is not varying around a lower value such as 160 pounds, he may need to consider another fundamental change, such as regular exercise, to reduce his weight.

Although Bill collected data on his weight for a month, he had been on a diet for only the last two weeks. Although the first two weeks of "baseline" data (that

## FIGURE 2.5. DATA ON AN ASTHMA PATIENT'S LUNG CAPACITY.

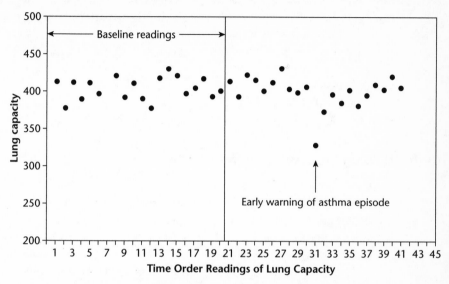

is, the level of performance prior to a change) are helpful, this is not necessary. If you don't have baseline data, don't wait to begin testing a change. It often takes time for a change to affect performance. Start collecting data when you start testing, and use the beginning data to understand the current level of performance.

# Developing a Change

Confronted with the need for change, many people first respond by attempting more of the same (more money, more people, more inspection, more equipment, more rules, and so on). If improvement results, it is usually costly and might not last long. The owners of the CanDew Cleaning Service could have responded to their need to improve by hiring more employees or increasing inspection. This would have added to their costs and might not have helped the service to their customers. The owners decided to develop and test a checklist to standardize the specific steps for cleaning a restroom.

Another ineffective response to the need for change is to try to define the perfect change. People often become so busy developing the perfect change that nothing gets done. You can imagine the owners of the cleaning service meeting for months, discussing what the perfect system for cleaning might look like. Although such planning might be useful, developing and testing a checklist quickly addressed the complaints of their customers in a short time period.

When developing a change, the focus should be on changes that alter how work or activity gets done. Changes developed should be detailed enough to test. For example, if "better communication" is suggested as a change, some detail around who, what, when, where, and how would be needed. We have found three approaches to be effective to develop a change that results in improvement:

1. An understanding of processes and systems of work
2. Creative thinking
3. Adapting known good ideas

## Understanding Processes and Systems of Work

A law firm was concerned that many of the talented new lawyers they hired each year did not perform up to their potential. Some of these new lawyers left the firm in the first year or two. After interviewing a variety of young attorneys at the firm and some who had left, it became apparent the orientation of new lawyers to the firm was haphazard and chaotic. It was obvious to the partners the firm did not have a standard way to bring new lawyers into the firm. They decided they needed to design a process for orientation.

The partners realized the importance of viewing all work as a process. A process is a set of causes and conditions that repeatedly come together in a series of steps to transfer inputs into outcomes. Driving to work, paying bills, and buying supplies are all processes people perform in daily life. Orientating new employees is a business process.

By thinking about daily activities as processes, we gain insights for making improvements. All processes have inputs, all processes have steps, and all processes have outcomes. An example of a process for obtaining blood analysis for a patient at a hospital is illustrated in Figure 2.6. The input to the process is a patient for whom blood analysis is needed, and the output is a report on the blood analysis delivered to the floor.

One could collect data on the performance of the inputs, steps, and outcomes of a process to help develop a change. For the process for obtaining blood analysis, one could learn what hinders patients from being ready for their blood work (input) or what the most common omissions are from the report that delay action (outcome). For each step, one could also identify where work is backing up or the reasons for rework or problems. Ideas for improvement could be developed and tested from this information. For an individual or organization just beginning to develop the skills of improvement, creating standard processes to replace chaotic and wasteful activity is an important source of improvement.

## FIGURE 2.6.  THE PROCESS FOR OBTAINING
## A BLOOD ANALYSIS.

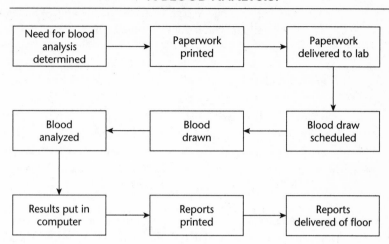

As people advance in their skills at making improvements, they realize that further improvements can be made by putting processes in the context of the system in which the processes are embedded. *A system is an interdependent group of items, people, or processes with a common purpose.* Driving to work is a process. Getting a family out of bed, fed, dressed, and transported to work and school is a system. Orienting a new employee is a process; creating satisfied, productive employees takes a system. In a system, not only the parts but the relationships among the parts become opportunities for improvement. The process of obtaining a blood analysis is part of the bigger system of delivering health care for a patient in a hospital. The process for obtaining the blood analysis may be flawless, but care will be affected by the timely and effective action taken for the patient on the basis of the analysis.

In a system, everything affects everything else. One area could make a change that results in improvement for some people but harm the overall system. From the customer's viewpoint, things could be worse. For example, the purchasing department may change suppliers of a raw material to reduce costs, which results in a lower-quality product and more returns from customers. When fundamental changes are developed, the interdependencies within the system must be considered.

## Creative Thinking 2.3

A group of nurses and physicians wanted to reduce the time and cost associated with patients recovering from hip replacement surgery. They were asked to consider doing some of the hip replacement steps in a different order. The team first listed and then rearranged the steps in the current process. This led to developing a change to begin some of the rehabilitation before the operation (prehabilitation). The result was improvement in many aspects of the hip replacement process. The surgery itself went better because the patient's body was in better shape (thanks to the prehabilitation therapy). Consequently, the patients recovered more quickly, saving them both time and agony.

Before the idea of changing the order of steps in the hip replacement process was introduced, the nurses and physicians assumed the order was fixed. They assumed that rehabilitation always comes after surgery. To develop changes that result in improvement, we often need to change our normal thought patterns. To do this, we have found several methods to be useful.

*Challenge the Boundaries*  People can be limited in their thinking by the boundaries they impose in a particular situation. To challenge these boundaries, begin by listing the boundaries within which a change must occur. Many times, the boundaries define the current system or how people view it. Real changes to the system are often outside the original constraints. Once the boundaries are listed, think about how they can be expanded, or even eliminated.

During a discussion among the employees and owners of the cleaning service, someone mentioned that the cleaning was tailored to each type of house or business. When this boundary was challenged, people started to develop best practices that could be standardized across all locations. The idea of a checklist evolved from that discussion.

*Rearrange the Order of the Steps*  List the activities involved in a process in order, and then move them around. Seeing the steps in another order—for example, rearranging the steps in the hip replacement process—can provoke ideas for change that the regular order prevents. This idea is really a subset of the first idea, because the order in which things are done is a boundary. It is worth mentioning separately because it is so simple to do and often produces new ideas. Once the checklist is developed for the cleaning service, rearranging the order of the steps for cleaning may generate new ideas for improvement.

A bank decided to change the way their ATM processed money requests. They changed the order so that the last step was the release of money, instead of giving the person's card back. This change eliminated the problem of people leaving their cards behind.

***Look for Ways to Smooth the Flow of Work*** Fluctuation in flow of work causes a ripple effect in all other aspects of the system. When flow is smoothed, things can get done more predictably. Restaurants often have early bird specials from 5:00 to 6:00 p.m. to entice customer to avoid the peak dining hours of 7:00 to 9:00 p.m.

> Bills were routinely held by each department to the end of the month and then forwarded to the accounting department for payment. Having departments forward the bills when they received them lessened the end-of-the month rush.

***Evaluate the Purpose, and Challenge Why You Are Doing Something*** Take a close look at the reason activities are being performed. This approach often produces ideas for change such as eliminating steps that are not vital to the purpose. When people have been involved in an activity for a long time, it is found that steps often have been added to the process or system that were needed at one time but are no longer necessary.

> A director of quality control signed off on every release of product from a small manufacturing plant. On account of her other job responsibilities, there was often a backlog of documents to review, causing delays in releasing products to customers. She decided to rethink this policy because she had not found any important errors in the documentation in the past few years. She met with the technicians, who agreed there was no reason for this extra check. The technicians would take final responsibility for the release of product. The backlog created at the director's desk was eliminated, and after six months there were no additional complaints from customers about out-of-specification product.

***Visualize the Ideal*** Describing aspects of the situation in an ideal state can generate new ideas for change. The phrase "Wouldn't it be nice if . . ." is an example of a visualization that can start the formation of ideas.

> An organization was experiencing long delays in responding to the many requests for its brochures. The requests could arrive through various departments, and each department would generate forms documenting the requests. The forms were then passed around (or buried in someone's in-basket) before reaching the distribution center. A team working to improve the process asked themselves, "Wouldn't it be nice if no forms were needed?" This question helped them focus on the use of the computer networking system to allow anyone to forward requests for brochures directly to distribution, without the need for any paperwork.

***Remove the Current Way of Doing Things as an Option*** New ideas for change are needed if the current system is not an alternative. Begin by understanding the current system. Then declare that a part or all of the current way of doing things can no longer be used. Let people explore the possible alternatives.

> Everyone believed that George kept the place running. Each morning, George would get the manufacturing schedule and go from station to station to make sure everything was in place to accomplish the day's goals. If a packaging line was down, George would rearrange the schedule to keep everybody busy. It was hectic, but it seemed to work—except when George was sick or on vacation. Efforts by the plant manager to get the production department to improve the scheduling process had met with opposition. People were afraid to disrupt the fragile situation. So the plant manager announced that starting in three weeks George would no longer be involved in scheduling. People immediately began to develop a new way of scheduling that required increased cooperation among the planning, production, and quality assurance departments.

It is helpful, when using the approaches suggested here or others to develop a change, that people are optimistic in first exploring the possibilities. There will be time to express critical thinking as the ideas for change are further developed.

## Adapting Known Good Ideas

When we use creative thinking to develop changes, we think outside our normal thought pattern to develop new ideas. New ideas for us, though, could already be standard practice for someone else. One small business might pay its bills by check while another saves time and money by paying bills online. One hospital may experience long waits to transition patients while another hospital of similar size uses better scheduling, resulting in few delays.

We should be drawn to examples of a high level of performance in areas we are trying to improve. Wouldn't we want to learn more about a hospital with low waits for patients if that was our problem? Reading journals, visiting other similar sites, or talking with colleagues could generate new ideas. There are also existing models (for example, the Chronic Care Model for care of patients with chronic illness) that have been shown to improve performance. As with any new idea, we often cannot just copy it but need to adapt the idea to our situation by testing.

We discussed three approaches to develop a change: understanding processes and systems of work, creative thinking, and adapting known good ideas. Chapter Six explores methods for developing a change in greater depth.

To improve, it is not sufficient to just develop a change. One must also test, implement, and if needed spread the changes. These skills are defined below and explored briefly in the next sections.

- Testing a change: Running trials to adapt ideas to a local situation
- Implementing a change: Making a change part of the day-to-day operations
- Spreading improvements: Having the change adopted beyond the initial locations

# Testing a Change

Once a change has been developed, it should be further explored and refined by testing. Testing is a way of trying the change on a temporary basis and learning about its potential impact. The idea of testing a change does not seem to come naturally. People tend to want to make a change part of the day-to-day operations immediately. Being successful at making changes requires a very different approach. Tests should be designed so that as little time, money, and risk as possible are invested while at the same time enough is learned to move toward full-scale implementation of the change. The PDSA Cycle, introduced in Chapter One, is a useful framework for planning, carrying out, and learning from a test of change.

> Parents agreed to help the teachers at lunch and recess during the next school year. Many of the teachers and the administrator wanted to write a letter to the parents simply informing them of their responsibilities. Janet convinced them to test the change instead. Volunteers from each grade were asked to help at lunch and recess at the end of the current school year. Janet explained the responsibilities and assigned each parent to work closely with a teacher. Much was learned during the three weeks, and a small guide for parents was developed. Janet was much more confident parents would be successful in this new activity during the next school year.

Results of a test sometimes turn out opposite from what was predicted. Unfortunately, many see this as a failure. The success of a test lies in what is learned from it, no matter how it turns out. This learning increases the likelihood that the effort will lead to a change that improves performance and is permanent. The principles in the next section should help with running successful tests.

## Some Principles for Testing a Change

*Principle 1. If possible, keep your tests on a small scale initially and increase the scale of the test on the basis of learning.* There is usually some risk when making a change.

Changes developed in a conference room often don't perform as designed in practice. By using an approach of sequential testing that starts with testing on a small scale, we can learn about the impact of the change and its side effects. Small scale is not equivalent to small change; rather the test is initially tried with one person, for a short time period, or with one component (such as a new form) of the change. The scale of the test is then increased as the ability to predict the results of a test improves. Once it becomes possible to predict the results of a change in different situations, consideration can be given to making the change permanent (see the section on implementing a change). It can be difficult for people to consider fundamental changes because of the risk involved. Suggesting ways to test changes on a small scale minimizes risk and often alleviates people's initial fear of change.

> The owners of the cleaning service decided to keep their initial test small and use only one crew. The plan included using the last half hour of the day for a review of the test results. From the review, they decided to refine the form and test it again with all four crews.

*Principle 2. As the scale of the test is expanded, include differing conditions in your test.* The circumstances faced during the test will not be the same in the future. So even though the changed worked well, it may not work next month because some circumstances will have changed. As you are scaling up your change, possible circumstances (staff on vacation, new employees, or different days of the week) that could affect performance should be discussed and plans to learn about their impact should be included in tests.

> Ryan wanted to speed up his process of delivering newspapers every morning. He decided to test the idea of reversing the order of his deliveries. Even though this meant starting at the farthest point from his house, it made it possible for him to pick up more papers from a central location as he needed them. He did this for a week. The results were that it took him twenty fewer minutes each day. Two weeks later, on a rainy day, he saw the flaw in his change. His new route did not afford him a way to keep his central supply of papers protected from the wind and rain.

*Principle 3. Plan the test, including the collection of data.* A test of change may not be successful because the test was not well planned. To plan a test, people should explicitly document what is being tested and who will do what, when, and where. This should include a plan for the collection of data. They should also be clear on why they are testing the change and what they expect to happen as a result of the test. This will be helpful as a basis of learning when the results of the test are reviewed. While the test is being conducted, someone should monitor the test closely to ensure it is being carried out as planned.

Although in classical research methods there are many sophisticated methods for running and analyzing experiments, these methods normally bring a formality and expense with them that is not practical in many business settings. Chapter Seven explores the concepts and methods for testing a change in greater depth.

## Implementing a Change

Because of a change in the county tax laws, the clerks in the tax processor's office were given a new way to verify tax status and calculate changes in taxes owed. Six months after telling the clerks about the new procedure, their supervisor discovered about one-third of the taxes were still being verified and calculated using the old method.

Implementing a change means making it a permanent part of how things are done day-to-day. Implementation differs from testing in several important ways:

- To implement a change, permanent support structures (training, job descriptions, standardized procedures, and so on) need to be created that increase the chances the gains will be achieved and sustained. Some temporary supports might be needed during testing, such as assistance in data collection, but these supports might not continue.
- Although the results of a change being tested are uncertain, only a change you are very sure will result in improvement should be implemented. Plotting data over time and viewing the patterns will furnish the evidence that performance is being sustained at a new level.
- Implementing a change will affect more people than the tests of the change. The test normally involves far fewer people. Successful implementation requires activities to address the impact on people.

Depending on the situation, change can be implemented in a number of ways. In very simple cases, it might be a matter of "just doing it." Implementation could be as simple as asking people to follow a documented diagram of the flow of a new process. Even apparently simple changes, however, have an effect on the people involved. This impact needs to be considered.

If the change is not simple, it might be implemented in parallel with the present system to lower the risk. For example, an online registration system could be implemented while still having the paper system available. Keeping the old system does have some potential consequences. Some people might continue to use it routinely, so consider taking away any access to the old system as soon as possible.

Implementation can also be accomplished in phases if a change has multiple components, such as the changes needed to improve patient access to primary care. An individual change, such as reducing the number of types of appointment, could be made permanent in a clinic while other changes are still being tested.

In addition to creating the permanent support structures (such as training) mentioned earlier, ongoing measurement and audits should be used to ensure improvement is achieved and maintained. Those involved in testing should decide the data to collect and the frequency of collection in order to support the implementation. Audits can be done periodically to see if people are adhering to the new standard process. Managers in the area where the changes were implemented should arrange these audits. More details on methods for implementing a change are presented in Chapter Eight.

## Spreading Improvements

A team of physicians, nurses, and staff of a large primary care clinic developed a system to drastically reduce the amount of time physicians were behind schedule seeing patients in the office. The team had tested the changes with some success. They communicated the changes involved in the new system around the clinic. Two months later, they were discouraged to find the system had not been implemented by any other teams in the clinic.

Although it is difficult for even one team in a primary care clinic to test and implement changes that result in improvement, the difficulty and complexity increases when the aim is focused on multiple teams or multiple clinics. People in manufacturing or in the service industry face the same dilemma. In addition to the skills of testing and implementing a change, a large body of knowledge exists on methods to spread changes. Spreading a change means having the change adopted by a wide audience at multiple locations.

To make the decision to adopt a change, people first have to believe the change addresses an existing problem. In the example from the clinic, other teams might not be interested in the new ideas if they do not think there is a problem with being behind schedule. To increase awareness about the problem, the team—with support from leaders of the clinic—could share data on delays in the clinic and stories from patients and staff about how they are affected by the delays. Once others in the clinic realize there is a problem, they will be more inclined to make the decision to adopt new ideas.

When the team starts to share ideas, they should consider Everett Rogers's attributes of an idea that facilitate its adoption:

- *Relative advantage* over the status quo or other ideas to achieve the desired outcome
- *Compatibility* with existing values, experiences, and needs
- *Complexity* inhibiting an adopter's ability to understand and use the ideas
- *Trialability* allowing ideas to be tried on a small scale and reversed if desired
- *Observability* of the ideas in practice

The foundation of spread is communication. First, communicate the problem and then communicate the new ideas. The communication methods used are very important. More general communication methods (such as newsletters to convey patient stories on the problem or success stories about the solution) can get people to make the decision to adopt. Personal letters can be used to share data. Once individuals or teams make the decision to adopt, more direct contact with successful adopters (for example, face-to-face meetings, mentoring, visits) is usually needed. Peer-to-peer interaction allows details to be shared about how to make the changes and raises people's confidence they can make them.

Not everyone will make the decision to adopt at the same time. Rogers refers to those who embrace new ideas first as early adopters. Resources can then be focused on these early adopters to build evidence for making the changes. Others will follow as success grows and the perceived risks decrease. If the team in the primary care clinic had used good communication methods to attract one or two other teams and then given support to help them make the changes, they might not have been discouraged by the lack of adoption of their ideas. More information on the theory and methods for spreading improvements is presented in Chapter Nine.

## The Human Side of Change

We can see from the discussion of developing, testing, implementing, and spreading a change that most change will not happen without the support of people. Focusing only on the changes themselves and not on their effect on people will doom improvement efforts.

Because most improvement efforts involve an informal or formal improvement team, members of a team (or at the least the team leader) should have some knowledge of running effective meetings, active listening, and resolving conflict. Adhering to simple principles to run good meetings such as having an agenda, designating roles ( minute taker and the like), agreeing on how decisions will be made, documenting action items, and ensuring all members are heard can have a positive effect on progress.

People will usually have some reaction to change. This reaction can range from total commitment to open hostility. Here are some guidelines that can help people commit to change more readily:

- Begin by letting people know why the change is needed. This should begin as soon as the ideas for change are being developed.
- Gather input about the ideas from those affected by the change.
- Continue to inform everyone of the progress being made during testing of the change.
- Share specific information on how the change will affect people once it is implemented.

People need to cooperate to make effective change. An organization that keeps a constant focus on satisfying customers will more easily be able to achieve cooperation from its workforce. People, though, will still be concerned about how the change affects them. In some cases, a person or group of people will need to take a loss or give up some control when changes are made. The improvement team needs to elicit, recognize, and deal with such concerns. They could agree to collect and share data on multiple measures that include differing points of view.

The staff was very concerned that the new schedule meant to reduce delays for patients in the clinic would result in longer hours and work days. In testing the new schedule, in addition to tracking delays for patients, the improvement team decided to collect data on staff overtime and satisfaction with the new schedule.

Some theory and methods on the human side of change are introduced in Chapter Four within the discussion of psychology and also included in other chapters in Part Two of the book. Chapter Fifteen focuses on developing improvement capability within an organization.

## Key Points from Chapter Two

- This chapter has introduced six skills:
  1. Supporting change with data
  2. Developing a change

3. Testing a change
4. Implementing a change
5. Spreading improvements
6. The human side of change

- These skills will enhance one's effectiveness at making changes that result in improvement.

CHAPTER THREE

# IMPROVEMENT CASE STUDIES

This chapter presents five examples of improvement initiatives that use the framework in Chapters One and Two to structure the effort. These improvement stories are not meant to portray perfect applications of the methods presented in those chapters; rather, they are meant to convey realistic first attempts to use them. The five case studies are:

1. Improving the morning meeting
2. Improving service in a dental office
3. Teaching biology
4. Contamination in shipping drums
5. Reducing energy use in a school

Case studies 1 and 2 were created on the basis of experiences from multiple sources, while case studies 3, 4, and 5 were extracted from specific improvement efforts. A discussion of the use of the most relevant of the six skills from Chapter Two is included after each case study.

## Case Study 1: Improving the Morning Meeting

The owner of a construction company was frustrated by the recent difficulties experienced by managers and site supervisors at their daily morning meeting. For the last three years, this meeting had played a central role in making the business successful. All managers and key personnel attended the meeting in the warehouse next to the offices so that the work of the company would be coordinated. The department managers took turns furnishing breakfast at the meetings. It was this opportunity for everyone to experience and deal with the whole system that had made the company successful. Any issues and problems that needed to be addressed were surfaced and dealt with at the meeting. Also discussed at the meeting was the scheduling of materials and labor for the company's various projects and key changes requested by customers.

But recently, there never seemed to be enough time to discuss all the important issues. Arguments would sometimes occur, and tempers would flare. When this happened, the rest of the meeting would be devoted to resolving the issue and trying to get everyone to agree to move forward. Recently one of the best site supervisors stormed out in the middle of the meeting, saying, "We're just wasting our time here." The meetings would often run past the scheduled one and a half hours. The company had almost doubled its business in the previous year, but the frustrating morning meetings were affecting morale and beginning to visibly hurt the quality of the company's work.

The owner introduced the idea of improving their morning meetings to his management team. He asked the three improvement questions, and the discussion converged to these answers.

## What Are We Trying to Accomplish?

Investigate ways to make the daily meeting more effective, and to not run over scheduled time.

## How Will We Know That a Change Is an Improvement?

Monitor the length of time of each meeting, the number of items or topics covered, and a using scale of 1 to 5, "How was the meeting?" assessment as measures of improvement.

## What Changes Can We Make That Will Result in Improvement?

The attendees at the next morning meeting brainstormed a list of changes they thought would result in improvement:

Have fewer people at the meetings
Meet less often
Prepare and use an agenda
Give assignments to prepare for the meeting

Quit having the meetings, and everybody solve their own problems

Limit the meeting time for each issue

Make decisions by voting

End the meeting at eight o'clock, no matter what

Have the owner be more of a dictator during the meeting

Keep notes of the meeting and distribute for review and follow-up

Limit issues to critical ones (minor issues to be worked out in smaller groups)

The owner was originally upset by several of the ideas for change, which seemed negative about even holding the meetings. Then he realized he could use the suggestion "quit having the meetings" as provocation to himself and others to start thinking about ideas for improvement.

During a conversation with the purchasing manager after work that day, the owner suddenly saw a path to follow. The purchasing manager was talking about the process for ordering all their construction materials and equipment. He was describing changes that the purchasing staff had made to their process, and the owner realized there was no process for preparing and running the morning meeting. They just started the conversation and let things happen as they might. Compared to the process of ordering materials, their meetings were chaos. The owner wondered why the activities for ordering materials should be so clear to everyone, while a critical morning meeting was run in such a haphazard fashion. He saw that many of the ideas suggested to improve the meeting could fit together to form a standard process.

## PDSA Cycle 1

**Plan.** The owner and two of his managers spent a Saturday morning designing a meeting process. They incorporated several of the change ideas into the process, including setting an agenda, reducing the frequency of the meetings (Monday, Wednesday, and Friday), scheduling the meetings for two hours, making assignments before the meeting, submitting topics the day before the meeting to be included in the agenda, and assigning roles during the meeting (someone to take notes, keep time, and collect data). They predicted that this new process would increase effectiveness and cut the weekly meeting time in half. They decided to document the new process and give it out to all the other managers and supervisors for comment.

**Do.** It took more than a week to get comments back from everyone.

**Study.** Everyone was worried about the time to complete assignments before the meetings and having to submit agenda topics the day before. Most of the managers and supervisors felt that they would not know what the critical issues were the day before. Some were also concerned about being asked to fill a role (such as note taker) during the meeting.

**Act.** The owner felt that the concerns were due to fear of change, so he decided to go ahead with the new ideas for the meeting. He made a few clarifications to the meeting process and prepared copies to hand out at the Monday morning meeting.

## PDSA Cycle 2

**Plan.** At the Monday meeting, the owner handed out the updated description of the meeting process and asked everyone to participate in a test of the process on Friday (the process included meetings only on Monday, Wednesday, and Friday). If an agenda topic was not submitted ahead of time, it would not be covered in the meeting on Monday. Joe was assigned to take notes at the meeting, Mary agreed to keep the meeting on time schedule and collect data, and the owner volunteered to put together the agenda late in the afternoon. Everyone predicted a short meeting.

**Do.** Only one topic was submitted that Friday, so the agenda the owner wrote only two items: resolve scheduling problems for the construction site at the college, and figure out why only one agenda topic was turned in.

The meeting was indeed short. The scheduling problem took twenty minutes, but the discussion about submitting agenda topics was even shorter. People said there were issues they would like to have on the agenda but they were unsure of the format for submitting them. (Several people said they felt stupid giving the owner some notes scribbled on the back of a napkin, but was that OK?) Everyone agreed to test a form for the next meeting that Joe volunteered to design.

**Study.** The meeting was short, but for the wrong reason. Issues that should have been discussed were not because people were not comfortable and familiar with the new process. The quality ratings from the attendees ranged from 1 (not at all successful) to 3 (neutral) on the 1–5 scale. The owner saw that other pieces of the process would have to be defined and meeting attendees would need some time to get used to it.

**Act.** Joe designed a standard, simple form for submitting topics, which was used in preparation for the Wednesday meeting. Everyone was to submit at least one topic, even if it was not critical.

## PDSA Cycle 3

**Plan.** The owner would gather the submitted topics from everyone and construct an agenda on Tuesday afternoon for the Wednesday morning meeting. Everyone would receive a copy of the agenda to prepare for the meeting. Again, Joe volunteered to keep notes and Mary agreed to keep track of time and collect other data. Because everyone had been asked to estimate the amount of time for his or her topic, the owner used these estimates to set the timing for the agenda.

**Do.** The meeting went well. It lasted two hours. All fifteen topics on the agenda were covered, most in less time than planned. Only one topic was not finished in its allotted time. The group decided to finish it on Friday as per the process.

**Study.** One reason the meeting went well was that knowing ahead of time what the topics would be allowed people to study and bring information that was helpful to resolving the issue. Everyone agreed that this element alone made the new process worthwhile. They had never been able to resolve more than five issues at any one meeting before. In this meeting, fourteen issues were resolved, and one was to be continued. The quality ratings were all 4s and 5s—a very successful meeting (except for a 3 from a supervisor who did not like it that everyone would not stay longer to get his issue resolved).

**Act.** Everyone was ready to commit to the new meeting process. They would continue to refine the process, as appropriate.

## PDSA Cycle 4

**Plan.** The owner used this fourth PDSA cycle to implement the new meeting process in the company. Plans were made to make the process sustainable.

**Do.** The description of the process was included in the company procedures manual. A soft copy of the topic form was put on the intranet system. The orientation process was updated to include an overview of the process for future new managers. Run charts of the length of time, number of topics covered, and average quality rating were developed and updated at the end of each meeting.

**Study.** The meeting process continued to work well. Minor changes were made during the next six months and the process description was updated. The run chart for number of topics covered indicated a lower number during the period when contract negotiations were going on.

**Act.** Continue to reap the benefits of the improved meeting process:

- Effective issue resolution from this critical company activity
- Total time meeting each week reduced by 58 percent
- Improved morale for job supervisors, who now have a method to get their issues on the meeting agenda

Some of the managers began to think about other company activities that could benefit from some process thinking.

## Discussion of Case Study 1

The three improvement questions helped the owner focus his management team on improving their morning meetings.

**Supporting change with data.** Although the management team did specify measures they would track to measure the impact of any change they would try, initially they did not look at the data over time. Later, when they plotted the data, it was easy to see the improvement (the baseline data was developed from the owner's notes and calendar). Figure 3.1 shows the effect of the change and the pattern that developed after the change. The three weekly meetings lasted typically about one hour and twenty minutes and covered an average of 6.8 topics. The average quality rating ("How was the meeting?") stabilized above 4 on the 5-point scale.

**Developing a change.** The brainstorming session alone did not produce new ideas for change, but the attendees did avoid just adding more of the same (more time, more people, and so on). Further thought about change was stimulated by use of the provocative suggestion "Quit having the meeting." It was only when the owner was outside his normal area of thinking that he had the insight for a change. The breakthrough was his realizing that the morning meeting was a process. Improvement was achieved by designing and standardizing the meeting process.

**Testing a change.** The owner and his management team used multiple PDSA cycles to test the change. Their testing was very small-scale in cycle 1. They simply asked the meeting participants to visualize using the process and comment on it. Cycle 2 could have been on a smaller scale; they could have applied the new meeting process to a shorter meeting with fewer people. The problem with submitting topics would have surfaced and the Monday morning meeting would have been more productive. The risk, however, was relatively low. Once there was a lack of topics on the agenda, the problem was addressed immediately.

**Implementing a change.** The first three cycles all dealt with testing a change. Cycle 4 was used to implement the change. The implementation cycle addressed ways to make the morning meeting process permanent. Continuation of the run charts was used to provide ongoing feedback that the process was still working.

**The human side of change.** Working with others was a key issue in this improvement effort. How could the owner have created more cooperation? Is he still going to have trouble getting some of his managers and supervisors to fill some of the roles in the meetings (note taker, timekeeper, and so on)? Although the owner asked everyone to comment on the new process, if he had gotten other meeting participants involved in designing it then support and participation would have been stronger.

## Case Study 2: Improving Service in a Dental Office

Beth, a dentist, wanted to improve the service to her patients. She had a good reputation for quality of work; she was known for taking great care and time to see

# FIGURE 3.1. RUN CHARTS OF KEY MEASURES FOR MORNING MEETINGS.

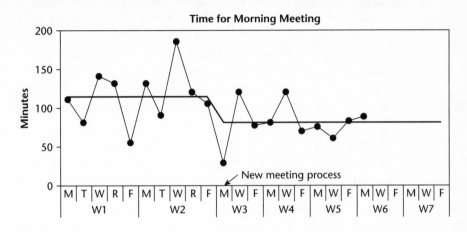

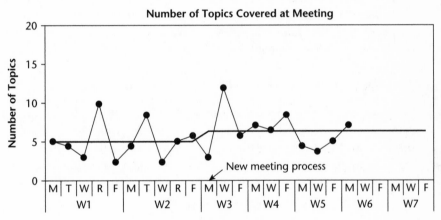

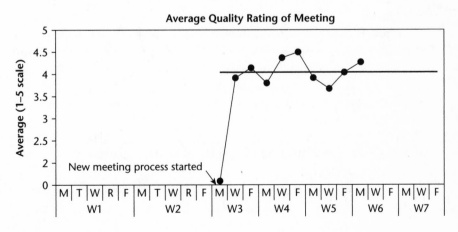

that the work was done right. She had two full-time and two part-time assistants, as well as two office administrators (one worked half-time). The two part-time assistants mainly did teeth cleaning, while the full-time assistants helped Beth with dental procedures other than cleaning. Beth was thinking about expanding the practice and creating a partnership with another dentist. Beth answered the three improvement questions:

## What Am I Trying to Accomplish?

Beth decided that if she could increase her patient base by 15 to 20 percent it would justify bringing a second dentist into the practice.

## How Will I know That a Change Is an Improvement?

Beth felt that the most important measure of her business was the number of people who consistently came to her office for their dental care. She had records of the number of patients she had seen since she started her practice. Because of her good reputation, many of her patients had been coming exclusively to her for the ten years she had been in business.

## What Changes Can I Make That Will Result in Improvement?

Beth was not sure how to answer this question. She felt the answer was probably to bring in the latest technologies, but she was worried that this answer could come from her thinking and technical training rather than from what might be best for her patients (existing and potential). She decided that she would need to talk to patients to be able to answers this question well.

## PDSA Cycle 1

**Plan.** Beth chose six names from her list of patients. She made sure the six represented both long-time and newer patients. The plan was to meet individually with each patient outside the dental office and ask three questions:

1. When you have chosen a dentist in the past (not just my office), what were the main things you looked for?
2. What are some aspects of the services you have received from me and my office that would make you recommend or not recommend my services to friends or relatives?
3. What are some improvements you would like to see in the service you receive from my office?

**Do.** Beth took three weeks to complete the six interviews. She found that two of the six patients were seeing another dentist. Beth realized that she did not have a good way to track the number of patients who had changed to another dentist. One of the patients who had quit coming to her offered several reasons: convenience of location, less expensive, a bad experience during a cleaning, and so on. The other ex-patient confided plainly that after two very painful cleanings she had said, "No more!" All six of the patients interviewed shared their ideas about what makes a good dental visit.

**Study.** Beth had not been aware of two important issues: (1) her patients were not as loyal as she had thought, and (2) her patients were having problems with the teeth cleanings they received at her office. Beth also learned that the patients were not very concerned about new technology. They assumed she would take care of that. They were more concerned about things that increased their anxiety and comfort before and during a dental visit.

**Act.** Beth decided to make some changes that would specifically affect how teeth were cleaned in her office. She had hired all four of her assistants and knew that the ones who did the cleaning were as well qualified as the other two. So the answer was not to blame the two assistants who did the cleaning, which would have been easy to do. She also decided to graph her past data on weekly visits to see if there had been any changes.

## PDSA Cycle 2

**Plan.** Beth discussed the results of her first cycle with her assistants. Although the assistants were not comfortable at first with the whole discussion, Beth kept pointing out that the reason they were working on this was to improve their service to the patients and that all five of them would benefit from a larger, more loyal patient base. "If patients enjoy their dental visits more or at least are not anxious about them, our work will be much easier," she told them. The assistants all had to agree with this and eventually got excited about their own involvement in the changes. They all agreed that the following changes would make the teeth cleaning process less of a pain for patients:

- Rotate assistants (between working with Beth and doing the cleaning)
- Standardize the cleaning process
- Get patients involved in the cleaning (such as have patients do their own flossing at cleaning with supervision, and use it as an opportunity to teach proper flossing)
- Use gentler cleaning tools (especially those that come in contact with the patients' gums)

## FIGURE 3.2. RATINGS BY DENTAL PATIENTS.

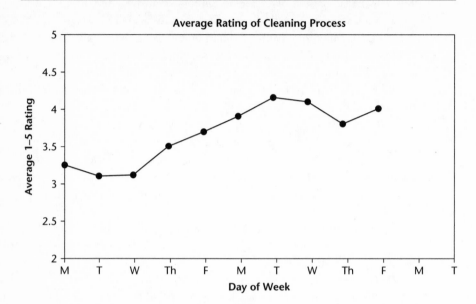

These changes would be developed and tested for two weeks. Also in the plan was to ask patients to rate the cleaning experience relative to past cleanings.

**Do.** It took more than two weeks to develop the new process. Beth and her staff seemed to have more fun at work as a result of all the interaction among them in making sure the plan was carried out.

**Study.** The forty-six patients who had cleanings during the two-week test also enjoyed the new process of getting their teeth cleaned, although three patients did not want to do their own flossing. The data from the patients' ratings clearly showed that they experienced less pain and anxiety at these cleanings. Figure 3.2 shows the average rating for each day.

The rotation of assistants between assisting Beth and doing the cleanings had a few problems related to scheduling and technical experience. Beth saw that she would have to set aside some time for training.

**Act.** The team decided to implement the new process, with the exception that patients were given the option of flossing themselves or having it done by the assistant. Beth asked the office administrator to work on the scheduling problems.

## PDSA Cycle 3

**Plan.** Steps to implement the new process were put in place. The standard procedure was changed so that patients were given the option of flossing themselves

## FIGURE 3.3. NUMBER OF PATIENT VISITS IN BETH'S OFFICE EACH WEEK.

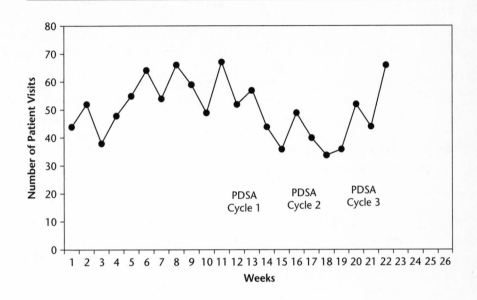

or having it done by the assistant. Beth asked the office administrator to develop a schedule for the assistants, looking three months ahead. Beth also scheduled training for all of the assistants during the next month. Patient satisfaction surveys were modified to monitor the cleaning process, with surveys conducted one day per week. An open-ended question was added to the questionnaire to collect additional feedback and ideas from patients.

**Do.** The training was completed. The training materials and process were standardized to use with new hires in the future. The rotating schedule for the assistants worked for everyone.

**Study.** Monitoring of patient satisfaction with cleaning procedures yielded five related suggestions from five patients about office hours. Beth also studied her graph of weekly office visits (Figure 3.3) and realized there had been some drop-off in the last few months. But the most recent data were looking much better.

**Act.** Beth was feeling more optimistic about plans to bring a partner into the office. She would monitor the number of visits for the next month to see if she got the 20 percent increase she would need if she were to bring on a new partner. She also scheduled a meeting to review the hours the office would be open.

## Discussion of Case Study 2

Beth was initially ready to follow her first idea, about bringing new technology into her practice. This would have cost a considerable amount of money and might not have helped with patient satisfaction at all. The framework of the three questions and the learning experience of the first cycle opened a new direction for her improvement efforts.

**Supporting change with data.** Beth collected specific data during each of her PDSA cycles, including the responses to the six interviews and the comments and ratings the forty-six patients gave the cleaning process. She also had data on her patient base and got a better understanding of the decline in visits after putting these data on a run chart.

**Developing a change.** This example, like the others, shows that it takes a different approach to come up with ideas that are not just more of what has been done in the past (for Beth, this would have been spending money on the latest technology), to develop a change that is new. Beth asked patients for input. Their feedback helped her realize that she needed to develop a standard process for cleaning that would result in improvement from the viewpoint of her patients.

**Testing a change.** The two PDSA cycles were both small-scale, yet they involved enough patients to explore a range of conditions. The cycle to test the change was run over a short period with a limited number of patients. The scale of the test could have been made even smaller, if the assistants had first tried the new procedure on themselves or on a small select group of patients.

**Implementing a change.** Beth learned in cycle 2 that training was needed. She also learned that to implement the changes she would need a process for scheduling her assistants. These and other maintenance issues were addressed in an implementation cycle.

**The human side of change.** It was necessary for the five people working together on this improvement effort to support each other in many aspects of their work: scheduling, skills, knowledge, and so on. They needed to cooperate to agree on a standard process. Each assistant had to change some aspect of his or her approach to cleaning to conform to the standard process. At the beginning, Beth was able to use the aim of the effort to keep everyone focused and cooperating. Once they all took ownership of the changes, cooperation grew.

# Case Study 3: Improving Methods for Teaching Biology

A teacher of an introductory college-level biology course was interested in improving the methods she used in teaching the course. In particular she identified the module on cellular respiration and protein synthesis as difficult for the students. She decided to focus on this first and use what she learned to improve other topics in the course. She used the Model for Improvement to guide her efforts.

Here is some background on the teacher's observations of students in this class over the last three years:

- In the past this module has been a difficult one for the students. This is especially true for those students not majoring in science. As a result, their interest has been low and it has had a negative effect on their enjoyment of the entire course.
- Typically there is quite a mix of students with regard to interest and ability in science. This has presented difficulties for teachers.
- Grades for the test on this module averaged about 65 out of 100.

## What Am I Trying to Accomplish?

Improve the teaching of cellular respiration and protein synthesis in the introductory course. The improvements should help those going into health professions to use this knowledge to understand the results of interventions that they make. The improvements should also help nonbiology majors understand and appreciate the world around them.

## How Will I Know That a Change Is an Improvement?

The primary measures that the teacher used to know whether the changes were improvements were test scores and observations of the students during class (questions, enthusiasm, posture, and so on).

## What Changes Can I Make That Will Result in Improvement?

The teacher ran two cycles to test improvements, one for each of two semesters. Her summary of the two cycles and some ideas for further cycles are given below.

## PDSA Cycle 1

**Plan.** A review of the lesson plan for the module indicated that the students may have been overwhelmed with detailed information on this subject before they had a grasp of the basic concepts. A rearrangement of the lesson plan to improve the progression of topics was accomplished. A simplified handout was developed to highlight the major points. During the next semester, the new approach was tested.

**Do.** The plan was carried out. During the semester, topics that could benefit from a similar approach to the one being tested were noted.

## FIGURE 3.4. TEST SCORES BY SEMESTER.

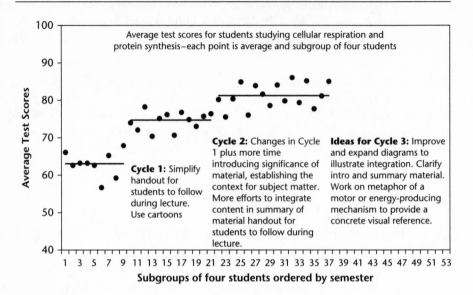

**Study.** The teacher observed some improvement in interest in the topic and about a 10 point increase in the average test scores (see Figure 3.4). She still was not satisfied with the teaching of the topic.

**Act.** Keep the changes made to the lesson plan and incorporate some new ideas for next semester.

## PDSA Cycle 2

**Plan.** The changes to the lesson plan that were made during the previous cycle were retained, and some other changes were included. These changes involved more time introducing the significance of the material and establishing the context for the subject matter. She also informally incorporated the learning from cycle 1 into other topics in the course in addition to cellular respiration.

**Do.** The plan was carried out. Substantial interest was observed in the topic relative to other classes. No obvious difference in the makeup of the class relative to other semesters was discerned.

**Study.** Interest was increased from the previous semester and the average grade for the test on this module was 80. The specific questions on the test changed from semester to semester, but the tests were believed to be of comparable difficulty.

**Act.** Retain the changes in the lesson plan and discuss them with other biology teachers. Enlist the other teachers to incorporate the learning into more of the biology curriculum. In the next PDSA cycle, build on the improvements made.

## Discussion of Case Study 3

**Supporting change with data.** The teacher relied on the traditional test scores as data. However, she did take note of other kinds of data, such as the interest of the students, participation, etc. She tracked these data over time. By plotting the averages of four students, she reduced the noise from variation between students in test scores, and the impact of the changes the teacher made is clear.

**Testing a change.** Both of the cycles required one semester, and the changes were strong enough to produce results that are obvious improvements. The teacher believed that the improvement was due to the changes because the makeup of the class was similar relative to other semesters.

**Spreading improvements.** A clear improvement has been made in one teacher's classes. How willing will the other biology teachers be to adapt the changes she made? There is a clear opportunity for spread, so the teacher should study the material in Chapter Nine to develop a spread strategy.

# Case Study 4: Contamination in Shipping Drums

A manufacturer of chemical products received complaints from customers that blue specks were being found in the product. Contamination from blue specks can occur when product is shipped in a blue plastic drum without a liner. The customers were offered the option to switch to drums with liners or drums made from fiber. Most customers did switch, but one larger customer continued to request product in blue drums without a liner. The manufacturer formed a team to resolve the quality problem with the blue drums. The team began their first meeting by discussing the three improvement questions.

## What Are We Trying to Accomplish?

Their aim was documented: "Eliminate blue specks from contaminating product shipped in blue plastic drums without liners." The solution should not result in any added resources to manufacture or package the product and should significantly reduce the amount of inspection currently done.

## How Will We Know That a Change Is an Improvement?

The key measure was the percentage of drums contaminated with blue specks. The goal was to have no drums rejected because of contamination. For any change developed, the team would monitor the amount of resources expended to eliminate the contamination.

## What Changes Can We Make That Will Result in Improvement?

The team believed the source of the contamination was the rough edge at the top of the drum. They decided to run a PDSA Cycle to verify this theory and learn about the extent of the problem. Then they would work with their supplier to rectify the issue.

## PDSA Cycle 1

**Plan.** Thirty drums will be packed with product that required blue plastic drums without a liner. The packers will use the current blue drum procedure for packing (that is, cleaning and deburring the drums with a rough cloth). Each drum will then be inspected for blue speck contamination. Any contamination will be removed and the product will then be shipped to the customer.

**Do.** The plan was carried out. After they were packed, the thirty drums were inspected before releasing the material.

**Study.** Approximately 25 percent of the drums contained blue specks. The specs were removed with a sterile tongue depressor. These lots were released, but extensive time and manpower was involved. It was noted the lid was creating the specks as it was fitted to the drum.

**Act.** The team shared the results with their supplier of blue drums to determine what actions they could take to eliminate the problem.

The supplier informed the team that it had just purchased a machine for removing excess plastic around the lid of the drum because of complaints from other customers. The machine used heat to cure the drum as a final step. The team requested some drums manufactured using the new machine. Once they received the drums, the team planned their next PDSA Cycle.

## PDSA Cycle 2

**Plan.** Test the new drums to determine if blue specks are created when lids are placed on drums. The plan was:

1. Four drums would be selected at random from drums produced with and without the new machine.

2. Drums would to be cut about five inches down from the lid. The cut edge would be flame sealed to eliminate the possibility that specks would result from the newly cut edge.
3. The top part of the drum would be placed on white paper in a well lit room.
4. Lids would be placed on the top half of the drums multiple times to simulate packing.
5. The white paper would be examined for blue specks from each drum.

**Do.** The plan was carried out without incident.

**Study.** The four drums produced without the machine revealed many blue specks on the white paper. The four drums produced with the machine revealed no blue specks.

**Act.** Order one shipment of the drums produced with the new machine.

When the order for drums was placed, the supplier informed the plant that because of orders from larger customers they could not produce drums with the new machine for the plant for a number of months. The supplier advised the team to flame-treat the current drums at the plant to eliminate the blue specks. Owing to safety and resource issues, the team agreed this was an unacceptable solution. They began to look for another drum supplier to treat the drum lids in a similar fashion. Within a month, they found such a supplier, and this company actually charged less per drum. The team requested drums from the company and tested them in a similar fashion as in Cycle 2. On the basis of the test results, the plant signed a contact. Since the plant began using the drums from the new supplier, there have been no complaints of blue speck contamination, inspection has been nearly eliminated, and the cost of drums has been reduced.

## Discussion of Case Study 4

**Supporting change with data.** Data on complaints from customers originally focused the plant on the problem of blue speck contamination. The team collected data on the "percentage of drums contaminated with blue specks" to share with their supplier. They continue to monitor complaints and have not had any due to blue specks since contracting with a new supplier.

**Developing a change.** The team did not want to develop a change that added resources at the plant, so they began to work with their supplier. Once they understood the cause of the blue specks, they were able to find a suitable supplier. Working with suppliers is an important activity in many improvement efforts.

**Testing a change.** The team used a PDSA Cycle to test whether the drums produced by their first supplier's new machine eliminated blue specks. After they switched suppliers, they ran a similar test on the new supplier's drums. The results of the tests gave the team confidence that the new supplier's drums would not produce blue specks.

**Implementing a change.** A contract was signed with the new supplier after the successful test. The blue drum procedure for packing was revised to no longer require deburring the drums with a rough cloth. New packers continue to be trained in drum cleaning procedures.

**The human side of change.** A formal improvement team was established to work on the blue speck contamination. The team consisted of representatives from production, maintenance, and quality control. The team agreed changes were needed to improve quality for one of the plant's key customers. The packers readily accepted the change of suppliers because it made their job easier.

## Case Study 5: Reducing Energy Use in School

Fifteen students in third through sixth grade at Hitch Elementary School, a public school on the north side of Chicago, were engaged in an after-school program to learn about energy and energy conservation. They put their knowledge into action to help lower energy use in their school.

### What Are We Trying to Accomplish?

Reduce energy use in our school without hurting the learning environment.

### FIGURE 3.5. ENERGY USE OVER A SEVEN-DAY PERIOD.

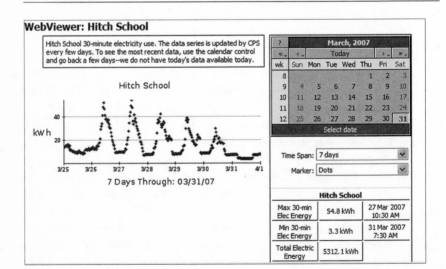

## How Will We Know a Change Is an Improvement?

Figure 3.5 contains the display from the project Website. It shows electricity use for Hitch school; each plotted point represents electric energy use, in kilowatt-hours, for a thirty-minute period ending at the location plotted on the time axis. The thirty-minute data are passed to the project Website from an energy management system. The energy contractor for Chicago Public Schools obtains the interval data from the local utility for several hundred school buildings.

## What Changes Can We Make That Will Result in Improvement?

The facilities staff of the Chicago Public Schools reminds school administers to "use daylight when possible" as a way to save energy. Another school in the EnergyNet project group, Armour Elementary, demonstrated the impact of substituting daylight for electric light in early June 2006. Teachers at Hitch learned about this test during a teacher professional development session. The Hitch energy team decided to find a way to put this idea into practice and sustain the gains. The team thought that the Hitch School was particularly well suited to take advantage of this idea because it has large windows, a hallmark of public schools built before World War II in Chicago.

With the support of their teachers, the Hitch energy team organized a series of schoolwide tests the last week in March. The objective of the tests was to learn if teachers and students could reduce energy use by changing lighting practices.

## PDSA Cycle 1

**Plan.** On Monday, March 26, 2007, teachers used their usual lighting. On Tuesday the twenty-seventh, the students asked teachers to use all the lights in their room (to turn on all the wall switches.) The objective was to estimate whether energy conservation practices were already in place and how much these practices might be saving.

**Do.** Some of the teachers did use all of their lights on Tuesday, but some forgot, so only partial implementation of the plan was accomplished.

**Study.** Energy use on Monday and Tuesday was about the same. The students concluded that energy conservation methods with respect to lighting were not widespread. They agreed that their conclusion could be wrong because not all teachers used all the lights.

**Act.** They decided not to repeat cycle 1 but to design a new cycle to make more use of natural lighting and determine its effect on energy use.

## PDSA Cycle 2

**Plan.** On Wednesday, March 28, the students asked teachers to use half the lights in their room (turn on only half the switches). On Thursday, March 29, the school had an in-service day and classes were not in session.

**Do.** The test was carried out as planned.

**Study.** A substantial reduction in energy use was seen in their graph. This level of energy use on Wednesday was about the same as on Thursday (when students were not attending school). The team took this as a good sign.

**Act.** Encouraged by the success of their test, they decided to push the use of natural lighting even harder.

## PDSA Cycle 3

**Plan.** On Friday, March 30, students asked teachers to try to run their classrooms using only natural daylight.

**Do.** Enthusiasm for the energy saving project was building in the school. The team got lots of cooperation from teachers and students for their test.

**Study.** Energy use was only about half of what it was during their Monday and Tuesday baseline. No complaints were received from teachers or students that lighting was insufficient for the classroom.

**Act.** They decided to implement the change permanently.

## PDSA Cycle 4

This cycle was used to implement the idea of using natural lighting and sustain the energy savings until the end of the school year.

**Plan.** When Hitch students returned to school on April 10, after the spring break, the energy team integrated natural light use into their EnergyNet "stakeouts" that they started earlier in the year. In the stakeouts, students toured the school daily and checked for energy waste and proper recycling practices.

Figure 3.6 contains a picture of the door-hanger checklist the students devised for classroom doors to remind teachers and students of proper management practices.

**Do.** The cycle was carried out as planned.

**Study.** Because energy use varies by season, by day of the week, and by hour of the day, the team compared energy use for approximately a one-month period this year to a comparable period last year. Table 3.1 contains the data for this comparison. Total energy use was down about 23 percent. This was a combination of the energy team reducing use during school hours by 16 percent and

## FIGURE 3.6. CHECKLIST FOR ENERGY CONSERVATION.

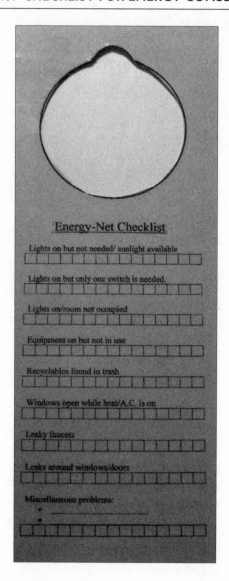

changes in the lighting configuration on the part of the school engineer during off hours and weekends.

The team also checked to see if any obvious differences between the two years—rather than their work—explained the reduction. They found weather temperature to be about the same in the two time periods. The assistant principal and the school

### TABLE 3.1. ENERGY USE ANALYSIS.

| Time Period | Total energy (kWh) | Total Energy 8:30–3:30 M–F (kWh) | Total energy off-hours and weekends (kWh) |
|---|---|---|---|
| 4/20/06 to 5/19/06 | 24,690 | 11,130 | 13,560 |
| 4/19/07 to 5/18/07 | 19,000 | 9,300 | 9,700 |
| % Reduction | 23 | 16 | 38 |

engineer confirmed that no major power outages or equipment upgrades were done that would invalidate their conclusions that their project was the primary source of energy savings. (The large saving off hours is interesting; the assistant principal said that the kids were always going up to the school engineer asking about energy use and ways to conserve. The changes from 3:30 to, say, 6:30 P.M. each day may be explained by lights being on before the cleaning crew came through the classrooms.)

**Act.** They maintained the approach as tested in this cycle. A communication plan was set up to let other schools know of their changes and savings to motivate similar work in other schools.

## Discussion of Case Study 5

**Supporting change with data**. The availability of data from the Siemens Energy management system was critical to the success of the project. Software that displayed the data over time allowed the school kids to easily understand the impact of the changes they tried. They were able to easily compare the energy use during their test periods with baseline data from the same time period the previous year. A key change they developed was a data collection form (the checklist) to monitor sustainability of the changes and serve as a reminder to the teachers and students in each classroom.

**Developing a change.** The students and teachers first learned the basics of energy management. Then they decided to work with a change concept (use daylight when possible) where they thought they could have the most influence.

**Testing a change**. The teachers and students designed a rather sophisticated PDSA test over one week to understand the impact of their changes. Each day of the week, a different scenario of light use in the classrooms was tested. From the results of this first test, they ran a pilot for seven weeks at the end of the school year and demonstrated a 16 percent drop in energy use.

**Implementing a change.** The pilot at the end of the school year demonstrated an important savings in energy use from the changes made. What will happen next fall when school starts again? There will be new staff members and new students who will have to learn the practices to reduce energy use. A formal procedure needs to be established in the school to pass on these changes and sustain the gains.

**Spreading improvements.** One school was able to develop and test changes that made significant reductions in energy use. There are hundreds of schools in the Chicago area and thousands in other parts of the country. How do good ideas like this get spread? Publication of the results of this improvement project is a first step. Campaigns built around science classes and parent-teacher projects could be used to accelerate spread to other schools.

**The human side of change.** The enthusiasm of the school kids' focus on energy use spilled over to the school engineer, who was able to make some additional changes that contributed to the reduction in energy consumption.

## Key Points from Chapter Three

- These five case studies illustrate the variety of opportunities to make improvements in the various organizations where we work.
- The improvement activities were very different in each of the case studies, but they were all framed and guided by three questions of the Model for Improvement.
- Each case study used multiple PDSA cycles to first test new ideas for change and then eventually implement the changes.
- One or more of the six skills were instrumental in the success of each case study.

PART TWO

# METHODS FOR IMPROVEMENT

Part One of this book discussed several key concepts for optimizing improvement, introduced the Model for Improvement as a framework for making improvements, and presented six skills to support improvement efforts. To demonstrate applications of the concepts and methods presented, five examples of improvement projects were included.

Part Two explores the concepts and methods discussed in Part One in more depth across a wider range of applications and complexity. Chapter Four begins Part Two by discussing the system of profound knowledge, the science that forms the foundation for making improvements. Chapter Five discusses the use of the Model for Improvement in more detail. Chapters Six, Seven, Eight, and Nine offer more sophisticated methods and applications for performing the key work of improvement: developing, testing, implementing, and spreading change. Chapter Ten discusses how one might integrate these methods to develop an effective and balanced approach to improvement. Chapter Eleven discusses more sophisticated use of the model and more advanced methods for accomplishing successful improvement projects in large and complex systems. Part Two ends with Chapter Twelve, which presents six case studies to illustrate the use of the methods across a range of topics.

We believe the material presented in Part Two will deepen your understanding of the science and art of improvement and its varied applications.

CHAPTER FOUR

# THE SCIENCE OF IMPROVEMENT

S cience (from the Latin *scientia,* meaning knowledge) is defined in *Webster's New Collegiate Dictionary* as "knowledge attained through study or practice." Science refers to a system of acquiring knowledge of the physical world. This system must be based on observable phenomena and capable of being tested through the scientific method for its validity. Acquiring knowledge is essential for improvement activities, whether it is a simple problem to solve, a work process to improve, a design or redesign of a product or service, or improvement to a complex system. What kind of knowledge will allow us to develop, test, and implement changes that result in improvement?

The most obvious answer is appropriate subject matter knowledge acquired through formal and informal learning and reinforced with experiences. Subject matter knowledge is basic to the things we do in life. Health care people should be able to improve health care. Sales people should be able to make changes that improve sales.

Subject matter knowledge is vital for developing changes that result in improvement. However, there is another kind of knowledge useful for developing effective change. W. Edwards Deming proposed a body of knowledge called a "System of Profound Knowledge." The word *profound* denotes the deep insight this knowledge offers into how to make changes that will result in improvement in a variety of settings. Deming defined the System of Profound Knowledge as the interplay of the theories of systems, variation, knowledge, and psychology.

## FIGURE 4.1. INCREASING CAPABILITY TO MAKE IMPROVEMENTS.

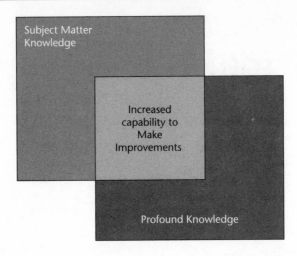

The ability to make improvements is enhanced by combining subject matter knowledge and profound knowledge in creative ways. This interplay is illustrated in Figure 4.1.

The first section of this chapter describes each part of profound knowledge and the relationship to making improvements.

## Profound Knowledge

Deming describes profound knowledge in four parts, all related to each other:

1. Appreciation for a system
2. Understanding variation
3. Building knowledge
4. Human side of change

A leader of improvement does not need to be an expert in all of these areas. The leader should understand the basic theories, how the areas interrelate, and why they are important for any improvement effort. Profound knowledge gives us a lens to view our organizations differently. The lens is illustrated in Figure 4.2; a brief description of each part follows.

## FIGURE 4.2. DEMING'S SYSTEM OF PROFOUND KNOWLEDGE.

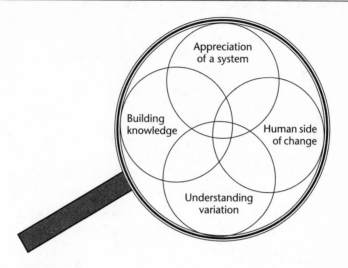

## Appreciation for a System

Because most products and services result from a complex system of interaction among people, procedures, and equipment, it is vital to understand the properties of a system. A system is *an interdependent group of items, people, or processes working together toward a common purpose.* The common purpose aligns the parts of the system, while interdependence considers the relationships and interactions among them.

Organizations are made up of departments, people, equipment, facilities, and functions. If each part of a system, considered separately, decides to operate as efficiently as possible, then the system as a whole will not operate to maximum effectiveness. Management's job is to optimize the system, that is, orchestrate the efforts of all components toward achievement of the stated purpose.

> Bill in the purchasing department was being congratulated on his ability to strike a deal with a new supplier that resulted in lower material costs. At the same time, the manufacturing department was being questioned about decreasing quality since they began using the new material.

Ultimately, the success of an organization will depend on integration, not the performance of individual parts such as the purchasing department. The principle of interdependence has important ramifications for improvement in terms of the aim of improvement efforts and selection of measures. In complex projects, multiple measures are almost always needed to understand the impact of changes on the components of the system and on the system as a whole.

Considering interdependence will also increase the accuracy of our predictions about the impact of changes throughout the system. A tool to help us see the interdependence of the components of a system and its boundaries is a linkage-of-processes diagram, or system map. By identifying where improvement efforts are to be made on this diagram, we can see the impact on the rest of the system. See Appendix B for more on systems maps.

In addition to the principle of interdependence, systems theory has contributed several other key ideas:

- *Boundary of a system.* A boundary separates the system of interest from the outside environment. The larger the system (a whole hospital versus one unit, one manufacturing plant versus all ten in the organization), the more difficult it is to optimize, but the greater the potential benefits.
- *Temporal effects.* Changes can have a different effect on a system in the short run than in the long run. We should expect and consider these delayed effects. Many of today's problems come from yesterday's short-term solutions to problems. For example, some organizations manufacture extra product at the end of the fiscal year to make budgets. Much of this extra product ends up in inventory, resulting in higher storage costs and damaged goods, which in turn affect next year's profits. This concept is often referred to as "dynamic complexity."
- *Leverage.* Small changes can produce significant improvement. For example, changing the order of the steps for getting cash from an ATM (user cannot get money until after card has been removed) eliminates the chance of people leaving their cards in the machine. Leverage points can prove especially effective when the change is directed at a constraint in the system (a key idea in complexity theory).
- *Constraint* (or bottleneck). A bottleneck is that component of a system that limits the overall performance or capacity of the system. Bottlenecks must be identified and managed (for example, off-loading work that can be done by a nonbottleneck resource.) Efforts spent improving a nonbottleneck will not improve the overall performance of a system. An emergency department could allocate a second nurse to its triage process, but not reduce the length of stay in the department because the physicians are the bottleneck in the system.
- *Types of change in a system.* See Chapter Six for more on the two types of changes:

  First-order: a change that returns the system to a normal level of performance. The system essentially remains the same.

  Second-order: a change that alters the system and results in a new level of system performance.

- *Every system is perfectly designed to deliver the results it produces.* This statement has been called the Central Law of Improvement. The implications of this statement are that if the system is not producing the quality of products or services needed and wanted by the customer, then the system must be changed in some fundamental way to produce improved results.
- *Unintended consequences.* Systems are not made up of simple linear cause-and-effect relationships. Making a change in one particular part of a system may well produce an unpredicted effect in another part of the system or at a later time. Unintended consequences are a common experience and in many cases lead to misinterpretation of the causes.

## Understanding Variation

Everything we observe or measure varies. We are forced to make decisions in our lives based on our interpretation of this variation. Do the latest standardized test scores indicate my child's school is improving? Does this month's change in sales mean we are losing market share? Do the two medication errors this month in our hospital indicate an undesirable trend? Was improved performance this week the result of the change we made or just luck? The ability to answer these questions and others like them is inseparable from making improvements.

A supervisor in the accounting department was very interested in making certain the staff who posted information to customer records did it right the first time. To help accomplish the goal, the supervisor sampled a total of sixty customer files from each of ten staff per month for two months and checked them for accuracy. Figure 4.3 is the control chart she created for the percentage of records with errors for each staff member.

What are we to conclude from these data? Which staff members should we question? Knowledge of variation is needed to take the appropriate action. Walter A. Shewhart was one of the pioneers in developing the theory to understand variation; his work dates back to the 1920s. It stresses the importance of plotting data over time. When we view data plotted over time, we can observe two situations: in some cases the patterns in the data are predictable, but in other cases unpredictable. Statistical theory can be used to develop a means to differentiate these two situations on the basis of the patterns of variation over time. The method comprises two definitions:

1. *Common causes*—those causes that are inherent in the process (or system) over time, affect everyone working in the process, and affect all outcomes of the process

# FIGURE 4.3. CONTROL CHART FOR ERRORS IN CUSTOMER RECORDS.

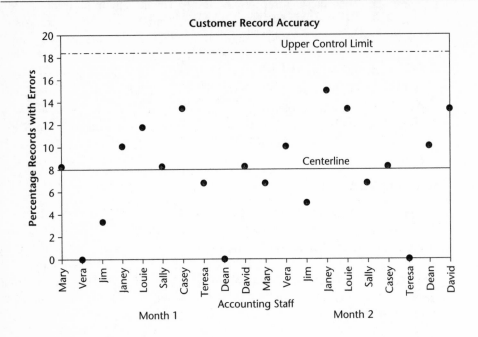

2. *Special causes*—those causes that are *not* part of the process (or system) all the time, or do not affect everyone, but arise because of specific circumstances

A process that has only common causes affecting the outcomes is called a *stable* process, or one that is in a state of *statistical control*. In a stable process, the causal system of variation remains essentially constant over time. This does not mean there is no variation in the outcomes of the process, that the variation is small, or that outcomes meet requirements. It implies only that the variation is predictable within statistically established limits. In practice, this means improvement can be achieved only through a fundamental change to the system.

A process whose outcomes are affected by both common and special causes of variation is called an *unstable* process. An unstable process is not necessarily one with large variation. Rather, the magnitude of variation from one period to the next is unpredictable. If special causes can be identified and removed, the process becomes stable; its performance becomes predictable. In practical terms, this implies that the system can be put back to an original level of performance by identifying the special causes and taking appropriate action. Once a change is made, continuing to plot data over time and observe the patterns helps to determine whether the change has eliminated the special cause. In addition to proposing the basic concepts, Shewhart developed the control chart method for determining whether variation in a system is dominated by common or special causes.

The concepts of variation create a structure for understanding the key mistakes that people make in dealing with variation. The first is to treat common cause variation as if it is due to special causes and adjust or reset the system, when in fact the only way to improve the system is by fundamentally changing it. The second mistake is to accept special cause variation as if it were all due to common causes and miss an opportunity to fix a problem.

> After viewing the control chart for the percentage of records with errors, the supervisor correctly concluded the data indicated a stable system. She decided to talk with all the staff to solicit suggestions about possible fundamental changes to the processing of records rather than singling out any individuals.

Although there are many situations in which the statistical formality of control charts is useful, it is often adequate to view patterns of data on run charts. A run chart is a simple plot of data from a measure over time. More on both run charts and control charts can be found in Appendix B.

Leaders in the science of improvement should speak the language of variation. Knowledge about separating variation of outcomes of a process or system into common and special causes helps to decide appropriate actions for that process or system. Inappropriate action may make things worse.

## Building Knowledge

In the context of improvement, a change is a prediction: if the change is made, improvement will result. The more knowledge one has about how the particular system under consideration functions or could function, the better the prediction and the greater the likelihood the change will result in improvement. Comparing predictions to results is a key source of learning.

Rational prediction requires theory. A theory represents our current knowledge about how some aspect of the system of interest works. Participants in an improvement effort articulate the basis of their predictions by making their theories (or hypotheses) explicit. Stating theories or assumptions helps us design tests to validate these theories; we can then improve our ideas for change on the basis of the results of the tests. If changes tested do not lead to the improvement predicted, we should identify the circumstances present and use this understanding to further refine our theory. For example, we may find that changes successfully made in some emergency departments are not successful in others. On investigation, we may theorize this is due to the size of the emergency department, the lack of support from consulting physicians, or inadequate inpatient capacity in the hospital. What changes will be successful under these circumstances?

Skillfully building knowledge by making changes and observing or measuring the results is the foundation of improvement. By repeating learning cycles, we can eventually categorize most circumstances for applying the theory, making the theory useful for predictions in future situations. This iterative deductive and inductive approach to learning and improvement is illustrated in Figure 4.4.

Deductive and inductive learning are built into Plan-Do-Study-Act (PDSA) Cycles (introduced in Chapter One and described in detail in Chapter Five). From Plan to Do is the *deductive* approach. A theory is tested with the aid of a prediction. In the Do phase, observations are made and departures from the prediction are noted. From Do to Study the *inductive* learning process takes place. Gaps (anomalies) to the prediction are studied and the theory is updated accordingly. Action is then taken on the new learning.

Deming classified studies (gaining knowledge through the use of data) into two types according to the action that will be taken:

1. An **enumerative study** is one in which information is produced and action taken on a group of items (for example, people, materials, invoices).
2. An **analytic study** is one in which action will be taken on a cause system to improve performance of a product, process, or system in the future.

## FIGURE 4.4. THE ITERATIVE NATURE OF LEARNING AND IMPROVEMENT.

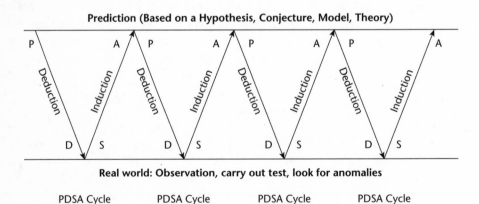

The aim in an enumerative study is estimation—estimation about some aspect of the group of items. Action will be taken on those items according to this estimate. An example of an enumerative study is the U.S. Census, which is carried out every ten years. The number of representatives in Congress from an area depends on the number of inhabitants in an area, as counted by the last census.

The aim of an analytic study is prediction—prediction that one of several alternatives will be superior to others in the future. The choice may encompass different concepts for a product, or materials, or conditions for operating a process. As part of the analysis of the data from an analytic study, it is generally useful to compare performance of the alternatives under various conditions. The ultimate aim is prediction of performance in the future. The improvement of quality is almost solely focused on analytic studies.

In addition to the idea of prediction in learning and improvement, the concept of operational definitions is an important contribution to building knowledge. Operational definitions are used to put communicable meaning to a concept. To develop an operational definition, consideration needs to be given to:

- A method of measurement or test
- A set of criteria for judgment

> Data on on-time arrival are used to compare the performance of airlines. To make comparisons, operational definitions of "arrival time" and "on-time arrival" are needed. The *arrival time* of a flight is defined as the time the wheels touch down on the runway. Time will be determined by the timepiece used for navigation for the flight. An arrival will be *on time* if the arrival time is not more than fifteen minutes after the scheduled arrival time.

One corollary to the idea of operational definitions is that there is no true value for any measurement, no matter how precise the instrument you are using or how careful you are in gathering data. The definition could change (arrival time could be when the plane is at the gate) or variation could exist in how the definition is applied.

## The Human Side of Change

Knowledge of the human side of change helps us understand how people, as individuals, interact with each other and with a system. It helps us predict how people will react to a specific change and how to gain commitment. It helps us understand the motivations of people and their behavior.

The fields of psychology and change management are very dynamic. New ideas are forthcoming continuously. Our focus on the human side of change (psychology) will be on ideas, methods, tools, and theories that help people better integrate changes into the social system. Some important contributions from psychology and change management:

- *Differences in people.* People have their own preferences, aspirations, motivations, and learning styles. People have varying levels of needs. If a person has needs at one level (for example, home-life balance), then appeals to another level (to work overtime to complete an assignment) have little impact. People may have differing beliefs and values. Most changes aimed at improvement will have to recognize the differences in people and account for them.

- *Behavior is driven by motivation.* We can observe the behavior of others. Observing behavior, though, does not often give us a clear window into what is motivating someone's behavior. We tend to perceive the behavior of others through our own filter. A person's disinterest at a meeting might make us conclude the person is not committed to a particular project being discussed. Rather than drawing such a conclusion, we should seek to understand the motivation underlying the behavior. Perhaps the person is concerned that similar ideas had been discussed in the past with no follow-through. Understanding what is motivating someone rather than relying on our interpretation of the behavior can help us take appropriate actions to build commitment to change.

- *Fundamental attribution error.* We make this error when we explain our behavior in terms of the situation or environment while holding other people accountable for their own behavior. For example, we may attribute the dissatisfaction of one of our customers to the lack of resources within our organization or theirs to support them. On the other hand, when we are the customer and experience dissatisfaction, we may attribute this to a salesperson's lack of dedication to customer satisfaction. It is often easier to blame people than to take a hard look at how the system affects behavior.

- *Intrinsic and extrinsic motivation.* When motivation is extrinsic, the satisfaction people derive from a work activity lies outside the work activity itself (as with motivation derived from bonuses or other rewards). Potentially, commitment to the activity will decline as these motivators are reduced or eliminated. When motivation is *intrinsic,* satisfaction comes from the activity itself and the fulfillment of social and personal needs. Leaders can motivate people intrinsically by aligning improvement work with what people believe in and are passionate about. People will have a tendency to adopt new behaviors more readily if the requested change is in line with existing attitudes and beliefs. This includes alignment with the organization's values, principles, or tenets. Therefore, when a change is proposed, leaders need to explain the *why* of the change in terms of the organization's values.

- *Attracting people to the change.* Building commitment to change requires leaders to understand that change involves more than just the tangible and technical aspects (a new product, a revised procedure, a modified form). Once a change has been developed, the desire is often to implement it immediately to capture the predicted benefits. However, people may resist if they do not feel included or truly understand the benefits of the change to the organization and to themselves. Everett Rogers proposed five attributes to facilitate adoption. They give us a good framework to ensure effective communication to attract people to a change:

1. Relative advantage of the change over other changes or the status quo (What is in it for me?)
2. Compatibility with current culture and values (as discussed above)
3. Minimal complexity in explaining the change
4. Allowing people to try and test the new change
5. Opportunities for people to observe the success of the change for others

Some knowledge of psychology is essential to understand the human side of change. Leaders of improvement plan for the social impact of technical change and make people part of the solution. They look for fundamental (unspoken) assumptions and beliefs behind decisions and actions taken. They appreciate differences in people and the importance of the fundamental attribution error. They understand the value of teams and that cooperation, rather than competition, is necessary if changes are to be successful. Leaders use reward and recognition systems that rely more on intrinsic motivation than extrinsic motivation. Commitment to change is built through sharing of information. Leaders understand that we have bad systems, not bad people.

## Interaction of the Components of Profound Knowledge

Although the four components of profound knowledge have been described separately here, their importance in improvement is derived mainly from their interaction. Focusing on appreciation for a system without considering the impact that variation is having on the system will not produce effective ideas for improvement. Similarly, the interplay of the human side of change and the building of knowledge, as seen in areas of study such as cognitive psychology, is critical for growing people's knowledge about making changes that result in improvement.

# Milestones in the Development of Profound Knowledge

Table 4.1 details many of the important milestones in the development of profound knowledge. These contributions have advanced the theories of variation,

TABLE 4.1. IMPORTANT MILESTONES FOR PROFOUND KNOWLEDGE COMPONENTS.

| | Variation | Systems | Psychology | Knowledge |
|---|---|---|---|---|
| 1900 | | | | *Realism of Pragmatism,* John Dewey, 1905 |
| 1910 | | Scientific management, Frederick Taylor, Frank and Lillian Gilbreth | | |
| 1920 | Control chart, Walter Shewhart, 1924; Design of experiments, Sir Ronald Fisher, 1925 | | Lewin's equation $B = f$ (pe), Kurt Lewin, 1920; participatory management, Mary Parker Follett, 1925; Hawthorne experiments, Elton Mayo, 1927 Constructive conflict, Follett, 1924 | *Mind and the World Order,* C. I. Lewis, 1929 |
| 1930 | Shewhart books on control chart methods, 1931, 1939; Shewhart lectures at USDA organized by W. Edwards Deming, 1938 | | Anthropology experts apply theory to business; motivation drives behavior, Edward Tolman, 1932 | *How We Think,* John Dewey, 1933 |
| 1940 | Sampling methods, H. F. Dodge; use of statistical methods to support war effort, 1941–1945 | *General Systems Theory,* Ludwig von Bertalanffy, 1949 | | |
| 1950 | | Holistic management, Stafford Beer, 1959 | Tavistock Institute, Eric Trist, 1951; sociotechnical system; organizational development, Douglas McGregor | |

|  | | | | |
|---|---|---|---|---|
| 1960 | Enumerative vs. analytic studies, Deming, 1960 | *Principles of Systems*, Jay Forrester, 1968 | *Human Side of Enterprise*, McGregor, 1960; hierarchy of needs, Abraham Maslow, 1962; motivation theory, Frederick Herzberg, 1968 | *Experiential Learning Theory*, Carl Rogers, 1969 |
| 1970 | | | *Relationship Awareness Theory*, Elias Porter, 1971; attribution error termed by Lee Ross, 1977 | Adult learning theory, Malcolm Knowles, 1973; Double loop learning in organizations, Chris Argyris and Donald Schön, 1974 |
| 1980 | | *Creating the Corporate Future*, Russell Ackoff, 1981; open systems, Fred Emery; *The Goal*, Eliyahu Goldratt, 1984 | | |
| 1990 | | *The Fifth Discipline*, Peter Senge, 1990; *Theory of Constraints*, Goldratt, 1990 | | |
| 2000 | | | | Paul Carlile and Clayton Christensen, 2005 Descriptive and Normative Learning Models |

systems, knowledge, and psychology. Many of these influenced Deming during his lifetime. His major contribution was to have us look at these theories as a system and use this outside view as a lens by which to understand the organizations we work in. The methods and concepts described in this book are based on the science of improvement discussed in this chapter. The rest of the book expands and furnishes the details of this science, which guides improvement efforts in such a way as to lower risk and improve results.

## Key Points from Chapter Four

- Leaders of improvement need some understanding of the four parts of profound knowledge and their interactions. They should use this knowledge as an outside view or lens to develop effective change.
- Management's job is orchestrating the efforts of all components in an organization toward achievement of the stated purpose. The success of an organization will depend on the integration of its components, not their individual performance.
- Knowledge about separating variation of outcomes of a process or system into common and special causes helps to decide appropriate actions for that process or system. Inappropriate action may make things worse.
- Improvement takes the application of knowledge. Because knowledge is built on theory, our theories need to be systematically revised and extended by comparing predictions and observations (deductive and inductive learning). The Plan-Do-Study-Act (PDSA) Cycle helps facilitate this process.
- Leaders understand we have bad systems that need to be improved, not bad people.

CHAPTER FIVE

# USING THE MODEL FOR IMPROVEMENT

Change and improvement are never easy. Even an apparently simple system appears much more complex when change is contemplated or introduced. This chapter explores in more depth the use of the Model for Improvement introduced in Chapter One (see Figure 1.1). We rely on the operational definition of improvement presented in that chapter. Fundamental changes that result in improvement:

- Alter how work or activity is done or the makeup of a product
- Produce visible, positive differences in results relative to historical norms (from the viewpoint of those served by the system)
- Have a lasting impact

We consider this definition of improvement as we discuss using the three fundamental questions of the Model for Improvement to guide our efforts.

## What Are We Trying to Accomplish?

When the business owners from Chapter One decided to improve their cleaning service, they may have been able to discuss and agree on the aim of the project over a cup of coffee. They may even have been able to come up with some ideas for changes. This was possible because so few people were involved in the effort, those initiating the effort were also doing the work, the system was relatively simple, and unintended consequences were easily identified.

As the scope of an improvement effort increases, an improvement team or individual should answer the question "What are we trying to accomplish?" by writing down what the aim of the effort is. This written statement of the aim is sometimes referred to as a *charter*. The charter can be discussed and circulated for comment to a variety of people who have a stake in the work or the outcome of the project.

## Using a Charter to Start an Improvement Effort

Charters can take many forms. We first present a basic version of a charter developed by a team in an accounting department. In this department, the invoice process was plagued by rework and late payments.

---

Improve how the organization handles the billing of customers. Complexity and waste should be identified and removed so that turnaround time for invoices is reduced and there is less cost due to late payments.

---

Although a charter documents the answer to the first fundamental question of the model, it can begin to address all three questions. Following is a charter aimed at improving (reducing) waiting time in a dental office.

The first charter includes a general description of the activities to improve the invoice process. The second charter includes more information about the improvement effort in the dental office. It has these elements:

- The system to be improved: the flow of patients in the dental office
- The setting or population of focus: all patients
- What is expected to happen: reduce patient complaints, reduce waiting time, reduce expense associated with schedule slips (with associated measures)
- Timeframe: within the next twelve months
- Goals (predictions of improved performance): for example, reduce waiting time from thirty minutes to less than five minutes
- Guidance for the activities (such as strategies for the effort, what to include what to ignore, limitations): for example, up to twenty hours a week of part-time personnel for one month to collect data, make additional reminder calls, and consider matching the schedule for the dental assistance to periods of high demand

## General Description (What Are We Trying to Accomplish?)

Within the next twelve months, we will reduce the average amount of time patients spend waiting to be seen by a dentist or one of our staff to less than five minutes.

## Expected Outcomes and Measures (How Will We Know That a Change Is an Improvement?)

- Reduce patient complaints
- Reduce waiting time
- Reduce expense associated with schedule slips (overtime hours)

Following are measures for the improvement.

## Performance Measures and Goals

| Measure | Current Performance | Goal (prediction) |
|---|---|---|
| 1. Waiting time (actual time started minus scheduled) | 30 minutes | <5 minutes |
| 2. Percentage of overtime hours | 22 | <10 |
| 3. Percentage of patients who leave | 5 | 0 |
| 4. Percentage of patients late for appointment | 15 | <5 |
| 5. Number of patient complaints per 10 visits | 3 | 0 |

## Guidance

These are the boundaries of the project:

- Appointments for the dentists and the hygienists could be included in the project, but the team may choose to limit the scope to one or the other.
- Up to twenty hours a week by part-time personnel for one month to collect data, make additional reminder calls, and so on.

Some initial activities and potential cycles:

- Interview and observe dentists, hygienists, and support staff
- Interview patients concerning use of reminders and their timing
- Consider matching the schedule for the dental assistance to periods of high demand
- Consider ways to decrease the non-value-added work of the dentists and hygienists

## Use of Numerical Goals

In the example of the charter for the dental office, the team established goals for the measures used to answer the question, "How will we know that a change is an improvement?" Advice about the use of numerical goals in setting an aim for an improvement project could include "Never use them" or "Always provide one and let other people figure out how to achieve it." This book's authors recognize the abuses associated with numerical goals and the potential unintended consequences when people are held responsible for results they are not capable of achieving. One unintended consequence is falsifying figures or distorting the measurement system, as illustrated in this example:

> In a manufacturing plant, the production department was given a goal to reduce defective product by 20 percent. To achieve this goal, they stopped counting as defective any unit that could be reworked for another application.

Another unintended consequence is achieving the goal at the expense of other parts of the system (appreciation of a system; Chapter Four), as in this instance:

> A hospital was given the goal to increase admissions by 5 percent. They immediately instituted a no-diversion policy that caused long delays and potential safety issues in their emergency department.

We do not believe these instances of poor practice or abuse should preclude beneficial use of numerical goals. We also recognize some hardy souls need only the challenge of a numerical goal to find ways to actually improve the system. Our experience indicates that a middle ground between these two extremes is achievable and useful.

First and foremost, numerical goals must be connected to methods for achieving the goals. Leaders should understand that to improve a stable system beyond the current level of performance a fundamental change is needed. Developing such changes is discussed in Chapter Six, but here are some initial considerations to develop methods for achieving numerical goals:

- Observe other organizations that have accomplished similar goals.
- Give some basic concepts or ideas that could feasibly result in achieving the goal.
- Draw out ideas from participants themselves by asking questions such as, "What would it take to get a 50 percent reduction in time to ship an order?"

- Ask experts on the changes being considered what level of improvement is possible.

Numerical goals can also be a convenient way to communicate expectations. What are the consequences of not meeting the numerical goal? Are small and incremental improvements expected, or are large breakthrough changes necessary? If the numerical goal is used well, it communicates not only the expectation but also the support that will be offered. Large changes to big systems usually require investment of time and capital. When first using a goal to break the current bounds of the status quo, leaders must furnish:

- An explanation of the need for and feasibility of the goal
- Assurances the goals will be used to cause new thinking and learning, and not for judgment

## Removing the Current System as an Alternative

Change is difficult. The current system pulls innovative changes toward more familiar ground like a giant magnet. What begins as a large change can result in only a small adjustment. Frequently, it is implicitly or explicitly assumed that if changes resulting in the desired level of improvement cannot be easily developed, then remaining with the current system is an option. This may be comforting, but it inhibits improvement.

The charter can be used to prevent this assumption from being made by including:

- A statement of fact, such as, "Remaining at the current level of twenty-one days is not an alternative if the custom business is to remain viable."
- A numerical goal that clearly is not attainable with small changes to the current system.
- Some ideas for changes to be pursued, if no better alternative is developed.
- Logical consequences that follow from failure to make the improvements, such as discontinuing the product or service. A statement that takes part of the present system away can be useful: "Computer Services will delete the old version of the accounting package from all computers on the tenth of the month."

# How Will We Know That a Change Is an Improvement?

An effective answer to this question lays the foundation for learning that is fundamental to effective improvement. Changes to large and small businesses, government, or social systems are frequently made without thoughtfully answering this question. Consequently, valuable opportunities to learn and accelerate improvement are lost.

In simple systems, it is often easy to discern a change is an improvement by informally observing the system. In more complex systems, measurements or other types of data are almost always necessary to answer this question. For example, measures of improvement in redesigning a hospital's medication system might be medication error rate, patient satisfaction, timeliness of administration, and costs associated with the system; measures for reducing labor costs in the lab might be hours of overtime, costs for temporaries, turnaround time, accuracy, and staff satisfaction; and measures for developing a new flooring tile might be whether it holds a shine, its ease of installation, durability, and visual attractiveness. Some guidelines for developing measures are:

Make sure the interests of the customer of the product, process, or service are strongly represented in the list of measures.

> A company that makes garage door openers learned from their 800 number survey that ease of installation was one of their customer's measures of quality. This measure was then included in their manufacturing requirements.

It is useful to look at data collected both before and after a change; however, don't disregard an important measure if this is not possible. Often, looking at data collected after a change is enough to justify calling the change an improvement.

> Sally was quite happy. The chart of the number of medical errors for the health system showed they were producing consistently fewer errors each month as changes were being made. Each change was annotated on the chart. The improvement team decided they could not afford to wait for baseline data on account of patient safety, so they started making changes that had been effective in other health care settings. From their weekly meetings of the previous year, Sally knew more than five errors per day occurred. Although she did not know precisely the effect of the changes that would be made, she had high belief that it would be substantial. Figure 5.1 shows the data and the changes that Sally's team made.

In many situations, the data needed to measure the impact of a change will not be available for a long time. If this is the case, select a surrogate outcome measure related to the measure(s) you most want to affect.

> The leaders of a large health care organization wanted to make some changes that would result in reduced occurrence of lung cancer. They decided to start a clinic for helping people stop smoking. Obviously, what they wanted was to

## FIGURE 5.1. ANNOTATED RUN CHART OF MEDICATION ERRORS.

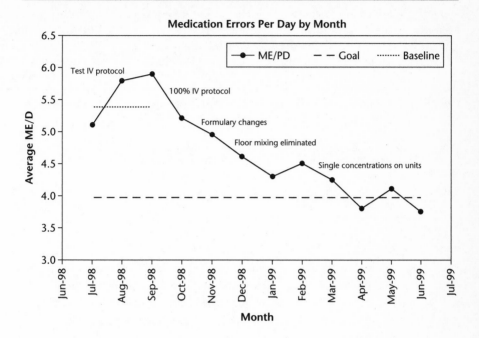

see the rate of lung cancer go down. It would take many years, however, for this result to be detectable. They decided to focus on a measure that could be measured immediately and one they strongly believed is related to a reduction in lung cancer. They measured the success rate of people trying to quit smoking (specifically, the percentage of people who went through the workshops and were still not smoking six months after the program).

Multiple measures are almost always required to balance competing interests and to help ensure that the system as a whole is improved. Try to keep the list to six measures or fewer. Strive to develop a list that is useful and manageable, not perfect.

A state's secondary education system was interested in increasing the scores its high school students achieved on the Scholastic Aptitude Test, necessary for admission to most colleges. Some people were concerned some high schools would achieve the aim by discouraging the poorer-performing students from taking the test, thus hurting their chances of going to college. To accommodate this concern, the percentage of students taking the exam was included in the list of measures. This measure was then monitored to determine whether at least the current level was maintained.

### TABLE 5.1. EXAMPLES OF MEASURES.

| Type of Measure | Education: Increase the Percentage of Students Passing the State-Mandated Test | Health Care: Redesign the Processes by Which Patient Flow Is Managed Within Our Hospital | Inventory: Reduce Costs of Inventory While Maintaining or Improving Service Level to Customers |
|---|---|---|---|
| Outcome | Percentage of students passing state-mandated tests | Diversions from the hospital; transfer time between units | Cost of inventory |
| Process | Percentage of students who took a review course | Number of units conducting bed huddles | Number of inventory checks |
| Balancing | Percentage of students who took the test | Admissions; patient satisfaction; cost per bed | Stockouts; customer satisfaction |

In answering the question "How will we know that a change is an improvement?" different levels of measurement are useful. We should consider three levels of measurement to facilitate learning while improving a complex system. The levels are described below; Table 5.1 gives some examples relative to improvement efforts.

***Outcome measures.*** Outcome measures are measures of the performance of the system under study. They relate directly to the aim of the project. Outcome measures offer evidence that changes are actually having an impact at the system level.

***Process measures.*** Process measures are measures of whether an activity has been accomplished. For example, process measures could be whether inventory checks were made or whether patients received evidence-based interventions. Process measures are often used to determine if a PDSA Cycle was carried out as planned.

***Balancing measures.*** To achieve an improvement in some measures while degrading performance in others is usually not acceptable. In making changes to improve outcome and process measures, we want to be sure any related measures are maintained or improved.

## What Changes Can We Make That Will Result in Improvement?

Answering this question requires developing changes to test. For relatively simple systems, a list of changes may be developed and tested almost immediately. For larger, more complex systems, or for efforts that require fundamental design or redesign, it is advantageous to answer the question in two parts. First, give some broad concepts for the system (for example, better match of capacity to demand), and second, offer more detail on the actual changes that will be made (for example, reallocating nursing resources from the day to the evening shift). Chapter Six presents methods for developing changes.

## The Plan-Do-Study-Act Cycle

Once the three fundamental questions are answered, the PDSA Cycle can be used to turn ideas into action and connect action to learning. Using the cycle effectively takes some discipline and effort. Figure 5.2 furnishes some detail on what should be considered in each phase of the cycle.

Ryan and his team planned a cycle to evaluate the participation of suppliers during the early concept design phase for a new computer. This cycle was part

### FIGURE 5.2. THE PLAN-DO-STUDY-ACT CYCLE.

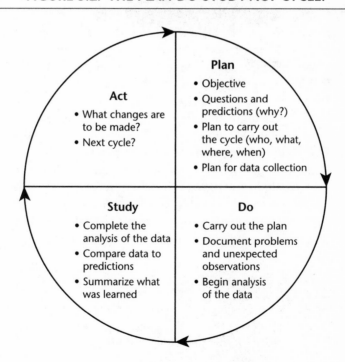

**Plan**
- Objective
- Questions and predictions (why?)
- Plan to carry out the cycle (who, what, where, when)
- Plan for data collection

**Act**
- What changes are to be made?
- Next cycle?

**Study**
- Complete the analysis of the data
- Compare data to predictions
- Summarize what was learned

**Do**
- Carry out the plan
- Document problems and unexpected observations
- Begin analysis of the data

of their project to increase the quality and lower the cost of their computers and associated products through better supplier relations. In theory, the idea of including suppliers in the design phase was appealing. However, it did take more work, it made the meeting arrangements more complex, and it required additional time for technical people from the suppliers. The team wanted to learn about the return on this investment.

The plan for the cycle was to invite suppliers to three upcoming design meetings. Each meeting was concerned with a different product, so a few people would be at all three of the meetings. In some cases, more than one supplier for the same component would be at a meeting and the team was interested in seeing the effect of having competitors at the same meeting. Two members of the team were assigned to attend all three meetings to observe and record their observations. In particular they were to record (1) attendance from the suppliers and their level of technical expertise, (2) ideas that came from the suppliers that would be pursued in the design, and (3) the willingness of suppliers to perform further investigative work after the meeting. After the meeting, a survey would be sent to each person who attended to get general impressions of the meeting and the usefulness of including suppliers at this phase in the design of a new product.

The improvement team would study the data for the three meetings. According to the results, they would take some action, such as changing the criteria for who gets invited, structuring the meetings differently, changing the timing for when to invite the suppliers, or continuing the meetings in the same format. More than likely, they would need to continue testing some of these ideas.

Contrast what Ryan and his team did with a more familiar scenario: have the meetings; after the meeting, hear some anecdotes about how the meetings went during a weekly staff meeting; from the most compelling anecdote, decide whether to keep inviting suppliers; and regardless of the decision, neglect to set up a good process to carry out the decision. Although in this scenario action could occur, it should not be considered a cycle. To be considered a PDSA Cycle, four aspects of the activity should be easily identifiable:

1. **Plan:** the learning opportunity, test, or implementation was planned and included:
   - Questions to be answered
   - Predictions of the answers to the questions
   - Plan for collection of the data to answer the questions
2. **Do:** the plan was attempted. Observations are made and recorded, including those things that were not part of the plan.

3. **Study:** time was set aside to compare the data with the predictions and study the results.
4. **Act:** action was rationally based on what was learned.

The PDSA Cycle is a vehicle for learning and action. The three most common ways for using the cycle as part of an improvement effort are:

1. To build knowledge to help answer any one of the three questions
2. To test a change
3. To implement a change

Not all improvements require PDSA cycles; some just happen. However, purposeful improvements in large or complex systems will usually require one or more cycles. Filling out a worksheet for each cycle is a convenient way to document the project. Appendix B contains worksheets proven useful for establishing a degree of discipline and thoughtfulness in carrying out a cycle. Examples of PDSA Cycles are in the case studies in Chapter Twelve.

In the improvement effort to reduce medication errors described earlier, the team was unanimous in their prediction that the changes would reduce errors. Sally then asked *why* they believed the changes would be successful. To the team's surprise, there were contrasting reasons for their unanimous prediction of "yes." A few thought it was because of the use of a protocol; others thought it was where the medications would be mixed or how they would be stored. The act of making a prediction and considering the basis for the prediction resulted in a much deeper understanding of why the changes were being made. It also caused the data collection plan to change for certain PDSA Cycles. (For example, data collection on where the medications were mixed was included.) The team felt better prepared to learn from their tests as a result.

PDSA cycles facilitate learning through an iteration of cycles spurred by predictions. We make predictions in the Plan phase of a PDSA Cycle to:

- Make the *why* underlying the prediction clear
- Surface differences in assumptions among team members before collecting data or running a test
- Prevent hindsight bias ("I knew it all along")
- Improve the Plan phase of the PDSA Cycle relative to how we collect data, develop, test, or implement changes
- Enhance the learning in the Study phase of the cycle when results are compared to predictions

The next sections clarify the use of the cycle as an aid to answering the three questions. The use of the cycle to test a change is discussed in Chapter Seven, and the use of the cycle for implementing a change is discussed in Chapter Eight.

## Using the Cycle to Build Knowledge

Although the primary use of the PDSA Cycle is to test changes, we can use the cycle when current knowledge or readily available background information is not sufficient to answer one or more of the three questions. The primary use of data in answering the question "What are we trying to accomplish?" is to determine why a particular aim should be chosen from among many initiatives. The data might be warranty claims, responses to a customer survey, an analysis of defects or complaints, plots of measurements over time, or documented comments from employees. An example illustrates the use of a cycle to set the aim for an improvement effort.

A manufacturer of garage door openers established an 800 phone line to assist customers. As input to their quality planning process, management planned a cycle to collect and analyze data from the calls to the 800 number according to this procedure:

- For one week, a summary of each call was logged.
- The calls were classified into six categories: installation, warranty, parts, new model, billing, and cosmetics.
- The data were collected for three more weeks by using a form with the six categories. Space was allocated for summaries of calls that did not fall into any of the categories.
- The analysis of the data was used as input to planning for improvement.

Figure 5.3 contains a Pareto chart (a graph that illustrates the relative frequency of occurrence of an activity; see Appendix B for more on Pareto charts) of the number of calls for assistance from customers received on the 800 number. Two aims were adopted as a result of analyzing the data: (1) to improve the ease of garage door installation and use of accompanying instructions, and (2) to make warranty information more understandable.

A PDSA Cycle can be used to answer the question "How will we know that a change is an improvement?" by assisting in determining a balanced set of measures for a process or system. Such a cycle might consist of a survey of customers or interviews with a sample of people who have a stake in the system. Four other cycles that might be completed to help answer this question include:

## FIGURE 5.3. PARETO CHART OF CALLS FROM CUSTOMERS.

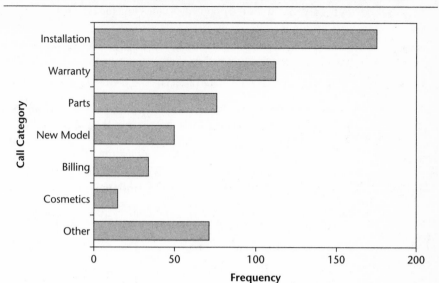

- Testing the feasibility of using a new measurement device, such as a color-measuring instrument
- Testing the clarity of survey questions
- Assessing the ability of workers to routinely collect data
- Testing the accuracy of a lab result

The question "What changes can we make that will result in improvement?" can be answered by using existing knowledge or some creative activity (see Chapter Six for more detail on developing a change). If ideas for specific changes are not available, one or more cycles can be used to build the knowledge necessary to develop the changes. An example illustrates the use of a PDSA Cycle to build knowledge to support the development of a change.

The management of a rapid rail transportation system in a large metropolitan area designed a cycle to help set priorities for improvement. The cycle included soliciting suggestions from riders of the subway as to how the system could be improved. More than eighteen hundred replies were received. The replies were analyzed in a variety of ways (most frequent, most creative, relative merit). The output of the analysis was a list of changes to be tested in subsequent cycles:

- Pay telephones on station platforms
- Better lighting in the stations

- More directional signs
- A twenty-four-hour telephone assistance line for riders
- Use of credit cards to buy fare cards
- Transit system information on display near the convention center
- Selling the family/tourist pass at all stations
- Indicators showing the color of the next scheduled train (by track)

When using PDSA Cycles to build knowledge to answer any of the three questions, it is important that the knowledge gained be subsequently translated into action. Do not forget the A in PDSA.

## Using the PDSA Cycle Sequentially to Test Changes

The Model for Improvement is based on an iterative, trial-and-learning approach to improvement. We advocate the testing of changes on a small scale initially to reduce risk and then, from the learning, use of subsequent cycles to scale up the changes. Even trials that are not successful can add to the learning if they are thoughtfully reviewed. Although the use of small-scale, sequential cycles for the design or redesign of large or complex systems is counterintuitive, it is an effective approach. The bigger the system, the more uncertainties there will be. In our experience, spending time in a conference room trying to perfect a change and then trying to "install" it is not an effective way to make improvements.

One criticism of this iterative approach is that for large systems the small cycles will not be coordinated and therefore will not result in real change to the system. This potential weakness is overcome by using broad concepts for the system design (see Chapter Eleven and Appendix B for more discussion on driver diagrams) to set the context for all the smaller cycles. It is important to note that *small-scale* refers to the size of the test. The change tested could be quite innovative and a significant departure from current practice—in this sense, a very large change. Figure 5.4 shows cycles to test the use of a scribe to offload paperwork from the dentist and hygienist. The team used these cycles with the aim to reduce waiting time in their dental office.

In large systems, it is often needed to test multiple changes. For example, in the dental office they might also be using a series of cycles to test extending the interval between appointments for certain patients. We will address this issue in Chapter Eleven, "Improving Large or Complex Systems."

## Using Data in a Cycle

To support an iterative approach, we need to establish a "learning loop." This can be thought of as consciously building on what we have learned from a previous

## FIGURE 5.4. REPEATED USE OF PDSA CYCLE TO TEST USE OF A SCRIBE.

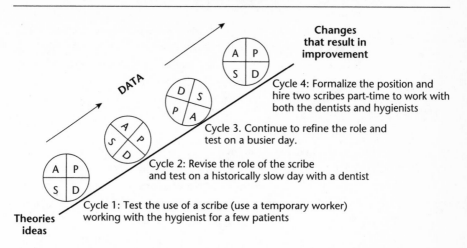

**Changes that result in improvement**

Cycle 4: Formalize the position and hire two scribes part-time to work with both the dentists and hygienists

Cycle 3. Continue to refine the role and test on a busier day.

Cycle 2: Revise the role of the scribe and test on a historically slow day with a dentist

Cycle 1: Test the use of a scribe (use a temporary worker) working with the hygienist for a few patients

DATA

Theories ideas

cycle or test. When we started riding a bicycle, we learned about our technique the hard way: we fell. Most of us learned quickly from the clear and immediate signals we received—two important characteristics of a good learning loop. Our experiences learning to ride a bicycle indicate that learning does not have to be based on data; few of us probably documented learning about our falls. But data can be a good source of feedback in PDSA Cycles to understand if we are having an impact on the system. We establish a learning loop in the Study phase of the cycle by comparing data to predictions. Data can take many forms but need to produce learning to serve as input to the next cycle. This learning ultimately leads to making changes that result in improvement. The use of data in a cycle to facilitate learning and action is an important aspect of the approach presented in this book.

> Theresa was a midlevel manager in a large corporation. Her department was responsible for processing hundreds of complex forms every day. To improve the performance of her group, Theresa purchased new high-speed computers and new software. She was quite sure these changes had produced improvement in the department's performance. But some of the clerks complained the new programs were too hard to use. Others talked about how fast the new computers were "once you learned the new system." Theresa's boss was not happy that errors were still being made, and the department's work was backed up worse than before they "invested all that money."

Theresa's problem could have been greatly reduced if her plan for the change (new computers and new software) had included the use of data collection and analysis. Data collected on measures such as errors made and time to process could be used to answer the fundamental question "How will we know that a change is an improvement?" Instead, Theresa relied on observation, memory, and feelings to judge the success of the changes being implemented in her department. The feedback she received might have been immediate, but it was not clear. In Chapter Two, we defined data as documented observations, including those that result from a measurement process. The only difference between observations and data is that data are thoughtfully documented. Data offer a more balanced and objective view of the behavior of the systems you are trying to improve.

Earlier we discussed the three levels of measurement: process, outcome, and balancing. In a cycle or sequence of cycles, each should be considered. Process measures can be used to learn whether the cycle is being carried out as planned. Theresa could collect data on whether the computers and software were being used correctly. She (and her boss) might expect an impact on outcome measures (that is, errors and time to process the forms) at the department level after a number of cycles have been run. Outcome measures might be affected in initial cycles if the cycles are focused on part of the population, such as a few of the clerks. Theresa should consider the feelings of staff as they learn to use the new computers and software to be important balancing measures. Collecting data on personal experience is discussed in Appendix B.

## Some Suggestions for Proper Collection of Data

Since data are usually collected as part of the PDSA Cycle, here are some suggestions for collecting data:

1. *Explicitly state the questions to be answered by the data.* Data are collected to facilitate learning. The data collection will be most efficient if the questions to be answered by the data are stated in the planning phase of a cycle. Deciding how the data will be analyzed (perhaps by sketching some "dummy" tables and graphs) gives those planning the cycle a check on whether they are collecting the data necessary to answer the questions posed. To make predictions more explicit, the questions "How much?" and "Why?" should be considered. Questions that elicit only yes-or-no answers should be avoided. Column 1 in Table 5.2 contains some questions for PDSA cycles. Column 2 shows the questions reworded to help make predictions more useful.

See the application of the tree diagram in Appendix B for identifying questions for a PDSA cycle.

2. *Use sampling to collect data.* To conserve resources, people can study a sample rather than all available items. For example, rather than recording every call

## TABLE 5.2. CRAFTING QUESTIONS FOR MORE USEFUL PDSA CYCLES.

| First Question Proposed for PDSA | More Useful Questions for Prediction |
|---|---|
| Will the new roles of the care team members result in more efficient and effective encounters with patients? | How much (as measured by a survey) will the new roles of the care team members improve encounters with patients? Why? |
| Will the new physical set-up of the manufacturing plant allow easy movement of materials? | How much time and resources will the new physical set-up of the manufacturing plant save in moving material? Why? |
| Will use of the new form reduce errors in billing? | How much will use of the new form reduce errors in billing? Why? |

to an 800 number, analyze every twentieth call in more detail. Much can be learned from samples, especially if they are collected over time. Reducing the burden of collecting a large amount of data also enables people to do a better job of studying the items selected. Studying a *sample* therefore often furnishes better information than studying all of the items available.

3. *Design and test a form for collecting the data.* Using a form carefully designed and tested to collect data will make collection easier and reduce the opportunity for error. The form should contain the necessary instructions for collecting the data and definitions of terms.

4. *Train those who will collect the data and give them understandable instructions.* In most cases the collection of data to aid improvement efforts requires some new tasks for those collecting the data. Do not assume people will know how to do these tasks. Conduct training that includes the reasons for collecting the data and the importance of the data. The specific process of measurement or recording should be reviewed and practiced.

5. *Record what went wrong during the data collection.* As the data are collected during the Do phase of the PDSA Cycle, some things may not go as planned. Be sure to require, in the instructions to those collecting the data, recording the unplanned occurrences. The people analyzing the data can then assess the impact of these occurrences on the conclusions drawn from the data.

Note that the appropriate rigor and formality of the application of these five suggestions for proper data collection will vary. With more complex measures and changes, more formality is useful. In simpler situations, especially those of shorter duration, less formality can be applied.

## Display and Analysis of Data

Good data analysis begins with clarifying what questions are being asked of the data. Are we trying to predict future performance, determine the extent of a problem, find out where we should focus our efforts, or determine a relationship? The questions we want to answer guide us not only to the appropriate data but also to what type of data display is appropriate. Of the many ways to analyze data, visual displays are a particularly useful form. There are five basic types of data display (more on these tools and considerations for constructing visual displays of data can be found in Appendix B):

1. Plots showing data over time (run chart and control chart)
2. Plots showing the distribution (shape and spread) of data (Pareto chart, histogram, stem-and-leaf plot, box and stem plot, pie chart)
3. Plots showing the relationship between different characteristics (scatter plot and response plot)
4. Plots showing location of data (map and physical layout)
5. Plots showing results for multiple measures (radar chart and spider diagram)

Of all the displays, the plots showing data over time play the central role in making improvements. Change is a prerequisite for improvement, and people experience change as a time-related phenomenon. The answer to the question "How will we know that a change is an improvement?" is often that one or more measures will increase or decrease over time. By plotting data over time, we can discern patterns that indicate improvement.

## Guiding Teams and Projects Using the Model for Improvement

Good charters will help individuals and teams ensure they are guided by the Model for Improvement and assist in team selection, sponsorship, and project management. Possible roles are team member, team leader, improvement advisor (sometimes referred to as a "black belt" or internal consultant), subject matter experts, and the management sponsor.

Table 5.3 describes the roles of team members with regard to various responsibilities during a project using the Model for Improvement.

# Key Points from Chapter Five

- Numerical goals contained in aims for improvement efforts must be connected to methods for achieving the goals, or else they can cause unintended consequences.
- In answering the question "How will we know that a change is an improvement?" assure the interests of the customer of the product, process, or service are strongly represented in the list of measures.

- During improvement efforts, multiple measures are almost always required to balance competing interests and help ensure the system as a whole is improved.
- Data collection will be most efficient and effective if the questions to be answered by the data and predictions are stated ahead of time.
- The Model for Improvement is based on an iterative, trial-and-learning approach to improvement. This iterative approach is spurred by prediction and feedback loops for learning. Even trials that are not successful can add to the learning if they are thoughtfully reviewed.

## TABLE 5.3. VARIOUS ROLES AND RESPONSIBILITIES OF A TEAM DURING THE LIFE OF AN IMPROVEMENT EFFORT

| Team Responsibilities | Team Member | Team Leader | Improvement Advisor | Subject Matter Expert | Management Sponsor |
|---|---|---|---|---|---|
| Using the charter | Accept and work toward the aim of the team | Keep team meetings focused on charter | Use the charter to focus the team and give input to the team | Learn what the team is trying to accomplish | Work with team to reach consensus on the aim |
| Education and training for the team | Learn the model, tools, and teamwork principles; apply these methods and ideas | Communicate need for additional help | Teach or coach the team on improvement and teamwork methods | Assist with required education and training on the subject matter; help assess needs | Help supply resources (time, schedules, use of experts) for the team |
| Organizing and conducting effective meetings | Attend and participate in meetings; complete assigned tasks | Plan meetings; distribute agendas, minutes; conduct good meetings | Focus on the team decision-making process | Observe meetings and help leader and sponsor | Periodically, attend meetings and participate, if needed |
| Using the Plan-Do-Study-Act Cycle | Participate in planning, data collection, study, and action | Organize team activities and assignments using the cycle | Assist the team to collect and analyze data and run effective tests | Furnish knowledge about the change being tested | Allocate resources and remove barriers to help teams take action for improvement |
| Communicating the status and results of the team | Share experience with coworkers | Serve as liaison to others outside the team | Help leader and sponsor summarize status |  | Keep abreast of team progress and report status to management |

CHAPTER SIX

# DEVELOPING A CHANGE

All improvement requires change, but not every change is improvement. Where do changes that result in improvement come from? Sometimes people are just lucky. For instance, a change in the business environment may open up new opportunities for a company. Unfortunately, organizations cannot count on luck; opportunities for change need to be pursued purposefully.

> Fred had managed the distribution department for eight months. When he first started the job, he sat down with some of the people in the department to get an understanding of how things were going. What he heard gave him a headache! Orders were not being filled promptly, and many were returned because of mistakes. Fred encouraged everyone to focus more on the quality of their work and hoped that things would get better, but eight months later similar things were still happening.

Fred needs to begin pursuing purposeful change. People usually make changes to improve the quality of their work or lives. For a change to have this kind of impact, it will involve altering an existing activity or product, or developing something new. In business terms, this is called the design or redesign of a process, product, or service.

Change should be developed considering those who will benefit from the results of the change. When people make changes in their lives, they, their families, and their friends can benefit. When changes are made in an organization, the focus should be on benefits to the customer. Other stakeholders should be considered, but in answering the fundamental questions the customer's voice should stand out. Fred heard the customer's voice loud and clear: complaints about the time it took to ship orders and the number of errors that were made. Fred will learn that complaints are perhaps the least desirable way to hear the customer's voice.

The Model for Improvement, introduced in Chapter One and further explored in Chapter Five, supplies the framework for making effective change. The three fundamental questions and the PDSA Cycle offer a framework for making changes that result in improvement. Sometimes, confronted with the question "What changes can we make that will result in improvement?" we think the answer seems obvious. The knowledge to support a specific change has existed for some time, but the conditions, resources, or inclination needed to make the change have not existed. Many times, however, a change that will result in improvement is not obvious. In such cases, people have a tendency to resort to some common, though often ineffective, ways of developing change.

## Some Typical Problems in Developing Changes

Once Fred decided that something had to be done with the problems causing customer complaints, he set up a meeting with Susan, the vice president. Fred requested that an additional person be hired to work in the distribution department, or at the very least that the current people be allowed to work overtime. Susan was somewhat skeptical about this approach; an additional person had been hired a little more than a year ago. She asked Fred about some of the other things he had tried in order to improve the timeliness of shipments. He said he had tried encouraging people to work harder. He had even tried to enforce daily work quotas; nothing was working. Susan would not agree to hire another person. She suggested that Fred try having people inspect one another's work to reduce the number of errors made.

Both Fred and Susan employed some common, ineffective approaches to improvement. They resorted to doing more of the same—more people, more money, more time, more exhortations to work harder. Susan also suggested adding inspection. Although such changes are commonly used, none of them will alter the basic way work is accomplished in the distribution department. They may result in some improvement in the short run, but they will also probably add costs and complexity to the system. Such changes can often contribute to the problem, or actually become a worse problem:

- Trouble with meeting customer requirements: add more resources (more money, more time, or more people)
- Trouble with performance of a product: introduce or add more inspection
- Trouble with variation in a process: make more adjustments
- Trouble with adherence to procedures: add more procedures or define them more rigorously
- Trouble with discipline: add more restrictions

It is also common for some people to look for perfection when they are developing a change, a tendency known as the *utopia syndrome*. This syndrome causes individuals, teams, and organizations to suffer paralysis of action. This search for perfection can slow down the consideration of changes that could be readily tested and adapted today. Part of the motivation of looking for the perfect change is fear of failure. To make a change is to take a risk; the change might not result in improvement and in fact might actually make things worse. As long as people are busy working on perfection, they will not have time for testing new ideas. The fact that doing nothing may be a bigger risk is little consolation. To support the development and testing of change, people must be willing to embrace the unexpected (things not working out as planned) as an opportunity for learning. Many of the ideas and techniques described in this chapter and in Chapter Seven on testing are meant to give the reader an approach that minimizes risk in making changes.

## Reactive Versus Fundamental Change

The noun *change* is defined as the process or result of making or becoming different. For example, making your facial expression different is a change. But "different" is not the same as "an improvement." Developing a change that is an improvement from the viewpoint of the customer is not always easy. It invariably requires that a fundamental alteration or modification be made to the system of interest. The change need not be expensive or time-consuming; it just needs to involve design or redesign of the process, product, or service.

There is an important connection between appreciation of a system and ideas for change. In developing changes, it is useful to distinguish between changes that are needed to keep the system of interest running day-to-day at the current level of performance (reactive changes) and changes that are needed to create a new system of performance (fundamental changes).

## Reactive Changes

Reactive changes are required to maintain the system at its current level of performance. Here are some aspects of reactive change:

- They are often made routinely, to solve problems or react to a special circumstance.
- They often result in putting the system back to where it was some time before.
- Typically they take the form of a trade-off among competing interests or characteristics (such as increasing quality but also increasing cost, reducing errors but also reducing volume, or speeding up delivery but reducing customer service).
- Their impact is usually felt immediately or in the near future.

When one deals with problems, making a reactive change is often the best strategy. A customer may not receive a shipment when expected because a truck broke down; a physician may be called away on an emergency, affecting the waiting time of scheduled patients; or bad raw material may result in a faulty product. In each case, there is a need to make changes to remove the immediate problem and bring the performance of the system back to where it was. Special circumstances could also affect costs. Materials may run out, resulting in a company having to pay retail prices; a faulty machine could increase waste; or a pipe could break, causing excessively high water bills.

> When Fred looked more closely at the work being done in the distribution department, he noticed that the postal meter broke down quite often. This added to delays in fulfilling orders. Fred brought this problem to the attention of the company that supplied the meter. They promised to get a repairman there quicker the next time the meter was out of order.

Another example of making a reactive change illustrates *why* sometimes we have different perceptions about whether changes are reactive or fundamental. To reduce infections and other side effects, hospitals are trying to minimize the number of days an intensive care patient has to spend on a mechanical ventilator. The ICU director in one hospital was asked to investigate why the vent days per patient were high in the last quarter's management report. In August, she put together an improvement team that investigated and learned that some of the standard procedures were not being followed. The team conducted staff training to review the standard procedures and by the end of the year reported a 50 percent reduction in average ventilator days in the unit, with the rate now running below the goal of four days. The top graph in Figure 6.1 shows a run chart the QI team used to report their results.

## FIGURE 6.1. RUN CHARTS OF AVERAGE NUMBER OF VENTILATOR DAYS PER PATIENT IN ICU.

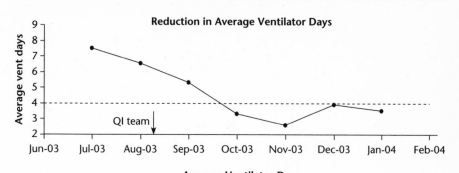

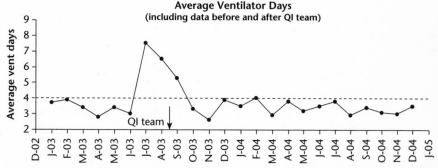

At the end of the year, the management team was reviewing the annual performance and noticed that the average of the ventilator days was not much different from the previous two years. They were concerned that the days had crept back up after the QI team's work. They prepared a run chart of the last two years to better understand what was going on. This second run chart shows the system had deviated from its expected performance in July 2003, and the work of the QI team brought the performance back to norm (a reactive change). Monitoring processes and reacting to deviations in performance are important components of effective quality control in any organization, but not the same as improving the system by making a fundamental change.

## Fundamental Changes

The ability to make reactive changes is very important for any organization. If the broken postage meter were not repaired quickly, customers would experience delays. Reactive changes should not, however, be confused with fundamental changes, which prevent problems from recurring. After a reactive change has been made, customers will perceive an immediate problem has been solved.

After a fundamental change, customers should also perceive an improvement has been made. Fundamental changes are required to improve the system beyond historical levels. Here are some important aspects of fundamental change:

- They result from design or redesign of some aspect of the system (process, product, or service) or the system as a whole.
- They are necessary for the improvement of a system that is not plagued by problems.
- They fundamentally alter how the system works and what people do.
- They often result in improvement of several measures simultaneously (quality and cost, or time-to-ship and errors).
- Their impact is felt into the future.

> Fred was happy that the supplier of the postal meter was being more responsive when the machine broke down. He was not happy, though, that he did not see a significant impact on service to customers. So he decided to have discussions about improvement with the people who worked in the distribution department. After a few meetings, they agreed there were many times during the year when their workload surged because of special offerings. If they could only find out about these specials earlier, they might begin to prepare them for shipment during their slow work periods. The people were sure this would reduce the time to fulfill requests and that it would also reduce the number of errors. They used a couple of PDSA Cycles to test this change. The result was a reduction in the average time to fulfill requests and in the number of orders that were returned because of errors. What made the group even happier was that the improvement was often mentioned by customers on the company's monthly survey. The people in the department were so encouraged they began to think about other changes they could make to improve performance.

A fundamental change can be made by redesigning part of the current system or by designing an entirely new one. In redesigning a system, you should consider first whether the system is even needed; eliminating part or all of a system is one possible fundamental change. Second, be aware that big improvements can often be realized by making small changes directed at the right places in the system.

> Fred's group decided to focus on the system of order fulfillment for large orders (see the system flow diagram in Figure 6.2). Two departments played a major role in the system. The customer service department took the orders and printed the picking tickets. Fred's distribution department then pulled the items,

packaged them, and loaded them onto a truck. After the picking tickets were printed in customer service, someone walked the tickets down to distribution twice a day. This resulted in alternating periods of light and heavy workloads. If the heavy period was in the afternoon, shipments often were not completed that day. Operation of this system resulted in only about 40 percent of orders being shipped on the same day they were received.

Guided by the flow diagram they created, Fred's group worked with customer service to make two small but significant changes to improve performance. The first change was to move the customer service printer into the distribution department. The picking tickets could then be printed in distribution every hour. The second change was to move the final time at which a truck left the distribution department from 4:00 P.M. to 5:00 P.M. These two small changes resulted in same-day shipments being made more than 85 percent of the time. The group is now considering whether customers can enter certain orders directly into a computer in the distribution department, which could result in a fundamentally redesigned system.

Making fundamental change has now become the focus of the people in the distribution department. It is their aim to continuously improve the system. They must keep in mind, however, that once fundamental changes are made, unanticipated problems can occur. It is important to make the reactive changes required to remove any immediate problems until the appropriate fundamental changes can be developed to eliminate them.

## FIGURE 6.2. THE SYSTEM OF ORDER FULFILLMENT.

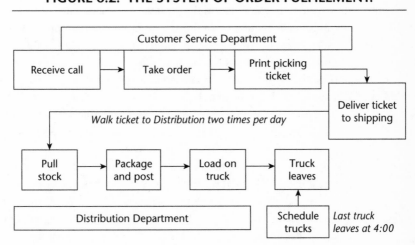

Fred noticed that once in a while the picking tickets would pile up in the printer. When he asked his group what was going on, they said that sometimes they forgot the picking tickets were no longer being delivered to them by customer service. Fred wrote himself a reminder to get the picking tickets from the printer. He could not be there all the time, however. He realized that he needed to get his group together again to develop a way to ensure that the picking tickets were picked up every hour.

## Theory for Change

How do we develop fundamental changes that lead to good system improvements? What is the relationship between our theories of how our organization works and effective ideas for change? Sometimes changes are made without any understanding of the theories behind the change. We might do what our parents, teachers, or other mentors did when faced with a similar problem. But if we want to develop fundamental changes that go beyond the performance of our current system, it is useful to enumerate theories about why we think our proposal will be a good change. Making theories (or hypotheses) explicit helps all participants in an improvement effort to articulate the basis of predictions that changes will result in improvement. Stating our theories or assumptions also helps us design tests to validate these theories and improve our change idea from the results of these tests. A theory represents our current knowledge about how some aspect of the system of interest works. When is our theory valid enough to begin testing our ideas for change?

Fred's success in increasing same day shipments for large orders from 40 percent to 85 percent and the positive customer feedback that resulted from this improvement got him thinking about the remaining 15 percent of the shipments that did not make it the same day as ordered. The IT department had informed him that direct entry of orders from customers could not be done prior to a system upgrade scheduled to be completed in two years. Could he do something about the late shipments now, or would he have to wait two years? Fred decided to make some observations and collect some data.

The next morning, Fred asked for some information on any large orders received the day before that had not yet been shipped. He learned there were three orders, so he went out to the warehouse to see what he could learn about them. He noted that all three of the orders included three or more stock items, and all were waiting on an item that was currently not available in the warehouse. Fred wondered if the complexity of an order (number of items) might lead to late shipments. He decided to test his idea the next day on other shipments that were shipped today. The next morning he was told that five large shipments did not go out the previous day. He was tied up in meetings, so he asked the data clerk to check to see if these late shipments all included more than three separate stock items. He bet the clerk a soft drink that he would find all five were complex shipments (a prediction). When Fred returned from his meetings, there was a note and a soft drink bottle on his desk; all five orders were complex, with one of them containing twelve stock items. Fred had confirmed his theory and was ready to share his information on the association of complexity and late shipments with his boss.

Fred's boss was impressed by his finding and his theory that the 15 percent late large shipments the department was experiencing were all associated with complex orders. This was logical to her because more items in the order meant more opportunities for stockouts and other problems to occur. One missing item would hold up the order. Fred's data (eight out of eight late shipments were complex) were pretty convincing. They began to brainstorm some ways to reduce the complexity of customer orders. This discussion led to questions about which of their customers were making the complex orders. Fred agreed to collect customer information on any late shipments the next day.

There were four orders not shipped, each from a different customer. But one of the late orders was for only one stock item. Fred's investigation found that the order for this item was unusually large and required more than what was stocked to fill it. Fred had found another attribute of order complexity: unusually large quantities of a single item ordered. He updated his theory: either a large number of items or an unusually large quantity of an item means a complex order that is not shipped on the same day. His data now showed twelve large complex orders (newly defined) were associated with the twelve late shipments during the past three days.

Fred was ready to apply his "complexity theory" for the causes of late shipments for large orders and develop some changes on the basis of the theory. But when he reviewed the data on the twelve late shipments and presented his theory to the distribution group, they were not as impressed as his boss. The dock supervisor pointed out that a majority of their orders contained more than three items and most orders (85 percent) were currently shipped the same day. Another team member objected that the sales department already had guidelines to keep a customer from ordering more than the amount stocked for a specific item. Fred realized from this feedback that he had only focused on the late shipments and should have also tested his theories with on-time shipments. He was pretty discouraged until another member of the group pointed out something interesting in the twelve late orders. There was a ticket from the assembly group in eleven of the twelve orders. From memory, the group agreed that fewer than 20 percent of orders contained items that required assembly. This observation led the group to begin making plans for some data collection that would help them better understand the association between items requiring assembly and late shipments.

Fred's experience with developing a theory on which to base changes is not unusual. When he attempted to make the leap from his original ideas about large orders, he discovered that causal relationship was not as strong as he thought. He discovered he needed to further develop his theory about late shipments. Once he learns further about the association between items requiring assembly and late shipments, he will be ready to design a series of appropriate tests to continue to build his theory. Chapter Seven discusses approaches to the design of tests using PDSA Cycles.

It is not always necessary to understand the theory behind a change that leads to improvement. This is especially true when we are interested only in specific local applications of a change idea. Sometimes we accidentally stumble on a new way to do something that gives better results and we are not sure why. Many early advances in medical care occurred this way; sometimes it was years later that someone was able to describe the theory of why the change worked. But it is difficult to transfer this type of change to other applications or spread it to other organizations. Others will ask "Why?" and want to know our theory.

Communicating their theories about changes that will lead to improvement is an important function of an effective improvement team. Without a common understanding of the working theory, the team may be working on changes for various perceived reasons. Making a prediction in the Plan step of every PDSA Cycle, and then discussing the basis of the predictions, is one way to keep theories for improvement in the project out in front of everyone.

Another way to make a theory explicit is to develop a concept design for the change of interest. Actually describe, at a conceptual level, the redesigned product, service, or system that you are envisioning to the rest of the improvement team. This might take the form of a picture, a physical model (prototype), or a computer simulation.

The cause-and-effect diagram seen in Appendix B is an improvement tool that can be used at the beginning of theory building. It is often associated with a brainstorming session; subject matter experts can build the diagram by describing all the ideas they have that might be causing a particular problem or that could potentially affect a specific opportunity for improvement. The ideas are recorded on the diagram, organized by categories of causes.

Another approach to describing our theories of improvement is to construct a driver diagram (Appendix B). The initial driver diagram for an improvement project might illustrate the team's current theories and ideas and hunches of improved outcomes that can then be tested and enhanced with PDSA Cycles. The diagram can be updated throughout an improvement effort and used to track progress in theory building in answering the question "What changes can we make that will lead to improvement?"

Figure 6.3 shows a driver diagram for the initial theory Fred presented to the group for reducing late shipments of large orders.

After Fred's initial theory of "managing complex orders" was found to be invalid, the group started developing a new theory for late shipments. Figure 6.4 shows the status of the driver diagram for the new theory.

For more complex projects, the driver diagram will have multiple primary and secondary drivers. (An example is presented in Chapter Eleven.) Specific ideas for change can then be connected to these drivers. This gathering of concepts and ideas useful for improvement in a particular context is, at times, referred to as a change package or bundle. As knowledge is built, the changes in the package are supported by evidence that suggests adaptation and implementation of the changes will lead to improved results.

## FIGURE 6.3. DRIVER DIAGRAM FOR FRED'S PROJECT.

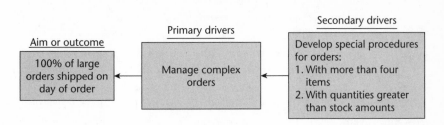

## FIGURE 6.4. UPDATED DRIVER DIAGRAM FOR DISTRIBUTION DEPARTMENT LATE SHIPMENTS.

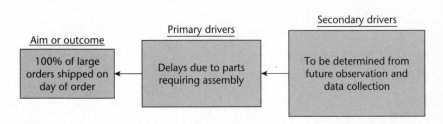

# Methods for Developing Fundamental Change

The remainder of this chapter describes five approaches for developing fundamental changes:

1. Logical thinking about the current system
2. Benchmarking or learning from others
3. Using technology
4. Creative thinking
5. Using change concepts

## Logical Thinking About the Current System

Sometimes it just takes a little time to develop good ideas for change by reflecting on the system of interest (perhaps with the use of a flow diagram, as described in Appendix B, or a video or other pictures) and using already-existing knowledge of the subject matter. Talking about or documenting how a process is currently performed or how a product works or is used might be sufficient to identify ideas for change. This is the approach Fred took with his group in the distribution department. Reflection on what is wrong with a system can be enhanced with knowledge of some principles of good system design (which is introduced in the discussion on change concepts later in this chapter) to develop good fundamental changes.

Figure 6.5 contains an example of a flow diagram created by a group working in a blood plasma donation center. Their aim was to improve the process by which new donors were selected. Once the group had spent some time reviewing the flow diagram, it became obvious to them that there were some potential improvements to the current process. The fact that donors could be rejected at three separate steps in the process added complexity.

After thinking logically about this current system, the group made some simple changes that resulted in the physician and phlebotomist working more as a team. Consequently more plasma was collected and customer satisfaction increased. The changes made are shown in the flow diagram at the bottom of Figure 6.5.

The collection and analysis of data contributes significantly to identifying problems with the current system and their causes so that changes can be developed. These changes can then be tested in later cycles. An example of collecting data in a rapid rail transportation system to help develop a change was included

# FIGURE 6.5. FLOW DIAGRAM OF ORIGINAL AND REDESIGNED PROCESS FOR SELECTING PLASMA DONORS.

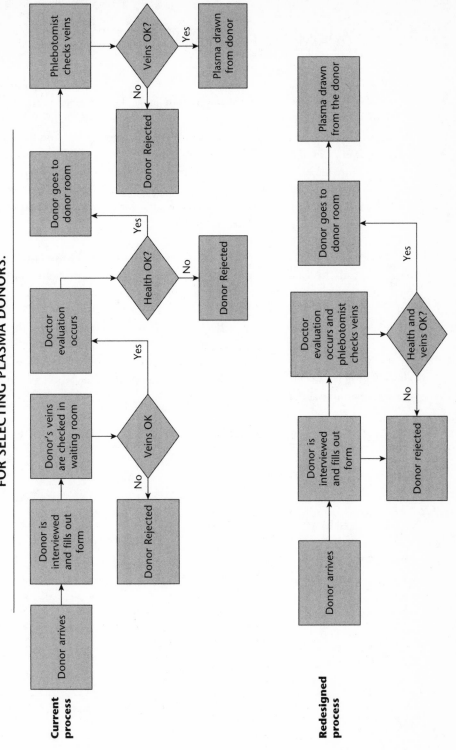

in Chapter Five. Here is another example of logical thinking about the current
system.

> The nurses at a Midwestern hospital felt that certain blood serum measures
> made by the hospital's laboratory were unreliable. They decided to run a
> PDSA Cycle to better understand the nature of the variation in the blood mea-
> surements. They sent the lab a sample of blood from one large stored bottle
> once every shift for two weeks. The data obtained was plotted on a run chart
> (see Figure 6.6). The nurses learned from the plot that the B shift consistently
> produced higher results than the A and C shifts. From this knowledge, they
> determined that any change made to reduce the variation in blood testing
> should be related to the differences in shifts.

Another strategy to uncover issues and opportunities in the current system is to study in detail a "sample of one" (or case study approach). We might
take one customer order and follow it all the way through the system. Or take
one diabetic patient and use the medial record to review the patient's history in
the health care system for the past five years. Or we could take one product and
walk it through the assembly line to see what would be required to eliminate all
delays. The learning from this one experience often encourages logical thinking
about high-leverage changes that could have an impact on the whole system, not
just the one sample that was observed.

## FIGURE 6.6. BLOOD MEASUREMENTS FOR ONE SOURCE.

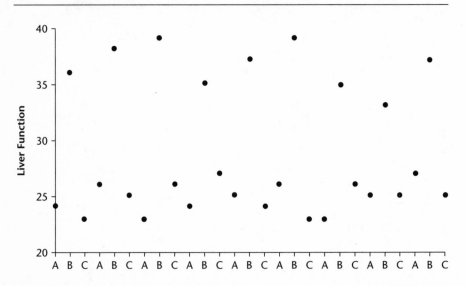

More sophisticated approaches to support logical thinking, such as statistical analysis (regression analysis, data mining, time series analysis, simulations, and so on), can also be used to develop ideas for change. These methods rely on using data generated from the current system.

## Benchmarking and Learning from Others

In many cases, the improvement we want in our organization has already been made by others. The changes may not match our exact context, but the aim would be to adapt the ideas they used to our environment. How can we learn about these change ideas from others?

In recent years, the practice of "benchmarking" has been popularized and used by many organizations as a method for both setting goals for improvement and learning about "best practices" or change ideas that result in a high level of performance. The term *benchmarking* comes from land surveying and refers to a marker of a previously determined position, which can be used to establish a new position. A popular book by Robert Camp defines benchmarking as "the process of identifying and learning from best practices or best performance from any industry to identify potential changes for improvement."

It is in this sense we use the term *benchmarking* in improvement work. Benchmarking in its simplest form is merely looking around at how others are doing things and trying to learn new approaches and possibilities. A formal benchmarking process furnishes a method with some structure for making these observations and then using this information for improvement.

Benchmarking can compare how things are done differently (practices), or it can compare measurements taken from processes (metrics). For example, benchmarking might look at a process such as accounting, compare some key measures from the accounting processes of several organizations, and try to learn from these differences. Benchmarking might also look at how the accounting processes in organizations are carried out and try to learn from these differences.

Anyone in the organization can participate in a benchmarking process. Some organizations assign specific individuals to make regular visits and learn new ideas about their organizational core processes. It does not take any particular sophistication to go on a visit and learn how someone else is doing things; being curious and interested in learning new things are the key personality traits. Spending time listening and asking questions, instead of talking, are the key behaviors that result in successful benchmarking efforts. But it is useful to have a basic process to increase the chance of success and furnish a platform for improving future visits. Without a thoughtful process, a benchmarking exercise can turn into just an industrial tour. An example of a benchmarking process could be to:

1. Identify organizations that are high performers in the type of system we want to improve (distribution, new product development, employee development, and so forth)
2. Make initial contact with these organizations:
   - Explain the rationale for our desire to visit (or "benchmark")
   - Request information about their current outcomes in the areas of interest
   - Explain how we want to use the information and our process for learning from their system
   - Discuss options of how we may want to share information in the future or what they might be interested in learning about our system.
   - Discuss potential times for a visit.
3. Develop a plan to obtain the information of interest during the visit (organize the visit as a PDSA Cycle):
   - What questions do we want to answer? What are our predicted answers to these questions?
   - Who do we need to visit to get this information?
   - What parts of the organization do we want to physically visit to make observations (knowing that front-line observations can often supply the most useful information)?
   - How will we successfully collect the data and information needed to understand best practices and bring back the information required to develop change ideas (using checklists, cameras, video, written reports, example of forms and tools, and so on)?
   - Ask for feedback and suggestions from the host site on the plan, and make adjustments accordingly.
4. Conduct the visit according to the plan (Do in PDSA).
5. Share the information gained from the benchmarking visit with the members of the improvement team that did not attend ("Study" in PDSA).
   - Collect additional questions for follow-up.
   - Develop a list of potential ideas to test.
   - Collect information requested from the benchmarking host.
6. Prepare a thank-you response to the benchmarking host.
7. Consider improvements to the process for future benchmarking.

Why would anyone allow you to benchmark their organization? Sometimes your closest competitors would not be comfortable with you doing that. But many find that the best benchmarking opportunities are outside of their industry or type of organization. Winners of the U.S. Malcolm Baldrige Quality Award are required to describe their outcomes, processes, and approaches in their business as part of the award process. They also present at a formal meeting and set up formal site visits the year after they win the award.

The idea behind benchmarking can be applied in a number of other ways to develop change ideas. Activities such as interviewing, field visits, volunteering to work in an organization, and shadowing someone in his or her job are all variations of observing others to develop new ideas for change.

Many people practice benchmarking in a way that leads to copying something they have seen without understanding the underlying theory. This is usually not successful and in fact can lead to disastrous results. The key to making benchmarking worthwhile is to focus on learning about the *causal mechanisms* (why something works well) more than the *what*.

## Using Technology to Develop Changes

For the purposes of this discussion, *technology* is defined as the practical application of science, including equipment, materials, information systems, and methods. Technology can be used to generate fundamental change. For instance, Fred's group in distribution might try using automation to pick and package orders. If approached correctly, new technologies offer organizations opportunities for making big improvements by just applying what others have developed. However, large amounts of money and time are often necessary to make a technology-related change happen, especially in a capital-intensive industry such as manufacturing. In some situations, the change may not even result in improvement.

> A transportation company introduced a computerized reservation and routing system. The system left thousands of potential passengers unable to get through on the phone and thousands of actual passengers stranded in terminals. Ridership and the company's stock price plummeted.

This company is not alone when it comes to the introduction of new technology. Companies have invested countless dollars in new information systems alone. These systems have created opportunities to solve quality problems, reduce costs, and develop new products and services. Some would question, however, whether they have resulted in all of the improvements desired. By considering methods for improvement in acquiring and using new technology, we increase the likelihood that the technology will result in an improvement.

To take advantage of new technology, processes for recognizing relevant technological breakthroughs should be in place within the organization, along with processes for bringing in beneficial technology. In some situations, an organization might also consider getting involved during the early stages of the development of the new technology. This might be done by establishing partnerships with other organizations or by allowing the developers to test the technology in one's own organization.

One of the pitfalls an organization can fall into is "acquisition of technology for technology's sake." Application of the three questions of the Model for Improvement can help protect against this.

Organizations must determine ways to test the new technology on a small scale, which should help reduce the risk involved in bringing it in. Renting or leasing new equipment, having a supplier furnish a few lots of a new material, and using the technology in a pilot process are examples of ways to test new technology.

Some people will find it difficult to change to using new technology. When computers were first introduced, some people felt more comfortable using more familiar typewriters and file cabinets. The appropriate training is often not conducted. Even if it is, people sometimes find ways to avoid it. To lessen these problems, management must have a plan to help people transition to use of the new technology. The guidelines for implementing a change discussed in Chapter Eight should prove useful when integrating technology-related changes into a system.

Here are some cautions for making changes that involve technology:

1. Do not automate a bad system.

   A professional association processed more than two hundred requests for materials each week. Most of the requests were initiated by a form that appeared monthly in the association's journal. In an attempt to reduce the long delays in responding to these requests, a scanner was purchased that allowed the form to be read directly into the association's computer system. Unfortunately, this did not speed up the process very much. The same information was still missing from or incorrect on the form.

   It appears the association is attempting to automate a bad system. This just allows errors to be made faster! Simple redesign of the system using changes such as mistake proofing, simplification of the form, minimization of the number of handoffs, and standardization of the system should be considered. Cycles might be run to redesign the system first before a change involving automation is developed and tested.

2. Try to reserve technological solutions for improving stable systems rather than fixing special causes.

   The variability of the semifinished product coming from a particular operation in a large manufacturing facility was so great that the product was difficult to process at further operations. This resulted in large scrap and rework costs. To reduce the variability, the plant manager proposed to the division vice president that they purchase a new piece of equipment. Although the new equipment was expensive and more costly to maintain, the plant manager felt the savings in scrap, rework, and the like would offset most of this extra cost.

Before a change involving technology is developed, it should be understood whether special causes affect the variability in the system. If this operation were studied by the people in the plant, they might discover that special circumstances were the source of much of the variation. Special circumstances might include changes in lots of raw material, substitute operators, or changes in operating conditions. Although the new equipment might mitigate the effect of these special causes (or might not), a more cost-effective change may be possible. Once the special causes have been identified and removed, if further reduction in variation is needed then a more fundamental change will be required. Only then should the use of new technology be considered.

3. Direct changes that involve technology at a bottleneck (or constraint).

A hospital invested in a new computer system to speed up the paperwork required for admissions. New patients could now be processed in half the time. They did not get into their rooms any faster, however, because they still had to wait until a room was available.

A bottleneck is the component of a system that limits the overall performance or capacity of the system. Because the throughput of the system is dictated by the capacity at the bottleneck, changes should be directed at increasing the flow through that resource. Using technology to increase capacity in areas that are not bottlenecks will not result in increasing the throughput of the system. It will just result in greater waiting time at the bottleneck. The hospital used new technology to increase patient flow through admissions. This did not decrease the total time for patients to get to their rooms because the discharging of patients was the bottleneck in the system.

4. A technology that is unreliable is worse than none at all.

A new machine to fill drums with product was installed at a manufacturing plant. The next week, however, it failed to work on a very busy day at the plant, delaying the shipment of product.

Once a change involving technology is implemented, people rely on the performance of that new technology. The new technology should therefore be thoroughly tested so there is no doubt about its reliability.

## Creative Thinking to Develop Changes

In its simplest form, creativity is the inventing of a new idea. Where does the new idea come from? How does one go about getting more creative ideas? Creativity is not something that a few gifted people possess, but rather a capacity everyone possesses. How can people begin to unleash that capacity?

The nature of the mind that makes it a bountiful source of creativity is also the force hindering creativity. A way to think of the mind is as a self-organizing information system. As perceptions and experiences occur, the mind attempts to find meaning and order. This organizing process uses existing thought patterns to judge the meaning of the new experiences. Using existing thought patterns severely restricts the options for change people consider. It is one of the primary reasons individuals or groups who are not skilled in improvement usually produce ideas for improvement that are more of the same.

The normal thought patterns occurring in a particular situation have a logic sharpened over time (Figure 6.7). Because a new idea does not yet have an acquired pattern of logic to support it, it can easily be defeated by this more well-developed logic. Thus a promising new idea can be squelched before it has had a chance to be refined into a change that would result in improvement.

Breakthroughs in creativity are often produced by recognizing and using new modes of thinking. Recognizing the different modes is especially helpful in group

## FIGURE 6.7. NORMAL THOUGHT PATTERNS (LOGICAL THINKING).

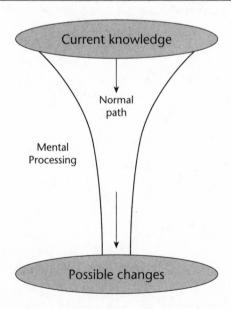

or team settings. Three modes of thinking are usually present when changes are being developed:

1. Creative thinking, which results in new ideas and possibilities
2. Logical positive thinking, which is concerned with how to make a new idea work
3. Logical negative (critical) thinking, which is focused on finding problems in the new idea

All three modes of thinking are important and play a role in developing changes that result in improvement. Without creative thinking, some incremental improvement may result, but there is often only more of the same. Without logical positive thinking, good concepts for change will not result in practical, workable changes to the system. Critical thinking is needed to surface problems.

These three modes of thinking must be recognized and managed by teams developing changes. It is usually better for a group to engage in one type of thinking at a time. When new ideas for change are being developed, creative and logical positive thinking should be used. This allows logical thinking to enhance creative thinking rather than stifle it.

Methods for creative thinking have their foundation in provoking new thought patterns, which lead to new ideas for change. (Figure 6.8 illustrates this concept.)

## FIGURE 6.8. PROVOKING NEW THOUGHT PATTERNS.

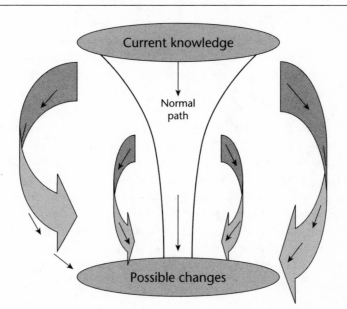

Without new thought patterns, a very limited set of potential changes will be produced.

Provoking new thought patterns opens up a limitless variety of changes that can result in dramatic improvement. Here are some general methods for provoking new thought patterns:

*Take time.* This is the simplest method. Spend perhaps even just five or ten minutes to expressly do some creative thinking.

*Be in the right place at the right time.* A story claims that Isaac Newton was provoked into thinking about gravity by an apple falling on his head as he sat under a tree. Spending time observing customers or taking the role of a customer can allow a person to be in the right place when serendipitous events occur that provoke new ideas.

*Challenge the boundaries within which the change can be developed.* People are often limited in developing changes by implicit or explicit boundaries. To challenge these boundaries, begin by listing them; then eliminate or expand the boundaries. One of the boundaries listed by a group working on improving service in an office cafeteria was that the food was always paid for after it was selected. When the team challenged this boundary, the use of prepaid meal tickets or a set-price buffet was suggested as a possible change.

*Attack the solution.* Make a list of the suggested changes and identify what they have in common. As in challenging the boundaries, attack the common themes as hindrances to new ideas. Look for a change that does not possess this commonality. A group working on improving efficiencies in their order fulfillment process examined previous changes made. Although some of the changes were successful, all of them were focused on reducing paperwork and handoffs within the organization. A review of these solutions resulted in someone suggesting that customers enter their orders directly into a computer in the distribution area.

*Use "unrealistic" goals.* When the current way things are done is clearly inadequate to meet the goal, ask, "What would it take to____?" (Fill in the blank with a seemingly unrealistic goal.) This will help people abandon the current way of thinking.

*Focus on the need.* For any particular product or service, articulate what the need is that the product or service is meant to match, and then—as with attacking the solution—discard the current products and services as options. There will be many ways to match the need with new products and services. For example, a landscaping company offered the service of mowing lawns. After they articulated that keeping the grass short and neat was the need for this service, they began to experiment with regulators that slowed the growth of the grass. This greatly reduced the service demand for mowing, but also created a platform to build a highly profitable business around care of lawns using appropriate regulators and enhancers.

When new thought patterns are provoked, new ideas for change should result. These ideas can often be brought to life through some form of expression, such as giving an example, drawing a picture, storytelling, or acting them out. Ideas are slippery things, and the act of representation tends to stabilize them, allowing them to be studied and improved. Representation is also a way to share the idea with others.

After Tony drew a picture of the new handles he had been talking about, everyone was able to see why it would help with lifting large pots. Mary added some detail to the picture, and they took it down to engineering to see if they could install the handles on one pot to test.

Appendix B summarizes some of the creativity tools that facilitate these ideas for creative thinking.

## Using Change Concepts to Develop Changes

A change concept is a general notion or approach found to be useful in developing specific ideas for change that result in improvement. When Fred and the group in the distribution department began to consider changes to improve service, they took time to think critically about how work was being accomplished. This did result in some improvements. Suppose, however, that to provoke new ideas Fred was able to apply already existing concepts for change to his situation. He would have been able to start with a concept such as "smooth the work flow." Then, to develop a specific change, the team could have combined this concept with their knowledge of how the distribution department worked. Starting with such a concept can help people accelerate the quality and quantity of new ideas.

Included in Appendix A of this book are seventy-two "change concepts" that are at the heart of changes that result in improvement. Many are based on the elements of W. Edwards Deming's System of Profound Knowledge, discussed in Chapter Four: appreciation for a system, understanding variation, building knowledge, and the human side of change. Others have been collected over time by this book's authors. Regardless of the origin of the concepts, their usefulness to improvement makes them valuable. Using change concepts will provoke new ways of thinking about how to improve the situation at hand.

Here is a list of the seventy-two change concepts. Appendix A gives detailed discussion of each concept. As you review these concepts, many will be familiar. Some of the concepts have been grouped and packaged by others as a particular approach to making improvements, as is seen in the items following the list.

## Complete Listing of Change Concepts

1. Eliminate things that are not used
2. Eliminate multiple entry
3. Reduce or eliminate overkill
4. Reduce controls on the system
5. Recycle or reuse
6. Use substitution
7. Reduce classifications
8. Remove intermediaries
9. Match the amount to the need
10. Use sampling
11. Change targets or set points
12. Synchronize
13. Schedule into multiple processes
14. Minimize handoffs
15. Move steps in the process close together
16. Find and remove bottlenecks
17. Use automation
18. Smooth workflow
19. Do tasks in parallel
20. Consider people as in the same system
21. Use multiple processing units
22. Adjust to peak demand
23. Match inventory to predicted demand
24. Use pull systems
25. Reduce choice of features
26. Reduce multiple brands of the same item
27. Give people access to information
28. Use proper measurements
29. Take care of basics
30. Reduce demotivating aspects of the pay system
31. Conduct training
32. Implement cross-training
33. Invest more resources in improvement
34. Focus on core process and purpose
35. Share risks
36. Emphasize natural and logical consequences
37. Develop alliances and cooperative relationships
38. Listen to customers
39. Coach customers to use product/ service
40. Focus on the outcome to a customer
41. Use a coordinator
42. Reach agreement on expectations
43. Outsource for "free"
44. Optimize level of inspection
45. Work with suppliers
46. Reduce setup or startup time
47. Set up timing to use discounts
48. Optimize maintenance
49. Extend specialist's time
50. Reduce wait time
51. Standardization (create a formal process)
52. Stop tampering
53. Develop operation definitions
54. Improve predictions
55. Develop contingency plans
56. Sort product into grades
57. Desensitize
58. Exploit variation
59. Use reminders
60. Use differentiation
61. Use constraints
62. Use affordances
63. Mass customize
64. Offer product/service anytime
65. Offer product/service anyplace
66. Emphasize intangibles
67. Influence or take advantage of fashion trends
68. Reduce the number of components
69. Disguise defects or problems
70. Differentiate product using quality dimensions
71. Change the order of process steps
72. Manage uncertainty, not tasks

- "Lean" (aka Toyota Production System) includes most of concepts 1 through 27 and number 71, which deal with eliminating waste, improving work flow, and optimizing inventory.
- "Six Sigma" includes most of concepts 51 through 62, which focus on managing variation and designing systems to avoid mistakes.
- Throughput and Cycle Time programs include concepts 46 through 50, which deal with ways to better manage time.
- Customer service programs usually contain many of concepts 28 through 40, which are related to enhancing the producer-customer relationship and changing the work environment.
- Supply Chain Improvement programs contain some of the concepts numbered 12 through 27 and 40 through 45, relating to improving work flow and optimizing inventory.
- Product Design Programs contain many of the change concepts 63 through 70 and 72, which focus on a product or service.

Fred and his group in the distribution department were having difficulty developing additional ideas for change to further improve the flow of work. A friend who was familiar with Fred's dilemma passed on to him a book. In the appendix, Fred found concepts that could be used to develop ideas for change. In fact, there were a number of concepts that dealt directly with improving work flow [concepts 12 through 14 in the list seen here]. Fred was very excited about sharing these concepts with his group. He felt the concepts would help to generate some specific ideas for change.

At the next meeting, Fred explained what he was going to do and asked them to think positively while changes were being suggested. He started by presenting the change concept "minimize handoffs" [number 14]. Immediately Mike said they did have a tendency to hand off a particular job, from picking to packing to postage. There would be fewer holdups if one person could both pick and package the order. Others nodded in agreement and offered some other suggestions. Fred was starting to feel good about this approach. He tried another concept: "smooth workflow" [number 18]. Karen said they had smoothed the flow by starting to prepare orders earlier. She wondered why they had not been given this concept before they spent so much time trying to come up with the idea. Next, Fred tried "do tasks in parallel" [number 19]. John enthusiastically suggested, "Let's get the paperwork going at the same time we are preparing the order." Fred was very happy about how the meeting was progressing. They had begun to develop a number of good ideas for changes, and he still had more change concepts left. The possibilities for improvement now seemed almost endless.

## FIGURE 6.9. USING CHANGE CONCEPTS TO DEVELOP SPECIFIC IDEAS FOR CHANGE.

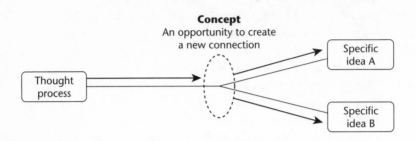

Fred employed a good approach for using the change concepts. He first picked some of the concepts related to his issues of improving flow of work. Then he used some of the change concepts from that grouping to provoke specific ideas for change. His approach is not the only way that the change concepts can be used.

The change concepts listed here are designed to be context-free and at a similar level of abstraction. So by themselves, these concepts are not ready to be applied directly to making improvements. Rather, a concept must be considered within the context of a specific situation and then turned into a change idea. Figure 6.9 illustrates this thought process; the idea will need to be specific enough to test and implement in a particular situation.

The diagram also suggests another way to use change concepts. Observe a specific idea (idea A in diagram) in another context (see earlier discussion of benchmarking). Then extract the concept(s) behind the idea. Next apply the concept to the context you are interested in, and create a new idea (idea B) that is potentially useful for improvement in your system.

Sometimes, a new idea seems at first to be a new change concept; often, with further thinking, it is seen to be an application of one of the more general concepts. Figure 6.10 uses Fred's earlier experience with developing a change to illustrate an example of moving from strategic yet vague concepts for change to specific ideas for change. Note the change concept "move steps in the process closer together" in the third position moving down the diagram. The next step in becoming more specific requires the concept to be applied to a specific context ("Move order receipt and warehouse closer together"). In the last step, the idea becomes specific to the context of interest: "Move the printer that prints orders into the warehouse."

How is a particular change concept selected for focus in a session to generate ideas? The aim of the improvement effort will give some direction. Here are some ways that have been found useful:

- Select a group of change concepts that are related to the aim of the improvement effort (the list in Appendix A can help with this). Then randomly choose one of the change concepts in that category.
- Choose a change concept someone on the team thinks might generate some ideas that would be useful to the aim of the improvement effort.
- Choose change concepts that have not been previously considered by the team.
- Randomly choose a change concept from the list of seventy-two.

When a concept is randomly selected, more creative ideas can be expected to come from the session because people might get further away from their usual thought processes. Conversely, it might take a longer session before the relevance of ideas from a randomly selected concept is discovered. A concept, or concept category, that is obviously relevant to the aim of the improvement effort can be expected to yield a higher number of useful ideas in less time, but it may not generate a completely new approach to the activity of interest.

Fred kept a list of the ideas for change developed using the change concepts. The list was very impressive. Although the group believed all the changes had potential, they also realized the changes needed to be tested to determine if they actually would result in improvement. So, they prioritized the different change ideas, considering such things as predicted impact, the cost, and the ease of testing and implementation. The group was excited, but Fred was worried. He had never thought about testing changes before. Fortunately,

## FIGURE 6.10. MOVING FROM CONCEPT TO SPECIFIC CHANGES.

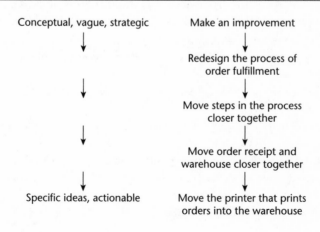

Mary was familiar with the use of PDSA Cycles to test new ideas and helped the group learn how to do this.

As discussed earlier, the seventy-two change concepts have been considered from the perspective of Deming's system of profound knowledge. However, it is still useful to critique new ideas developed from the concepts through the lens of profound knowledge before initiating testing.

Others have described the use of concepts to generate ideas. Edward de Bono made concept thinking a key strategy in his approaches to creative thinking. His writings include a number of tools (see Appendix B) to formally use concept thinking. Another use of concepts is called "TRIZ." This is a Russian acronym meaning "the theory of the solution of inventive problems." The list of inventive principles contains concepts that are more technical and connected to the physical sciences than the change concepts in our listing. Similar to the change concepts for improvers, the concepts in TRIZ attempt to take the engineer out of the box of limited thinking and put the person in a world of creative or inventive thinking.

## Key Points from Chapter Six

- All improvement requires change but not every change results in an improvement.
- Fundamental change results from design or redesign of some aspect of the system (process, product, or service) or the system as a whole. They are required to improve the system beyond historical levels. They often result in improvement of several measures simultaneously.
- A strategy to uncover issues and opportunities for change in the current system is to study in detail a "sample of one." For example, take one customer order and follow it through the system.
- Some cautions for making changes that include technology:
  - Do not automate a bad system.
  - Try to reserve technological solutions for improving stable systems rather than fixing special causes.
  - Direct changes that involve technology at a bottleneck (or constraint).
  - A technology that is unreliable is worse than none at all.
- To provoke new thought patterns to develop fundamental change:
  - Spend time observing customers or taking the role of a customer; this can allow a person to be in the right place when serendipitous events occur that provoke new ideas.

- Challenge the boundaries within which the change can be developed.
- Attack the solution.
- Use "unrealistic" goals.
- Focus on the need for a particular product or service.
- Use change concepts to provoke new ways of thinking. Seventy-two change concepts were introduced in this chapter. They are discussed in the later chapters and in Appendix A.
- Changes developed need to be tested to determine if they actually result in improvement.

CHAPTER SEVEN

# TESTING A CHANGE

Chapter Six discussed methods for developing a change. When a change is developed, how should the potential improvement from the change be evaluated before the change is implemented? How can we accelerate the learning as we test the change? How can the risk of making a change be minimized?

> Jim was a supervisor in a lab. He had recently become aware of a new procedure that could be used to measure the amount of a key ingredient in a product. Another lab that used this procedure reported improvements in accuracy and time to complete the test and attributed it to the fact that the new procedure eliminated complexity. Jim decided to test the new procedure in his lab.

Jim thought the change had some promise. He made a wise decision when he decided to test the new procedure rather than just implement it. In making improvements, it is important to distinguish between testing and implementing. Testing is used to evaluate the change on a temporary basis. Implementing the change means making it part of the day-to-day operations for a process or system or incorporating it into the next version of a product. An important practical consequence of testing before implementing is that some tests are expected to fail, and we can learn from those failures. This is why testing on a small scale to build knowledge while minimizing risk is so important. Once a change is implemented, we should expect very few failures. (Implementing a change is discussed in Chapter Eight.)

## Applying the Science of Improvement to Testing

Chapter Four laid a foundation for the science of improvement by using Deming's profound knowledge along with subject matter knowledge to develop effective change. The use of this science of improvement as an outside view or lens offers important guidance in testing changes. Some insights for testing changes:

- Understand interdependencies in the components of the system where the changes are being made
- Understand the relationship between prediction and knowledge of the system being changed and how predictions about the changes build knowledge
- Understand the temporal effect of changes made in the system
- Understand how separating variation of outcomes of a process or system into common and special causes helps to decide appropriate actions (inappropriate action may make things worse)
- Understand how to integrate changes in the social system (especially when planning for implementing the changes)

Testing changes builds knowledge about the causal mechanisms at work in a system. A process of building knowledge emphasizes the importance of rational prediction. If during testing a prediction is incorrect, the theory that was used to generate the prediction must be modified.

When considering making predictions about a change, it is important to recognize that a very limited set of conditions will be present during the test. Circumstances unforeseen or not present at the time of the test will arise in the future. Will the change still result in an improvement under these new conditions? In the opening example, Jim is interested in learning whether the new procedure will be an improvement in his lab when used by different technicians for different batches. To move forward with the change, he is making a prediction that the change will result in improvement once it is implemented. Extrapolation of the test results to the future is the primary source of uncertainty when testing a change. Determining whether the change actually resulted in improvement during the test is important, but this determination is usually much less difficult than considering the effect of the change in the future.

A government agency was concerned about the low rate of immunization (shots for measles, polio, and so on) among children. The agency proposed a change that consisted of the agency buying the available vaccine and distributing it free of charge to physicians. Their prediction was that this would substantially increase the rate of immunization among children. The prediction was based on the theory that the cost of the shot is a primary reason people do not have their children immunized and that free vaccines would eliminate this reason.

The formulation of a scientific basis for prediction has its beginnings with W. A. Shewhart. Shewhart's concept of "degree of belief" presents a way to think about and assess the depth of an improvement team or individual's knowledge about a change. In making any prediction, one has some degree of belief (high, medium, or low) the prediction is correct. One's degree of belief in a prediction depends on two considerations: (1) the extent to which the prediction can be supported by evidence, and (2) the similarity between the conditions under which the evidence was obtained and the conditions to which the prediction applies.

The government agency made a prediction about a change to increase immunization rates. Is the cause of a low rate the cost of the vaccine, as the agency suggests? Perhaps it is something else, such as lack of knowledge the shots are important, or neglect, or complacency because no one gets certain diseases anymore. What is the evidence to support the theory that cost is the issue? Do poor people have a lower immunization rate? What about people with low income who have the shots paid for by a government program, by an employer-supplied insurance plan, or by an HMO? Data related to the prediction will help answer these questions. The government agency should consider this as it makes decisions on testing in numerous areas.

How could you quantify degree of belief? Unlike a probability, confidence level, or statistical significance level, degree of belief is a concept, not a calculated value. The belief is about a prediction, not a past occurrence. There is not a proven theory to make quantitative statements about the future. Degree of belief is increased as tests of changes are conducted and predictions begin to agree with the results of the tests. If a prediction is incorrect, our theory must be modified and hence learning takes place. We propose a "gold standard" for building evidence in testing changes:

> *Gold standard: Satisfactory prediction of the results of tests conducted over a wide range of conditions is the means to increase the degree of belief that the change will result in improvement.*

Achieving the gold standard for testing changes requires accelerated learning on the part of an improvement team or individual. Methods to accelerate the learning are discussed in the next section.

## Accelerated Learning

As one moves from changing simple work processes to more complex systems, the rigor for learning must be increased, as well as the rate of learning. Teams often spend too much time thinking about all of the possible options, ramifications, and implementation issues before proceeding with a test of a change. Can one learn more by diagnosing the current process or system, or by changing something? Improvement efforts are frequently stuck in the diagnostic journey (analysis paralysis). The alternative is to very quickly run a test. Experience has shown this latter approach leads to accelerated learning and improvement. However, it does require a structured approach to testing and learning.

## Use the PDSA Cycle to Accelerate Learning

Knowledge is built through a systematic revision and extension of theory based on comparisons of predictions and observations. The PDSA Cycle, discussed in Chapters Four and Five, facilitates this iterative (that is, deductive-inductive) approach.

The four steps in the cycle used for testing consist of planning the details of the test and making predictions about the outcomes (Plan), conducting the test and collecting data (Do), learning from comparing the predictions to the results of the test (Study), and taking action based on the new knowledge (Act).

Developing a good plan for a test is critical to its success. The plan begins with a statement of the specific objective for the test. The objective of the cycle clarifies the specific focus of the testing of the change. Cycles to test a change will have varying objectives depending on the current degree of belief. Some objectives of test cycles might be:

- Increasing degree of belief that the change will result in an improvement
- Deciding if one or more changes will lead to the desired improvement
- Deciding which combination of changes will lead to the desired improvement
- Evaluating how much improvement can be expected if the change is implemented
- Deciding if the proposed change will work in the actual environment of interest
- Evaluating cost implications and possible side effects of the change
- Give individuals a chance to experience the change to minimize resistance upon implementation

After agreeing on the objective, we can identify the changes to be tested. The specific questions to be answered in the cycle are stated by the team (or individual) involved in the improvement effort and a discussion of the theories related to these questions occurs. A plan to answer these questions is developed. The plan includes who, what, when, and where. Where will the test be conducted? When will the test be done? These details need to be specific before a plan can be carried out. The principles for testing a change and various test designs are presented later in this chapter.

How will the results of the test be evaluated? Should outcome, process, and balancing measures be included? How will the data be collected? Who will be involved? Finally, the team makes predictions for the questions based on the plan. As discussed in Chapter Five, the predictions should be stated such that the results of the tests conducted in the cycle can be compared to the predictions.

Here are hints for planning useful cycles in testing changes:

- Think a couple of cycles ahead of the initial test (future tests, implementation).
- Scale down the size and decrease the time required for the initial test.
- Do not require buy-in or consensus as a prerequisite for the test (for instance, recruit volunteers, or run tests to evaluate conflicting ideas).
- Use temporary supports to facilitate the change during the test.
- Be innovative to make the test feasible.

In the Do step of the cycle, the test is performed and data are collected. Two types of data should be collected during the Do step: (1) data that are useful for answering the questions in the plan and can be compared to the predictions, and (2) data about problems and unexpected occurrences during the test. Although much of the learning will come from the Study step, the Do step has its own unique learning opportunities. Documenting problems and unexpected occurrences during the test will promote learning about aspects of the change that studying the planned results will not.

The information obtained during the Do step should prepare for the effective learning in the Study step. What if the test of a change is not successful? There are a number of possible reasons:

1. The change was not properly executed.
2. The support processes required to make the change successful were not adequate.
3. The change was executed successfully, but the predicted results did not occur.

Information should be obtained during the Do step to clearly differentiate which situation occurred.

The third step, Study, brings together the predictions made in the Plan step and the results of the test conducted in the Do step. This synthesis is done by comparing the results of the data analysis to the predictions. If the results of the test match the predictions, the team's degree of belief about their knowledge is increased. If the predictions do not match the data, there is an opportunity to advance their knowledge through understanding why the prediction was not accurate.

In the Act step of the PDSA Cycle for testing a change, the team or individual must decide on the next course of action:

- Is further testing needed to increase the team's degree of belief about the change (for example, testing under different conditions)?
- Do alternative changes need to be tested?
- Is it important to learn about other implications (such as costs) of the change?
- Is the team ready to implement the change on a full-scale basis?
- Should the team modify the proposed change or develop an alternative change?
- Should the proposed change be dropped from consideration?

A change should be abandoned only if the current theory (updated from the Study step) no longer predicts that the change will result in improvement. A common reason many initial tests fail is that the change was not executed properly. In these cases, the next cycle should focus on better execution. The decision on a specific course of action will lead to developing the next PDSA Cycle. The use of multiple cycles allows knowledge to increase as the team progresses from testing to implementing a change, while at the same time minimizing risk. As the degree of belief that the change will be successful is increased, the scale of the test can be increased. See Appendix B for a PDSA form.

Figure 7.1 illustrates changes in degree of belief as a team or individual uses PDSA Cycles to go from the development of a change to testing and implementing it. Degree of belief changes in the three cases illustrated, depending on the results of the test of the change. The next section discusses some basic principles that should be applied to all PDSA Cycles used to test a change.

## Principles for Testing a Change

Anyone who has tested a change has probably pondered whether the same results will be obtained when the change is implemented in the future. Considering three basic principles helps reduce this uncertainty:

## FIGURE 7.1. DEGREE OF BELIEF WHEN MAKING CHANGES TO IMPROVE.

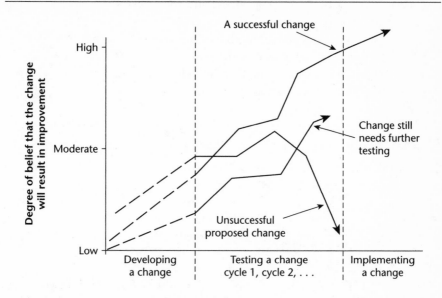

Principle 1: Test on a small scale and build knowledge sequentially.
Principle 2: Collect data over time.
Principle 3: Include a wide range of conditions in the sequence of tests.

## Principle 1: Test on a Small Scale and Build Knowledge Sequentially

Knowledge is built iteratively by making predictions that are based on the current theory, testing the predictions with data, improving the theory according to the results, making predictions on the basis of the revised theory, and so forth. The building of knowledge in a series of tests is illustrated in Figure 7.2.

It is important to minimize the negative impact that can result from a change that does not result in improvement. Table 7.1 summarizes the appropriate scale of the test for a number of situations. Very small-scale tests are needed if the degree of belief is low and the consequences of failure are large. Planning one large cycle in an attempt to get all of the answers with one test should always be avoided. Moving to implementation (discussed in Chapter Eight) should be considered only if:

- The team has a high degree of belief that the change will result in improvement, and
- The cost of failure is small (losses from a failed test are not significant), and
- The organization is ready to make the change.

# FIGURE 7.2. SEQUENTIAL BUILDING OF KNOWLEDGE WITH MULTIPLE PDSA TEST CYCLES.

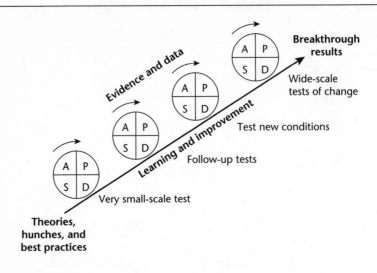

## TABLE 7.1. DECIDING ON THE SCALE OF THE TEST.

| Current Commitment Within Organization | | No Commitment | Some Commitment | Strong Commitment |
|---|---|---|---|---|
| Low degree of belief that change idea will lead to Improvement | Cost of failure large | Very small-scale test | Very small-scale test | Very small-scale test |
| | Cost of failure small | Very small-scale test | Very small-scale test | Small-scale test |
| High degree of belief that change idea will lead to Improvement | Cost of failure large | Very small-scale test | Small-scale test | Large-scale test |
| | Cost of failure small | Small-scale test | Large-scale test | Implement |

During the design of PDSA Cycles to test a change, those responsible for developing the change should be asking themselves how they can reduce the risks of the test and still gain some knowledge. Here are some ways to design a test on a small scale:

- Simulate the change (physical or computer simulation).
- Have others with some knowledge about the change review and comment on its feasibility.

- Test the new product or the new process on the members of the team that developed the change before introducing it to others.
- Incorporate redundancy in the test by making the change side-by-side with the existing process or product.
- Conduct the test in one facility or office in the organization, or with one customer.
- Conduct the test over a short time period (one hour or one shift).
- Test the change on a small group of volunteers.

Testing a change on a small scale is an important way of reducing people's fear of making a change. When small-scale tests are not considered, people procrastinate. They try to develop the perfect change because of the potential consequences of a failed test. This approach might be particularly prevalent in some big corporations or government agencies where any change to programs or policies is usually scrutinized. When planning a cycle to test a change, much thought should be given to developing ways of building knowledge through small-scale tests.

On the basis of what is learned from any cycle, a change might be:

- Implemented as is (adopt)
- Dropped (abandon)
- Modified (adapt)
- Increased in scope (expand)
- Tested under other conditions

One should never move quickly to implementation after one successful small-scale test. In most situations, additional cycles for testing the change are needed. As the degree of belief in the success of the change is increased, the scale of the test can be increased with less risk.

Similarly, one should never move quickly to abandonment of a change after one "failed" small-scale test. One must first understand why the prediction is incorrect. Is the observed outcome an anomaly? There is much to learn from failure. The whole point of performing a small-scale test is to minimize the risk from failed tests and maximize the learning.

A company that manufactures tiles for floors and ceilings was experiencing some difficulties with the accuracy of inventory records. A computerized material control system (MCS) was used to keep track of the amount of inventory on hand. Actual physical counts to verify the computerized records were made frequently by a variety of people. Discrepancies were often found between the MCS and the physical counts. Adjustments made to reconcile the discrepancies seemed to make the problem worse; the situation was having an effect on the schedule for manufacturing. A team was therefore formed to make improvements to the process of monitoring inventory. The team had great success in increasing inventory accuracy by using numerous cycles to test and implement changes. The objectives of some initial cycles were as follows:

Cycle 1 Test changes to standardize procedures for the physical counts for residential tile.

Cycle 2 Test the revised counting procedures (based on the learning from cycle 1) for physical counts for residential tile.

Cycle 3 Implement the new counting procedures for the physical counts for residential tile.

Cycle 4 Test the new counting procedures for other products.

Cycle 5 Test the revised counting procedures (on the basis of learning from cycle 5).

Cycle 6 Implement the new counting procedures for other products.

Cycle 7 Collect data to determine the impact of adjustments to the MCS, from physical counts of the inventory of residential tile.

Cycle 8 Test the use of the control chart to determine when adjustments to the MCS for residential tile should be made.

Cycle 9 Implement the use of control charts to determine when adjustments to the MCS should be made for all products.

## Principle 2: Collect Data over Time

In conducting PDSA Cycles, there will be variation in the measures of the product or process due to causes and conditions unrelated to the change being tested. The effect of the change must be distinguished from these uncontrolled or extraneous conditions. Viewing the patterns of the data over time can assist in this distinction. It is also helpful to analyze data over time to determine whether a system is stable after a change has been made. A stable system constitutes a rational basis for predicting that the change will result in improvement in the future (see Appendix B on the use of control charts to evaluate stability of a system).

Figure 7.3 shows the results of data collected for fourteen weeks. For the top graph, data was collected on week 4, the change was made after week 7, and then data was collected again on week 11. The reduction in cycle time from eight hours to three hours was considered very significant for the process of interest. Does this test, summarized in this way, afford an adequate degree of belief that the change, once implemented, will lead to an improvement? Are there other feasible explanations of the reduction in cycle time after the change was introduced?

## FIGURE 7.3. RESULTS OF A BEFORE-AND-AFTER TEST.

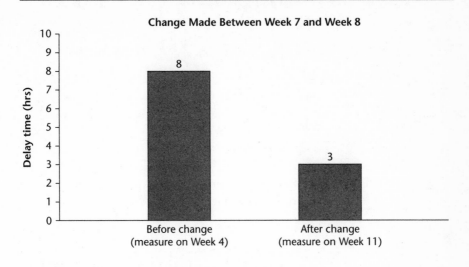

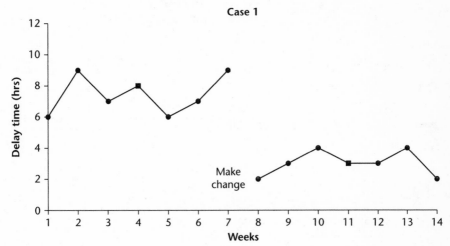

The run chart at the bottom Figure of 7.3 (case 1) shows one possible scenario that could have yielded the results observed in the test. The run chart shows results for cycle times for weeks 1 to 14 (three weeks before the change was made until three weeks after the second test observation was made). The run chart in case 1 confirms the conclusion the change did result in a meaningful improvement.

Figure 7.4 shows five run charts for other possible scenarios that offer alternative explanations of the test results. In each case, a run chart of cycle time for weeks 1 to 14 is shown. The test results for week 4 (cycle time of 8) and week 11 (cycle time of 3) *are the same* for all cases.

# FIGURE 7.4. RUN CHARTS FOR BEFORE-AND-AFTER TESTS.

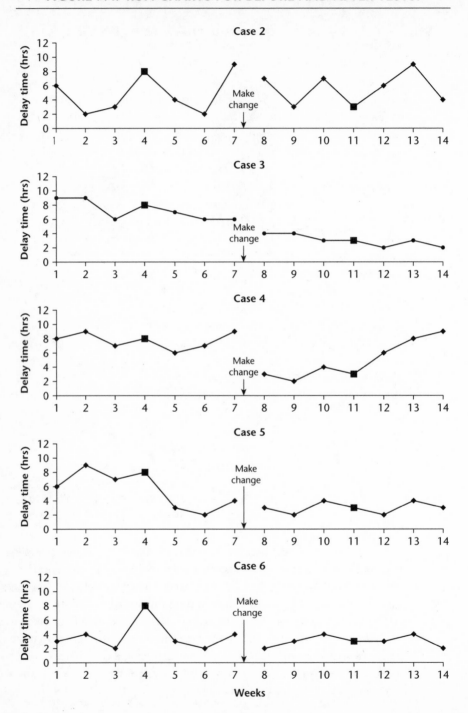

In case 2 there is no obvious improvement after the change is made. The measures made during the test are typical results from a process that has a lot of week-to-week variation. The conclusion from analysis of the run chart is that the change did not have any obvious impact on the cycle time.

In case 3 it appears that the process has been steadily improving over the fourteen-week period. The rate of improvement did not change when the change was introduced. Although the cycle time for the process has certainly improved, there is no evidence that the change made any contribution to the steady improvement in the process over the fourteen weeks.

In case 4 an initial improvement is observed after the change is made, but in the last three weeks the process seems to have returned to its pre-change level of cycle time. The results may be due to a Hawthorne effect. (This is named after some tests on productivity conducted at the Western Electric Hawthorne plant in the 1920s. During the test, the people involved may be more careful or diligent in their work, and this extra diligence may be the cause of the improvement rather than the change being tested.

In case 5, an improvement in the process cycle times has occurred, but it appears that the improvement occurred in week 5, before the change was made after week 7. The improvement in cycle time should be attributed to some other phenomenon, not the change of interest.

In case 6 the process appears to be stable, except for a special cause that occurred in week 4 when the pretest results were obtained. The unusually high result on week 4 made it appear that the typical result on week 11 was an improvement. Once again, there is no evidence that the change contributed to any improvement.

If a statistical test of significance (for example a t-test, described in books on statistical methods) for difference in means was used, would there be significant results in cases 2 through 6 in Figure 7.4? In performing a t-test on the fourteen points of data from each of the cases, case 3 was significant with a p value $< .001$, case 4 was significant with a p value $< .034$, and case 5 was significant with a p value $< .030$. That is, using a statistical test of significance would lead to an incorrect decision for three of the six cases.

Incorporating time into the test will be a more important consideration than the sample size. There is almost always more information in small samples selected over a long time period than a larger one collected over a relatively short period of time. A large sample taken in the winter to determine the results of a test may not increase degree of belief about the effect of the change in the summer.

## Principle 3: Include a Wide Range of Conditions in the Sequence of Tests

Including data spread over time is also a convenient way to include a range of conditions in the cycle, the third principle for testing a change. How can a team increase their degree of belief that the change will be effective in the future? Including a wide and varied set of conditions in the test is the best way to increase degree of belief.

Too often, tests of change are not conducted over a broad range of conditions. Some reasons given for limiting the conditions are limited resources, time constraints, difficulty in analysis of the data, lack of knowledge of how to efficiently include different conditions, and too many possible conditions to consider. Degree of belief in the results of a test increases as the same conclusions are drawn for a variety of test conditions. The time required to increase the degree of belief that the change will result in improvement and persist is a matter of judgment.

If a particular supplier's material proves to be the best in various environmental conditions and on different days and shifts, one feels much safer to use the results to select a supplier than if the test was run on one day under constant environmental conditions. The experimenters might also consider running the test using material from more than one lot provided by the supplier. Incorporating some or all of these conditions will increase the degree of belief in the results if similar conclusions are seen for all conditions.

Consider a PDSA Cycle to choose one of four types of instruments for use by operators in the plant to replace the current instrument. The objective of the cycle is to choose an instrument for future use that will yield the best precision when used by any operator. Resources are sufficient to allow seven of the thirty operators presently working in the plant to participate in the test. How should the seven be chosen?

The seven operators in the test could be randomly selected, and the magnitude of measurement variation under the conditions of the test could be estimated. But it is important to remember that the conditions of the test will not be seen again. There will be new operators working under new conditions, training may change, and so on. A judgment selection of operators will permit a higher degree of belief concerning the performance of the instruments in the future. One option is to choose some operators who have the most experience *and* some with the least experience. If an instrument performs best when used by experienced and inexperienced operators alike, the degree of belief that a good choice of instrument has been made will usually be greater than if the instrument performed best when used by seven randomly selected operators.

In this example, selecting seven operators from the most and least experienced was a type of judgment sample. It is rare in a test of a change that a random selection of people or things to test is preferred to a selection made by a subject matter expert—that is, a judgment sample. Another way to include a wide range of conditions in a test is to bring in different conditions in a systematic way. These conditions potentially can affect the results of the test but are not part of the change (lot, shifts, seasons, temperature, noise levels, and people).

In the next section, several types of designs to test changes are presented. Choice of a design depends primarily on the objective of the test and one's degree of belief about the change.

# Designs for Testing a Change

A *test design* is the arrangement of the changes being tested and the people or things on which the changes will be tested (people, manufacturing runs, primary care clinics) in the test. Designs of various types can be used within a PDSA Cycle. The individual or team involved in testing a change should select a level of formality and complexity relevant to their situation.

The test designs introduced in this section are:

1. Observational
2. Before-and-after
3. Time series
4. Factorial

These designs are widely applicable and occupy the midrange of formality and complexity. More advanced test designs are beyond the scope of this chapter. Many books are available for further study of more advanced designs.

## Observational Design

A team was considering a new method of measuring patients' temperatures in a hospital. The new method was advertised to be quicker than, and just as accurate as, the current method they used. Instead of testing the new method in their hospital, the team decided to collect data from two other hospitals using the new method. They would then compare results (time and accuracy) to similar data from their hospital using the current method. It appeared that the new method is better.

If the results of this "test" look promising, the team can then design a test of the new method in their hospital. The advantages of such an observational design are simplicity, low cost, and low risk. The disadvantage is that one must make assumptions about the conditions where the observations were made. In the example, the team might assume the two hospitals were similar to theirs, although the hospitals may have been better off with their current method as well. The relevance and importance of these assumptions determine how much degree of belief is increased by an observational PDSA Cycle.

A team can also learn from an observational cycle that includes studying individual cases. These individual cases can be compared to a standard process, for example the treatment of asthma at a children's hospital, or the certification of raw material from a supplier. This would allow learning about deviation from the process or improvements to the standard process itself.

## Before-and-After Design

One of the more popular designs for a test of change is the "before and after test" (or pretest, posttest design). In this design, a comparison is made of the circumstances after the change to the circumstances before the change. The collection of data before the change furnishes the historical experience that is the basis of the comparison. The data before the change could be collected as part of the test or be already available (baseline).

In some situations, it might be practical to collect data only once before and once after the change. For example, scores on a pretest and posttest might be used to evaluate the effect of new audiovisual materials in a history class, or a group of patients undergoing rehabilitation might be asked to evaluate the amount of pain they are feeling before and after a new exercise program. Displaying on a histogram the data collected prior to and after a test offers a comparison of the evidence. However, because the histograms are snapshots in time of the process (before and after), the effects that occur over time cannot be discerned just by analyzing the histograms.

A landscape maintenance organization purchased mulch in bulk quantities. The mulch was delivered to a central location. It was used around trees, shrubs, and flower beds at various sites. Bulk purchasing was the cheapest way to buy the mulch, but it resulted in waste and cleanup problems. A team was formed to consider alternative ways to purchase and use mulch. After some research, they decided to test the use of mulch supplied in bags.

Customers at the sites were asked to rate the appearance of the mulch on a scale ranging from poor to excellent, both before the test of bagged mulch and after the bagged mulch was used. The responses before and after the change were compared on a histogram (Figure 7.5). Data on the cost of mulch during the test were kept by the purchasing department and compared to past expenditures.

After reviewing the histograms in Figure 7.5, the team concluded that appearance was improved with the use of bagged mulch. The members of the crews did not feel that any change other than the use of bagged mulch delivered to the site resulted in the improvement shown. Purchasing reported that the cost for mulch was only slightly higher when the bagged mulch was used. Considering ease of application and delivery, the total cost to the system was considered to be less. The degree of belief of the team was high that the use of bagged mulch was an improvement. Purchasing was asked to arrange with the supplier to provide the mulch required. The team decided to track any problems encountered during the implementation of this change.

The rating question used in this example could have been "Regarding appearance, how would you rate the bagged mulch versus the bulk mulch?" A "much worse" to "much better" scale could have been used. Data would then need to be collected only after the change.

The advantages of a before-and-after design are that it is simple and easily understood. Because the basis of comparison in a before-and-after test is historical experience, the test is vulnerable to misinterpretation if something unrelated to the change occurs at or about the same time the change is made. Perhaps other enhancements to some of the customer's sites were made at the same time the bagged mulch was used. A short-lived Hawthorne effect can also occur immediately after a change is made (see case 4 in Figure 7.4 and discussion in time series designs). It is up to those conducting the test to make the judgment that the effect

## FIGURE 7.5. DATA ON THE USE OF MULCH.

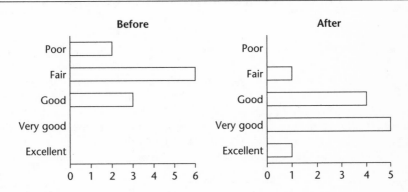

seen is due to the change being tested. One should also consider the issues with the use of histograms identified in Figures 7.3 and 7.4 when evaluating the evidence of a test of change.

To increase the rigor of the test design, one could collect and plot data over time on run charts for each of several measures (outcome, process, and balancing) before and after the change. Several designs that do this will be discussed in the next category of time series designs.

## Time Series Designs

Time series designs require collecting observations over time. Run charts or control charts can be used to assess whether an improved level of performance has been achieved and is being maintained. Four time series designs are introduced in this chapter and are described in Table 7.2. Each design is focused on studying only one change at a time.

***Before-and-After Time Series*** This design consists of a baseline period where data are collected on the measures at various points in time. If no baseline data are available, it can be collected as part of the test. Data are then collected at various points in time after the change is made. Collecting data over time makes it possible to see whether patterns indicating improvement coincide with the time of the change. Those conducting the test must make the judgment whether any effect seen is due to the change being tested. There is a rational basis for this judgment if there are no obvious external events and the system has been stable in the past.

Figure 7.3 showed the results of a before-and-after time series design with a run chart at the bottom (case 1). It shows that the simple before-and-after test

### TABLE 7.2. ALTERNATIVE TIME SERIES DESIGNS.

| Time Series Designs | Description |
| --- | --- |
| Before-and-after time series | Testing a change where before (baseline) and after data are collected over time |
| Time series with replication | Testing a change over time where the before and after data are repeated to see if the process returns to the initial level |
| Time series with a control group | Testing a change over time where there is no baseline for comparison |
| Time series with planned grouping | Testing a change over time under a wide range of conditions |

using only a histogram to analyze the data is often not rigorous enough to increase degree of belief about the change (cases 2 through 6 in Figure 7.4).

Figure 7.6 presents a run chart used to analyze the results of a time series design to test a change conducted by a group of physicians. The test was designed to determine whether a new instrument (change) to obtain cell samples from patients would be an improvement over the existing instrument.

One of the measures used in the evaluation was the percentage of inadequate samples. An inadequate sample does not contain enough cells to proceed with the diagnostic test. Data were obtained on the percentage of inadequate samples before and after the use of the new instrument. In the run chart in Figure 7.6, the reduction in inadequate samples coincides with the use of the new instrument. The physicians believed the improvement in the percentage of inadequate samples was the result of the new instrument.

The design for a before-and-after time series design is given in Table 7.3. Italicized numbers represent the order of the observed data from one or more measures. Data are aggregated and plotted on a run chart at specified time intervals (daily, weekly, monthly).

As discussed in the last section, the data collected during a before-and-after time series design are susceptible to the Hawthorne (or sentinel) effect. This challenge can be reduced by testing over time so the initial novelty of the test wears

## FIGURE 7.6. DATA FROM A BEFORE-AND-AFTER TIME SERIES DESIGN.

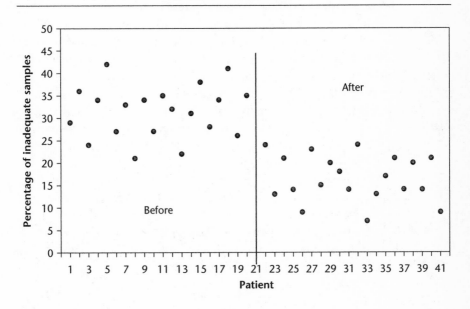

### TABLE 7.3. TESTING PATTERN FOR A BEFORE-AND-AFTER TIME SERIES.

| Before Change | After Change |
|---|---|
| 1 | 11 |
| 2 | 12 |
| 3 | 13 |
| 4 | 14 |
| 5 | 15 |
| 6 | 16 |
| 7 | 17 |
| 8 | 18 |
| 9 | 19 |
| 10 | 20 |

off. Also (if it is possible and ethical) people might not be informed that they are part of a test. Open communication, however, is often the better alternative. If the Hawthorne effect is suspected, the data collected during the test can be used to provide feedback to people. This feedback allows them to change what they are doing so that the improvement seen during the test can be sustained.

Repeat observations (*replication*) are used to increase the rigor of the test. The design given in Table 7.3 has ten replications before and ten replications after the change, yielding a total number of points of twenty. Is this number enough? The number of data points needs to be adequate to detect patterns that are indications of improvement. Table 7.4 contains some guidelines for selecting the number of data points (sample size).

Usually fifteen to thirty data points on a run chart will be sufficient to recognize patterns indicating improvement. From fifty to one hundred points would be necessary in situations where the variation in the measurements themselves is large or the variation among people (students, patients, or customers as experimental units) can mask the effect of the change.

If a change is intended to affect a rare event, such as the side effect of a new drug or a serious but rarely occurring defect, an alternative measure of "time between" or "event between" should be considered. In the new drug example, the rare event measure could be "days without a side effect of the new drug" or "number of doses given without a side effect of the new drug." A statistician might be consulted in such situations.

### TABLE 7.4.  GUIDELINES FOR NUMBER OF DATA POINTS TO TEST A CHANGE.

| Total Number of Points | Situation |
|---|---|
| Fewer than ten | Expensive tests, expensive prototypes, or long time periods between available data points. Large effects anticipated. |
| Fifteen to fifty | Usually sufficient to discern patterns indicating improvements that are moderate or large. |
| Fifty to one hundred | The effect of the change is expected to be small relative to the variation in the system. |

A clinical team wanted to determine what sample size would detect a 30 percent reduction in average waiting time in their clinic. They had been collecting a random sample of fifty patients per week. Is this sample size necessary to detect a 30 percent reduction? They developed run charts showing the average of samples of five, ten, twenty, and fifty patients' waiting time per week over twenty-four weeks.

As shown in the graphs of Figure 7.7, as the sample size increases the variation in the data around the average level of performance decreases. A sample size of five or ten, when twelve weeks of data are collected before and after the change, begins to provide convincing evidence of improvement. A sample size of fifty per week is probably unnecessary overkill. The team concluded that small samples over many points in time permit an adequate degree of belief that the change is an improvement. Also, they concluded that sample size issues in improvement efforts are a balance between resources (time, money, energy, slowing improvement efforts) and the clarity of the results desired.

Evidence for testing a change with a time series design can be increased by removing or alternating the change to see if the process returns to its initial level (time series replicated), using multiple baseline time series or adding a control group. Each of these options is now discussed.

***Time Series with Replication***  One method to increase degree of belief in the change being tested is to remove the change and see if the process returns to its initial level. This can be repeated as many times as necessary (make the change, observe results over time, remove the change) until an adequate degree of belief is obtained. This design is shown in Table 7.5. It merely includes a repeat of the before-and-after design shown in Table 7.3.

## FIGURE 7.7. EFFECT OF A CHANGE IN SAMPLE SIZE.

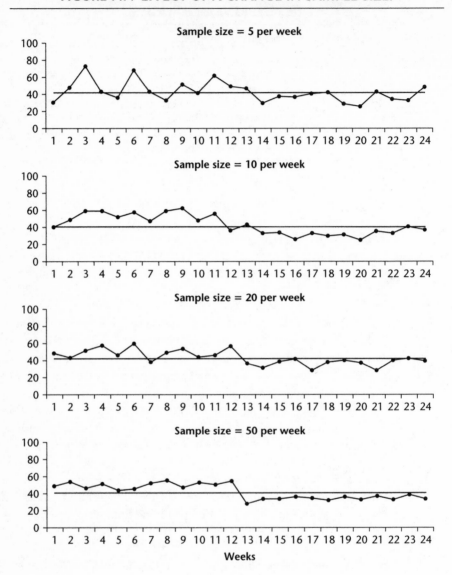

In this design there are four phases:

Phase 1: baseline
Phase 2: after change
Phase 3: replicated baseline
Phase 4: replicated after change

**TABLE 7.5. TESTING PATTERN FOR A TIME
SERIES DESIGN WITH REPLICATION.**

|  | Before Change | After Change |
|---|---|---|
| **Replicate 1** | 1 | 11 |
|  | 2 | 12 |
|  | 3 | 13 |
|  | 4 | 14 |
|  | 5 | 15 |
|  | 6 | 16 |
|  | 7 | 17 |
|  | 8 | 18 |
|  | 9 | 19 |
|  | 10 | 20 |
| **Replicate 2** | 21 | 31 |
|  | 22 | 32 |
|  | 23 | 33 |
|  | 24 | 34 |
|  | 25 | 35 |
|  | 26 | 36 |
|  | 27 | 37 |
|  | 28 | 38 |
|  | 29 | 39 |
|  | 30 | 40 |

By comparing the replicated baselines (phases 1 and 3) and the replicated period after the change (phases 2 and 4), one can assess the effect of uncontrolled conditions that varied between replicate 1 and replicate 2. Does performance return to its initial level when the change is reversed? Also, degree of belief is increased if the change shows improvement in both phases 2 and 4. There may be situations where the change can be alternated from observation to observation instead of having multiple observations before and after the change. For example, the use of a new instrument in a lab might be alternated with the current instrument in analyzing specimens.

There are disadvantages with replicating the time-series design. Besides additional cost of a longer test, return to the prior conditions in phase 3 may not be possible or desirable. If the experimenter can return to the situation before the change, replication is a powerful tool for increasing degree of belief that the change is an improvement. If one cannot return to the conditions before the change, having multiple baselines is an alternative.

***Time Series with a Control Group*** An approach to create a basis of comparison without collecting data before a change is to add a control group to the design. In a control group, no changes are purposefully made. Performance on the outcome of focus in the control group is then compared to performance in the group where the change is tested. Data are displayed on run charts. The design is shown in Table 7.6. The order of the observed data is numbered one through ten for both groups to indicate the data are collected during the same time period. An example is testing a new process for discharge planning in a medical-surgical unit in a hospital and comparing the length of stay (LOS) over the same time period to another medical-surgical unit using the current process. If another variable was present that affected LOS, it should affect performance on both units.

There are potential problems that can occur with the use of a control group. Something may happen within the control group that does not occur with the test group (or vice versa). For example, turnover of one or more key nursing staff in the medical-surgical unit during the test could affect the outcomes.

***Time Series with Planned Grouping*** The designs just discussed assist in reducing the threat uncontrolled conditions pose to the interpretation of results from a test. If we want to include a wide range of conditions in a test in a systematic way, we can use planned groups. Planned groups are formed when important contextual variables are held constant within each of two or more groups, but varied between the groups. Although planned groups can be used with other designs,

**TABLE 7.6. TESTING PATTERN FOR A TIME SERIES DESIGN WITH A CONTROL GROUP.**

| Group | Change | | | |
|---|---|---|---|---|
| | No | | Yes | |
| Control | 1 | 6 | No observations | |
| | 2 | 7 | | |
| | 3 | 8 | | |
| | 4 | 9 | | |
| | 5 | 10 | | |
| Test | No observations | | 1 | 6 |
| | | | 2 | 7 |
| | | | 3 | 8 |
| | | | 4 | 9 |
| | | | 5 | 10 |

## TABLE 7.7. TESTING PATTERN FOR A TIME SERIES WITH PLANNED GROUPING.

| Planned Groups to Test Under a Wide Range of Conditions | Change | |
| --- | --- | --- |
| | No (or Current) | Yes (or New) |
| Group 1 | 1 | 4 |
| | 2 | 5 |
| | 3 | 6 |
| Group 2 | 7 | 10 |
| | 8 | 11 |
| | 9 | 12 |
| Group 3 | 13 | 16 |
| | 14 | 17 |
| | 15 | 18 |

we will focus on their use with time series. A pattern for such a design with three planned groups is shown in Table 7.7. An example follows.

On the basis of the results of a previous test, Dr. Smith believed the new rehabilitation procedure had an impact on rehabilitation time. She was now interested in learning whether the procedure would prove successful when used by other therapists, in other hospitals, and with young and old patients. She decided to run another cycle to consider a wide range of conditions in her test. She planned to set up two groups with extreme conditions to determine whether the new procedure would result in improvement in both groups. She selected two hospitals, one small and one large; two therapists, one with two years of experience and one with ten years; and two sets of patients, one under thirty years of age and one sixty and older.

Dr. Smith purposely set up two groups with very different conditions for her test.

| *Group 1* | *Group 2* |
| --- | --- |
| Small hospital | Large hospital |
| Therapist with two years of experience | Therapist with ten years of experience |
| Young patients | Old patients |

Her degree of belief would be high that the change would result in improvement in the future if the new procedure resulted in improvement in both groups in the test. Five patients were selected for each group. They were randomly assigned to receive the new or old procedure. *Randomization* gives each patient an equal chance of being assigned to a group. This might be done by selecting a card for each patient marked either 1 or 2 from a shuffled deck. Dr. Smith used the pattern in Table 7.7 with two groups and five observations in each of the four cells. The results of the test are plotted in Figure 7.8.

The run charts are arranged to show the new procedure resulted in improvement in both groups. Although the rehabilitation time was generally higher in group 1, the new procedure still resulted in shorter times. Dr. Smith's degree of belief that the new procedure would result in improvement under the different conditions to which it would be applied was higher. If Dr. Smith wanted to study the effect of two new rehabilitation procedures, the time series with planned grouping would follow the same procedures as discussed but now would have a third set of data with the addition of the results from the second new approach.

In the example, the new procedure resulted in improvement in both groups. If the new procedure showed improvement in one planned group but not the other, Dr. Smith could focus her next PDSA Cycles on the effect of the specific conditions in the group on the impact of the new rehabilitation procedures. For example, suppose group 1 did not show a better result for the new procedures. Dr. Smith might test an experienced and inexperienced therapist using the new procedures in the small hospital with old patients to better understand the impact of experience on results.

## Factorial Designs

This category of design includes tests where multiple changes (which can also be called factors) are included. Table 7.8 below describes the factorial designs considered in this chapter.

***Two-Factor Design*** Including two changes (factors) in a test is an alternative to testing one change at a time. It allows study of possible interaction of the changes. An interaction results if the impact of a change depends on which alternative of the second change is used. For example, a teacher might want to test two teaching methods, such as having students learning in teams versus a standard lecture format, and at the same time test the impact of class size on student learning. Perhaps, the team approach will result in improvement in learning only when the class size is small—an interaction between the two changes. In manufacturing, engineers might want to learn whether some combination of temperature and pressure has the optimal effect on an important characteristic of a product.

## FIGURE 7.8. RUN CHARTS OF REHABILITATION TIME FOR TIME SERIES WITH PLANNED GROUPING.

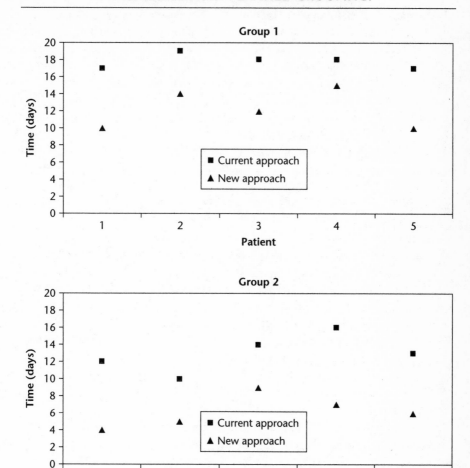

### TABLE 7.8. ALTERNATIVE FACTORIAL DESIGNS.

| Factorial Design | Description |
|---|---|
| Two-factor design | Testing change 1 and change 2 together |
| Two-factor design with planed grouping | Testing change 1 and change 2 under a wide range of conditions |

The pattern for a two-factor design is given in Table 7.9. One of the alternatives could be the current way things are done. Although the table shows two alternatives, there could be multiple alternatives for each change.

From the educational example, the changes and alternatives would be:

| | | |
|---|---|---|
| Change 1: Teaching method | Alternative 1: Team learning | Alternative 2: Lecture |
| Change 2: Class size | Alternative 1: Small | Alternative 2: Large |

Randomization could be used to assign the combinations of the alternatives of the two changes (for example, standard lecture format with large class size) to the people or things selected for the test (one of four classes of students in this example) or to select the order of performing some aspect of the test (team learning with a small class size tested first). One should always construct a run chart that plots the observations in the order they are collected. A run chart allows a check of possible special causes (nonrandom pattern of points) that may have occurred during the testing that are not associated with the changes made. Then a graph (interaction chart) can be constructed to show the effects of the changes and whether there is an interaction between them. The data in Table 7.9 are used to illustrate the run chart and interaction chart. The data are from a two-factor design used to test changes to have an impact on the time to process an order.

Change 1 represents the method used to process orders. The current method is a clerk processing the total order, and the alternative is a team approach to processing orders. Change 2 introduces the use of technology. The current approach is paper-based, and the alternative is processing by computer.

Three replicates of each of the four cells (combinations of two alternatives of each of the two changes) were observed. The run order was randomized throughout the four cells. The run chart and the interaction chart (using averages of the three numbers within each cell) are given in Figures 7.9 and 7.10.

#### TABLE 7.9. TESTING PATTERN AND RESULTS FOR TEST OF TIME TO PROCESS AN ORDER.

**Two-Factor Design (Time to Process an Order, in Hours)**

| | | Change 2 (Technology) | | | |
|---|---|---|---|---|---|
| | | Paper-based | | Computer-based | |
| | **Clerk processing** | 10 | 6 hrs | 8 | 5 hrs |
| **Change 1 (method)** | | 4 | 8 | 5 | 4 |
| | | 7 | 7 | 3 | 3 |
| | **Team approach** | 11 | 9 hrs | 12 | 3 hrs |
| | | 2 | 7 | 1 | 1 |
| | | 6 | 8 | 9 | 2 |

## FIGURE 7.9. RUN CHART FOR DELAY TIMES.

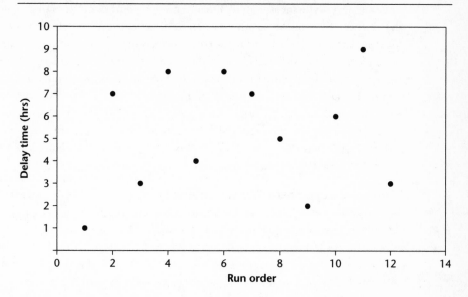

## FIGURE 7.10. INTERACTION PLOT FOR DELAY TIMES.

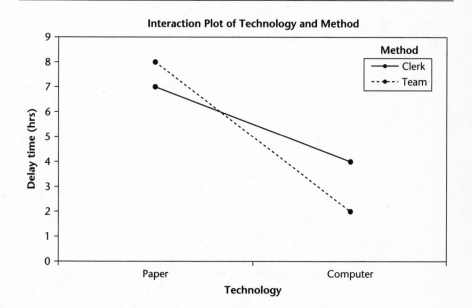

The plot of the run order does not indicate any nonrandom patterns over time that need to be investigated. The interaction chart (see Appendix B for more on this type of graph) shows the reduction of process time when using the computer, no matter what method is used to process orders. The impact, though, is greater when a team approach is used because the line for "change 1 team" has a steeper slope. In general, if the slopes of the two lines in the interaction chart are not the same (nonparallel lines), an interaction exists between the two factors. No interaction exists if the lines are "nearly parallel."

The process could be studied further by determining if the results will be similar under a variety of conditions. This can be accomplished as shown below by using planned grouping in a fashion similar to time-series designs.

**Two-Factor Design with Planned Grouping** In this design, the same layout as the design in Table 7.9 is used but now completed with each of two (or more) planned groups. The pattern is given in Table 7.10.

For the testing of reducing processing time for orders, group 1 could be new employees on second shift and group 2 could be experienced employees on first shift. Analysis is similar using run order plots and interaction charts but now is done within each group. Just as in time-series designs, if there are differences in results between the groups then the next cycles should be used to study the relationship between the change being tested and the conditions in the groups.

## Strategies for Testing

Developing an overall strategy for testing a change or changes is an important activity. We suggest using the structured format of the PDSA Cycle to accomplish each test. The aim should be to gain knowledge and increase degree of belief rapidly with minimal resources. Table 7.11 provides some guidance.

Here are some important questions to consider in planning your testing strategy:

- Are historical data available to act as a basis of comparison? If so, take advantage of this in the first test cycle.
- How likely are threats to misinterpretation of the results because an external event is present on or about the same time the change is made? A historically stable process makes this threat less likely.
- Can data continue to be collected over a long period of time after the change is made, mitigating the Hawthorne effect or misinterpretation of external events?
- How large an improvement is expected? Large improvements are much easier to isolate with simple tests.

### TABLE 7.10.  TESTING PATTERN FOR TWO FACTORS WITH PLANNED GROUPING.

| Planned grouping to test under a wide range of conditions **Group 1** | | | **Change 2** No | Yes |
|---|---|---|---|---|
| | **Change 1** | No | 1 | 2 |
| | | | 3 | 4 |
| | | Yes | 5 | 6 |
| | | | 7 | 8 |
| **Group 2** | | | **Change 2** No | Yes |
| | **Change 1** | No | 9 | 10 |
| | | | 11 | 12 |
| | | Yes | 13 | 14 |
| | | | 15 | 16 |

### TABLE 7.11.  STRATEGIES FOR DESIGNING PDSA CYCLES FOR TESTING.

| Degree of Belief | No. of Changes Considered | Objective of Test | Possible Design |
|---|---|---|---|
| Low | One | Selecting a change | Observational |
| Low | One | Small scale testing | Before-and-after |
| | | | Before-and-after time series |
| Moderate | One | Increase degree of belief | Time series with replication |
| | | | Time series with control group |
| Moderate | Two | Increase degree of belief | Two-factor design with planned grouping |
| Moderate | One | Learn about wide range of conditions | Time series with planned grouping of conditions |
| Moderate | Two | Learn about wide range of conditions | Two-factor design with planned grouping |
| Moderate | Two | Understand interactions | Two-factor design |
| High | One | Test different conditions | Time series with replication |
| | | | Time series with planned grouping |
| High | Two | Test different conditions | Two-factor design with planned grouping |

- Can a wide range of conditions be thoughtfully included in the test?
- Are there two changes that might be studied in a factorial design?

The methods for the analysis of data from tests of change are almost exclusively graphical. The aim of graphical methods is to visually display the impact of a change on the data being collected. Run charts and histograms (or Pareto charts for qualitative data; see Appendix B) are commonly used because of their simplicity. Using graphical methods also has the side benefit of allowing everyone involved with planning the test to be involved in the analysis. Five elements are usually part of the analysis of all tests of change(s):

1. Plot the data in the order in which the tests were conducted. This is an important means of identifying the presence of trends and unusual results in the data.
2. For time-series designs, clearly indicate on the graph when the change was introduced.
3. Rearrange the plot as appropriate (as by shift) to study effects included in the design but not directly related to the change(s) being tested.
4. If planned groups are used, analyze the data separately in each group.
5. Studying unexpected results (for instance, a change showed improvement in one hospital unit but not another) to build theory is a key part of the analysis.

Chapter Twelve includes case studies that demonstrate the use of the key ideas developed in this chapter as well as the data analysis for testing a change. A form to help develop the plan for a test cycle appears at the end of this chapter. When designing a PDSA Cycle for testing a change, this form can supplement the general PDSA form in Appendix B.

## Key Points from Chapter Seven

- The concept of "degree of belief" is used to describe one's conviction the change will lead to improvement in the future. Degree of belief can be increased by testing.
- Adopt the gold standard for testing a change: "Satisfactory prediction of the results of tests conducted over a wide range of conditions is the means for a team to increase their degree of belief that they are ready to implement a change."
- Conduct a sequence of PDSA test cycles to accelerate the rate of improvement.
- Small scale does not mean small change but rather refers to the initial scope of the test.

- Knowledge of the subject matter is important in studying the results of tests of a change.
- Graphical analysis with run charts should be used to analyze data.
- Testing before implementing is almost always important for successful implementation.

## Form for Developing the Plan in a PDSA Test Cycle

1. Objective of the test
2. Key background information
3. Change(s) being tested
4. Questions to be answered (discuss the theories or hunches relative to these questions)
5. Measure(s)
6. Design of the test
   - People or things selected for the test
   - Scale of the test and the risks involved
   - Likely influential uncontrolled conditions
   - Type of test design
   - Method of data analysis
   - How will a range of conditions be included?
   - Has randomization been considered?
   - Has replication been considered?
   - Has planned grouping been considered?
7. Who, when, where for the test (table to describe test design)
8. Predictions about the change(s) based on the questions in item 4 above

*Note:* Planning for a PDSA Cycle is not a linear process. It is often useful to revisit steps repeatedly, as needed.

CHAPTER EIGHT

# IMPLEMENTING A CHANGE

The term *implementation* has been used to describe many aspects of making a change. In its broadest sense, implementation has been used to mean the execution of a plan for a change. From this broad perspective, the term would include developing, testing, and activities to sustain and spread the change. However in this book, we use the term "implementation of a change" in a narrower sense. Specifically, in implementing a change our focus is on the activities one takes after testing has shown the change is positive and leads to improvement, but before spreading the change to brand new areas of the organization.

The aim of this narrower scope of implementation is to make sure the infrastructure is in place to make the change long-lasting and successful. This includes issues such as training, documentation, standardization, adequate resourcing, and social considerations. To summarize, testing is about learning if the change will result in an improvement, and implementation is about how to make the change an integral part of the system.

The PDSA Cycle creates the structure for both testing and implementing change. Besides the similarities between testing and implementation (making predictions, collecting data, and documenting things that go wrong) that result from use of the cycle, there are also important differences. First we summarize the differences between testing and implementing a change.

## Testing a Change

- The change made during testing is not permanent and therefore does not need supporting processes to maintain it beyond a brief period.
- The opportunities for learning about many aspects of the change from testing are expected to be significant, including learning from failures. Some percentage of tests—perhaps 25 to 50 percent—is expected to result in no improvement, to "fail," but to result in substantial learning nevertheless.
- The number of people affected by a test is usually smaller than the number that would be affected if the change was implemented. Thus, the awareness of and reaction to a test of a change is often much less.

## Implementing a Change

- A change that is implemented is expected to become part of the routine operation of the system. Therefore, supporting processes to maintain the change will usually need to be designed or redesigned. Supporting processes include feedback and measurement systems, job descriptions, procedures, new employee training, and so on.
- Because learning can occur anytime action is taken, implementation should be carried out as part of a cycle. However, assuming that testing has been effective, implementations are expected to result in no improvement.
- The increased permanence of a change that is a result of moving from testing to implementation is usually accompanied by increased awareness of and reaction to the change.
- Implementation cycles generally require more time than testing cycles.
- Normally, the same team that tested the changes will be involved in implementing the changes. However, the implementation team often has to be supplemented with others needed to support the more permanent nature of the effort.

> Sally Hudson, a second-shift nurse, had a great idea for increasing quality and reducing the cost associated with documenting patient information in the medical records. She encouraged everyone to start using the idea. But nothing happened! The other nurses continued to enter the data using the old procedure.

It is a common mistake to go straight to implementation and skip testing. This is the reason so many implementation efforts fail or create innumerable problems. The learning that occurs in testing cycles is vital to successful implementation. Changes can be tested under a variety of conditions to raise one's degree of belief that improvement can be sustained in the future (recall achieving the gold standard, defined in Chapter Four). Also, the learning from test cycles that did not go as planned is very important and differs from the learning from successful cycles. Organizations cannot afford to learn from failed implementation cycles.

Why is it so hard to implement change? During the early phases of developing and testing changes, the existing system remains in place. Though these early investigative stages may arouse people's interest, the fact remains that nothing has yet been permanently altered. Once the development and testing of changes are finished, it is time to implement the changes on the basis of what was learned. To many people, this implementation would appear to be a matter of simply "installing" what was developed and tested. If implementation did not involve people, then the physical, emotional, and logical challenges that hinder most planned changes might not be an issue. However, most changes in an organization have a social component. The social challenges that usually accompany the implementation of a change (that is, when there is a need for people to change behavior permanently) can surprise the sponsors of the improvement effort.

Implementing change can be very challenging to many organizations, especially when the scope of the change is broad. This chapter focuses on the implementation of changes that involve some complexity, as opposed to simple changes, which can be made with little interdependence on other processes, people, procedures, or structures. Simple changes can be implemented with little formality, and the steps for implementing them are usually readily apparent to the person or persons making the change. For example, improving procedures for reordering supplies might involve simply posting a reorder list on the bulletin board. To implement complex changes, however, it is generally useful, if not necessary, to develop a formal plan involving procedures and training.

These ideas have been found to be important in implementing complex changes effectively:

- Managing implementation as a series of cycles
- Providing support during and after the implementation to ensure that improvement is achieved and maintained
- Recognizing and addressing the social aspects of implementing a change

## Implementation as a Series of Cycles

For some changes, people do not even have to be told about the change in order to implement it. For example, a computer service department added additional memory chips to all of the computers in the office over the weekend. On Monday, all of the employees noticed that their applications performed much faster. This change resulted in an increase in productivity of the office.

> Bob tested the use of safety gloves for the truck loaders. Through the testing, they learned that one specific glove met their needs in terms of protection yet was thin enough that the loaders felt they had control of the equipment, tools, and boxes. They tested it with experienced, inexperienced, small, and large loaders. Bob felt sure that they had isolated the best choice. How should he implement this change with all the loaders? He obtained the hand sizes of all twelve loaders, bought a dozen pairs of gloves, and handed them out to all the loaders on Monday morning.

Bob used a one-cycle approach to implementation. Was he finished with implementation of the change to all loaders using safety gloves? He later found he had to run several more cycles, one for glove replacement due to lost, misplaced, or damaged gloves, and in the second cycle he offered training on the use and care of the gloves. He also arranged for a change in orientation so that when a new loader was hired the person would be given training on the use and care of the gloves and be given his or her own pair.

For many changes, multiple cycles are required for implementation. For example, changing the type of wrapper on a food item to make it environmentally safe may be viewed as simply changing the material. However, when the implications of the change are viewed from production, legal, and customer perspectives, the change becomes relatively complex. Changing the food wrapper may take months, and several cycles.

> Customers of a grocery store chain complained for several months about chicken packages that leaked. Gertrude, the manager of the butcher department, decided to contact the vice president of sales for the Chicken King Company to voice her dissatisfaction with the leaking packages. Dave, the vice president, made a visit to the grocery store and learned about the leaking package situation from the viewpoint of the customer. Gertrude also told Dave that her customers generally preferred the competition's shrink-wrapped package to Chicken King's simple plastic wrap. The visit resulted in Chicken King conducting research on the technology needed to use the shrink-wrap. A series of cycles were conducted to develop and test changes in equipment and materials. Chicken King was now ready to implement changes at their processing plant.

The plan for the first implementation cycle appears in the box that follows.

Depending on the complexity and the risks involved, implementation can be conducted in a number of ways. Three approaches are considered here, all relying on the use of the PDSA Cycle:

---

## PDSA Cycle for Implementation of a Change

### Objective:
Implement the new shrink-wrap equipment and process at the Chicken King processing plant.

### Questions:
1. Will the equipment operate as effectively as under test conditions?
2. Will the new process be easy for our operators and maintenance personnel to learn?
3. What difficulties will we experience with the implementation?

### Predictions:
1. Yes. The tests were conducted under similar plant conditions at Oscar Equipment Co., and all the equipment being used is manufactured by Oscar.
2. No. The new equipment is computer controlled. Many of our people will require training in the use and maintenance of this complex equipment.
3. The computer equipment will add some complexity. The acceptance of new setup methods by maintenance will add some challenges. The equipment looks sufficiently different that the operators may find it difficult to learn at first. Training will be essential to this effort. This plant was selected because of its ability to embrace change.

### Who:
Hank Duval's people will carry out the implementation at the plant.
The shrink-wrap and equipment suppliers will be available if needed.

### What:
New equipment installation, shrink-wrap material, and necessary training.

### When:
Training will begin in October. Equipment will be installed in November.

### Where:
Chicken King processing plant

---

1. The "Just do it!" (or "cold turkey") approach
2. The parallel approach, which implements the change while the old system is still in place
3. The sequential approach by time

## The "Just Do It!" Approach

Many times, implementing a simple change is a matter of doing it—for example, following a flow diagram for a new process. After a successful test on a relatively low-risk change, implementation can often be accomplished by running one more cycle to ensure that the predicted results are achieved and the changes are made so as to be irreversible. The effect of the change on the people involved should also be considered.

If unforeseen negative consequences occur, the "Just do it!" approach will maximize their negative impact. If the change is complex and the system is large, one of two types of a phased-in approach should be considered (the parallel approach or the sequential approach).

## The Parallel Approach

Sometimes changes must be phased in by operating them parallel to the existing system. Business cannot just stop during implementation. Changes must be accomplished while the business is running so that customers will be satisfied while the changes are being implemented. Implementing complex changes while trying to satisfy normal business demands has been compared to changing the fan belt on a car while the motor is running. Planning and phasing in the changes parallel with the existing system should reduce some of the risks. This type of implementation will take a bit longer than the "Just do it!" approach, but it is usually less risky. If changes are planned and implemented properly, then the implementation will produce the expected results.

A manufacturing organization historically had maintained control of its schedule and inventory with a manual system of documentation, a schedule, expediters, and a "war room" to control work in the shop. A computer system for materials management was purchased and tested and was ready for final implementation. Although some of the work was already being completed with the aid of computers, the change to complete automation of the paperwork tracking system represented a major change for the business. To ensure that orders were not delayed or missed, the new system was installed while the manual system was used for backup in the event of a failure during the implementation cycle.

## The Sequential Approach

Often a change comprises multiple components. The third approach is to implement the components of a change sequentially over time. For example, if a medical practice was implementing a system to improve access to primary care (based on the results of several months of testing, of course), they might choose to first reduce the appointment types and then work down the backlog, before opening up the scheduling to all same-day appointments. These components could be implemented sequentially. After the first few cycles, all the components of the change may not be implemented, but there is no risk of 100 percent failure. When determining whether to use a sequential approach, consider this:

- Identify people and circumstances that will adopt the change. What strategy will best use the skills and capabilities of the people involved, consider the environment (other changes that are going on and the *will* and support that exists for the change), and minimize geographical issues?
- The impact. Will a sequential approach result in improvements early in the implementation process?
- The potential learning. Will a sequential approach permit learning that can then be used in the next phase of implementation?
- Resources. Will a sequential approach allow the best scheduling and use of available resources?
- Interdependence. A sequential approach should not be used if the change cannot work without all of its components.

# Implementing Changes to Achieve and Maintain Improvement

Dave picked up the receiver of his ringing telephone. It was Gertrude. "Dave, the ink from the new package is flaking off the plastic wrap." Dave thanked Gertrude for the information and called Hank Duval immediately.

Everything had gone so well for several months. The plant was now online with the new equipment and shrink-wrap packaging. The grocery store chains were happy, and more important their customers preferred the new package to that of the competition. However, now a whole shipment of chicken had been rejected. After some investigation, it was determined the purchasing people had managed to get a better price on some ink. This ink worked fine with the other package, but not with the new film composition.

Once improvements are implemented, practices need to be established to ensure that the change becomes the normal way the business is run. Holding the gains usually requires some change in the system to ensure that the change is maintained. Many organizations make improvements on the job only to discover later that the improved performance has degraded to the old level or some new problem has been encountered. Many times this occurs because management did not establish the structure to sustain the change.

Some of the practices that help make improvements permanent in an organization are standardization, documentation, training (both current and new employees), measurement, and appropriate resourcing. Periodic self-audits can be useful in determining whether these practices are being followed. PDSA Cycles can be used to ensure that the appropriate aspects of the infrastructure are engaged in the change. Table 8.1 shows a sample Project Team Worksheet for managing PDSA Cycles for implementation of the change. Some objectives of PDSA Cycles are contained in the example.

### TABLE 8.1.  PROJECT TEAM WORKSHEET.

| Key Implementation Areas | Changes to Support Implementation | Lead | Cycle No. | Objective of PDSA Cycle |
|---|---|---|---|---|
| Standardization | Policies and procedures | | | • Update P&P doc. Test with a few techs and engineers. |
| | Hiring procedures | | | • Test use of SDI screening tool.<br>• Try new orientation process. |
| Documentation | Job descriptions | | | • Develop and test process tech job descriptions.<br>• Test description of new position for a lab analyst. |
| Training | Staff education/ training | | | • Offsite vs. onsite vs. Web-based (in three cycles)<br>• Learn about mentoring and shadowing approaches. |
| Measurement | Information flow | | | • Integrate time measurement into standard checksheet. |
| Resourcing | Equipment purchases | | | • Test one server.<br>• Investigate two types of networking. |

## Standardization

A hospital's records showed much variation among patients in recovery time from knee operations. To reduce variation in practice, a team of doctors and therapists worked with the administration to develop and test a standard rehabilitation process for patients who have a knee joint replaced.

Standardization is the method of establishing specific recognized policies and practices that act as a model or guidelines for a process. The actual documented policies, materials, methods, equipment, and training are usually called "standards" or "best practices."

Organizations that effectively use standards exhibit many of these conditions:

- Management requires the use of standards, especially to document improvement efforts.
- Different employees and shifts use the same standards and expect similar results.
- Employee training focuses on the documented standards for materials, methods, and equipment. Critical elements and impact on internal and external customers are discussed.
- Employees document and compare steps, procedures, and results to an easily accessed standard for each when solving problems.
- Standards are regularly updated and changed on the basis of new knowledge about better methods. To avoid suboptimization, conditions that get similar results are reviewed for least cost and best results for the overall system.
- Employees share information with co-workers and managers in ongoing efforts to improve.
- Variability in the outcomes of processes is reduced, resulting in more predictability.
- To assist in maintaining improvement, work can be periodically audited to determine whether standard processes are being adhered to.

## Documentation

After implementing the new rehabilitation process, recovery times were more consistent and the hospital's costs were in line with other systems. Two years later, however, costs were creeping back up and a variety of procedures were again being used. What happened to the improvement that had been made?

There may have been numerous causes resulting in the improvement not being sustained, but one possibility is that the standard process was not appropriately documented. Documenting a change (including the standard process) after each implementation cycle is most important, but more often than not it is the least-appreciated task. The term *documentation* has a bureaucratic ring to it and usually means more paper. More paper means more work: filing it, maintaining it, and so on. Unfortunately, many changes are only as good as their documentation. Organizations depend on the documentation for education and training during the implementation of the change, for consistency from one group to another, for understanding a method or process, for a common definition of the change, for instructions, and so forth. For many changes, the documentation represents the "deliverable;" it is what the organization bought with all its efforts and resources aimed at gathering data, testing, and implementing cycles. The final product is sometimes a simple document defining the change.

> An organization in the international construction industry recently reengineered its ten major subsystems. When the task was finished, they had ten volumes of materials describing the new processes. Several million dollars were expended in gathering information, benchmarking other companies, testing, purchasing software, and finally implementing the system. Much learning occurred and many changes in policies, structures, and procedures were implemented. One person observed, "If we don't have a process to update our process books, pretty soon we will have ten process books that are no longer useful. We would then risk losing all of the investment we have made in these major improvements.

It is not enough to document a change when it is implemented; documentation will soon be out of date if there is not a system for keeping it fresh and reflective of new knowledge. This requires an active process with assigned roles and responsibilities.

## Measurement

Good documentation of a process does not mean the process is always performed as documented. Visible measurement of the process is a good way to ensure the changes implemented are in fact being carried out.

Measurement is a source of learning during implementation and a method of maintenance after implementation. Some of the measurements developed and used in testing and implementation cycles should be considered for permanent use after implementation, although data may be collected and summarized less frequently. Viewing measurements over time allows an organization to determine whether it is continuing to get the desired results and whether those results can be predicted to continue in the future. Is there a need to update the process, make changes, and so on?

In addition to the obvious measures of improvement, it is often useful to measure the extent to which the support processes needed to maintain the improvement are running as planned. For example, what percentage of the employees have successfully completed the training? How well are the new standards being followed?

The tools for tracking data to support implementation included run charts, as with testing. However, implementation can also make use of control charts, a tool more focused on aspects of maintaining a change rather than testing. (See Appendix B for more information about run charts and control charts.)

## Training

Some form of training is usually required to implement a change. If the change to be implemented is a simple extension of the work currently being performed, then a one-time discussion of the change with the workers affected may be all the training required. Such training could be done on the job or by reviewing the new standards at a meeting.

If the change is complex (as when it involves the use of new technology), then extensive, formal classroom training may be required to implement the change. The type of change that is being proposed, who will be asked to implement the change, and the skill level and work experience of the target group are all considerations in how much training is done. The training required for testing a change is minimal, often only requiring a "watch one and do one" approach. Training to support implementation requires a broader, longer-term approach.

People are motivated to learn when they perceive a need or reason to learn something new and when they believe that training will satisfy this need. Leaders of the change effort must again be ready to explain the *why* of the change. Also, the timing of the training is essential. If the training is given too early, people will stall on the learning curve because of nonapplication. If it is given too late, people will be rushed, force-fed, and ill-prepared. Treating the training as a series of PDSA Cycles can help create a learning environment where the trainees are motivated and the result is improved training.

The discussion here has focused on training of current employees on the changes. If the change is not standard to the industry or formal education programs, then development of training modules for new employees is critical to sustaining the gains from the change. New employees will view the ("new") process not as change but as just one of the unique ways business is conducted in their new organization.

Figure 8.1 shows a checklist that can be used for review whenever a change is being implemented. The form can be completed while the Plan for a PDSA (or series of PDSAs) is being developed. The use of the form will ensure that predicted results are evaluated; that communication with people affected by the implementation has been considered; and that the necessary training, documentation, and measures are completed to effectively implement and sustain the change.

## Resources for Implementation

Implementation of a change often requires new forms, training, a piece of equipment, or something else that requires resources to be allocated. Needed resources may not be thought through and included in the plan. This is one of the areas where the shift from testing a change to implementing a change is not fully appreciated. The testing is done small–scale, where resourcing is not an issue. Therefore, PDSA Cycles to learn about the required resources to maintain the change should be planned into the series of implementation cycles.

Understanding how a proposed change will be maintained should be part of the implementation plan. This approach should apply to all changes. Even small changes can sometimes cause big effects, some desirable and some quite undesirable.

These general points should be considered in developing a system to maintain changes implemented in the organization:

- A process should be developed to capture all important changes in the organization:
  - In deciding if the change needs to be documented, consider if the change will have a small (localized) or large (interdependent) effect on the system.
  - Who has the authority to implement a change? What will his or her responsibility be in seeing that the change is properly implemented and documented? Who will be the process owner?
- How will the change be communicated to those affected inside or outside the defined system?
  - How will improvements and learning be shared with interested people in other departments, divisions of the same company, suppliers, and customers?
  - Will training and education be required to implement the change?
- What will the process be for updating flow diagrams, best practices, measurements, and other important process or product information?
  - Information technology offers an opportunity for real-time updates to documentation of procedures to all parts of the organization.

## FIGURE 8.1. IMPLEMENTATION CHECKLIST.

| Description of change: | | | | | |
|---|---|---|---|---|---|
| Implementation dates: From          to | | | | | |

**Predicted impact of change on key measures:**

| | Measure | Current level of performance | Predicted level after change |
|---|---|---|---|
| 1 | | | |
| 2 | | | |
| 3 | | | |
| 4 | | | |
| 5 | | | |
| 6 | | | |
| 7 | | | |
| 8 | | | |

**Processes or products affected by the change:**

| | Processes or products affected | Process or product owner | Number of people affected | Change in standard? Yes/No | Predicted acceptance High/Med/Low |
|---|---|---|---|---|---|
| 1 | | | | | |
| 2 | | | | | |
| 3 | | | | | |
| 4 | | | | | |
| 5 | | | | | |
| 6 | | | | | |
| 7 | | | | | |
| 8 | | | | | |

**Documentation of change:**
  Materials/forms defined. Comments:
  Procedure defined. Comments:
  Equipment defined. Comments:
  Change request procedure. Comments:
  Changes in job descriptions or role statements. Comments:

**Impact on training:**
  Training procedure defined for implementation. Comments:
  Training resources allocated. Comments:
  Training schedule complete. Comments:
  New employee training procedure complete. Comments:

**Measurements required:**
  New measurements defined. Comments:
  Measurement procedures defined. Comments:

  Measurement responsibilities defined. Comments:
  Measurement review scheduled with responsibilities. Comments:

  Analysis of data responsibility assigned. Comments:

| | | | | | |
|---|---|---|---|---|---|
| | | | | | |

# The Social Aspects of Implementing a Change

*There is nothing more difficult to carry out, nor more doubtful of success, nor more dangerous to handle, than to initiate a new order of things. For the reformer has enemies in all those who profit by the old order, and only lukewarm defenders in all those who would profit by the new. . . .*

NICCOLÒ MACHIAVELLI

Dealing with change in many organizations has become an everyday challenge. There are constantly new methods, tools, products, and sometimes a meeting of very different cultures as our world becomes smaller. How can we deal with these changes successfully? Not too many years ago, it was common for people to raise an issue about the monotony and sameness of the work world. Many people considered it their responsibility to maintain the status quo. Now more and more thoughtful people are agreeing that managing change is one of our more important tasks. Despite this, there remains much that is misunderstood about how people and organizations undergo change.

## Reactions to Change

After an improvement team has developed and tested a change that it is convinced will lead to improvement, it will expect people to accept the implementation of the change. It is only natural, however, that people will seek to maintain control of their environment. Some sort of reaction should be expected when a change is announced. This is the stage at which the leaders of the change must explain the *why* and *how* of the change. Properly addressing concerns and questions helps people commit to the change. The behavior of the people affected by the change might range from open resistance to commitment, depending on how the change is communicated and what the circumstances are surrounding the change (that is, the degree and relevance of the change, the current situation in the organization, the credibility of management, how changes were handled in the past, the style of leadership, and the organization's culture). A number of behaviors may be observed:

- Resistance: responding with emotions or behaviors meant to impede change that is perceived as threatening
- Apathy: feeling or showing little or no interest in the change
- Compliance: publicly acting in accord while privately disagreeing with the change
- Conformance: changing behavior as a result of real or imagined group pressure
- Commitment: becoming bound emotionally or intellectually to the change

People have a need to understand the physical implications of the change ("How much smaller will my new office be?"), the logical implications ("Why is this change necessary?"), and the emotional aspect of the change ("How do I feel about this change?"). The leaders of the change should not view people's initial reactions as negative resistance; however, if these reactions are not properly dealt with, they can develop into full-blown resistance.

One common mistake is to think of change as only a technical issue. This view would confine us to consider only the new methods and equipment to ensure that they function as planned. For every technical change in a system, there are usually social and economic changes as well. These changes must be planned and managed if we are to gain the predicted benefits of the change. Figure 8.2 describes the relationship among technical change, social change, and improvement in quality and cost.

Chapter Four introduced the human side of change from knowledge of psychology. This component of profound knowledge, and its interaction with the three other components, helps us predict how people will react to a specific change and their motivations during implementation. This helps us learn how to implement a change more effectively.

## Initial Results of Implementation

The initial impact of a change that involves people learning a new skill or doing something differently (new behavior) is often disappointing. Figure 8.3 illustrates the familiar learning curve that often accompanies a technical change in the

### FIGURE 8.2. TANGIBLE AND SOCIAL CHANGE FOR IMPROVEMENT.

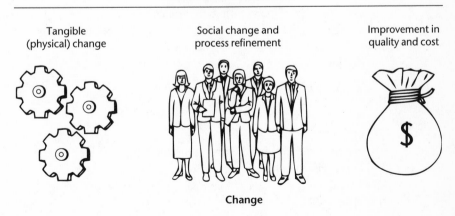

| Tangible (physical) change | Social change and process refinement | Improvement in quality and cost |

Change

## FIGURE 8.3.  DISAPPOINTING INITIAL RESULTS WHEN BEGINNING IMPLEMENTATION.

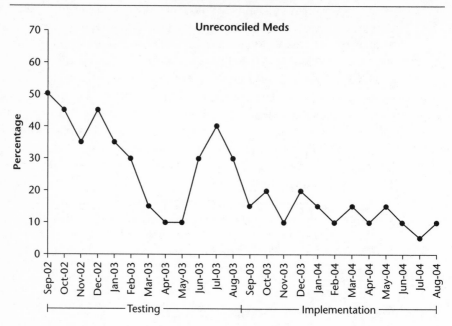

work environment. In this example, methods for reconciling medications in a hospital were developed and adapted in numerous PDSA test cycles. When the methods were implemented housewide in June 2003, the percentage of cases measured with unreconciled medications increased back to the pretesting-period level. After three months, the hospitalwide data were closer to what was expected from the testing.

People who are implementing change need to plan for this potential result. Many changes have been needlessly stopped or tampered with because of the results of the first or second trial of a new change.

To sustain a change that has been implemented, we need to create structure that makes it easy for people to do the right thing (use the new system) and hard to the do the wrong thing (go back to the old system). Some inhibitors to sustaining a change:

- We met our goals
- We assumed the improvement would hold
- Other priorities took all resources away
- The change is not on senior management's radar screen
- The organization did not learn how to maintain the gains
- Infrastructure was not put into place

Many of the ways to enlist people to support a change begin before implementation is started. They start with the purpose and strategic direction of the organization, the specific areas that are selected for improvement, the testing of changes to bring about the improvement, the training of employees, and so on. With that said, it is with implementation that the impending impacts of change become more real. Aligning and giving people the opportunity to be involved in change that they care about becomes vital. Organizations do not empower people; people empower themselves once they see the opportunity and understand how their values and aspirations are aligned to the needs of the organization. The leadership of the organization has the primary responsibility of aligning the will of the people involved to the purpose of the organization.

Organizations sometimes have a written statement of values, principles, or tenets (see Chapter Thirteen). These statements describe the behaviors expected and necessary to carry out the organization's purpose. How can these statements be used to give people the opportunity to support change? When a change is being proposed, the *why* of the change should be explained in terms of the organization's values, principles, or tenets. If the change is consistent with these statements, then the logic of the change will be understood and accepted. If the change violates these values or tenets, then people may have a very difficult time adapting to the change.

Many experts would advise us that cultural change takes time and requires that the beliefs of the organization be changed. Challenging beliefs or attitudes directly can create more resistance to change efforts. Introduction of a change that appears to match the beliefs of the organization usually facilitates adoption of the change. For example, safety at chemical plants throughout the world is usually perceived as important. Much time and effort is usually spent to ensure that the plants are operated in a safe manner. Any improvement that is introduced that also is linked to plant safety will usually find a quick path to adoption.

## Guidelines for Getting Commitment to Change

Here are guidelines that have proved useful in helping people minimize resistance to change and get the desired commitment of those affected by the change:

- Create the will in the organization to adapt the change. The leaders in the organization can help with this by communicating in four ways:
  - *Dissatisfaction.* People need to be unhappy about the current state of affairs. If unhappiness with the status quo isn't there, create it.
  - *Direction.* Relentlessly communicate what the change is, why it is necessary, and what people ought to be doing right now with as much clarity as possible.

- *Overconfidence* (punctuated by self-doubt and updating). Express excessive faith that the change will succeed and be worth the pain, time, and money in the end. Create a self-fulfilling prophecy, regardless of the success rate anywhere else.
- *Embrace the mess.* Accept that there will be errors, setbacks, miscommunication, frayed nerves, and frightening rumors when an organization tries to do something new, no matter how well the change is planned.
- Provide information on why the change is being made:
  - Empathize with the anxiety created by the change (but do not expect to eliminate it).
  - Show how the change supports the purpose of the organization.
  - Put the change in historical perspective.
  - Link the change to the outside customer.
  - Reframe the change as an exciting opportunity, not something being forced on people.
  - Establish a special hot line for recording questions and comments during implementation.
- Offer specific information on how the change will affect people:
  - Use the results from the testing cycles to share visual displays of data and test results.
  - Discuss how the change will benefit people (that is, make their job easier).
  - Be prepared to discuss questions, requests for clarification, and ideas about the change.
  - Study rational objections to the change and be prepared to address them.
  - Include in presentations representatives from the organization who actually carried out the tests or implementation.
- Get consensus on solutions, resources, and other necessary support to implement the change:
  - Decide on a plan of action with defined milestones and dates.
  - Ask leaders and key people in all parts of the organization to publicly show their support.
  - Express confidence in the ability of those who must carry out the change.
- Publicize the change:
  - Use symbolism (stories, analogies, pictures, staged events).
  - Summarize all key points and agreements as they are made.
  - Show appreciation for the efforts of everyone who was involved in the development and testing of the change.
  - Take advantage of significant events (record sales, loss of a big customer) and tie the implementation of the change to these events.

Following these guidelines help an organization enlist people to support changes being implemented. If commitment is not achieved in the face of the facts, then the sponsor, or possibly a higher-level manager, must deal with the situation by direct measures:

- Modifying the planned change to increase commitment
- Using incentives
- Using logical consequences
- Demanding conformance as an expectation of continued employment

## What If the Resistance Cannot Be Mitigated?

If the resistance continues in the face of the facts, then the sponsor, or possibly a higher-level manager, must deal with the resistance by direct measures. In this unhappy situation, the resister or resisters should be confronted as candidly as possible. Typically, this means that management will state expectations and offer incentives, or spell out what the consequences will be if certain behaviors are not demonstrated. This story of implementing a change in a zoo illustrates how difficult making a change can be. As you read the story, consider how the workers were involved in implementing the change. What would you have done differently if you had been leading the change?

> After one of its elephant keepers was accidentally stepped on and instantly killed, the San Diego Zoo decided to change how its elephants were trained and handled.
>
> Experts in the use of behavior modification with animals were brought in to work with the elephant keepers. None of the experts had any experience with elephants. The purpose of the change was to improve safety for the keepers, to improve the methods used to discipline the elephants, and to permit better access to veterinary care for the elephants.
>
> Gary Priest, head of the Department of Animal-Behavior Management at the Zoological Society of San Diego, reported that at first the keepers accepted the work with the elephants as "an amusing diversion not to be taken too seriously. But as we began to see results, we discovered that to propose significant change is to invite ridicule." Priest discovered what many people learn as they try to make changes.
>
> The method that the elephant keepers were currently using to train and discipline the elephants had been in use for thousands of years. It was based on the elephants' social behavior of being led by the dominant cow of the elephant herd. This cow was usually the oldest and most experienced of the herd.

Challenges to the authority of this dominant cow were met with swift retali-
ation. The elephants understood this hierarchy of control, and it was on this
hierarchy that the ancient training methods were based. The elephants were
taught to be subordinate to the trainer, as they would be to the lead elephant.
Priest reported, "The elephants' unquestioned acceptance of the pecking order
was a matter of life and death for the trainer. Unfortunately, elephants do
sometimes challenge the pecking order . . . often with disastrous results."

The proposed changes differed from the traditional method in a number
of ways:

- Trainers would no longer go into the elephants' enclosure.
- There would be a protective barrier between the trainer and the elephant.
- The elephant would present various body parts on command in exchange
  for a reward.
- No physical discipline of the elephants would be permitted.
- Training would rely only on positive reinforcement and "voluntary" cooper-
  ation from the elephant.

This strategy of training was predicted to work because the elephant is a very
social animal and appears to enjoy interaction with human trainers and keepers. Within a few days, the elephants had discovered the connection between
their behavior and the reward of a carrot or apple. The elephant with the
worse behavior, Chico, was chosen for the first cycle. Within six months of
using the new method, Chico would voluntarily submit to a pedicure on all
four of his feet. He had not had a pedicure for ten years under the old method,
even though foot infections are the leading cause of death for elephants in
captivity.

Although the new method of control proved successful with Chico and
the other elephants, the keepers still insisted that "the new system wouldn't
work, that it was stupid, and they [the animal behaviorist and management]
were being unrealistic." Priest observed the keepers stubbornly trying to prove
the new methods would not work, rather than practicing the new system of
training. After exhausting various positive reinforcement methods to entice the
keepers to voluntarily change their approach, management was left with no
alternative but to step in and make the new method a contingency of employment. Priest reported, "It was especially ironic to me that we had abandoned a
discipline-oriented, negative training system with our elephants only to adopt it
with our employees."

The new parameters were enforced using twelve-week review periods. The
first review identified multiple incidents of keepers not operating within the new
training parameters, and it was a negative experience for everyone involved in

the review. However, as each review was conducted, incremental improvements were noted. Each new improvement and behavior conformance created an opportunity for management to recognize and reinforce the new behavior. After one year, all keepers were using the new training methods, and the elephants were performing beyond expectations. "The atmosphere during the review was transformed from bristling hostility to informal, relaxed and open discussion of the program, its direction, and the keepers' participation in it." Now, positive reinforcement plays an important role in managing and maintaining the program.

The elephants accepted the change much more easily than the workers in the zoo. The shift in attitude that took a few months for the elephants did not take place in the workers until after more than two years. This story illustrates how resistance was formed in a group and how the zoo management had to resort to some rather harsh measures to implement a change.

What can we learn from the zoo story? Change is an uphill battle, no matter who is leading it. In this case, "outsiders" were brought in to teach some new methods to a group of keepers who were practicing methods that had been used successfully for centuries, and these experts did not have prior experience with elephants. Perceiving them as coming in to correct things would in itself have created a movement toward resistance to the change. How were the new keepers informed of the change? Did they get a chance to help with the experiment? The involvement of the keepers in testing and implementing the change should have been critical; people have a tendency to support what they help create.

If the zoo's management had used some of the guidelines given earlier, they might have had a chance to mitigate the resistance. Involvement of the keepers in testing the change, using some of their ideas from experience with the elephants, and explaining the *why* of the new methods could have resulted in much earlier commitment to the change. Because these issues were not addressed appropriately, resistance developed, resulting in the need for incentives, negative twelve-week reviews, and threats of job loss.

## Key Points from Chapter Eight

- Implementation is about how to make a change an integral part of the system.
- A common mistake is to go straight to implementation and skip testing.
- Implementation should be managed as a series of cycles.
- Once improvements are implemented, practices need to be established to ensure the change becomes the normal way the business is run. Some of the

practices that help make improvements permanent in an organization are standardization, documentation, training, measurement, and appropriate resourcing. Periodic self-audits can be useful in determining whether these practices are being followed.

- The increased permanence of a change associated with moving from testing to implementation is usually accompanied by increased awareness of and reaction to the change.
- Many of the ways in which people become motivated to support a change begin before implementation is started.

CHAPTER NINE

# SPREADING IMPROVEMENTS

D an and Carol Dixon noticed a new restaurant was preparing to open in town. The Dixons were always a bit tentative about trying a new restaurant and were very comfortable with their "regular" establishments. For this restaurant, they also worried whether there would be sufficient parking because it was in a rather crowded part of town. Their interest in the new restaurant increased when they read a favorable review in a local paper that included a coupon for 10 percent off the bill. If the Dixons decide to try the restaurant, they can then judge the quality of its food and service. Is the experience worth the price? Would they recommend the restaurant to others?

This chapter is focused on spreading improvements. Spread happens when people decide to try something new. When people adopt a new idea, their decision is based on many of the same factors as making a decision to try a new restaurant: awareness of a better alternative, letting go of current behavior, incentives to change, and overcoming issues that impede action. However, adopting a new idea may not be as easy as deciding to dine at a new restaurant. It may require significant changes in behavior and investment of resources.

Spreading improvement means having people implement good ideas beyond some initial locations. Spread is supported by the improvement capabilities of testing and implementing a change discussed in the preceding chapters, but now multiple sites are involved so execution is more complex. For example, an aim for an improvement initiative might be "Reduce the average time to schedule a primary care medical appointment from sixty days to less than three days within fifteen months by implementing changes associated with advanced access." No doubt, it would be challenging to achieve such an aim under any circumstances, but the complexity of the initiative would increase as the focus changed from a clinic with one physician to a group of ten clinics with forty physicians, to a system with more than one hundred clinics located in multiple states.

There is a large body of knowledge on the theory and methods to spread changes that can be applied in even the most challenging situation. We will explore some of the theory and methods in this chapter. Our attention is on spread within organizations. However, anyone with an aim to spread change, no matter what the scale, can easily tailor the methods for the application. The methods can also be applied between organizations or in a community, if an appropriate entity exists to provide leadership to the spread project. Examples of such entities are a trade association, a government agency, and even a coalition of organizations.

## A Framework for Spread

In 2000, the authors along with colleagues began testing approaches to spread through projects in health care and other industries such as chemical, landscape maintenance, and building products. Figure 9.1 presents the "framework for spread" that evolved. The framework is based on Everett Rogers's definition of diffusion ("a process by which new ideas are communicated over time through a social system") and draws

**FIGURE 9.1. A FRAMEWORK FOR SPREAD.**

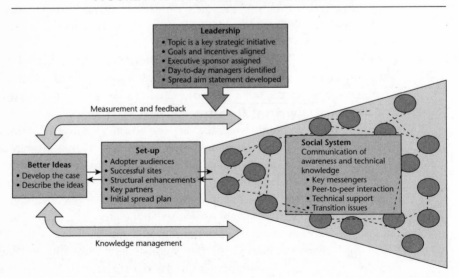

from the literature (including social learning theory, social marketing and the theory of self-change) and our experience in spread projects.

The framework identifies some general areas to consider for any spread initiative:

- Strong *leadership* is essential to undertake a large spread project in an organization or a community. Executive leaders need to connect the work to a strategic initiative, align incentives with the work, and allocate appropriate resources. A special leadership role to give this work priority falls to an executive sponsor. The executive sponsor is the leader in the organization who is responsible for improved performance from the spread work.
- A succinct description of the ideas being spread and the evidence to support them are the key elements of *better ideas.*
- The elements contained in *setup* are important inputs to the development of the spread plan. For example, understanding the audience (information about potential adopters) will be needed when the communication plan for spread is formulated. A spread plan should include a communication plan, a measurement plan, and a work plan. We believe to make spread happen in a timely fashion the spread process needs to be managed.
- Development of the *social system* is founded on communication. Communication is twofold, both raising awareness to attract adopters and sharing the technical content needed by adopters to make improvements.
- *Measurement and feedback* and *knowledge management* systems are used to continuously monitor the spread work and make it easier for others to adopt the changes.

To use the framework for spread to develop and execute a spread strategy, people have found it useful to consider the framework in terms of three connected phases: organizational readiness for spread, developing an initial spread plan, and executing and refining the plan. The elements contained in each phase are shown in Table 9.1. The sections that follow explain each phase in some detail.

# Phase for Organizational Readiness for Spread

A decision to undertake a spread project should not be taken lightly. Before an organization proceeds, people should ensure they are ready. This section discusses some of the key elements to judge organizational readiness for spread.

## Strategic Topic

The challenges faced in a large spread initiative are difficult to overcome without purposeful leadership. Purposeful leadership is more likely to exist if a spread

## TABLE 9.1. PHASES FOR DEVELOPING AND EXECUTING A SPREAD STRATEGY

| Organizational Readiness | Developing an Initial Spread Plan | Executing and Refining the Plan |
|---|---|---|
| Strategic topic | Organizational structure | Communication of awareness |
| Executive sponsorship | Communication plan | Identification of early adopters |
| Project manager | Measurement plan | Knowledge transfer/application |
| Spread team | Work plan | Feedback loops |
| Better ideas | | Maintaining the gains |
| Spread aim | | |

project is connected to a strategic objective in the organization. People are then more willing to give a spread project the oversight, resources, support, and attention needed for success. Leadership activities that indicate the spread project is strategic are:

- Aligning systemwide and local goals and incentives with the spread aim. This may require changes to an organization's reward and recognition systems.
- Communicating a compelling message of why the initiative is needed rather than mandating involvement.
- Scheduling time to review progress and provide advice.
- Being visible to those making the changes.
- Assigning high performers to the effort and allocating them sufficient time.

## Executive Sponsor and Project Manager

Not every member of the senior management team can oversee progress and understand the support needed for every project. Therefore, the senior management team should designate an executive sponsor to be responsible for the work and the results. The executive sponsor's role should include these four activities:

- Playing an active role in the development of the spread plan and its revisions
- Offering assistance to overcome barriers
- Helping other leaders, middle managers, and staff understand the importance of the initiative
- Keeping the executive leadership team aware of the progress and the success of the work

Leaders should identify a project manager and allocate sufficient time to this role (at least 25 to 50 percent of their time for larger projects). Adding this role to existing responsibilities is not advisable. Depending on the size of the organization, the project manager may have assistants to help manage the work within the organization. The project manager's role should include these activities:

- Overseeing the development, execution, and revision of the spread plan
- Connecting adopters to others who can assist them
- Sharing important issues with appropriate leaders
- Managing the expanding knowledge base
- Reporting on progress
- Organizing and leading the spread team

## Spread Team

A spread team is an important structure to guide and support the spread work. The project manager serves as the spread team leader and the executive sponsor furnishes oversight. Members of the team should have some expertise in the area being spread (sales, access to primary care, analytical procedures). The team should include representatives from sites where the changes being spread were successfully tested and implemented. Representatives from support services such as information technology, human resources, and quality improvement can be added to the team or brought in to offer advice when needed. Customers or patients should also be considered.

The size of the spread team depends on the size of the organization and the complexity of the changes being spread. The core spread team, though, should not grow so large that it becomes difficult to manage. The project manager and executive sponsor should organize formation of the team but not mandate participation. Examples of spread teams in health care and the hotel industry:

## Spread Project: Access to Primary Care for Sixty Clinics in Three Regions

*Executive sponsor:* chief medical officer
*Project manager:* director of quality improvement for the system
*Other members of the team:*
   A physician and nurse manager from a high-performing clinic
   The clinic administrator or director responsible for each region
   A clinician from each region
   A patient

## Spread Project: Service at the Registration Desk for Forty Hotels in Two States

*Executive sponsor:* vice president with responsibility for registration
*Project manager:* manager with the responsibility for service quality
*Other members of the team:*
  A front desk employee from a high-performing hotel
  A hotel manager from each state
  Two front desk employees from each state
  A regular customer

The executive sponsor, project manager, and spread team ready the organization further for spread by overseeing the gathering and packaging of the better ideas and finalizing the spread aim.

**Better Ideas**  Obviously, a spread project will not be successful if an organization does not have ideas worth spreading. Rogers proposed five attributes to assess the "worthiness" of ideas:

1. *Relative advantage* over the status quo or alternative ideas
2. *Compatibility* with existing values, experiences, and needs
3. *Complexity* diminishing the ability of ideas to be adopted
4. *Trialability* allowing ideas to be tested and abandoned if desired
5. *Observability* of the ideas in practice

The spread team can use the worksheet contained in Table 9.2 to assess their ideas on the five attributes. They can assess the ideas as a group or individually.

The spread team should consider the relative advantage of the ideas to be the most important attribute influencing the rate of spread. Relative advantage is based on existing evidence the new ideas will achieve the desired results. In gathering the ideas, the spread team should review the literature and the experiences of high-performing sites to understand the strength of the evidence and its application to their situation.

The spread team should not be discouraged if the evidence of improved performance is not strong for all situations where the ideas will be applied. This would be a concern if leaders mandated the adoption of the ideas. Evidence is built as success is realized in different situations. Adopters will also generally view ideas that make their work easier as having a relative advantage. The spread team should try to make this case in their description.

## TABLE 9.2. WORKSHEET TO ASSESS IDEAS FOR SPREAD.

**Key Ideas:**

| Attributes | Relative to the Attribute, the Ideas are: | | | | | Comments |
|---|---|---|---|---|---|---|
| | Weak | | OK | | Strong | |
| | 1 | 2 | 3 | 4 | 5 | |
| Relative advantage | | | | | | |
| Compatibility | | | | | | |
| Simplicity | | | | | | |
| Trialability | | | | | | |
| Observability | | | | | | |

To reduce the number of leaky drums, a manufacturing company wanted to spread the use of an improved procedure for packaging product that included using a thicker liner for the drums. Most packers were willing to try the new procedure because currently they used two liners for each drum and the new procedure required just one.

Adopters will be influenced by how compatible the new ideas are with their beliefs, values, and experiences, so the spread team should try to make such connections. For example, if health care workers believe patients should have more control over their own health, they will be attracted to ideas that make more information available to patients. The spread team should also try to connect the spread project to existing successful initiatives in the organization.

The description of the ideas should be succinct. Adopters will most likely view a fifty-page book of ideas describing, for example, a new orientation program as overly complex. For more complex changes, some broad concepts for the system design, possibly using a driver diagram (described in Chapter Six), or a one-page overview or graphic might be provided. This overview can then be connected to the actual changes that will be made.

Fabricators manufacture and install countertops for homeowners and commercial organizations. When data were reviewed by a company for what caused their fabricator crews to return to job sites, they discovered that damage to the site was the primary reason. Returns averaged about two per month for each of the seventeen branches. One branch designed a process for site protection. When the process was tested, the fabricator's degree of belief was increased that use of the site protection process would reduce damage at the site. The new process was then made available to the other sixteen branches. The description of the ideas is shown in Figure 9.2.

Another structured way of packaging changes in health care is to provide a "bundle." A bundle is a small, straightforward set of practices—generally three to five—that, when performed collectively and reliably, have been proven to improve patient outcomes. The changes in a bundle are all necessary and together sufficient. They occur at a specific time and in a specific place. An example of a bundle in health care is a set of five changes to help prevent catheter-related blood stream infections (central line bundle). Bacterial infections can be introduced through an IV in a patient's vein supplying food, medications, blood, or fluid. This bundle is shown in this list:

Hand hygiene
Maximal barrier precautions on insertion
Chlorhexidine skin antisepsis
Optimal catheter site selection, with subclavian vein as the preferred site for non-tunneled catheters
Daily review of line necessity with prompt removal of unnecessary lines

In many research studies in health care, individuals involved do not know the intervention they are trying. In a spread project, the approach is quite different. Ideas should be made observable so potential adopters can see the ideas in use. This will build confidence that they also can make the changes.

A consideration in describing the ideas is whether the ideas included in the description are scalable. Some initial sites may be given additional resources, such as people or equipment, when they adopt the changes. These additional resources may not be available as the ideas are spread.

An organization with multiple primary care sites had an aim to improve care for the chronically ill. At some initial sites, an educator was used to educate patients on their chronic illness. As care for chronically ill patients spread, the spread team realized that educators could not be deployed to all sites. The spread team planned to provide patient education within available resources by using a video with some support from current staff.

**Aim of the Spread**   Once leaders of an organization are ready to begin spread, they should develop an aim for the project. An aim for spread is an explicit statement documenting what the organization expects to achieve. Leaders could draft

## FIGURE 9.2. DESCRIPTION OF A SITE PROTECTION PROCEDURE.

## PROCESS # 9610—SITE PROTECTION PROCEDURE (TOPWRIGHTS)

**Purpose:**
To have the installers be prepared to protect the "homeowner's" property during our installation process. To reduce property damage or the impression of damage during delivery and install. To build a level of trust with the customer that we will care for their property. To set up a noncombative atmosphere to correct damage if it still does happen.

### Installers Job-Site Damage Protection Check list

| Floor protection – | Quantity |
|---|---|
| 3' wide x 20' long canvas runner (painters tarp) | 1 |
| Rubber membrane, 3' wide x 10' to 12' long | 2 |
| Rubber membrane, 6' x 6' | 1 |
| Padded moving blankets | 2 |
| Disposable booties (clean) | 6 |
| Countertop protection – | |
| Rubber membrane, 2' x 3' | 1 |
| Wall and Cabinet protection – | |
| Plastic laminate or backer board cut to 2' x 1' | 2 |
| Formed cardboard corners | 6 |
| Formed cardboard edges, 3' to 4' long | 6 |
| Low stick "Blue" masking tape roll | 1 |

### Installers Job-Site Damage Protection Procedures

1. Wear clean disposable booties or remove shoes/boots when entering site.
2. Check for the best route to install area.
   - Inspect for preexisting damage or conditions and notify customer and/or document before starting.
3. Place protection on floor, walls, wall corners, stair rails, cabinets, fixtures or other items as needed around entire area of delivery and installation.
   - Use the canvas runner on carpet and the rubber membrane on solid floors to reduce slipping (tape in place if needed for safety).
   - No tops, tools, foot traffic or anything that does not belong to the owner should be set down without a protective covering under it.
   - Put the 2' x 3' piece of rubber membrane on the countertop after it is installed for a place to carefully set tools in use. If another trade sees you setting tools directly on the tops (no matter how carefully you did it) they will assume that it is OK for them also.
4. Padded blankets can be used on tops while they are being transported, and/or used as floor or countertop protection as needed.
5. Ask customer to move personal items (furniture, wall hangings) to a safe place if they may get in the way or could be damaged during delivery and install. (We should avoid moving customer items as much as possible. We take responsibility if they are damaged while we are moving them.)
6. When using Blue masking tape to hold protection in place, exercise extreme caution on wallpaper or loose plaster. You may have to use non-adhesive solutions (gravity, leaning or propping up, manual holding) to hold the protection in place. Even Blue masking tape may pull off or tear some wallpaper and plaster. Remove the Blue masking tape as soon as it is not needed.

the aim as part of strategic planning or assign the task to the spread team. If the task is assigned, leaders should review and comment. The aim can be used to raise awareness of the project within the organization.

Organizations have found it useful to include four elements in a spread aim:

1. The ideas, processes, or systems being spread (for example, a system for improving access to primary care clinics, new sales processes, a system for designing new products, or new manufacturing methods)
2. The target population for spread (the units expected to adopt the new ideas or processes)
3. The time frame for the spread activities
4. The target level of system performance to be achieved (for example, reduce adverse drug events in all medical and surgical units by 75 percent; reduce the cost to manufacture a product by 20 percent without affecting quality; increase sales to $50 million)

Some examples of spread aims are given in this list:

## Examples of Aims for a Spread Project

1. *Spread project:* Improve patient flow in a hospital
   - Ideas to spread
     - Scheduling capacity to match patient demand
     - Daily capacity management
     - Collaboration with extended care facilities
     - Admission unit
   - Target population and time frame
     - Within the next eighteen months, we will spread the ideas to the five hospitals within our system.
   - Target levels of system performance
     - Increase admissions by 5 percent
     - Left without being seen (LWBS) from the Emergency Department < 2 percent
     - Emergency Department length of stay for patients admitted to the hospital reduced to less than four hours
     - Readmissions to the hospital within thirty days at least maintained at current level
2. *Spread Project:* Significantly reduce returns to job sites due to damage to the customer's site
   - Ideas to spread

- Site protection procedures when installing countertops (see Figure 9.2)
- Target population and time frame
  - Within the next year, the procedures will be spread to sixteen separate branches
- Target level of system performance
  - Eliminate job returns due to damage to the customer's site

# Phase for Developing an Initial Spread Plan

After the elements of organizational readiness are in place, the spread team should develop a plan to achieve the aim of the project. The spread team will often need to revise the initial plan as the plan is executed. In the sections that follow, we discuss the key components of a spread plan: a communication plan, a measurement plan, and a work plan. The size and structure of the organization will influence the spread plan, so first we share some considerations on organizational structure.

## Organizational Structure

In developing a spread plan, the spread team should consider key dimensions of its organization's configuration or structure. Two important considerations:

1. *Leverage existing groupings.* In large organizations, units are often grouped in some fashion. For example, an organization may have a Southwest region, a Northeast region, and so on. Although each region may report to a central authority, much authority often resides with leaders in each region. Leaders can play a central role in managing spread within their region. If the organization is large and formal groupings do not exist, the spread team could consider how some grouping (for example, by product produced or service rendered) might be established to allow spread to commence in multiple areas. The spread team should consider a number of questions about organizational groupings in developing their spread plan:
   - Can we use existing groupings within the organization to accelerate the rate of spread?
   - What is the geographic distribution of the units involved?
   - Where are the authority or influence centers?
   - What groupings might be established to assist with spread?
   - Are there some groups (such as regions) that could be focused on first because there is better chance for success? (This might be the case if leadership in specific regions is willing and ready to begin spread.)

2. *Structural enhancements needed to facilitate and support spread.* Sometimes ideas cannot be replicated from unit to unit without support from enhanced organizational structures. For example, to facilitate spread, multiple sites might need to be linked together electronically to share information, or scheduling systems might need improvement. The spread team should take a proactive view of structural enhancements that could make the transition to the new system easier for adopters. Depending on the extent of the structural enhancements considered, senior leaders might need to be directly involved with these decisions.

The health care system with the spread project to improve patient flow in five hospitals tested an admission unit to facilitate admissions from the emergency department. If run correctly, the unit would reduce LWBS. This structure was included as an idea to be spread to the other four hospitals.

## Communication Plan

Communication is the foundation of spread, so developing a communication plan is a key activity of the spread team. Entities within an organization such as union representatives, or outside the organization such as suppliers, professional associations, or government entities, can be engaged to support the communication plan. The communication plan should assist adopters to make the transition from *awareness to decision* and from *decision to action*.

**From Awareness to Decision** To raise awareness, the spread team should first plan to communicate why change is needed; in other words what is the problem? Consistent with social marketing, the team should tailor the message about the problem to the segments of potential adopters. In a health care setting, physicians, nurses, and schedulers may need differing messages. To raise awareness, the spread team could use stories about the effects of the current system on patients or customers. They could also use feedback (data) to adopters on their performance. The spread team should include a general overview of the new ideas to show that change will overcome the problem. The spread team can use various communication methods:

- General methods such as flyers, newsletters, or posters
- Methods that convey a more personal touch, such as letters or cards
- Interactive methods such as e-mail and telephone

Table 9.3 can help to organize this part of the communication plan. An example is used from a health care system, with the aim to improve patient flow

## TABLE 9.3. WORKSHEET FOR COMMUNICATION OF AWARENESS ON IMPROVING HOSPITAL FLOW.

| Target Audience | Message | Methods |
|---|---|---|
| Physicians | Get your patients admitted more easily | Letters to MDs that include data showing the delays on certain days and certain times |
| Nurses | Better control of your day | A newsletter that includes a theme of getting the day under control |
| Other staff | Fewer patient problems | Newsletter includes stories of patient situations that could be avoided |

in their five hospitals. The general message to raise awareness focused on patient satisfaction and patient safety, but specific messages were also developed for physicians, nurses, and other staff.

The spread team should define measurable objectives for outcomes for this part of their communication plan (for example, percentage of the target population that should make the decision to adopt within three months, six months, and so on.) The timeframe for such objectives can be established on the basis of the timeframe included in the organization's aim for spread.

*From Decision to Action* Once individuals make the decision to adopt ideas, they are more likely to listen to the technical content needed to actually make the changes. This content knowledge is best conveyed during peer-to-peer interactions using such methods as educational outreach, visits, and discussions among groups of individuals with like jobs and interests. Many health care organizations have used a method referred to as a collaborative to bring together groups with a common aim to adapt and spread good ideas.

Besides planning the methods that best fit their organization's situation, the spread team should consider five ideas in developing this part of their communication plan:

1. *Leverage the natural connections between sites in the target population.* Adopters listen to those they know and respect, so existing relationships are powerful connectors in a social system. The spread team might plan visits or discussions between potential adopters and a high-performing site with which they have a working relationship.
2. *Leverage the existing organizational structure.* The spread team should use the existing organizational structure when designing their communication plan. For example, if an organization is grouped in regions, peer-to-peer interactions can start simultaneously in the several regions.

3. *Focus on only a few of the ideas initially.* There may be multiple ideas to spread to achieve the desired outcome. The spread team could plan to spread one (say, reducing appointment types in a primary care clinic) or a few ideas initially across all units in the target population. This approach allows the involvement of more adopters early on and makes it easier for the spread team to increase awareness of the project. This is especially powerful if some benefits can be seen from adopting these initial ideas. An alternate approach would be to spread all changes to one or two sites. The spread team needs to use this approach if the ideas are interdependent, that is, one cannot be made without the others.

4. *Arrange for technical support.* Adopters often need ongoing help and support to adapt the changes successfully to their local areas. The spread team should consider arranging technical support for the content and for quality improvement methods.

5. *Identify messengers.* The spread team may also need to identify people to assist them in executing the communication plan. Persons who are influencers or opinion leaders in the social system serve as the best messengers. The spread team can ask potential adopters, "Who do you go to for advice on a particular topic?" to identify opinion leaders. As the spread team identifies and enlists opinion leaders, they should:

   - Focus on peers of the potential adopters rather than their managers
   - Not overly formalize the role of an opinion leader and disrupt their informal leadership position
   - Arrange for the coaching needed to make the messengers effective
   - Understand and address the issues of opinion leaders who decide not to participate

## Measurement Plan

As was mentioned, four components should be included in a spread aim:

1. The ideas, processes, or systems being spread
2. The target population for spread
3. The timeframe for the spread activities
4. The target level of system performance

The spread team can base its measurement plan on the measures being used to evaluate system performance (number four in the list) and the target population for spread (item two).

First, the spread team should develop a plan to collect and plot data over time on a run chart or control chart for the key outcome measure (for example, adverse

## TABLE 9.4. FORM FOR DOCUMENTING THE IMPLEMENTATION OF IDEAS.

Month: _____

Please indicate with an X the ideas you have implemented.

|  | Site #1 | Site #2 | Site #3 | Site # . . . | Summary |
|---|---|---|---|---|---|
| Idea #1 |  |  |  |  |  |
| Idea #2 |  |  |  |  |  |
| Idea #3 |  |  |  |  |  |
| Idea #4 |  |  |  |  |  |
| Idea #... |  |  |  |  |  |
| All ideas |  |  |  |  |  |

drug events in hospitals, reportable injuries at manufacturing plants, or revenue for work orders for a landscape maintenance company). They should include data from the entire target population identified in the spread aim even though some units might not be adopting the changes initially. For example, data on reportable accidents should be plotted monthly in aggregate for all manufacturing plants in an organization. As the plants adopt change to improve safety, the total number of reportable accidents for all plants should decrease over time. The spread team could plot data on individual units, in this case each manufacturing plant, to monitor the impact on the outcome measure by those units currently adopting the changes. If a system to measure the key outcome is not already in place, a key initial activity of the spread team is to develop such a system.

Along with the key outcome measures, an organization should also collect information on the rate of spread of the key ideas within the target population. Here are some options to collect the data:

- Each site in the target population could use a form, similar to the one shown in Table 9.4, to document its progress monthly on implementing the ideas.
- The spread team could develop a sampling scheme to capture the information from sites (for example, sample one-third of the sites monthly and summarize the information quarterly).
- The spread team could gather the information through verbal reports from sites.

Whatever method is used to collect the data on the rate of spread, the spread team could plot monthly or quarterly the percentage of sites that have adopted all the ideas or the percentage of sites that have adopted a particular idea.

## Work Plan

Because spread is founded on attracting people to the work using will effective communication, the spread team will not know the specific units that will adopt the ideas first, second, and so forth until their plan for communication of awareness is deployed. The spread team can, though, document the what, when, and who for each part of their communication and measurement plan and how they will keep track of which units make the decision to adopt. The template in Table 9.5 can be used to document a spread work plan. In developing a work plan, the spread team should consider available resources. Resources, both dollars and time devoted to the project by the spread team and messengers, have to be matched to the communication methods used and when they are deployed.

# Phase for Executing and Refining the Spread Plan

In this phase, the spread team executes the work plan so adopters will test and implement the new ideas. Things rarely go as planned, so the spread team needs a good feedback system to help them support adopters and revise the plan. Details on key activities for this phase follow, including suggestions on feedback that may be useful at various points.

## Communication of Awareness and Identification of Early Adopters

Rogers placed adopters in five categories—innovators, early adopters, early majority, late majority, and laggards—according to when in time they adopt new ideas. Figure 9.3 depicts the theoretical cumulative rate of spread of a new idea.

Similar graphs could be generated for the rate of awareness and the rate of decision to adopt. If those curves were placed on the graph in Figure 9.3, they would, of course, be shown prior to the curve of the rate of spread.

Although the actual curve of the rate of adoption will vary, the spread team can draw some lessons from the theoretical curve:

- Individuals do not make the decision to adopt changes at the same time. Spread is a temporal process, with the curve being rather flat initially. The spread team should not get frustrated if the initiative starts slowly.
- Early adopters are the foundation for spread. They are the first in the target population to make the decision to adopt. They don't necessarily have the best results initially. Resources should be dedicated to the early adopters to make them successful.

## TABLE 9.5.  SPREAD WORK PLAN.

| Spread Activity | What Will Be Done | When: Start Date | Who: Responsible Person(s) |
|---|---|---|---|
| **Developing an Initial Spread Plan** | | | |
| • Leveraging the structure of the organization (e.g., Will the spread plan be focused on certain regions initially?) | | | |
| *Communication* | | | |
| • Target audience(s) and "messages" for each (see Table 9.2, Worksheet to Assess Ideas for Spread) | | | |
| • Communication methods for awareness | | | • Identify methods<br>• Deploy them |
| • Communication methods for knowledge transfer (including technical support) | | | • Identify methods<br>• Deploy them |
| • Identifying key messengers | | | |
| *Measurement* | | | |
| • Data on outcomes | | | |
| • Rate of spread | | | |
| **Executing and Refining the Plan** | | | |
| • Keep track of adopters who have made the decision | | | |
| • Provide feedback to adopters who are testing the ideas | | | |
| • Identify "transition issues" (i.e., barriers to adoption) | | | |

- The early and late adopters will be viewing the success of the early adopters. Making the success of early adopters visible reduces the risk for the majority and makes their decision to adopt easier.
- Those termed laggards are reluctant to adopt the changes. They should not consume the resources of the spread team. Some connection though needs to be made with those identified as opinion leaders.

## Feedback Loop for Communication of Awareness and Identification of Early Adopters

As the spread team executes the plan for communication of awareness, the team members should have methods (such as response to a mailing, sign-ups at a presentation) to keep track of those who make the decision to adopt the changes,

### FIGURE 9.3. THEORETICAL CURVE OF THE RATE OF SPREAD.

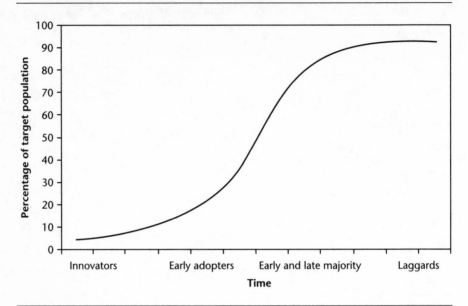

*Source:* adapted from Rogers, *Diffusion of Innovation*, and Bass, "A New Product Growth Model for Consumer Durables."

especially early on (the early adopters). From the curve in Figure 9.3, the spread team might anticipate at least 15 percent of the target population making the decision to adopt in the first quarter of the time frame contained in their spread aim. For example, if an organization sets a three-year time frame to accomplish their spread goals, in the first nine months at least 15 percent of the target population should transition from awareness to making the decision to adopt the changes. This is a very crude marker, but if the identification of early adopters falls short of this, it should at least serve as a signal to the spread team and senior leaders to review the spread plan. The spread team could ask a handful of questions to assist in the review:

- Does the message for certain groups need improvement?
- How capable are the messengers?
- Are the communication methods effective?
- Are transition issues affecting those making the decision?

This last point is an important one. Adopters may realize they have a problem and even believe in the benefits of the new ideas but be slow to make the decision to adopt because of issues getting in their way. Issues might include understanding how to work new equipment, or the belief they will get more work if they become more efficient. While the plan is being executed, the spread team should take an active role in listening to the target population to understand these issues.

> A chain of hardware stores trialed a new process that had proven successful to more accurately and efficiently keep track of inventory. Although both the managers and staff of the stores talked about the problems they were experiencing and the advantages of the new process, few made the decision to adopt. The spread team decided to discuss this with some managers. They found out that many of the staff were worried about learning new procedures because the inventory process required slight changes to some of the screens on the computer.

To accelerate the rate of spread, the spread team needs to resolve such issues or bring them to the attention of leadership for resolution. In the case of the inventory process, managers should make training available and assure staff they will not be penalized while they are learning the new procedures.

## Knowledge Transfer and Application

The spread team now executes the activities in its communication plan to move people who have made the decision to adopt to action. This part of the plan should include peer-to-peer interactions. Early adopters who improve performance by adopting the new ideas are critical to the success of the spread project. Not only can they serve as examples but they can also assist with the peer-to-peer interaction (mentoring, visiting, group discussions) others will need at this stage.

Most adopters adapt the new ideas to their situation. They may change a particular step in a process or how a piece of equipment is used. This active role of adopters in the spread process is a good thing. Most adopters are more inclined to make changes if they have some control over them. It also gives them the opportunity to optimize performance in their local setting. Because capability to make improvements is important during this phase, the spread team should offer quality improvement support to assist adopters in testing and implementing changes.

The spread team should develop a system for ongoing capture of the increasing knowledge base. They might ask adopters to post new materials or refinements to the ideas to a Website. The spread team could also visit sites to understand and document how the ideas are being adapted.

## Feedback Loop for Knowledge Transfer and Application

The spread team can now focus the feedback system on the measures contained in the spread aim. Team members should monitor the data on outcomes and the rate of spread. The spread team will find data at the unit level (for example, individual primary care clinics, manufacturing plants) very useful, especially early in the project. The spread team should conduct detailed reviews of a unit if it:

- Makes the decision to adopt but is slow in actually adopting the changes, or
- Reports making the changes but shows no improvement in outcomes, or
- Shows improvement in outcomes but reports not making the specific changes being spread

The spread team could ask these questions to assist in the review:

- Do the methods to assist adopters to take action need to be improved?
- Are managers at the local level supporting the work?
- Do adopters have sufficient time to test and implement the changes?
- Do adopters possess sufficient understanding of improvement methods (that is, testing and implementation)?
- Is technical support sufficient?
- Are there transition issues preventing adopters from moving to action?
- Do the changes proposed need refinement?

The procedures for site protection by the fabricators were made available to the other sixteen branches. Each agreed the procedures were worth testing to address the problem of site damage. Discussion of the procedures took place at meetings regularly scheduled to share what was being learned at the branches. One branch suggested an enhancement to the procedures that was based on a type of site damage not addressed in the initial procedures.

The rate of spread of the site protection procedures and the number of returns due to damage at a customer site are shown in Figure 9.4 and 9.5. Two of the seventeen branches did not implement the procedures. Data on the total number of job returns per month were used because the total number of jobs stayed approximately the same over the time period.

## Maintaining the Gains

As the rate of adoption increases and performance of the system improves, the spread team should ensure structures are in place to maintain the gains achieved. Middle managers who will have ownership of the new system are ultimately

### FIGURE 9.4.  RATE OF SPREAD OF THE PROCEDURES.

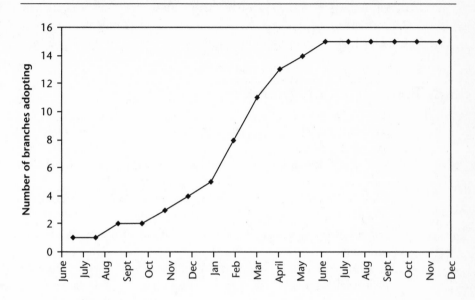

### FIGURE 9.5.  NUMBER OF JOB RETURNS PER MONTH
### FOR ALL BRANCHES.

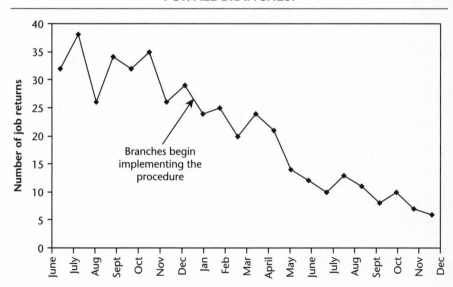

responsible for feedback to staff on performance. The spread team should involve middle managers in each phase of the spread strategy and assist them to develop appropriate processes for measurement and audits. Implementing a change (See Chapter Eight) is an important improvement capability at this point.

## Key Points from Chapter Nine

- For the spread of new ideas to happen in a timely fashion, the spread process needs to be managed.
- Spread is founded on communication—communication to raise awareness, attract adopters, and share the technical content with them.
- Leaders should assign high performers to a spread effort and allocate them sufficient time.
- Evidence for the ideas being spread is built as success is realized in different situations.
- Adopters will usually progress through stages of change, from awareness to decision and from decision to action. The spread team should develop communication tactics to assist adopters to make these transitions.
- Persons who are influencers or opinion leaders in the social system serve as the best messengers.
- Making the success of early adopters visible reduces the perceived risk of the majority and makes their decision to adopt easier. Spreading Improvements

CHAPTER TEN

# INTEGRATING METHODS FOR THE IMPROVEMENT OF VALUE

In the previous chapters, we discussed methods to make changes that result in improvement. In this chapter, we integrate those methods to assist practitioners in developing an effective and balanced approach to improvement. This approach can guide efforts to produce products and services that customers want and are willing to pay for. Whether the organization is a restaurant, a hospital, a manufacturing company, or a bank, customers are constantly judging products and services by their quality and their price.

Because of the importance of quality and price to success in business, we begin this chapter by exploring these terms.

*Quality* is the measure of how well a product or service matches a need. Quality is defined very broadly in this book, to include such dimensions as product features, timeliness, personal interface, reliability, durability, and consistency. *Price* is what the customer has to pay for a product or service (usually in money). This concept of price includes the price tag as well as the "cost to use" the product or service. For example, if a product must be repaired or adjusted in some way before it is used, the price includes the purchase price as well as the cost to repair or adjust. The "cost to purchase" (including time, shipping charges, travel expenses, and so on) might also be considered part of the price component. So there is a total cost of ownership:

*Total Cost = Price Tag + the Cost to Use*

*Value = Quality/Total Cost*

The concept of value combines quality and total cost: We have given a qualitative relationship here emphasizing the direct influence of quality and the inverse effect of total cost on value, but the precise relationship is usually more complex. Fortunately, to be effective at improving value at a system level, one does not need to be concerned with these relationships for each improvement effort. Leaders can develop an effective approach to improving value by balancing improvement efforts in three categories:

1. Eliminating quality problems that arise because we fail to meet the expectations of customers
2. Reducing costs significantly while maintaining or improving quality
3. Expanding customer expectations by providing products and services that customers perceive as unusually high in value

The improvement methods in previous chapters can be applied in each category. In this chapter, we suggest some *measures* related to each category, *change concepts* on which to base improvement ideas, and *infrastructure* to support the work. We conclude the chapter with some *operating principles* for developing an environment that is conducive to the improvement of value.

## Eliminating Quality Problems

Steve made an appointment with the car dealership to have the light on his passenger side door fixed. He called Sally, who worked with him and lived nearby, to ask for a ride to work the next day. She agreed but said that they must leave by 7:00 because she had an important meeting to attend.

When Steve arrived at the dealership the next morning, he found that six people were ahead of him in line. None of them was happy, but two were particularly upset because they were returning with problems that had not been fixed correctly the first time. It seemed the person who normally checked in the cars was sick and his replacement could not find the necessary forms. At 7:30, a half hour later than he had promised, Steve and Sally left for work.

Everyone has experienced such quality problems in their lives. We may also have encountered:

• Delivery of furniture two hours later than promised
• Long lines at the post office, bank, or grocery store

- A missing part for a child's toy (discovered at 5:00 P.M. on Christmas Eve)
- Incorrect information in the newspaper
- Poor advice from an accountant that resulted in an IRS audit
- Wrong drug administered in the hospital
- College classes filled at registration
- An electronic device too complex to use
- Bugs in computer software
- Electrical power outages
- Lost baggage on an airplane flight

These are all quality problems because the product or service did not perform according to the customer's expectations. Such expectations are developed through past experience with the product or service or by promises made by the seller. Steve's experience with the repair departments of car dealerships led him to expect the time to leave his car and complete the paperwork would be about fifteen minutes. One of the most basic tasks for any organization seeking to improve value is to eliminate quality problems.

> George arrived at work at 7:30 to find a long line of unhappy customers waiting to leave their cars to be repaired. He had been the manager of the department for three years, and it seemed every day he had a problem to solve. George realized he could not let this continue any longer; he had to take some action. The next day he instituted three actions:
>
> 1. The supervisor must test-drive and approve each repair job after the mechanic completes it. For repairs costing more than $700, George must give his approval after the supervisor has given approval.
> 2. The mechanic to whom the fewest cars were returned for repair of the same problem would receive a cash award.
> 3. Any mechanic with three or more returns in a month would be put on probation, and he or she would be fired if performance did not improve in the next month.

The assumption underlying George's actions was that most of the problems were caused by people (poor workmanship or lack of focus on the job). This is a manifestation of the fundamental attribution error described in Chapter Four. Although attention to the task and putting forth an earnest effort is obviously needed, lack of attention or effort is not usually the major source of quality problems. The causes of these problems are most often found in the processes of work, in the design of the product or service, or in unrealistic promises about the performance of the product or service.

When quality problems are viewed as people problems and not system problems, managers and supervisors resort to ineffective changes such as blaming and punishing the employees involved, instituting some form of checking or inspection, reacting only to resolve immediate problems, or denying that the customer had a right to the expectations in the first place. Progress will be made when system and process changes prevent the problems or mitigate their impact on the customer.

> Three months after implementing the actions, the situation was not any better. In fact, George felt that it was actually worse, because returns were about the same and two of his better mechanics were on probation. Also, he had just been reprimanded by his boss because complaints about the service department were up for two months in a row. Fortunately, George had just read an article in a trade journal about a service department that significantly reduced the number of returns by redesigning some of the processes in the department with the help of the supervisors and mechanics. They were also using something called the Model for Improvement, which was based on three simple questions.

## System-Level Measures Related to Quality Problems

Many improvement projects will be needed over time to continually reduce quality problems. These projects, if they follow the Model for Improvement, will have aims, measures, and changes associated with them. To measure whether all of these individual efforts are accumulating to have an impact at the business or system level, it is important to have aggregate measures. Some examples of aggregate measures associated with quality problems:

- Customer retention
- Contract renewals
- High school dropout rate
- Dollar value of warranty claims
- Return of products shipped incorrectly
- Replacement costs
- Complications in surgery
- Total cost of rework
- Backorders and stockouts
- Delays, as with flights

- Late deliveries
- Total customer complaints

## Process and System Changes to Eliminate Quality Problems

To prevent quality problems from occurring, products, services, or processes within the system must be redesigned. In Table 10.1 are a few change concepts that have proven to be particularly useful in the redesign work. These change concepts and others to eliminate quality problems are discussed in Appendix A. (The numbers in the third column correspond to the change concept number in the appendix.) Using change concepts to develop a change was discussed in Chapter Six.

George decided to use the Model for Improvement to eliminate some of the quality problems that were occurring. The aim was to significantly reduce the number of cars brought back for the same problem. George decided to run a cycle to analyze the company's records on repairs. He was amazed at what he found in the records. More than half of the returns were on repairs for leaks in the engine or transmission. The mechanics informed George that repairing

### TABLE 10.1. CHANGE CONCEPTS USEFUL FOR REDESIGN.

| General Grouping | Change Concept | Concept Number |
|---|---|---|
| Address customer problems | Listen to customers | 38 |
| | Coach customers | 39 |
| | Reduce wait time | 50 |
| Meet customer expectations | Focus on the outcome to a customer | 40 |
| | Use a coordinator | 41 |
| | Reach agreement on expectations | 42 |
| Eliminate mistakes | Reminders | 59 |
| | Differentiation | 60 |
| | Constraints | 61 |
| | Affordances | 62 |
| Manage variation | Match the amount to the need | 9 |
| | Standardization | 51 |
| | Improve predictions | 54 |
| | Contingency plans | 55 |
| | Sort product into grades | 56 |
| | Exploit variation | 58 |

the leaks is not the problem; *finding* them was. The mechanics suggested testing three changes as part of PDSA Cycles:

1. Every morning, designate one of the lifts for cars brought in to have a leak fixed. Put the car up on the lift and have the customer explain where he or she thinks the leak is. (Change concept 44: Optimize level of inspection)
2. Rent a piece of equipment that allows a probe to be inserted into the engine to display the inside and identify the source of a leak. (Change concept 27: Give people access to information)
3. For any customer who returns with an unfixed leak, mix a fluorescent dye into the oil so that if the repair is still unsuccessful the dye can be used to trace the source of the leak. (Change concepts 44 and 27)

After one month, the results were studied and the group agreed to some changes:

• Buy the equipment to probe the inside of the engine.
• Extend the policy of using the dye to first-time repair of leaks when the probe does not result in a definitive location of the leak.
• Drop the procedure of putting the car on the lift and asking the customer to point out the location.

Another cycle was planned to implement these changes. After two months, returns were down 20 percent, productivity was up, and George held another meeting after work to talk about the next opportunity to reduce returns.

## Infrastructure

A manager who believes that most quality problems are caused by faults of the system and whose workers are capable of using the Model for Improvement to improve processes will most surely make progress on eliminating these quality problems. The manager's efforts will be enhanced if three components of infrastructure are in place.

• Processes for identifying and analyzing quality problems and complaints
• An approach to recovering the customer's goodwill after the customer is affected by a quality problem
• Initiatives related to quality problems included in strategic or operations planning and execution

Many consumers who experience problems with products or services do not complain. Customers who complain are more likely than those who do not complain to do repeat business with the company that upset them, even if the problem is not solved to their satisfaction. For those customers who formally complain, most do business with the organization again, depending on the potential financial loss to the customer, if their complaint is addressed and solved. Among the reasons consumers experiencing product or service problems do not complain:

- Complaining was not worth their time or effort.
- They did not know how or where to complain.
- They believed that complaining would not do any good; no one wanted to hear about their problems.

Every day, frontline employees observe the frustration of customers who experience quality problems. In good organizations, these employees have the capability to empathize with the customer and solve the immediate problem. If improvement of value is strategic for an organization, then infrastructure to capture the information associated with the customer interaction will be in place and used for setting priorities for improvement.

In Table 10.2 is the outline of a system for collecting and analyzing data from product that was returned by the customer.

Once a customer experiences a quality problem, the damage has been done. However, an organization can compound the damage or decrease it, depending on how it handles the situation. A good example of handling of a quality problem is the reaction of airlines to overbooked flights. The airlines at one time would

## TABLE 10.2. SYSTEM FOR COLLECTING AND ANALYZING DATA FROM RETURNED PRODUCT.

| | |
|---|---|
| Definition of a return | Customer contacts the company asking that the product be returned or replaced. |
| Recorders of data | Any employee, but usually people in technical service and order processing. |
| Data collected | Customer information, product type, and lot number; information on the order, such as date, person who ordered the product, description of complaint, checklist on where the complaint should be routed. |
| Storage medium | Computer database. |
| Analysis methods | Control charts on the number of returns each month, and Pareto diagrams of the type of complaint. Data can be organized by business unit, type of customer, type of complaint, product, or service. |
| Action | The information on the individual return is routed to the appropriate group for resolution. After action is taken, the customer is contacted to confirm that the problem has been solved. |
| | The data from all the returns are analyzed and used to set priorities for improvement. |

explain to the people who did not make the flight why they had to overbook, and the angry customers would be put on the next available flight. Now, the gate attendant asks if there is anybody willing to give up their seat in exchange for a free trip anywhere in the United States. There are usually several people willing to take the offer.

Here are some guidelines for dealing with customers who have experienced problems with quality:

*Do*

- Have a process for dealing with quality problems.
- Listen empathetically while allowing the customer to vent.
- Acknowledge problem, sympathize with customer, and apologize.
- Go overboard to solve the problem.
- Keep the customer informed of the status of the resolution of the problem.
- Give the customer something that they would not have been entitled to if the problem had not occurred (such as refunds, credits, a product).
- Give people who respond to customer complaints the authority to compensate the customer within certain guidelines without supervisory approval.
- Train people who interface with customers.

*Don't*

- Tell the customers they should have read or followed the directions.
- Make the customer feel stupid.
- Make excuses by explaining your system and why the problem happened.
- Create a new problem or the same problem from the quick solution.
- Get angry at the customer.
- Have the customer assume the inconvenience caused by the problem.
- Tell the customer "Its not our policy to . . . ."
- Blame the customer.

## Reducing Costs While Maintaining or Improving Quality

George was pleased that the number of cars returned for repair because the problem was not fixed had decreased substantially. He had other quality problems to address, but most of his customers seemed to be reasonably satisfied for the time being. His major worry was that his costs were too high and that he was making only a meager profit.

Income from his automobile service business was extremely important to George if he was going to continue to provide high-quality service.

Automobiles were getting more complicated all the time. The equipment for solving the problem of identifying leaks was not cheap. His business could use other sophisticated (and expensive) electronic diagnostic equipment. To do a good job, a mechanic required training in electronics. All of this required investment, and there was not enough income to keep up even minimum standards, much less invest in providing extremely high-quality service.

George was experiencing a problem faced by most people who run businesses: keeping costs under control while providing quality products and services to customers. Without cost reduction and control, a business does not generate sufficient profits to invest in new technology or improvements. Almost any time a quality problem is solved by changing the system to prevent the problem from occurring in the first place, cost will go down because of elimination of rework and other waste associated with quality problems. Once George and his mechanics solved the problem of returns for leaks, quality went up and cost went down.

The cost reduction that occurs from the reduction of quality problems may not be enough, however, to improve a company's cost profile. Some resources usually need to be focused on changing the system, with the primary aim of cost reduction while maintaining or improving quality. In addition to financial costs, organizations are concerned with reducing the social costs related to their business. Typical areas of concern are occupational health and safety, and preserving the environment.

George was almost totally absorbed by the need to reduce costs. He felt the only alternative left to him was to put in a productivity incentive system. From his experience with eliminating the returns for leaks, he was concerned about this approach. But he did not have any realistic alternatives. Shop standards existed for each of the jobs that the mechanics performed. The standards specified the time it should take to perform the job (for example, an engine tune-up). The incentive system was based on performance to standard. Each mechanic would sign in with the supervisor when the job was started and sign out when it was completed. At the end of the month, the mechanics were paid a bonus based on the extent to which they beat the standard times for the jobs they performed.

Although productivity was increasing after two months, overall costs were up. George was perplexed, so after closing one evening, he invited the mechanics and the supervisors to discuss the cost figures. They mentioned they often had to wait to get a car on the lift in order to begin their work. Many of the mechanics had specialties they performed. Some could do the oil changes and engine tune-ups but could not do major repairs. Others who were specialists— for example, in electronics—thought that routine repairs were beneath them.

Because of this specialization, a car often had to be put on and taken off the lift several times to complete the work requested by the customer. The

mechanics tried to coordinate their work, but there was no satisfactory scheduling process available. Besides, since the new incentive system was put in place,
mechanics were paying less attention to coordination and focusing primarily on
getting their part of the service job done quickly. Parking fees were also increasing. Because more cars were waiting for repair, they had run out of space in
their normal parking lot and were using one down the street for the overflow.
They paid for the additional parking spaces at market rate.

George needed to make significant cost reductions, and he was not finding
it easy. His first cycle to test the incentive system was not encouraging. Anyone
can reduce costs if willing to sacrifice quality, but it takes substantial skill and
knowledge to reduce costs while maintaining or improving quality. Often, cost
reductions in one area of the organization just transfer costs to another area.
George considered or used some of the typical means that organizations use to
reduce costs:

- Instituting layoffs, leaving the remaining people to work harder or cut corners
- Using productivity incentives
- Cutting back on service—for example, having customers pump their own gas
- Giving people less product for the same price—for example, smaller candy bars

This is not to say that these approaches are wrong. In an organization that is
grossly overstaffed, across-the-board layoffs may be the only alternative. Sometimes this occurs because of major swings in the marketplace, but just as often
the organization was not planning for the future. The poor reputation of cost-
reduction efforts is mostly due to the methods used and the results obtained, not
to the aim itself.

## Measures Related to Cost Reduction

The system measures listed for eliminating quality problems have at least an indi-
rect connection to reducing costs. Some additional aggregate measures associated
with cost reduction are:

- Total cost saving associated with removing non-value-added work
- Utilization of assets, for example manufacturing capacity or equipment use
- Productivity
- Material costs for product rejected at final inspection
- Cycle time
- Injuries
- Hazardous waste disposal

## Process and System Changes to Reduce Costs While Maintaining or Improving Quality

Sources of waste are in every process. The practical matter is to find the time to redesign systems to eliminate the waste and the costs associated with it. George had learned what not to do, but what are some useful ways of designing or redesigning a system to make it more cost-effective? When people think about cost reduction, they often come up with decreasing some budget line item: people, materials, or inventory. There is no rationale for concluding that cost reduction done in this way results in quality being maintained or improved; systems associated with these line items have not been redesigned. In Table 10.3 are a few change concepts that have proven to be particularly useful in redesigning systems to reduce cost.

Reviewing the data on costs after two months of his productivity incentive system, George realized this change would not result in the reduction of costs for which he had hoped. He asked the mechanics to help him develop some

### TABLE 10.3.  CHANGE CONCEPTS FOR REDUCING COSTS.

| General Grouping | Change Concept | Concept Number |
|---|---|---|
| Eliminate waste | Eliminate things that are not used | 1 |
| | Eliminate multiple entry | 2 |
| | Recycle or reuse | 5 |
| | Match inventory to predicted demand | 23 |
| | Reduce wait time | 50 |
| Improve workflow | Synchronization | 12 |
| | Schedule into multiple processes | 13 |
| | Minimize handoffs | 14 |
| | Move steps in the process close together | 15 |
| | Find and remove bottlenecks | 16 |
| | Smooth workflow | 18 |
| | Do tasks in parallel | 19 |
| | Use a coordinator | 41 |
| | Optimize maintenance | 48 |
| Decrease cycle time | Reduce controls on the system | 4 |
| | Do tasks in parallel | 19 |
| | Use pull systems | 24 |
| Reduce costs | Optimize level of inspection | 44 |
| | Work with suppliers | 45 |

changes to the system that would increase the efficiency of the entire system and increase its capacity. They came up with these changes:

- Divide the mechanics into teams and assign each team one or more lifts, with the aim being to put the car on the lift only once. (Change concept 14: Minimize handoffs)
- Cross-train the mechanics so they can all do more jobs. (Change concept 32: Implement cross-training)
- Designate one lift for complicated jobs with uncertain time duration so that the inefficiency associated with these jobs would not slow down the more routine work. This lift could be used by any team. (Change concept 13: Schedule into multiple processes)
- Develop a scheduling system to support the coordination of work. (Change concept 41: Use a coordinator)

After six months, George was pleased with the progress. They had run several cycles that resulted in accomplishing a significant amount of cross-training and in removing most of the bugs from the team concept for repair of cars. The average cycle time (time from when the customer drops off the car until it is ready for pickup) was down from twenty-four hours to fifteen. Expenses for parking were lower than ever. George predicted that once the scheduling system was put into place, the cycle time would be reduced to ten hours. Thanks to the reduction in cycle time, the capacity of the system was increased. Customers were pleased with the quicker turnaround on repairs.

## Infrastructure

The manager's efforts to eliminate waste and its associated cost will be enhanced if three components of infrastructure are in place:

- Processes for taking cost out of the system while preserving employee morale after the waste has been redesigned out
- Initiatives related to waste reduction and its associated costs are included in strategic and operations planning
- An approach to measuring cost reduction at the system level

Those who redesign a system to take out waste create the potential for effective cost savings. However, the costs associated with the waste do not vanish without some intervention on the part of management. In George's situation, he might choose not to fill two vacant positions for mechanics.

The translation of waste reduction into cost reduction must be done in such a way that frontline workers and supervisors remain enthusiastic about improvement efforts aimed at waste reduction. The best situation is when the business is growing, because customers perceive that its products are of high value. In this environment, people whose non-value-added work is eliminated as a result of system redesign can be retrained to perform new jobs. This requires investment on the part of management and flexibility on the part of workers. If demand is steady or decreasing, management faces a more difficult job in converting waste reduction into cost reduction. If conditions demand some aggressive cost reductions to accompany the waste reductions, some of the means listed here can be considered to soften the trauma experienced in the organization:

- Reduce the use of contract labor
- Reduce the use of overtime
- Use attrition to reduce staff
- Find people jobs with suppliers
- Give incentives for people to retire early or voluntarily leave the organization

If the improvement of value is an important part of the business strategy for an organization, then strategic and operations planning will include initiatives relating to cost reductions. We believe organizations can set and achieve aims to reduce costs totaling 1 to 3 percent of operating expense yearly; an organization or business unit with a $100 million operating expense budget would set a cost reduction goal of $1 to 3 million each year. These savings might be used to offset salary increases or be reinvested in the business. If allowed to flow into profits or contributions to margin, these savings are substantial increases to the bottom line. For example, if the organization with the $100 million expense budget had a 10 percent profit margin, then the cost reductions would result in an increase in profit margin to approximately 11 to 13 percent. Of course, one-time cost reductions or focused efforts in narrow areas of the company may be able to accomplish greater results than 1 to 3 percent. However, 1 to 3 percent of total operating expense yearly over many years is a significant accomplishment, requiring everyone in the organization to contribute to the redesign effort.

To support a strategic initiative of cost reduction, the organization will need a way to measure the total cost reduction at the organization level. If cost reductions are occurring at many places in the organization, some principles and processes for counting savings will be needed. This is an area where the finance department can lend its expertise. To count true savings, actual budget costs should be used. For example, when George and his team reduced defects associated with leaks, the claim was that returns were down and productivity was up. How are these claims substantiated in the budget or financial reporting systems? There was also a new expenditure for dye to identify the leaks. These new expenses must be taken into account in computing total savings. George and his team redesigned the work

## TABLE 10.4. LABOR SAVINGS.

| 2005 | | | 2006 | | |
|---|---|---|---|---|---|
| Total jobs | Labor $ | Adjusted Labor $[1] | Total jobs | Labor $[2] | Saving $ |
| 3124 | 272,180 | 310,515 | 3564 | 269,135 | 41,380 |

1. Adjusted for yearly changes in total jobs.
2. Does not include 2.5% wage increase.

flow using teams and scheduling processes, and productivity gains were claimed. By not filling open positions the cost savings associated with the redesign seem at least intuitively to be realized. The reduced parking fees for cars in process should be an easily counted savings.

From readily available figures, George produced the analysis in Table 10.4 to count the labor savings from the improvement efforts.

To compute the labor savings, he compared the 2005 labor costs for the mechanics with the 2006 costs. In computing the 2006 costs, he did not include the 2.5 percent cost-of-living raise he had given to everyone in the company. His rationale was that he was able to afford the raise because of the savings from the improvement projects. He also made an adjustment for productivity. His shop had 3,564 jobs in 2006 compared to 3,124 jobs in 2005. For comparison, he adjusted the 2005 labor costs by multiplying by 3,564/3,124 to arrive at the labor costs if the shop had accomplished the same number of jobs in 2005 as in 2006. Using this approach, he computed that the labor savings associated with the improvement efforts were $41,380.

The third component of a strategic approach to increasing value is a strong external focus on exceeding customer expectation by innovating new ways to meet customer needs.

## Expanding the Expectations of Customers to Increase Demand

The elimination of quality problems and reduction of costs had brought success to George's repair shop. However, the increased capacity and reduction in rework meant the mechanics were not keeping busy full-time. A layoff as the consequence of everyone's efforts appalled George.

The next morning, George burst into the office and called a quick meeting. He had an idea for a new service to increase business and help preserve the jobs at the shop. He explained he had assisted a friend the previous evening who had experienced car trouble after work. He had done the repairs in the parking lot of his friend's office. He was sure that many people deferred routine maintenance because of the inconvenience of getting to work without their cars. Why not do the oil changes or other routine jobs right in the parking lot during working hours?

Initially, the idea was received with skepticism, but gradually the mood progressed to acceptance and even excitement. George put together a team to develop and test the new service. They would use the Model for Improvement just as they had done for the cost-reduction efforts. Once the team agreed on its aim, defined some measures, and developed a prototype of the new service, they planned the first cycle. The property manager at his friend's office complex agreed to a test for one week, so long as George would include her car in the test; it was badly in need of an oil change and some new wiper blades!

The third category of improvement—expanding the expectations of customers by providing products and services that customers perceive as unusually high-value—is often considered the most difficult category of improvement, but it is also the most strategic for an organization seeking to grow. It focuses on the mission of the organization and how it serves customers. It requires study of the customer beyond what is necessary for eliminating quality problems or for reducing costs. New, creative ideas are needed. Success in solving quality problems and reducing costs without developing new products and services to create more consumer demand results in short-term organizational gain but personal loss for the workers. The output of this category of improvement is a predictable stream of new products and services that raise the expectations of customers because of their very high value.

## Measures Associated with Increasing Demand

When the measures associated with reducing quality problems and the measures associated with cost are combined, they relate to the improvement of value for existing products. This increased value may result in increasing demand for existing products that still have a market. However, these measures must be supplemented by system measures that are more dynamic in nature and take into account attracting demand with new products or services. The measures include:

- Percentage of sales associated with products or services developed in the last three years
- Sales related to new customers

- Percentage of operating expense allotted to research and development (R&D)
- Number of new patents
- Sales from licensing of new technologies developed in R&D

## Process and System Changes to Increase Demand

For George's business, the primary changes related to where the repairs were done. The routine repairs were done at a place convenient for the customer. The same types of changes that might be done to eliminate quality problems (don't lose the car keys) or changes to reduce costs (efficiently schedule production) still apply. The new thinking comes from applying them in the customer's system rather than only in the producer's system. Thus an organization such as George's, which has built capability to reduce defects and costs internally, has an opportunity to increase demand by applying these same capabilities in the customer's system. Of course, this requires a customer focus and cooperative relationships with customers willing to test new ideas. In addition to applying change concepts for defect reduction and cost reduction in the customer system, the change concepts in Table 10.5 have been found useful to generate changes that increase demand. Others are included in Appendix A.

Change concept 70 (differentiate product using quality dimensions) can be one driver of new ideas if the definition of quality is expanded to include multiple dimensions. The list shown in Table 10.6 identifies and defines a number of generic "dimensions of quality" that may assist in defining quality for a particular product or service.

These dimensions support a broad definition of the concept of quality that can include all aspects of the performance, appearance, and variation associated with products and services. The dimension of "features" can be further divided to include such aspects as the size and location of a product or service.

## TABLE 10.5. CHANGE CONCEPTS FOR INCREASING DEMAND.

| General Grouping | Change Concept | Concept Number |
|---|---|---|
| Delight customers | Focus on core process and purpose | 34 |
| | Alliances and relationships | 37 |
| | Mass customize | 63 |
| | Offer product/service anytime | 64 |
| | Offer product/service anyplace | 65 |
| | Emphasize intangibles | 66 |
| | Differentiate product/service using quality dimensions | 70 |

## TABLE 10.6: DIMENSIONS OF QUALITY.

| Number | Dimension | Meaning |
|--------|-----------|---------|
| 1 | Performance | Primary operating characteristics |
| 2 | Features | Secondary operating characteristics, added touches |
| 3 | Time | Time spent waiting, cycle time, time to complete a service |
| 4 | Reliability | Extent of failure-free operation over time |
| 5 | Durability | Amount of use before replacement is preferable to repair |
| 6 | Uniformity | Low variation among outcomes of a process |
| 7 | Consistency | Match with documentation, forecasts, or standards |
| 8 | Serviceability | Resolution of problems and complaints |
| 9 | Aesthetics | Relating to the senses, such as color, fragrance, and fit |
| 10 | Personal interface | Punctuality, courtesy, and professionalism |
| 11 | Flexibility | Willingness to adapt, customize, or accommodate change |
| 12 | Harmlessness | Relating to safety, health, or the environment |
| 13 | Perceived quality | Inferences about other dimensions; reputation |
| 14 | Usability | Relating to logical and natural use; ergonomics |

## Infrastructure

Efforts to increase demand can be enhanced if three components of infrastructure are in place:

1. An approach to gaining knowledge in the customer's system
2. Investment in R&D
3. Initiatives related to increasing demand included not only in research and development but also in operations planning and execution

A start on an approach for gaining knowledge in the customer's system can be made through some simple behavior changes in the company. Here are examples of some behaviors focused on observing customers and assuming the role of the customer.

### Observing the Customer

- Travel agent taking a trip with a customer
- Engineer watching the customer install a garage door opener
- Designer watching the customer program a VCR
- Administrator spending a day with a patient who has just been discharged from the hospital
- Members of the IRS watching people fill out a new tax form

- Teachers observing the family life of students
- Programmers observing people using a newly acquired software program

### Assuming the Role of the Customer

- A new designer assembling the gas grill his company manufacturers
- Automobile company executives driving cars with fifty thousand or more miles on them
- Mayor of a city posing as a homeless person to use available government services
- An executive calling the company's main telephone number
- Manager returning a damaged product to one of his stores
- Physician spending time as a patient in her hospital

Most companies that sell products have well-defined R&D budgets and systems. However, this formal approach to developing new offerings is less common in service companies, or even in the service component of companies with mostly product offerings. Building an investment in service design and execution with dedicated staff accelerates improvements that increase demand.

New product and service offerings are supported and enabled by effective operations. Many improvements relating to internal operations are focused on defect reduction or cost reductions. Including initiatives in operations planning that enable new product or service offering is a vital part of sustained increasing of demand.

## Balanced Measures

A manager or executive intending to learn how improvement efforts in the three categories were affecting the organization could establish a "balanced scorecard" by choosing one, two, or three of the system measures in each category. For example, George might use this balanced scorecard for his auto repair business:

- Percentage of customers returning because the repairs did not fix the problem
- Percentage of repairs not finished on time
- Savings associated with removing nonvalue-added work
- Salary cost per repair job
- Percentage of revenue from new services
- Net promoter score (NPS)

The NPS is a measure that has been found to closely relate to increasing demand. It is a measure that integrates the impact of improvement in all three categories. It is computed as follows:

1. Randomly select a sample of customers and ask them to respond on a 0–10 scale: How likely is it that you would recommend (Company X) to a friend or colleague?

2. Zero represents the extreme negative end of the scale and ten represents the extreme positive end of the scale.
3. To calculate NPS, take the percentage of respondents who are promoters (9 or 10 on the scale) and subtract the percentage who are detractors (0–6 on the scale).

$$NPS = \% \text{ of Promoters} - \% \text{ of Detractors}$$

# Developing an Environment Conducive to the Improvement of Value

When an organization and its leaders make progress on improving value through system change in each of the three categories, their beliefs and assumptions also change and evolve as to what environment is needed to support these efforts. This supportive environment can be outlined in five operating principles:

1. *Quality problems almost always result from faults of the system, not the people involved.* Faults of the system are manifested as mistakes of people working in the system. Most people want to do a good job. Defects associated with their work are stressful for them. Change the system and people will make fewer "errors."
2. *Frontline workers are essential to the improvement efforts.* George's mechanics knew the issue was identification of the source of the leak, not fixing the leak once it was found. These mechanics faced the faults of the system every day and knew them in a level of intimacy that was vital to the improvement effort.
3. *System changes usually require action on the part of management.* Although the mechanics were vital to the effort, they did not have the authority or the means to make all the changes that were needed (for example, renting or purchasing new equipment). Managers who delegate the elimination of quality problems to the frontline workers are abdicating their responsibility.
4. *Reducing quality problems will almost always result in reduced cost.* If quality problems are eliminated by redesigning the product or service, then quality improves, costs are reduced, and productivity increases. Quality problems have costly side effects in the form of disruptions, rework, and other nonvalue-added work.
5. *Demand for product and service is built into the system through the organization's design processes.* Incentives for salespersons, increased advertising, and discounts may affect short-term demand. However, just as with defects and cost, demand over the long run is determined by the organization's ability to redesign its systems to produce products and services of high value.

## Key Points from Chapter Ten

- Methods to develop, test, implement, and spread improvements should be integrated within the three categories to achieve an effective and balanced approach to improvement.
- One of the most basic tasks for any organization seeking to improve value is to eliminate quality problems that arise because customers' expectations are not met. The causes of quality problems are most often found in the processes of work, in the design of the product or service, or in unrealistic promises about the performance of the product or service.
- Without cost reduction and control, a business does not generate sufficient profits to invest in new technology or improvements.
- Anyone can reduce costs if willing to sacrifice quality, but it takes substantial skill and knowledge to reduce costs while maintaining or improving quality.
- Success in solving quality problems and reducing costs without developing new products and services to create more consumer demand too often results in short-term organizational gain but personal loss for the workers.
- The new thinking to expand customer expectation to increase demand comes from the producer applying change concepts in the customer's system rather than only in the producer's own system.
- To develop a comprehensive approach to the improvement of value, leaders should consider the integration of the three categories of improvement into their business strategy.

# CHAPTER ELEVEN

# IMPROVING LARGE OR COMPLEX SYSTEMS

The approach to improving large systems builds on the methods to develop, test, implement and spread changes presented in previous chapters. Although projects focused on large or complex systems can use the Model for Improvement as a framework, successful large system improvement usually requires more sophisticated use of the model and more advanced methods. It is beyond the scope of this book to give an exhaustive treatment of the methods associated with improving these types of systems. The intent of this chapter is to give the reader an introduction to methods and approaches to improving larger and more complex systems and to point the way for further personal study.

Improvement work becomes more difficult when one or more of these elements are present:

- *Delayed response.* Significant challenges for learning exist because the temporal spread between making a change and observing its effect is substantial or because the complexity of the system makes it difficult to predict all the consequences of a change. Example: changes in a state law to legalize some forms of state-run gambling such as lotteries have immediate observable results in revenue. Other observations take longer to make, such as whether the change reduces illegal gambling or whether legalization encourages gambling by those who cannot afford it.

- *Integration, coordination, synchronization.* Systems that are to be improved across multiple organizational boundaries, and the components are separated by time or space so that the changes to the system are usually large in scope and often must be phased in. Example: "supply chain" is the name given to a large system that moves materials from suppliers to production to distribution and then finished product to the customer. The name recognizes the difficulty of coordinating geographically diverse entities to deliver a product to a customer reliably.

- *Behavior change.* The behavior of a large number of individuals working or living in diverse circumstances must be changed. Example: imagine the difficulty of changing the teaching of science in all elementary schools in a state or the entire country. Even if a superior curriculum and teaching method were available, the difficulty of reaching all schools and all teachers and changing their behavior as well as developing their skills would be a daunting problem of spread.

- *Disruption.* A new technology, market forces, or other circumstances negate existing business models or other aspects of the status quo and require the design of a new system on a large scale with accompanying transition issues. Example: the ability of customers to download music from the Internet caused fundamental change in an industry that relied on distribution of physical media (vinyl records, tapes, compact discs) to support its business model.

Figure 11.1 depicts the relative degree of difficulty of specific improvement projects.

Enhancement to the Model for Improvement in three areas is needed to overcome these difficulties:

## FIGURE 11.1. DEGREES OF DIFFICULTY OF IMPROVEMENT PROJECTS.

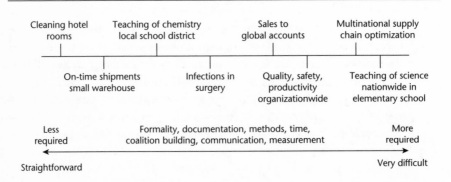

## TABLE 11.1. ENHANCEMENTS TO THE MODEL FOR IMPROVEMENT TO IMPROVE LARGE SYSTEMS.

| Elements That Make Improvement Difficult | Enhancements to the Model for Improvement to Overcome the Difficulties | | |
|---|---|---|---|
| | Project Set-up | Developing High-Impact Changes | Testing and Learning |
| Delayed response | | X | X X |
| Integration, coordination, synchronization | X X | X X | X |
| Behavior change | X | X X | X |
| Disruption | X X | X | X X |

*Note:* Impact of the enhancements on the difficulties: No X = little or no impact; X = some impact; X X = substantial impact.

1. Approaches to project setup and management that ensure coordination of effort and cooperation toward a common purpose
2. Methods to understand the relevant aspects of the system and the environment in which it operates to facilitate developing high-impact changes
3. Plans to design and execute complex testing and learning strategies

Table 11.1 illustrates how these enhancements contribute to overcoming the difficulties that are encountered when one attempts to improve a large system. The remainder of the chapter explores these enhancements to the Model for Improvement and their application to large systems.

# Project Setup and Management

As improvement projects become more ambitious and increase in scope, more attention needs to be paid to their setup and management. For example, many physician practices and other health care settings have improved the quality of care for patients with chronic conditions such as asthma and diabetes. Some of the projects are local in nature and focus on diagnosis and treatment based on the best medical evidence within a specific location such as a doctor's office, the emergency room, or a hospital. But suppose the focus is on a population of children with asthma who are living in poverty in a large metropolitan area. These children and their families have many challenges in daily life to overcome to properly deal with the treatment of asthma and the prevention of severe exacerbations that cause the child to need care in an ER or to be hospitalized. This larger focus has parts of all four of the elements that make system improvements difficult. Because asthma has a seasonal component to its severity, changes made in one part of the year may not produce observable improvement until later in the year. If the aim is to reduce ER visits and hospitalizations for this population, the system changes will require integration of many institutions and individuals, including pediatricians, hospitals, school-based health systems, and social workers. Some of these children live with adults who smoke in the home, which makes their symptoms worse. Behavior change of many individuals will be part of the improvement effort. Recognition of all the factors that might cause a child to be hospitalized could yield a major disruption of the current system for caring for these children, requiring a fundamental redesign of how care is given and paid for.

*Establishing a sense of urgency* about the aim can require honest disclosure and communication about the connection of the project to the strategic opportunities or threats the organization faces. Sometimes this can entail unpleasant discussion of problems that exist in the organization. For other projects, the challenge is getting others inside or outside the organization as excited as the leadership team about opportunities for growth or future success. Sometimes getting outsiders, such as suppliers or the board of directors, to share their perspective on the opportunity can be helpful.

The "improvement team" for a large system project can be much more complex than a project completed in a single division or department. There are often many subteams, possibly in various geographic locations, as is illustrated by the childhood asthma example.

*A steering team or guiding coalition* made up of senior leaders of the organization or representatives of cooperating institutions is recommended to keep the project team focused on the aim. Some of the tasks of the steering team are:

- Keeping a focus on the common purpose
- Assuming responsibility for success of the project
- Overseeing the resources needed to execute these complex projects
- Establishing and maintaining an appropriate sense of urgency
- Keeping the full executive team apprised of progress
- Establishing capital and expense budgets
- Specifying funding sources for the project

Any improvement project is nested in the political environment of the department, division, or organization in which it is embedded. That is, there exists people and groups with competing interests. It is essential in large-scale improvement projects to take this political context into account in establishing the steering team. Here are questions found to be useful in assessing the political context and establishing an effective steering team:

- Can the project be identified with a political agenda?
- What else of political significance is going on in the environment—for example, turnover of executives?
- Which persons or groups would like the project to succeed or fail for political reasons?
- Will there be winners or losers either in the end state or in the transition to that state?
- What coalition needs to be built?
- What system for relationship management is needed?

For the asthma project, the guiding coalition consisted of representatives from a number of institutions:

Metropolitan Housing Authority
Legal Aid
Health Department public health nurses, including school nurses
Mental health care, for family members in need
Community smoking cessation programs
Insurance companies
School-based health centers
Pediatricians
Emergency rooms
Hospitals

Some of the political issues to be addressed were how to pool resources and funding among the programs with varied revenue streams, how to cooperate efficiently, and how credit for the project would be communicated.

Throughout this book, we have emphasized the importance of answering the question, "What are we trying to accomplish?" Establishing the aim of a project for a large system poses some additional challenges to the ones we have discussed thus far. Because of the scope of the project, many people inside and outside of the organization must understand what is to be accomplished, why such an effort is needed, and what types of changes are required. The charter should be expanded to also include insights on the elements that make improvement difficult and suggestions on methods to overcome the difficulties.

A vision statement helps to integrate the many changes needed to affect the performance of a large system. An example of a vision statement for a company moving from an organization focused on regions or business units to a customer-focused organization: "Our global customers will be able to contact us in any part of the world and expect the same response to product and service availability. They can use the same systems to order and receive products from any of their locations." A large system project usually has a name or theme used to communicate the project to others; for example, "the 24–7 project" is about making customer service available anytime. A health care team working on end-of-life care could have "death with dignity" as a theme.

Stories can also be used to make the need or vision more compelling to all stakeholders. The asthma team chose to create a story about a child, Darryl, who was a typical member of the population they were addressing in their project.

> Darryl is eight years old and has moderate but persistent asthma. He lives with his mother, three siblings (who also have asthma), and his maternal grandparents in an apartment in the Cottage Hill neighborhood. His mother works and cannot bring Darryl for his doctor's appointments. He stays with his father on weekends. His father does not believe that Darryl has asthma. The boy has been admitted to the hospital multiple times since he was two months old, including one admission to the hospital's intensive care unit. He has recently been discharged from the hospital because of another severe episode of asthma-related symptoms.

The steering team will also form the *project operational team,* which includes a project leader with authority for execution of the project. The project leader should be able to commit 40–100 percent of her time to an effort of this size. Project leaders can come from a number of places:

- Dedicated improvers such as process engineers in chemical plants
- Middle managers who view this role as part of their development process
- Organizational opinion leaders with operating responsibility

The project leader will need support from others, including a day-to-day leader (at least half-time), technical or subject matter leader, plus others as needed.

Most projects to improve large systems require a series of integrated changes established over time to transition from the existing system to an improved one. Leaders of the project often break the work into subteams and then integrate the changes to optimize the system as a whole. There are exceptions to this—when there is a severe disruption in the environment—but almost always changes will be made to an existing system. This sequence of changes must be managed.

The credentialing case example in Chapter Twelve offers an example of laying out a plan for the project.

Laying out the project this way allows those working on the improvement initiative and those affected by it (especially the leaders of the subproject projects) to see how it all fits. The project plan also enables the steering team to establish interim goals and review them. Every 90 to 120 days is a good interval for an extensive review by the steering team. The improvement team will be reviewing progress more frequently, at least monthly. (Chapter Thirteen has suggestions for how to conduct project reviews.) Appendix B contains some project management tools such as PERT charts that are useful for managing large improvement projects.

# Understanding the System and Developing High-Impact Changes

In Table 11.1, methods related to understanding systems and developing high-impact changes were indicated to be essential in improving systems that require integration of several components or for changing behavior of many people working or living in varying contexts. A few rare individuals have a talent for intuitively or analytically developing insights into system dynamics and suggesting changes that can be based on these insights. The aim of the methods in this section is to increase significantly the number of people who can contribute to improving large or complex systems by making the task of understanding the system and the drivers of its performance less daunting.

The methods that are discussed here:

- Understand the structures and operating rules in the system
- Use frameworks
- Identify and remove bottlenecks
- Consider people in the same system (change concept 20)
- Define segments or paths in the system

## Understand the Structures and Operating Rules in the System

Improvement projects targeting large system change require consideration of changes to:

- Structures (concrete aspects of the organization)
- Operating rules (values, customs, habits)
- Processes (sequence of events to accomplish work)

*Structure* refers to the design of the organization through which the business is conducted. Structure includes the various frameworks that exist for organizations:

- Financial structures (pay systems, revenue streams)
- Administrative structures (the organizational chart)
- Responsibility structures (delegation of and accountability for tasks)
- Control and learning structures (management and improvement systems)
- Physical structures (buildings, equipment, supplies, raw material)
- Information structure (measurement systems, databases, computer systems)

The structure determines how the components of the system interact. The word *structure* implies stability and permanence, which is one reason changes directed at structure can be difficult. Use of the list of structures directs attention of the improvement team to make changes that will have an impact. The team members need lots of support and encouragement if they are going to make changes to the structural elements of the system.

*Operating rules* refer to the guiding principles, values, customs, or habits that explicitly or implicitly shape behavior in a system. In a project to improve a large system, spending time on clarifying or even changing one or more operating rules is often required. Examples of operating rules:

- The customer is always right (guides behavior of those interacting with unhappy customers)
- The patient is the source of control (moves the health care team away from a profession-based perspective on what is right for the patient)
- Board passengers on the plane from back to front (seeks to put some order and efficiency to the boarding process)
- When two or more customers are in line, drop what you are doing and open a cash register (seeks to generate the recognition in employees that the needs of the customer come first)

These operating rules lend guidance on how employees should behave or shape their decisions when faced with a new or difficult situation. The use of these operating rules leaves room for flexibility in dealing with situations as they arise. Operating rules are a very effective way for leadership to communicate the direction of a change without overspecifying how the change is to be executed in individual processes or circumstances.

The concept of a *process* is fundamental to improvement. Most of the improvement projects discussed thus far in this book were directed at one or more specific processes in an organization. Many of the approaches and methods for improvement are built around the process concept. For large system projects, many processes need to be redesigned at the local level to support the structural changes. In addition, there may be some high-leverage processes sufficiently important to performance that improving them will improve performance of the system. Figure 11.2 relates the concept of a nesting of processes within a system structure. In this picture, for example, the entire supply chain may be at the top level, inventory management is one of the processes that can be connected to production planning at level two, and purchasing raw materials can then be connected to inventory management at the bottom detailed level.

## Use Frameworks

A framework, as the word is commonly used, is a supporting structure or basic system. The use of a framework in large systems to generate system changes is analogous to the use of change concepts to generate process changes. Consider the framework prevent-identify-mitigate, which is useful for safety or defect-reduction applications.

## FIGURE 11.2. NESTED SYSTEMS.

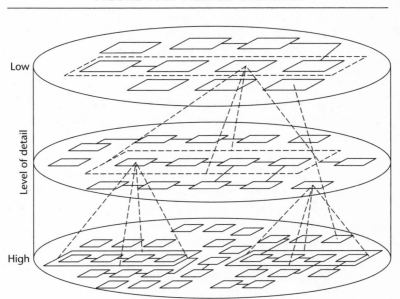

Signing up for an Internet account such as online banking or online purchasing of merchandise illustrates the use of this framework. A sign-in name and password are needed to use such as service. The operator of the site balances security and ease of use. One defect associated with the process of initial registration is that the customer may mistype her password. For most humans, this error will occur at a rate of parts per hundred. If this happens, the user will not be able to recreate the mistaken password easily, causing dissatisfaction and waste. Because the operator of the site may not have many ways to *prevent* this error, the process contains an *identify* step to recognize that an error is being made before it causes problems. It is now common to make the customer retype the password and have the software check for agreement. This perhaps brings the defect rate to parts per thousand or better. Although the password is now most likely entered correctly, the customer may later forget what password was entered originally. To *mitigate* this defect associated with the password, the user is prompted at the initial registration to pick a question (such as the city in which he was born) and answer it. If the user forgets the password when returning to the site, he is prompted to answer the chosen question and the password is e-mailed to the user. Perhaps this reduces defects associated with the password to parts per ten thousand or better. In the future, technology such as voice recognition or retinal scan may eliminate the need for all this manual entry. Until then, a system with a defect rate of parts per ten thousand or better can be designed using the prevent-identify-mitigate framework even though the humans are making errors at the rate of parts per hundred.

Sometimes frameworks are a collection of change concepts arranged in a logical order. Typing the password twice is an example of change concept 61 ("use constraints") and was part of the *identify* step in the framework. A contingency plan (change concept 55) was used in the *mitigate* step.

In Chapter Nine a spread model was described for replicating changes among individuals or locations. This model is built up from elements of social marketing that can be summarized in the framework list-offer-convert, meaning that there is a *list* of persons or locations (the social system in the spread model), the *offer* or suggestion of a change, and then a decision to *convert* the offer into practice. This framework is useful in sales and marketing situations in companies as well as in social services aimed at changing behavior of individuals or groups. Chapter Twelve contains a case study of increasing sales that used this framework.

Useful frameworks are also often developed in specific industries. One classic framework from the Toyota Production System aimed at reducing defects and increasing productivity contains three components:

1. Eliminating waste at the frontline
2. Reducing unevenness of work flow
3. Eliminating overburdening of people or equipment

At a specific production facility, the framework is a way to organize the many process changes that are needed in improvement of a large production system. The three components are nested in the manner depicted in Figure 11.2 relative to the level of the system at which changes are directed: waste at the most detailed level in the diagram, unevenness at the intermediate level, and overburden at the highest level.

This framework is often referred to as "lean manufacturing." The construction industry, seeing the merits of this framework but recognizing the differences between production and construction, adapted the framework and not surprisingly labeled it "lean construction."

## Identify and Remove Bottlenecks

A bottleneck is that component of a system that limits the overall performance or capacity of the system. The term *bottleneck* is derived from the neck of a bottle, which limits the flow of liquid from the bottle. If a bottleneck can be identified, then attention can be focused on making changes to the bottleneck component and thus improving the performance of the entire system. Focusing on the bottleneck simplifies the task of developing, testing, and implementing changes in a large system.

## Preoperative Visit at a Hospital

To illustrate the identification of a bottleneck, consider a clinic that is held for patients who will be undergoing surgery in the hospital within a week. At the clinic, the patient will be interviewed by a nurse and an anesthesiologist. They will have a blood sample drawn by a technician called a phlebotomist. The patient may also have an EKG of the heart. The clinic manager desired to reduce the total cycle time in the clinic. A first step was to determine the bottleneck resource; the data in Table 11.2 were collected. Figure 11.3 is a display of the data that relates capacity and average demand. The range of demand is designated by the vertical line. From the graph, it is seen that nursing is the bottleneck resource thus generating queues. Therefore the processes associated with the nursing work could be the focus for improving overall cycle time. Similar calculations and visual displays can be done for larger systems as a means of focusing the improvement work.

### TABLE 11.2. CAPACITY AND DEMAND FOR A PREOPERATIVE CLINIC.

|  | Anesth. | Nursing | Phleb. | EKG | X-ray |
|---|---|---|---|---|---|
| Total process minutes including paperwork per visit | 15 | 20 | 8 | 10 | 9 |
| Actual estimated capacity with breaks, calls, lunch (visits) | 45 | 30 | 38 | 30 | On-call |
| Range of visits per day | 27–44 | 22–36 | 22–37 | 11–27 | 7–21 |
| Average visit over four-day period | 35 | 27 | 29 | 20 | 14 |

### FIGURE 11.3. CAPACITY AND DEMAND FOR A PREOPERATIVE CLINIC.

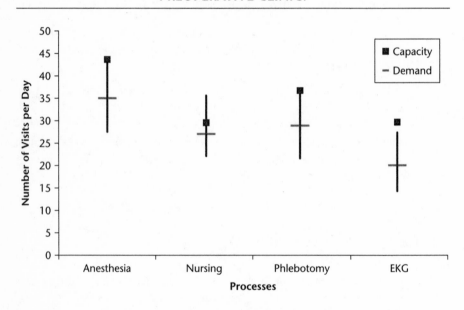

## Consider People as All Being in the Same System

Any of the change concepts in Appendix A could be applied to large systems, perhaps as part of a framework. However, change concept 20 is particularly useful in these settings. The change concept in the appendix is written as follows:

> People in different systems are usually working toward different purposes, all trying to optimize their own system. Taking actions that help people think of themselves as part of the same system can give them a common purpose and constitute a basis for optimizing the larger system.

## TABLE 11.3. PROCESS TO ENHANCE UNDERSTANDING OF THE SYSTEM.

| | |
|---|---|
| 1. | Gather representatives from the entities that must interact to optimize the larger system. |
| 2. | Reach consensus on a shared purpose. Using one or more stories about customers and their needs makes this task more concrete and puts a human face on the purpose. |
| 3. | Discuss the interactions among the participants that must occur to optimize the system for the customer. |
| 4. | Identify structures or operating rules that present barriers to cooperation and system optimization. |
| 5. | Define a plan for the short-term and long-term improvements to enhance interactions and make changes to structures and operating rules that cause suboptimization. |

One way a leader of a large system can take actions that help people think of themselves as part of the same system is to assemble a group of representatives from the several entities that will be optimized as a larger system. Table 11.3 contains a process for facilitating the event. For example, a team working on a charter for childhood asthma used Darryl's story as a focus for their discussion of purpose. They recognized the information transfer between the hospital and the pediatricians was flawed and resulted in less-than-optimal care for these children. Several of the representatives realized they all focused on the family and their living environment (among them smoking cessation programs, mental health providers, and legal aid), but their efforts were not coordinated. The team developed an action plan to test short-term changes and make the flow of money in the system match the needs of the children and families. In addition, the team agreed to count the new productive interactions between them each month as a result of their meeting.

## Define Segments or Paths in the System

The improvers of a large system face a dilemma of how to make the work of developing, testing, and implementing changes manageable while preserving the interdependencies in the system. Three useful ways to accomplish this are:

1. Segmenting individuals or locations into groups, for example grouping suppliers with respect to their level of sophistication with information technology.
2. Grouping by flow across various paths, for example products that are manufactured through unit operation 1, 2, 3 versus those that skip operation 2 and are processed through unit operations 1 and 3.
3. Using the 80–20 rule and defining the path for the most routine or high-volume 80 percent of products, services, or situations. Handle the other 20 percent in a customized way.

The segments or paths are used to assist with developing changes and make the testing of changes more efficient. For example, if the improvement aim is to process orders for product in a timely manner, the changes may depend on whether the order arrives by phone or by Internet. The project team might begin testing changes that arrive online to test the effectiveness of using information technology in processing the orders. They might then proceed to improving orders that arrive in other ways. The manufacturing team might choose to start its work on defect reduction for products whose path flows through operations 1 and 3. From the learning from those products, the team could reduce defects for the more complex products that flow through all three operations.

In Chapter Nine, "Spreading Improvements," the importance of establishing the social system within which peers can communicate with each other was discussed. As improvement initiatives requiring spread become large and ambitious (as with improving the teaching of science in all elementary schools in a country), the social system within which the spread is occurring becomes more diverse. Factors such as size of school, degree of urbanization, socioeconomic status of students, per pupil spending, and whether the school has a dedicated science teacher affect how attractive the changes are to individual teachers and schools. The improvement initiative can be made more tractable by using the factors listed above to establish some groupings of the schools:

Group 1: urban, low-socioeconomic, dedicated science teacher
Group 2: urban, high-socioeconomic, dedicated science teacher
Group 3: urban, low-socioeconomic, no dedicated science teacher
Group 4: urban, high-socioeconomic, no dedicated science teacher
Group 5: rural, dedicated science teacher
Group 6: rural, no dedicated science teacher

The leader of the project would be responsible for aggregating the learning across the groups.

## Testing and Learning Systems

The Model for Improvement emphasizes an approach to learning that relies on testing changes, preferably on a small scale, and observing whether the result is an improvement. As systems become larger and more complex, the relationship between cause and effect becomes more difficult to understand. Some experts in systems dynamics break the learning challenges into categories or contexts. A simple context is one in which the cause-and-effect relationship is known with a high degree of belief and a well-designed and executed test produces an observable effect. In Chapter One the owners of a cleaning company standardized the process of cleaning bathrooms and immediately observed a better result. The learning challenge in this context is to run a well-designed PDSA Cycle.

A complicated context is one in which the cause-and-effect relationship could be learned, but it may take an expert to learn it (for example, needing a doctor to learn the cause of pain in a patient or a mechanic to learn the cause of failure in an air conditioner). This is also the context in which sophisticated statistical analysis can be useful. Questions such as where to add capacity in a complicated supply chain may arise in this context. In health care, researchers at Dartmouth Medical School have studied data from large government databases to explain why the total per-person spending on health care varies dramatically in areas in the same region. Econometricians, epidemiologists, and statisticians operate in this context. A learning challenge that frequently occurs in this context is that the measures associated with the aim are not useful for learning in the short run. This occurs for at least two reasons: (1) the measure may not be affected until many changes are in place on a wide scale such as safety performance or hospital acquired infections, and (2) the effect of the changes on the measure may be delayed in time, as with warranty claims or sales to strategic accounts.

A complex context is one in which the cause-and-effect system is nonlinear and dominated by feedback loops. Systems in which people's behavior adjusts and adapts to a change make the results of changes unpredictable. In Chapter Ten, we discussed a situation in which the owner of an auto repair shop put in an incentive system to increase productivity and lower cost. The aim of the mechanics changed from fixing the car to obtaining the bonus. They adjusted their behavior in ways that the owner did not anticipate, and costs increased rather than decreased. The learning challenges in this context include the ones for the simple and complicated context as well as a challenge associated with lack of specificity of the change. The entire system change is the change in structure, operating rules, or process *plus* the system's adaptation to the change. The lack of predictability of the adaptation at full scale is the source of the learning challenge.

In large systems, all three contexts are usually present and the context changes over time. Skilled improvers of large systems will be aware of the contexts and the learning challenges associated with them, and have methods to mitigate the challenges. We discuss methods associated with:

- Measurement and theory building
- Using prototypes
- Learning during scale-up of changes

## Measurement and Theory Building

Projects to improve large systems require measures related to the aim of the project and balancing measures to detect unintended consequences. Developing these measures serves to bring a group of individuals into a true coalition with a common purpose. For large systems, these measures should be either the system measures of an organization's overall performance or very closely related to them to justify the investment of time and capital to accomplish the aim. Some examples of large system measures:

- Total salary cost to operate the supply chain
- On-time deliveries for all customers
- Safety performance companywide
- Sales from new products
- Percentage retention of contracts or customers
- Total cost savings in a business
- Warranty claims
- Volume of production per dollar of labor
- Customer complaints across all business units
- Rate of hospital-acquired infection
- Highway deaths
- Number of homeless in a city or region
- Sales to strategic accounts
- Variation in achievement in science among state elementary schools

These measures by definition are at the system level and may not be useful during early stages of the improvement work, even though they relate to the aim of the project. One approach is to use process or other measures associated with the system measure. The appropriate process measure to use depends on the theory that the team is currently using to develop the change. For example, a global specialty chemicals company had a strategic initiative to improve the supply chain. One of the teams associated with the initiative was integrating all components of the supply chain in one of their large locations. The primary aim of the project was to reduce backorders originating at that location. (A backorder occurs when a customer places an order but the product is not available in inventory.) The project was a challenging large system effort not only because it required integration and synchronization of components but also because the effect of changes on the primary measure (backorders) will not be affected immediately but decrease over time as backorders are avoided in the future. With help from experts in supply chain management, the team reviewed the structures

## FIGURE 11.4. DRIVER DIAGRAM FOR A PROJECT AIMED AT REDUCING BACKORDERS.

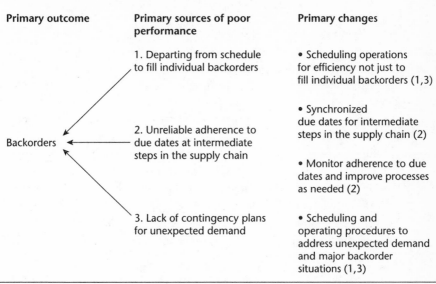

| Primary outcome | Primary sources of poor performance | Primary changes |
|---|---|---|
| | 1. Departing from schedule to fill individual backorders | • Scheduling operations for efficiency not just to fill individual backorders (1,3) |
| Backorders | 2. Unreliable adherence to due dates at intermediate steps in the supply chain | • Synchronized due dates for intermediate steps in the supply chain (2)<br><br>• Monitor adherence to due dates and improve processes as needed (2) |
| | 3. Lack of contingency plans for unexpected demand | • Scheduling and operating procedures to address unexpected demand and major backorder situations (1,3) |

*Note:* Numbers in parentheses indicate the driver to be affected by the change

and operating rules that were present at the location. Statisticians analyzed the large amount of data collected routinely on backorders, delivery schedules, and efficiency of operations to develop correlations among these variables and the amount of backorders. Through these activities, the team developed a theory of which faults of the system were causing backorders to occur. They summarized their theory using the driver diagram in Figure 11.4.

Three drivers of backorders in the current system were hypothesized:

1. An operating rule that required production to depart from the planned schedule to work on products on backorder. Because the original schedule was designed to make production most efficient, this operating rule caused efficiency to decrease and production schedules to be missed, causing more backorders, which were then made a priority. A reinforcing loop was set up.
2. Due dates for intermediate steps in the system, such as when raw materials should be ordered or when suppliers delivered them, were vague and thus not reliably adhered to.
3. Special circumstances, such as a sales promotion campaign or a large one-time order, caused predicted demand to be in error. There was no contingency plan for fulfilling this demand while continuing to meet routine, predicted demand.

Several projects were begun to address these drivers. Measures related to the team's theory about what caused backorders were used for each project. The projects were:

- Design processes to support a new operating rule to schedule for efficiency rather than backorders. The team was to take into account how to minimize disruption of filling backorders while transitioning to this new operating rule. *Measures:* (1) efficiency of production, (2) new products going on backorder each day
- A project to establish realistic lead times for each step in the system, monitor them closely, improve reliable compliance with the lead times, and eventually improve the capability of the system to achieve shorter lead times. *Measure:* compliance with lead times for each component in the supply chain
- A project to build contingency capacity into the schedule to deal with unexpected demand. This contingency capacity would need to be used in a way that maintained efficiency as much as possible. *Measures:* (1) efficiency of production, (2) Amount of contingency capacity built into the schedule each week

A quantitative approach was used in this example to develop theory about the dynamics of the system. Consider also the approaches a journalist or a writer of nonfiction articles might pursue. These methods are particularly useful in situations where the experience of the customer depends on the interaction or relationships among individuals, as in sales, education, and health care. Those seeking to improve their skills at theory building could profit from studying the methods these writers use.

## Developing and Testing Prototypes

One approach to overcoming the learning challenges associated with large or complex systems is to use prototypes or models of the system to be tested and then apply the methods found in Chapter Seven to these prototypes. Prototypes are not the real thing but are close enough for learning. Prototypes are essential when a disruption to the status quo is desired but the new system does not yet exist. Examples of prototypes are:

- Spreadsheet analysis of financial flows
- Computer simulations of large integrated systems such as a supply chain
- A process map or a spaghetti diagram of workflow and movement
- Miniature models such as those used by architects

- Test sites such as a hospital unit in which innovative ideas are tried without regard to efficiency initially and then scaled up to the entire hospital
- Computer games
- Role playing or rehearsals
- Informative case studies

All of these prototypes are aimed at making the new system tangible enough so that those involved in the development and their customers can discuss the merits of the evolving design. Developing useful prototypes often takes creativity and the ability to see associations, as can be demonstrated in a transportation example.

## Testing a Prototype for Emergency Evacuation

A fire drill is a rehearsal prototype. The alarm sounds and inhabitants of a building leave according to a defined process. Observations and measures of the evacuation are made by those responsible for the test and used to develop changes to the process. This is a standard PDSA Cycle. Let us suppose the system to be tested is the evacuation of a large city in response to a terrorist attack, chemical spill, or natural disaster. Getting the entire city to test an evacuation plan is probably not feasible. How could the team test the plan? In the early cycles, simulation of traffic flows can be useful to determine which routes might be best. The timing of lights at cross streets might also be determined by simulation. But these simulations will not test the many processes that must work well to make the overall evacuation effective.

The Department of Transportation of Washington, D.C. (DDOT), developed an innovative prototype to test some of these processes. Each year on July 4, Independence Day, the city holds a large fireworks display on the National Mall. Tens of thousands of people attend. They arrive at all hours of the day for sightseeing and picnicking, so getting to the mall is not difficult. However, all attendees leave at the same time: when the fireworks end. Members of the DDOT saw an opportunity to use the mass exodus as a prototype for testing an emergency evacuation plan. The objective of the test was to learn about regional communication and cooperation as well as to improve the emergency traffic signal timing for evacuation routes from the National Mall to the Beltway, a highway that circles the city. The plan for the test included:

- Changing traffic flow in the area around the mall to correspond to the evacuation routes in the emergency plan
- Delaying the traffic changes for fifteen minutes so some of the pedestrians could clear

- Setting the timing of green lights on evacuation routes to 240 seconds
- Getting every jurisdiction in the region on the same communications network
- Regional signal control
- Monitoring the patterns within the city
- Enlisting suburban jurisdictions to monitor the resulting traffic patterns in their jurisdictions

Here is some of the learning that was reported:

- Traffic cleared faster than usual
- Changes from one lane to two or from two to one were still troublesome
- Some problems with communication between Washington and Virginia
- Some pedestrian signals can only count down from ninety-nine seconds
- Better deployment of personnel to key intersections needed

Of course the prototype was not the real thing. One obvious difference is that the element of panic and fear that would accompany a real emergency was not present. However, one can assume cooperation among the multiple jurisdictions and discussion during the debriefing meeting will lead to a better system of evacuation in a real emergency.

The "natural experiment" is another opportunity for learning in a large system that is closely related to using prototypes. A natural experiment is a naturally occurring event or situation that introduces a change to the system beyond the control of the improvement team. A naturally occurring event might be a strike, a hurricane, a blackout, a fire at a supplier's manufacturing facility, or a gasoline shortage. It affords a unique opportunity for observing the innovative ways in which people respond to the event. Special causes on control charts (see Appendix B) can signal the occurrence of naturally occurring events that can be used for learning about the effect of naturally occurring changes to the system.

## Learning During Scale-up

In most initiatives to improve large systems, the changes cannot be made all at once on a large scale even if the team desires to do so. The scaling up of changes in a thoughtful manner is an opportunity for learning. Three methods for learning during scale-up are discussed in this section:

- Sequencing of components of the change
- Multiplicative scale up
- Cooperative testing

## Sequencing of Large Changes to Smooth the Transition

When a team improves a large system, the number of changes that they can develop is limited only by their imagination. However, testing and implementing the changes are limited by many practical considerations: the system is still in operation while the changes are being made, changes consist of multiple parts some of which are prerequisites for others, some parts of the change are more likely than others to produce motivational early successes, and so on. One method to help overcome these practical challenges is to plan the sequence of the changes effectively. A tool to help with this planning is a tree diagram; a template is given in Figure 11.5. In this diagram, we have four concepts that are driving the current changes. Following these current changes, other changes are planned, and depending on the learning from the PDSA Cycles of these changes other potential changes are predicted to be needed.

Consider an organization supplying machine tools to large manufacturers. The organization had a strategic initiative to improve its ability to partner with customers to co-design solutions to manufacturing challenges. This is a fundamental, disruptive change to the business, one in which people have no formal experience and there is no infrastructure. The improvement initiative was to last two years. The vision for the new system had three major components: understanding the needs of the customer, developing an internal team, and integrating execution with the customer's team. The company had a lot of learning to do. Could it develop the consulting and problem solving skills in the current employees, or should it hire new people or contract with outside experts? How should they build confidence in potential customers that they were capable of providing full solutions to manufacturing challenges, not just machine tools? They had a project management system for installation of a large machine tool, but this was not adequate for the uncertain nature of the collaborative services they were designing. How should they schedule and manage these new projects? They used the first year of the project to run small cycles to answer these questions.

Because of their expertise with a variety of manufacturing settings, customers informally asked them for advice in overcoming manufacturing challenges. They used some of these opportunities to test ideas and lay the foundation for the larger system changes. For example, they brought in an outside expert to help them in these situations and develop some of their employees. They tested the willingness of customers to pay for these services. By the end of the first year, they had answers to most of their questions and tested some of the components. They also obtained contracts for three medium size-projects that fit their new vision. They had a system capable of carrying out the projects, but it was untested at full scale.

## FIGURE 11.5. USING A TREE DIAGRAM FOR PLANNING CHANGES OVER TIME DIRECTED TO A VISION.

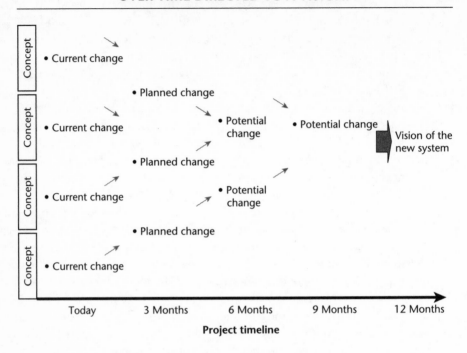

**Project timeline**

The steering team and the project leader decided they would use the three upcoming projects whose start dates were separated by two months as opportunities for full-scale testing. Table 11.4 contains a simplified version of the sequence of introducing the changes and testing them.

A ninety-day review cycle was used. At month 3 the test of the component for understanding the customer's needs would be in its second test cycle, and the component for establishing the internal team would be in its first test cycle. The second review, at month 6, could determine if the process for understanding customer's needs was sufficiently refined to make it the standard for new projects. The review would also have information from two tests of establishing the internal team and one test of full integration with the customer's team. At nine months, all three components would have had three test cycles, and two of the projects could be assessed for their outcomes. At the final twelve-month review, all three projects could be assessed for their outcomes. The steering team could assess whether to make the three-component system the standard for future projects of this type and what additional work (if any) is needed.

## TABLE 11.4. PLANNING CHANGES OVER TIME DIRECTED TO A DESIRED VISION OF CO-DESIGN WITH CUSTOMERS.

| System Component | Month | | | | | |
|---|---|---|---|---|---|---|
| | 0–2 | 2–4 | 4–6 | 6–8 | 8–10 | 10–12 |
| Understanding the customer | Tests for project 1 | Tests for project 2 | Tests for project 3 | Overall outcome project 1 | | |
| Developing the internal team | | Tests for project 1 | Tests for project 2 | Tests for project 3 | Overall outcome project 2 | |
| Full integration with the customer's team | | | Tests for project 1 | Tests for project 2 | Tests for project 3 | Overall outcome project 3 |

The test plan in the table illustrates three parallel sequences of PDSA Cycles, one for each of the three components as well as three replications of the entire system, one for each project.

## Multiplicative Scale up to a Large Number of Individuals or Independent Sites

In large systems, a sequence of PDSA Cycles is an important learning vehicle just as it is when the Model for Improvement is applied to small systems or processes. However, in large systems maintaining the pace of testing to match the size of the scale-up task is a vital responsibility of the team leading the effort. Without sufficient pace of moving from one cycle to the next, the efforts to incorporate improvement methods into large-scale change will be criticized for taking too long or missing the big picture. One way to establish an appropriate balance of learning and pace is to insist on multiplicative scale-up whenever replication of the change in different locations or involving various people is part of the implementation. Multiplicative scale-up means expanding the reach of the changes at an increasing pace—for example, from 1 customer to 5 in a month, then to 25 the next month, then to 125, 625 and so on. The sequence 1, 25, 125, 625 has been called "5x scale-up" because each number in the sequence is five times the number before it. The pace of scale-up depends on the multiplier (for example, five or ten) and the period between expansions (from 25 to 125 in one month or two).

At each 5x increment, new system issues are uncovered and can be dealt with sequentially. Take the example of the care for children with asthma. When the test includes only five children, very informal communication mechanisms might

## TABLE 11.5. 5X SCALE-UP FOR A SYSTEM TO CARE FOR CHILDREN WITH ASTHMA.

| Number of Children Affected | System Issues to Overcome or Questions to Answer |
| --- | --- |
| 5 | Can we make connections between the hospital and the pediatricians? |
| 25 | Can services outside the hospital be coordinated? |
| 125 | Can all team members have access to the same information? |
| 625 | How should the optimized system be financed? |
| 3,125 | Should we expand to overall child health rather than just one disease? |
| 15,625 | Can we reach our goal and sustain the performance? |

be used. The organizations involved might be willing to absorb the cost of the tests. As the scale grows, information technology and formal financial agreements are needed. Table 11.5 contains an example of the system issues that might arise at various population sizes.

The multiplicative scale-up allows the team to observe patterns as they emerge in the scale-up. They will have opportunity to learn how the people in the system adapt to the changes. Is the system truly being optimized, or are new forms of "gaming" the system emerging? This approach is especially useful when working in a complex context.

## Simultaneous Testing by Cooperating Entities

Frequently in working on a large system, many similar entities are involved, such as manufacturing locations, retail stores, schools, hospitals, sales regions, or police departments. Although structurally some aspects of these entities are similar, their operating rules, process, and environmental circumstances might be quite different. Thus the project team finds itself moving from what was assumed to be a simple context of like organizations to one that is complex and unpredictable. In these situations cooperative testing can be both an efficient way to learn and a means of studying emerging patterns. Consider an initiative to improve the teaching of science in elementary schools. One might assume that a simple context is present and mandate a standard state or national curriculum and teaching approach. More realistically, the team might acknowledge that one size doesn't fit all and engage numerous schools in a joint learning and improvement process. The potential changes at each school could include some combination of adoption of a standard curriculum, use of standard innovative exercises, or changes

### TABLE 11.6. COOPERATIVE IMPROVEMENT OF TEACHING SCIENCE IN ELEMENTARY SCHOOL.

**Two-Factor Design: Enjoyment and Achievement in Teaching Science in Elementary School**

|  |  | Curriculum | |
|---|---|---|---|
|  |  | Current | National standard |
| **Exercises** | Current | 1 | 2 |
|  | Innovative standard | 3 | 4 |

developed locally. Each school would be responsible for developing and testing some combination. They were free to choose what they wanted to test but were required to carry out the test in a PDSA Cycle and report the results to the oversight team. Table 11.6 contains a factorial arrangement for the cooperative testing. (See Chapter Seven for more on factorial experimental designs.)

Cell 1 contains schools that choose not to adopt either the standard curriculum or exercises but to develop their own change. Cell 2 contains schools that adopt the standard curriculum only. Cell 3 contains schools that adopt the innovative standard exercises, and cell 4 schools that adopt both curriculum and exercises. In each of cells 2, 3, and 4 the schools might also choose to add local changes and would report them to the oversight team.

The opportunities for learning in this cooperative approach include:

- Observe and analyze the patterns of choice and the reasons for them. This analysis would include the six segments defined early in the chapter by combinations of urban or rural setting, socioeconomic level, and whether the school had a dedicated science teacher or not.
- Determine which combinations in which segments were most promising.
- Determine which locally developed changes could be spread to other schools.
- Learn how the standard curriculum and exercises might be customized by segment.
- Learn whether a different segmentation would better explain the variation among the schools.

Subsequent cooperative cycles could follow on the basis of the learning. The spirit of sequential PDSA Cycles is the same as in other examples in this book. However, the design, execution, and learning from these cycles require a more sophisticated approach.

## Key Points from Chapter Eleven

- The approach to improving large systems builds on the methods to develop, test, implement, and spread changes presented in previous chapters. Although projects focused on large or complex systems can use the Model for Improvement as a framework, successful large system improvement usually requires more sophisticated use of the model and more advanced methods. These enhancements fall into three categories:

  1. *Approaches to project setup and management that ensure coordination of effort and cooperation toward a common purpose.* The improvement team focusing on a large system consists of members who cross boundaries within the organization, or perhaps even a coalition of members from multiple organizations. This requires some careful work to find a common purpose and define responsibilities for the team members. With such a varied group of participants, political issues will arise and must be addressed.

  2. *Methods to understand the relevant aspects of the system and the environment in which it operates to facilitate developing high-impact changes.* Effective large-system change requires that changes to structures or operating rules be made as well as changes to processes.

  3. *Plans to design and execute complex testing and learning strategies.* Recognizing when a change is an improvement is challenging because the measures associated with the aim are at a high level, and there is often a delay between making changes and seeing an effect. This requires the team to pick process measures on the basis of their understanding of the dynamics of the system. Prototypes and cooperative testing also are effective tools for learning in large systems.

CHAPTER TWELVE

# CASE STUDIES OF IMPROVEMENT EFFORTS

The case studies discussed in this chapter demonstrate a more structured approach than the examples in Chapter Three, but they are still guided by the Model for Improvement. The five improvement efforts are from health care, manufacturing, safety, and services in the technology business. The specific areas covered are:

- Reducing the occurrence of no-fault-found components (manufacturing)
- Improving the drill process (manufacturing)
- Reducing infection and mortality rates in a pediatric intensive care unit (health care)
- Improving safety at a manufacturing plant (manufacturing)
- Improving the credentialing process at CareOregon (health care)
- Improving sales at a specialty chemical company (manufacturing)

Each case study begins with a short introduction, followed by a description of the work done within the framework of the Model for Improvement. The emphasis in each case study is on the changes developed, tested, and implemented using a variety of the methods and tools for improvement that were discussed in Chapters Five through Eight. Not all of the case studies include all of the PDSA Cycles that were used to accomplish the aim, but they do include most of the key ones. The studies use various formats to document the cycles. Each case study concludes with a summary of what can be learned from the study about the concepts and methods that were used to make the improvements. The studies are meant to reinforce the concepts, methods, and other examples presented in the book, and to enhance the reader's ability to make improvements. Here are some key highlights to be found in the case studies:

- Although all the case studies use the Model for Improvement and the three questions, there are differences in use of the structure: approaches to charters, PDSA Cycles, and forms to provide documentation of the improvement journey.
- In all cases the questions under study drive the use of data and how data are collected and displayed graphically.
- For the most part, run charts and control charts are used to show the impact of PDSA Cycles over time. The case on drill quality employs the use of planned experiments and response plots to summarize the results of the experiments.
- People skills have figured prominently in all the case studies. However, the case on mortality rates explicitly discusses the impact of the social system on making improvements.
- Most of the cases discussed were working on unknown solutions, so it was important to develop, test, and ensure proper implementation of the changes. The project described in the PICU case study from a children's hospital began with a change package of solutions from adult populations. This change package was adapted and tested, taking advantage of the work of others to accelerate the rate of improvement.

# Case Study 1: Reducing the Occurrence of No-Fault-Found Components

An international technology company manufactures, sells, and services very complex electronic consumer products. During the service of these products, parts are sometimes replaced and sent back for refurbishment and reuse. Not all the parts are defective. A no-fault-found (NFF) occurs when a field replaceable part is removed from a customer's product (as part of a product repair) and returned to the depot for repair and refurbishment. At the depot, the unit is found to be operating within specs and is coded "no fault found." NFF results in waste for the company from doing unnecessary work and paying for transit of parts. The current process increases inventory needed to support the customers. It also creates the risk that customers might receive defective parts, causing repeat problems and decreased customer satisfaction.

No fault found for the new 80 gigabyte disk drive family has been much greater than expected. A team was chartered to look into the reasons for this high NFF rate and make changes to reduce it to a level similar to that of other products. Inventory is also high for a new product, and engineering is concerned about the return rate for this product. The box "Charter for No-Fault-Found Improvement Effort" describes the charter.

---

# Charter for No-Fault-Found Improvement Effort

## Project Name: No Fault Found, 80 GB Hard Drive
## Sponsor Name:

Start date: March 18, 2007                          End date: April 29, 2007

## What Are We Trying to Accomplish?

*General Description*  Redesign the field troubleshooting and depot repair processes to reduce no fault founds (NFFs) and spares inventory levels for the 80 GB hard drive. This project is linked to the division strategic objective to improve product quality and reduce cost.

*Customer Impact*  Customers will experience fewer perceived failures of this drive and have higher confidence that there is a real problem whenever errors are detected.

*Improvement Objectives*
- Reduce NFF at the depot repair facility
- Increase accuracy of field diagnostic tests (reduce false defects)
- Reduce spares inventory level
- Maintain or reduce warranty levels and re-repairs

*Estimated Business Impact* $285K annually, based on reduction of inventory churn and wasted repair cycles.

*Project Links to Other Teams, Processes, Systems, or Projects*
- Call Center: reduced customer calls
- Customer engineers: reduced trips to customer site
- Repair depot: reduced defective returns
- Linkage to overall division warranty reduction program

## How Will We Know a Change is an Improvement?

| Objective | Measure | Current Performance | Goals |
|-----------|---------|---------------------|-------|
| 1 | No-fault-found rate | Avg. 60% | Less than 25% |
| 2 | Months of supply | 4.2 | Less than 4.0 |
| 3 | Re-repairs per call | 0.1 | Maintain |

## What Changes Can We Make That Will Result in Improvement?

*Boundaries* U.S. only, leverage learning to other regions globally

### Possible Changes to Test
- Increase use of field diagnostic through CE training
- Extend testing capability of field diagnostics

### Initial PDSA Cycles

| PDSA No. | Objective of Initial Cycles |
|---|---|
| 1 | Validate baseline data (historical or sample current data) |
| 2 | Validate current diagnostic testing process and its use |
| 3 | Test if training and awareness of diagnostic use reduces returns and NFFs |
| 4 | Understand failure modes and determine if test covers observed modes |
| 5 | Test modifications to test coverage |

### Define the Improvement Team

| Team leader: D. A. Ta | Approvals and quality leadership: Homer Stove |
|---|---|
| Improvement advisor | |
| Team members: | Team members: |
| C. E. Johnston | |
| Norm Miller | |
| Barry Stern | |

### Review Schedule
- Every other week status report
- Monthly call with Homer

## First PDSA Cycle

The team decided to collect some historical data on the NFF rate, inventory levels, and re-repair rates. Figure 12.1 describes the historical data collected from the first PDSA Cycle.

# FIGURE 12.1. PDSA CYCLE 1—HISTORICAL DATA.

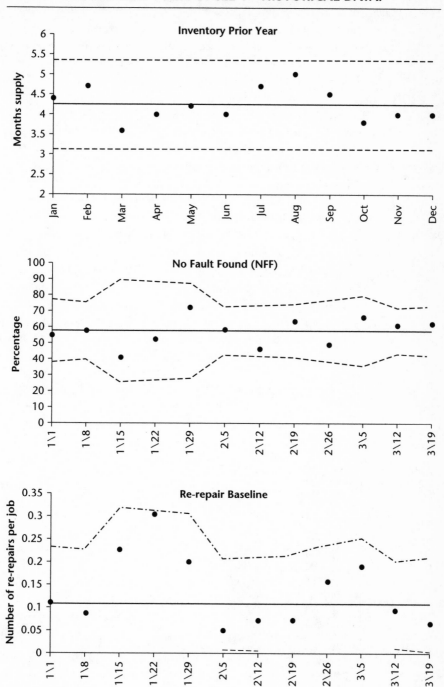

After reviewing the historical data (see NFF, inventory levels, and re-repair rates) the team, made up of people from product engineering, field service, procurement, and quality, studied the next thirty returns, quickly following up with the customer engineer and field logistics to understand why the drive was returned.

The Pareto analysis showed that the number one reason was a need to return unused parts for inventory rebalancing (19). The number two reason was not running the customer diagnostic due to pressures to complete multiple calls per day (9). Other reasons were system interactions (1), depot test coverage (1), and unknown (2). Figure 12.2 describes the Pareto chart from the first PDSA Cycle.

The team discovered that the return for credit process was not set up for this new product family and that field logistics was using the defective returns process for inventory rebalancing. It was decided to test the process used by other divisions. A very short test was run to validate the return process. This was verified and the change was implemented.

The team then tackled the second bar on the Pareto: scheduling calls. A major issue while scheduling a call is to do so without running the field test to verify the failure. Again, a test cycle was done to evaluate how the field testing could be ensured. The team thought there should be evidence the field diagnostic test was in fact run. An idea was developed to require that the test report be attached with the return as part of the return authorization. This requirement would act as a reminder for using the diagnostic. This was tested with one region and found to be effective enough to implement the change.

## FIGURE 12.2. PARETO CHART FOR NFF REASONS.

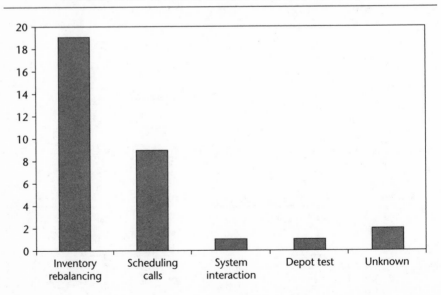

## Summary of Results

After implementing these two changes, NFF improved to a level that was similar to those for other disk drive products. In addition, the inventory levels dropped after several weeks. The project was deemed a success as the re-repair rate (balancing measure) remained consistent, demonstrating that reliability had not gotten worse. Figure 12.3 summarizes the key outcome, process, and balancing measures.

# Case Study 2: Improving the Drill Process

## What Are We Trying to Accomplish?

Determine the optimum speeds and feeds for drilling carbon steel tube sheets. A new machine was purchased in 2005 and was drilling three times faster than existing drills. Tooling was new and experiments were run to establish operating parameters. Because it was a new machine, operators were very careful with it. The new machine was producing the same output as three other drills and resulted in work patterns for the operators.

We were using Supplier K drills at slower speeds and feeds than the high speeds and feeds of the experiment. Supplier M tool representative wanted us to try a new drill they had and thought it would be competitive with the K drills we were using.

## How Will We Know That a Change Is an Improvement?

| Measures | Current | Goal |
|----------|---------|------|
| Tool life | 1,200 inches | 1,500 inches |
| Cycle time | 27 inches per min. | 30 ipm |

## What Changes Can We Make That Will Result in Improvement?

Based on the subject matter expertise of the team, it was decided to run a factorial experiment with three factors at two levels to test drills from suppliers K and M and learn about optimum drill settings. The first $2^3$ experiment would be run with the background variable of coolant concentration held at 7.5 percent. PDSA Cycle 2 would replicate the experiment with coolant concentration at 9.5 percent. Figure 12.4 describes the plan for the experiment, PDSA Cycle 1.

# FIGURE 12.3.  UPDATED CONTROL CHARTS WITH IMPROVED RESULTS.

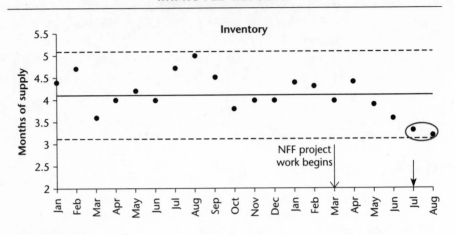

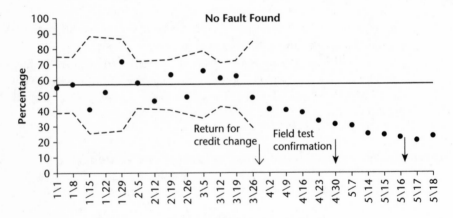

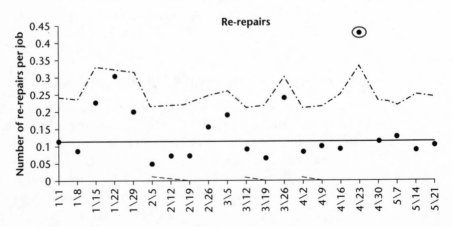

# FIGURE 12.4. PLANNED EXPERIMENT FOR DRILL STUDY.

1. Objective: Determine which combination of factors and levels will result in longer tool life and better cycle times. We need to understand what combination of feeds, speeds, and coolant concentration improves drilling production to reduce costs.

2. Background information: The team believes it has good results from K tooling. M tooling representative has approached us with a tool they claim will improve our results. After discussion it is believed we can improve tool life and machine productivity.

3. Experimental variables:

| | |
|---|---|
| A. *Response variables* | *Measurement technique* |
| 1. Tool life | Inches drilled before load indicator signals a tool change is required |
| 2. Cycle time | Inches per minute drilled |
| 3. | |
| B. *Factors under study* | *Levels* |
| 1. Feed | .008–.016 |
| 2. Speed | 1,258–2,159 rpm |
| 3. Drill supplier | K and M |
| C. *Background variables* | *Method of control* |
| 1. Coolant concentration | Check before and after each cycle |
| 2. Drill point | Measure point angle before and assess wear |
| 3. Drill new vs. regrind | Use new drills; need four each |

4. Replication: The design will be replicated at different coolant concentrations

5. Methods of randomization: Randomized runs with Study-it software

6. Design matrix (attach copy): See attached

7. Data collection forms (attach copies): Data will be collected on run charts

8. Planned methods of statistical analysis: Use of run charts and response plots

9. Estimated cost, schedule, and other resource consideration: Machine cost is $125 per hour plus 30% to run in manual mode. Tooling check at periodic intervals is $30. Tooling changeover time was $70 including study time. The total estimated cost per hour is $385.00 to run test.

**Do:** Overall, the experiment went as planned. Operator noted spray from coolant was not being contained by curtains. Engineer notes a fine mist escaping from drill containment. Tool life on Supplier M looks good; expected 1,200 and got 1,388 inches drilled.

**Study:** The team was thinking that Supplier M would perform better on carbon steel and was surprised to the see the dramatic results from Supplier K. Using the coolant concentration at 7.5 percent was also beneficial. Supplier K had better drill life regardless of speed. Supplier M performed better with high speed and high feed. The team was impressed with the results from Supplier K on drill life. Increasing time is a good result. Longer time between tool changes means more inches of metal are being removed. Tool changes cost time and money.

**Act:** The next PDSA cycle will be conducted with coolant concentration at 9.5 percent.

Figure 12.5 describes the results from the $2^3$ factorial experiments on carbon steel.

**Plan:** Run the same $2^3$ factorial experiment as in PDSA Cycle 1, holding coolant concentration at 9.5 percent.

**Do:** Engineer noted chip on drill tip at 1,800 inches and some burn on the drill coating at 2,000 inches. The operator noted some edge buildup at conclusion of the experiment at 2,145 inches. Supplier K drill performed very well. The operator now predicts higher speeds and feeds might be better. Foreman agrees.

**Study:** Supplier K with low speed and feeds is much better for tool life than M at high speeds and feeds. Prediction was that finished hole would be poor at slow feeds and speeds and turned out to be good. Tool life was better than we had seen before. The team decided to study the drill logs and past reports to understand why. The comments from the team were that we considered 1,200–1,500 inches excellent and 2,000 inches was beyond what was predicted. To summarize the learning for this cycle:

- The cost of Supplier K is 30 percent less than Supplier M.
- The Supplier K drill bit is superior to M with 53 percent more tool life.
- Production is up 15 percent with new feeds and speeds.
- We need to test load meter as a factor (optimize tool change) in a future cycle.
- Tool change is determined by load meter and visual test, not physical measures.

**Act:** After PDSA Cycle 2, the team decided on these actions:

- Need to standardize on K for carbon steel
- 7.5 percent coolant concentration is better for carbon steel
- Future test factor (coolant concentration for stainless steel)

## FIGURE 12.5. RESPONSE PLOTS FROM PDSA CYCLE 1.

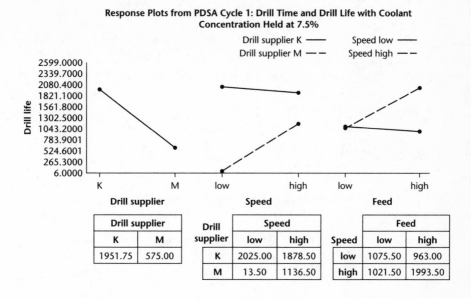

Response Plots from PDSA Cycle 1: Drill Time and Drill Life with Coolant Concentration Held at 7.5%

| Drill supplier | |
|---|---|
| K | M |
| 1951.75 | 575.00 |

| Drill supplier | Speed | |
|---|---|---|
| | low | high |
| K | 2025.00 | 1878.50 |
| M | 13.50 | 1136.50 |

| Speed | Feed | |
|---|---|---|
| | low | high |
| low | 1075.50 | 963.00 |
| high | 1021.50 | 1993.50 |

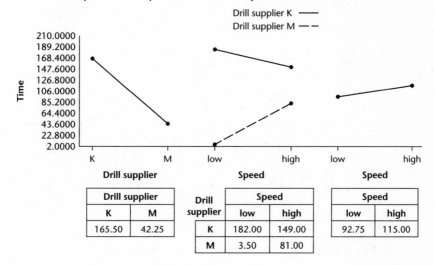

PDSA Cycle 2: Same Experiment as PDSA 1 Only with Coolant Concentration Run at 9.5%

| Drill supplier | |
|---|---|
| K | M |
| 165.50 | 42.25 |

| Drill supplier | Speed | |
|---|---|---|
| | low | high |
| K | 182.00 | 149.00 |
| M | 3.50 | 81.00 |

| Speed | |
|---|---|
| low | high |
| 92.75 | 115.00 |

- Future test factor (new drills vs. regrinds)
- PDSA Cycle 3: the confirmation run

Figure 12.6 describes the results from the $2^3$ factorial experiments from cycle 2.

## FIGURE 12.6.  RESPONSE PLOTS FROM PDSA CYCLE 2.

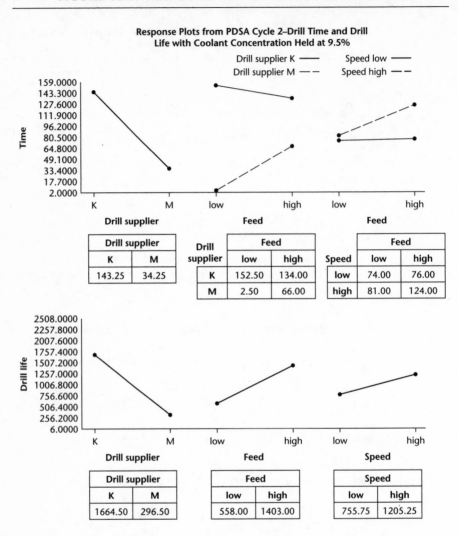

**Response Plots from PDSA Cycle 2–Drill Time and Drill Life with Coolant Concentration Held at 9.5%**

**Plan:** Do a confirmation run with the best settings:

- Supplier K
- High speed, .016 ipm
- High feed, 2,158 rpm
- Coolant, 7.5 percent; confirmed concentration not a factor; maintain lower cost (7.5 percent) setting

### Questions
1. Will we be able to replicate the results in a production run of Supplier K with high speed and high feed on drill life and time?
2. Will coolant concentration be an issue?

### Predictions
1. Shop foreman believes both high speed and feed are necessary to achieve tool life and cycle time goals. The operator believes this combination is better than we experienced in cycle 1.
2. Foreman and operators believe the coolant concentration is about right at 7.5 percent, on the basis of their observations of the experiments in cycles 1 and 2.

### Plan for Test
- Order enough drills from Supplier K; set up drill for high speed and feed. Data will be collected by operators on run charts.

**Do:** Engineer noted point looked fair at 1,400 inches; is thinking this won't be as good as last run. Operator noted that at 1,600 inches coating looked fair. Edge wear was noted at 1,905.

**Study:** We were drilling at 27 ipm and are now at 35 ipm. This is a 30 percent increase in productivity. Tool life was 1,200 inches on average before and about 1,800 now. That is a 50 percent increase in tool life. Although Supplier M was superior on stainless steel, we were surprised to see the difference in Supplier K on carbon steel. Coolant concentration at 7.5 percent worked best as predicted.

**Act:** The experiment was run, and results confirmed initial findings from earlier PDSA Cycles. As we implemented the new combination of factors in our daily operation, a new problem was discovered that did not arise during the experiment. This is discussed in the summary below.

## Summary of Results
- Over time the feeds were found to be correct, but speeds had to be modified in daily operation. The high speeds were causing problems with the tool holders.
- We are now researching the tool holders with the manufacturer.
- We slowed the drill speed and still achieved a 15 percent improvement in drill productivity.
- We have been able to sustain the improvement in tool life (50 percent).
- Supplier K remains the drill of choice on carbon steel. M is preferred on stainless.

- We noted the coating on the tool may be a factor and intend to research whether or not different coatings can be chosen. The engineer and the operator running the test noted in their observations that when the coating disappeared the drill life was nearly spent. (We did not anticipate this in our planning or design.)

# Case Study 3: Reducing Infection and Mortality Rates in a Pediatric Intensive Care Unit

*Note:* the following is an adaptation of a case study from Children's Hospital in Cincinnati. Some of the specialized language of health care has been removed to increase understanding for all readers.

Children's Hospital Medical Center in Cincinnati has used the Model for Improvement for a number of years to guide improvement work. It was decided in 2005 to take lessons learned from the Institute for Healthcare Improvement's (IHI) 100K Lives campaign (adult focus) and apply these changes to reduce infection and mortality rates for children in the Pediatric Intensive Care Unit (PICU).

The PICU cared for 1,982 patients in 2007, with an average daily census of 21.5. It began this decade with mortality rates that were average for PICUs of their size and patient mix. They were not satisfied with the *status quo* and sought to improve the outcome for these vulnerable patients. They targeted the infections that were key contributors to PICU mortality. An analysis of their 2005 data found that ventilator-associated pneumonia (VAP) and catheter-associated blood stream infection (CA-BSI) cases represented the highest reasons for mortality.

## What Are We Trying to Accomplish?

- Decrease the rate of VAP in the PICU by 50 percent (from a baseline of 5.6 per 1,000 ventilator days) and sustain this level of performance for at least two quarters
- Decrease the rate of CA-BSIs in the PICU to less than or equal to 1.0 per 1,000 central line days by June 2007

In our effort to reduce VAP rates, an internal improvement collaborative was organized among our three critical care units: PICU, cardiac critical care unit, and neonatal intensive care units. Unit physician and nurse leaders along with lead respiratory therapists from each ICU made up the team. Our CA-BSI project was carried out via an improvement collaborative with physician and nurse representation from several parts of the organization, including our three intensive care units (among them the PICU), our hematology-oncology service, our operating room and anesthesia services, and one of our gastroenterology floors.

## How Will We Know That a Change Is an Improvement?

We used four key measures to track our progress. They are described in Table 12.1 and appear in the graphs near the end of the study.

## What Changes Can We Make That Will Result in Improvement?

*VAP* We adapted the adult ventilator care bundle developed for IHI's 100K lives campaign for use in our pediatric intensive care population. This bundle of changes included several specific changes that were proven to be effective in other health care organizations in earlier improvement efforts and offered as a proven practice to members of IHI.

### TABLE 12.1. MEASUREMENTS, DEFINITION, BASELINE, AND GOALS FOR THE PROJECT.

| Measure | Calculation | Current Performance | Goal |
| --- | --- | --- | --- |
| PICU Mortality rate | Number of actual deaths in the PICU/number of predicted deaths (quarterly) | 5.78% | |
| PICU VAP rate | Number of ventilator associated pneumonias/ total number of ventilator days during the time period * 1,000 (monthly) | 5.6 cases per 1,000 ventilator days | Reduce by 50% and sustain for two quarters |
| PICU CA-BSI rate | Number of infections/ Total number of catheter days during the time period * 1,000 (monthly) | 5.2 per 1,000 line days | 1.0 per 1,000 central line days |
| Overall PICU infection rate | Number of infections, including surgical site infections, tracheitis, VAP, and other infection sites (monthly) | 16 per 1,000 patient days | |

*CA-BSI* Our organization has also been involved in multiple efforts to reduce CA-BSI rates over the past several years, including involvement in a 2003 collaborative with ten other local hospitals. We began by implementing small PDSA tests of change around specific bundle elements for both insertion and maintenance bundles that have proven successful in reducing infection rates in other collaboratives.

*Supporting Changes* In addition to the focus on the two bundles of changes to affect both VAP and CA-BSI, we found it necessary to add additional changes to impart the necessary structure to sustain the improvements. Table 12.2 describes these changes for both VAP and CA-BSI.

Here is a description of one series of PDSA Cycles used to adapt, test, and implement these changes:

**Plan:** Having developed a draft pediatric ventilatory care bundle, we determined that compliance with the bundle components needed to be tracked to ensure compliance by ICU staff.

The team developed a draft monitoring tool and developed a process whereby one RT and one RN would test the tool for one month.

**Do:** The team developed a checklist to assess the extent to which the components of the pediatric ventilatory care bundle were carried out—The first draft of this checklist was tested by one respiratory therapist and one RN on selected day shifts for one month.

**Study:** The team assessed the extent to which the checklists were completed, as well as the compliance indicated.

On the basis of feedback from the RN and RT, the team determined that it made more sense for the RT to complete the checklist than the RN. The RT had

## TABLE 12.2. ADDITIONAL CHANGES TO SUPPORT THE ADHERENCE TO BUNDLES.

| Change | VAP | CA-BSI |
|---|:---:|:---:|
| Use of checklists | ✓ | ✓ |
| Policy changes | ✓ | ✓ |
| Real-time analysis of causes of cases | ✓ | ✓ |
| Building adherence with the bundle into job descriptions for RNs and respiratory therapists | ✓ | |
| Rounds to assess bundle compliance | ✓ | |
| Adopted data transparency through use of charts that were posted on each unit in highly visible locations and updated weekly; report monthly on hospital intranet; monthly report to executive leadership and the patient care committee of the board of trustees | ✓ | ✓ |

more direct involvement with the bundle components. However, the team also determined that because many of the bundle components involved collaboration between the RT and RN, the RT had to engage the RN in conversation regarding bundle compliance. The team determined that small wording and formatting changes would lead to a more user-friendly tool.

**Act:** Having determined that the checklist was a viable way to assess compliance with the bundle components, the team decided to test a slightly revised version on a larger scale—with more patients and on additional shifts.

Through subsequent PDSAs, the team:

- Tested the monitoring tool on various shifts
- Tested the tool with additional caregivers
- Made additional revisions to the tool (including adding a space to note issues and challenges, and adding notes regarding contraindications to implementing the bundle components with particular patients)

**Implementation**  After numerous PDSAs to adapt the changes, the items included on the compliance form were eventually added to RN and RT flowsheets.

## The Social Impact of Change

As with any attempt to transform deeply entrenched care processes with the goal of dramatically improving outcomes, this work was not without challenges. Here are examples of the challenges that we faced, along with our methods for overcoming them. As these challenges were overcome, our belief that the changes we had tested would lead to improvement was bolstered.

*Challenge*: Convincing clinical colleagues to adapt changes that did not have substantial evidence in the pediatric population.

*Solutions*: Shared improving rate data with colleagues as it became available.

*Challenge*: An initial reticence to share outcomes data with the broader organization, as well as patients and families.

*Solutions*: Shared improving rate data with colleagues as it became available. Staff became eager to show off results of excellent care.

*Challenge*: Perception among staff that improvement activities were adding to already substantial clinical care for very ill patients.

*Solutions*: Shared improving rate data with colleagues as it became available demonstrated that changes actually led to enhanced efficiency.

*Challenge*: In collaborative improvement efforts with other units, reticence among these units to test changes suggested by the PICU with "their" population.

*Solutions*: Allowed other units to adapt changes to their own environment and devise tests of change that were acceptable to their staff.

## TABLE 12.3. SUMMARY OF MEASUREMENT RESULTS COMPARED TO BASELINE AND GOALS.

| Measure | Baseline Performance | Goal | Actual Result |
|---|---|---|---|
| PICU mortality rate | 5.78% | | 2.6% |
| PICU VAP rate | 5.7 cases per 1,000 ventilator days | Reduce by 50% and sustain for two quarters | 0 cases per 1,000 for fifteen of the last seventeen months |
| PICU CA-BSI rate | 5.2 per 1,000 line days | 1.0 per 1,000 central line days | 2.0 per 1,000 line days |
| Overall PICU infection rate | 16 per 1,000 patient days | | 8.6 per 1,000 patient days |

## Summary of Results

The improvement activities presented in this case study helped us achieve the outcomes described in Table 12.3.

We have also achieved important improvements in efficiency:

- Mean hospital length of stay for VAP patients was $26.5 \pm 13.1$ days compared to $17.8 \pm 4.7$ days for non-VAP patients
- Mean hospital attributable costs for VAP patients were $156,110 \pm \$80,688$ compared to $104,953 \pm \$59,191$ costs for non-VAP patients

The use of run charts with control limits has helped us identify the points at which improvement in our outcomes is likely to be significant and not due to special causes in our system. For both VAP and CA-BSI, we saw a significant shift in the average PICU rate following the launch of the improvement initiatives:

For VAP, a shift in the PICU average rate from 5.6 per 1,000 ventilator days to .50 per 1,000 line days occurred in April 2006.

For CA-BSI, a shift in the PICU average rate from 3.1 per 1,000 ventilator days to 2.8 per 1,000 line days occurred in October 2006.

Figure 12.7 shows the control charts and run charts that were used to monitor progress of the changes tested and implemented for the PICU.

## Lessons Learned That Can Be Spread to Others

Here are specific lessons learned from our effort that would benefit other hospitals:

## FIGURE 12.7.  FAMILY OF MEASURES FOR PICU IMPROVEMENT EFFORT.

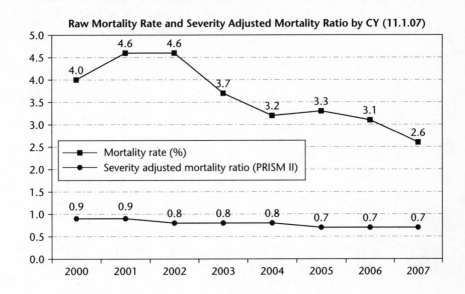

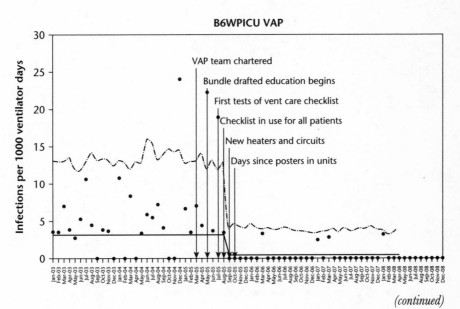

*(continued)*

## FIGURE 12.7. (*continued*)

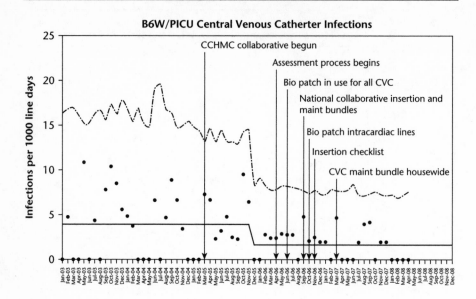

**B6W/PICU Central Venous Catherter Infections**

CCHMC collaborative begun

Assessment process begins

Bio patch in use for all CVC

National collaborative insertion and maint bundles

Bio patch intracardiac lines

Insertion checklist

CVC maint bundle housewide

*Infections per 1000 line days*

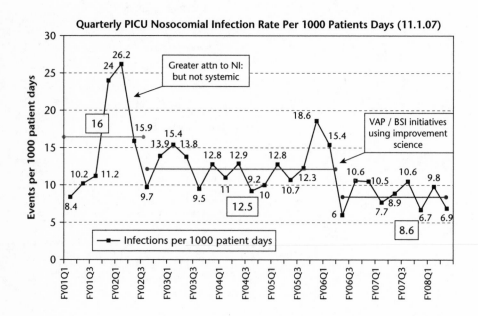

**Quarterly PICU Nosocomial Infection Rate Per 1000 Patients Days (11.1.07)**

Greater attn to NI: but not systemic

VAP / BSI initiatives using improvement science

*Events per 1000 patient days*

— ■ — Infections per 1000 patient days

# FIGURE 12.7. (continued)

## Housewide Ventilator Associated Pneumonias (VAPs)

Chart type: p-chart

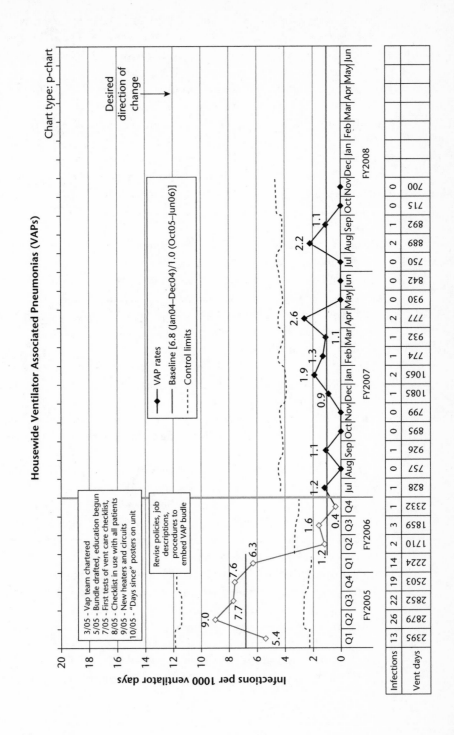

**Infections per 1000 ventilator days**

3/05 - Vap team chartered
5/05 - Bundle drafted, education begun
7/05 - First tests of vent care checklist,
8/05 - Checklist in use with all patients
9/05 - New heaters and circuits
10/05 - "Days since" posters on unit

Revise policies, job
descriptions,
procedures to
embed VAP budle

Desired
direction of
change

◆— VAP rates
——— Baseline [6.8 (Jan04–Dec04)/1.0 (Oct05–Jun06)]
- - - - - Control limits

| | FY2005 | | | FY2006 | | | | | | | | | | | | FY2007 | | | | | | | | | | | | | FY2008 | | | | | |
|---|---|---|---|---|---|---|---|---|---|---|---|---|---|---|---|---|---|---|---|---|---|---|---|---|---|---|---|---|---|---|---|---|---|---|---|---|
| Infections | 13 | 26 | 22 | 19 | 14 | 2 | 3 | 1 | 1 | 0 | 1 | 0 | 0 | 2 | 1 | 1 | 2 | 2 | 0 | 0 | 2 | 1 | 0 | 0 | 1 | 0 |
| Vent days | 2395 | 2879 | 2852 | 2503 | 2224 | 1710 | 1859 | 2332 | 828 | 757 | 926 | 895 | 799 | 1085 | 1065 | 774 | 932 | 777 | 930 | 842 | 750 | 889 | 892 | 715 | 700 |

- An intensive focus on reduction of infections in pediatric intensive care units can result in substantial and sustained improvement. The reductions in morbidity, family stress, and cost are real and measurable, as are improvements in family and staff satisfaction, and staff retention.

- Engaging frontline caregivers from the beginning of these projects helped ensure that the interventions reflected the practicalities and realities of daily care and also helped ensure their buy-in and enthusiasm for this work.

- Embedding the improvements into routine clinical care is essential. Building the work into daily routines instead of layering it on as "extra" work promoted efficiency and caregiver buy-in. Examples of this are adding the bundle components to RN flowsheets and making discussion of central line issues part of daily PICU rounds.

- Adult "bundles" of changes can be adapted to the pediatric setting with few modifications, leading to dramatic results.

- Once initial success in reducing infection rates is achieved, it is essential to continue random chart audits to review compliance with bundle components. Success could potentially lead to complacency with new care processes, so the knowledge that the care being provided may be audited can increase the likelihood of compliance by staff members.

- Celebrate successes! When the PICU reached milestones (such as one hundred days or six months) for *the time between infections,* staff appreciated celebrating with a party and cake.

- The use of real-time case notification and immediate analysis of causes was one of the best ways to identify compliance issues with the bundles, patient factors that might require additional interventions, and steps to be taken to avoid similar cases in the future. The staff now "huddle" at the bedside to discuss cases and learn from the results of the analysis.

- Staff previously untapped for improvement work, such as respiratory therapists involved with our VAP reduction work, were extremely effective change agents for improvement projects in the intensive care setting thanks to their real day-to-day ownership of and experience with the clinical care processes.

- Implementing bundles aimed at reducing infection rates can be accelerated by the involvement of multiple units within the hospital. This leads to cross-fertilization of ideas and economies of scale in terms of financial, human, and improvement resources and ensures that patients in different parts of the organization benefit from the best possible care.

- There is likely to be a strong business case for a variety of improved outcomes in the PICU, as our analysis of our VAP improvement work demonstrates.

# Case Study 4: Improving Safety at a Manufacturing Plant

A manufacturing plant that produced cabinets experienced a number of unprofitable years. Lack of standardized and optimized processes resulted in poor performance in safety, productivity, claims, and quality. Customers were unhappy due to delays in shipments and product defects. Because there was no formal system to make improvements, poor performance persisted. Facing the possibility of a plant closure and the loss of jobs, leaders of the parent organization set an objective to improve performance in the key measures of the plant: safety, on-time deliveries, productivity, and quality. This case study is focused on the work at the plant that began in 2006 to improve safety.

A new management team was given leadership of the plant at the end of 2005. They established objectives for key plant measures. For safety, the management team established objectives to reduce lost time accidents and OSHA recordable injuries by 50 percent in both 2006 and 2007. To achieve these objectives, the management team needed to make safety a priority, so they immediately instituted a support structure to foster effective changes:

- Improvement in safety measures was imbedded in all managers' goals.
- Safety was made an agenda item at all management meetings.
- A multidisciplinary safety team was formed. Engineers, managers, supervisors, and hourly workers from production and representatives from maintenance were members of the team. Meetings were held regularly to discuss safety issues and improvement strategies.

The management team also took steps to ensure the responsibility for safety did not reside just with them or members of the safety team.

- All supervisors, leads, and hourly workers were given safety training. Leads are staff who work on the line but are also cross-trained to fill in at other positions. One result of the training was that each morning when the group huddled to discuss issues for that day, safety was included.
- Maintenance issues with safety implications were given priority.
- Three engineers were hired and dedicated part of their time to eliminating hazardous conditions as sources of injuries.

The management team instituted benchmarking within and outside the company to identify best practices, ongoing safety audits to identify hazardous conditions and unsafe behaviors and the analysis of all safety events. Informed by this

## FIGURE 12.8. DRIVER DIAGRAM OF SAFETY PROBLEMS AND AREAS FOR IMPROVEMENT.

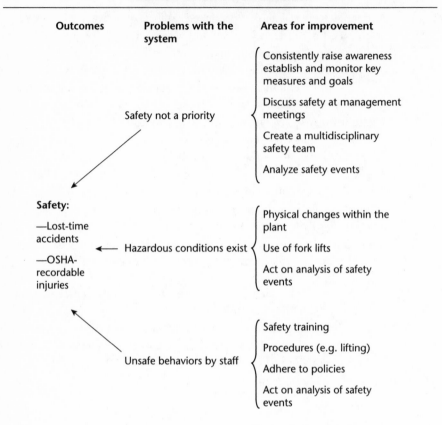

information, the safety team summarized the problems producing poor safety outcomes. This summary, referred to as a driver diagram, is shown in Figure 12.8. In the driver diagram, the safety team also included areas for improvement to address the problems.

The management team established an organized system of improvement to address the safety problems identified. They set goals; dedicated resources to developing, testing, and implementing changes; and established time to review progress. To focus the work, they developed a charter for the safety team for their improvement efforts in 2006. Seen in the box "Charter for Improving Safety at a Manufacturing Plant," it answers the question "What are we trying to accomplish?"

# Charter for Improving Safety at a Manufacturing Plant

## General Description

Reduce lost time accidents and OSHA recordable injures by 50 percent in 2006 by focusing on hazardous conditions and unsafe behaviors

| Measures | 2005 | 2006 Goal* |
|---|---|---|
| Lost-time accidents | 29 | 14 |
| OSHA-recordable injuries | 8 | 3 |

*Hours worked were budgeted to be similar in 2006 as in 2005.

## Guidance

- Analyze data from 2005 to identify specific areas of focus
- Clearly separate work areas from fork lift aisles

Guided by the charter, the safety team used an initial PDSA Cycle to summarize and analyze safety data to assist in answering the question, What changes can we make that will result in improvement? A Pareto analysis of the data indicated the most frequent injuries were:

- Lacerations from machines with rotating shafts
- Strains from lifting

The safety team, with the involvement of supervisors and leads, planned cycles to test changes focused on these areas. The leads, with the support of hourly workers, then carried out the tests. A summary follows of some of the PDSA Cycles.

## PDSA Cycles for Testing a Change

### Cycle 1: Plexiglas Guards

*Plan Objective:* Test the use of a Plexiglas guard installed on equipment with rotating shaft for sanding and cutting

*Questions:* Would a Plexiglas guard prevent workers from lifting the guard to perform cutting or sanding and thus reduce lacerations? Why?

*Predictions:* This unsafe behavior will be greatly reduced once workers can see through the Plexiglas guard to perform the work. The old guards did not allow a clear view of the work area. Keeping the guard down when cutting or sanding will reduce lacerations.

***Who, what, where, when:*** Maintenance will install a Plexiglas guard on one machine. Two operators on the day shift will perform sanding and cutting operations with the guard on Monday. The operators will be asked to comment on the ease of performing the operations with the guard.

***Do*** Test was carried out as planned.

***Study*** Both operators commented that the Plexiglas guard did not hinder their work and saw no reason not to keep it down. They believed it would greatly reduce the number of lacerations that occur when cutting and sanding is performed with the guards up.

***Act*** Thanks to the success of the test, plans were made to install the Plexiglas guards on all equipment with rotating shafts. Before the guards were installed, a few workers on the evening shift were asked to perform cutting and sanding with the Plexiglas guard.

## Cycle 2 and Cycle 3

In cycle 2, two workers on the evening shift were asked to perform cutting and sanding with the Plexiglas guard. Results were similar to cycle 1. In cycle 3, guards were installed throughout the plant on equipment with rotating shafts. Data collection included compliance with keeping the guards down, satisfaction of the operators with use of the guards, and the number of lacerations that occurred during sanding and cutting operations.

Installation of Plexiglas guards addressed a hazardous condition. To achieve the full impact on improved safety, worker compliance with using the new guards was still required. The management team understood they needed to balance a "blame free" environment with individual accountability. They would always place the initial focus on making timely changes to have an impact on hazardous conditions. If a hazardous condition existed and resulted in an unsafe behavior, a worker would not be disciplined. Once the hazardous condition was eliminated and a policy for safe behavior established, workers would be disciplined for not following the policy. This Progressive Discipline System is described next. Cycles to test and implement the system began in parallel with the cycles to test the Plexiglas guards.

## Progressive Discipline System

1. Hazardous condition identified (for example, guards difficult to see through, resulting in workers lifting guards)

2. No discipline for unsafe operation or injury until hazardous condition addressed

3. Priority given to a physical change to correct the hazardous condition (such as Plexiglas guards)

4. Policy on safe behavior established if not already existing (Plexiglas guard must remain down when working)

5. Policy enforced with violations, with or without injury, resulting in discipline

## Cycle 1: Progressive Discipline System

The Progressive Discipline System was reviewed with supervisors, leads, and hourly workers. They requested that short but formal training sessions be conducted prior to a policy being enforced. The safety team was given responsibility for this.

## Cycle 2

The safety team developed a short training session on the use of the Plexiglas guard. The session was tested with a few workers and some minor clarifications made. The session was then required for all workers who use equipment with rotating shafts.

## Cycle 3

To formally implement the Progressive Discipline System, the safety team documented the system and shared it with all staff at scheduled meetings. Discussion of the system was included as part of orientation for new staff. The safety team kept and reviewed data on those disciplined, the unsafe behavior, and comments from both the lead and the staff member disciplined. They used this information to ensure the system was functioning as designed.

# Other Areas of Improvement

1. *Lifting procedures.* To reduce the number of strains from lifting, training on lifting was conducted. Weight limits were also established for workers. For example, two men were needed to lift anything weighing over fifty pounds. This and other lifting procedures were tested and adherence monitored. After some minor changes to the procedures, a policy was developed that spelled out the lifting procedures at the plant. Once the policy was agreed on, lifting procedures became part of the progressive discipline system.

2. *Use of forklifts.* A worker, whose work station was within an aisle used by forklifts, was hit by a forklift and injured. Neither the worker nor the driver was disciplined for the existence of this hazardous condition. But from the incident, the management team chose to include guidance in the safety charter that work areas and forklift aisles should be clearly separated. As part of the improvement work, all work stations near forklift aisles were relocated. Forklift aisles were clearly marked and walking lanes indicated. The new layout was tested over a short time period. Once agreement was reached to make the layout permanent, a policy was developed for safe driving of forklifts and safe behavior of workers. Use of forklifts became part of the progressive discipline system.

## Summary of Results

The plant achieved its aim for 2006 to reduce lost time accidents and OSHA recordable injures by 50 percent. The improvement continued through 2007. Although a 50 percent reduction in lost time accidents was not achieved from 2006 to 2007, the overall reduction from 2005 to 2007 exceeded the strategic goal. The number of staff who needed first aid and the number of near misses also decreased. The data are shown in Table 12.4.

### TABLE 12.4. SUMMARY OF RESULTS.

| Measures | 2005 | 2006 | 2007 |
|---|---|---|---|
| Lost-time accidents | 29 | 12 | 7 |
| OSHA-recordable injuries | 7 | 3 | 2 |
| First aid, near misses | 12 | 5 | 1 |

*Leadership is essential to improve safety and other system measures.* Leaders both at the parent organization and at the plant committed to improve the plant's poor safety record. Strategic objectives focused on safety were established, and improvement in the safety measures was imbedded in management goals. Thanks to the actions of leaders, everyone understood that safety was a priority. Maintenance, for example, began prioritizing issues with safety implications.

*Appropriate structures should be established to facilitate the improvement of safety.* A multidisciplinary safety team was formed at the plant to manage the improvement work. Both management meetings and daily huddles conducted by staff included formal agenda items on safety. The management team established policies for safe behavior.

*All staff should be involved in making improvements.* The safety team developed a driver diagram to document knowledge of problems affecting safety outcomes. The team reviewed data to determine the initial areas of focus. Supervisors, leads, and hourly workers all had input into developing changes. The time of hourly workers was used efficiently by bringing them together in twenty-minute huddles, with supervisors and leads filling in on the line as needed. Engineers supplied technical input. Leads ensured that tests were carried out as planned.

*To improve safety, there should be a balance of system improvement and individual accountability for unsafe behavior.* The progressive discipline system was developed at the plant to achieve this balance. A policy for safe behavior was enforced only after hazardous conditions were eliminated. Policies were reviewed and approved by supervisors, leads, and hourly workers. Once the policy was in place, individuals were disciplined for unsafe behaviors.

# Case Study 5: Improving the Credentialing Process at CareOregon

CareOregon is a not-for-profit organization that is committed to improving and protecting the health of low-income and vulnerable Oregonians. One area CareOregon identified for improvement was workflow between the credentialing and provider services departments. The credentialing department is responsible for ensuring the quality of the health care facilities and medical providers contracted with CareOregon. Provider services manages the contracts, relationships, and system data for health care facilities and providers that participate with the health plan. The aim for improvement identified was the method by which each department identified and communicated the credentialing status of providers.

## Background

The current process involved seven people in the two departments. They tracked multiple calls to providers in a complicated, time-consuming spreadsheet, which when printed was more than *five feet wide*. Each department functions independently, using its own reports and access to information. The system dominated decisions and actions, while relationships suffered. Sponsors from both departments identified key staff who had intimate knowledge of the process. During a two-day workshop, the team was introduced to the Model for Improvement. Chapter Fourteen has an example of the agenda that was used to get the team going (under "Getting Started"). During the workshop, relationship awareness theory was explored with a method called the Strengths Deployment Inventory (SDI), which was a critical factor in helping team members understand each other's differences and create a foundation for building trust in a historically low-trust situation.

The team used the Model for Improvement charter to create a picture of the three questions with the addition of change concepts, which were identified by the team for generating ideas to test. Questions generated by the team were grouped into the initial cycles and prioritized for learning. Figure 12.9 describes the tree diagram to summarize the approach to the project.

During a twelve-week period, the team met weekly, running concurrent PDSA Cycles by subgrouping members of the team to "divide and conquer PDSA Cycles." The team created a flow diagram of the credentialing process; it is presented in Figure 12.10.

Assumptions were tested and team members learned each other's processes by cross-training, discovering missing information (available to only one department but presumed available to both) which caused individuals to personalize and misinterpret actions. The most important cycle was to test the elimination of the five-foot-wide spreadsheet, as shown in Figure 12.11.

## Summary of Results

At the conclusion of the team project, the entire five-foot-wide spreadsheet was eliminated. The project team included eight members, two sponsors, and three ad hoc members for developing and testing this change. The process is now done as a daily task by one credentialing administrative assistant and one provider information specialist rather than seven persons. The streamlined process eliminates work duplication and improves the clarity of communication processes, documentation, and integration of processes. Figure 12.12 shows the impact of these changes on the control charts kept by the two people involved before and after the changes.

Most important, the interdepartmental relationship has grown to have greater respect and trust. New issues and processes are now openly discussed and identified for additional improvement opportunities.

# Case Study 6: Improving Sales at a Specialty Chemical Company

A specialty chemical company had an objective to increase sales in a certain product line. The chemicals in this product line were processed further by other companies; they were then used in the manufacture of equipment that relied on the detection of radiation, such as diagnostic imaging in medicine or detection

# FIGURE 12.9. MODEL FOR IMPROVEMENT IN A TREE DIAGRAM.

| What are we trying to accomplish? | How will we know a change is an improvement? | What changes might cause improvement? | |
|---|---|---|---|
| | | Change Concepts to consider | Questions To Consider |
| Describe project: (check one)<br><br>XX Redesign existing product process or service<br>__ Design new product, process or service Improve system as a<br>— whole (drivers, mainstay, support) Collaborate and<br>— share an existing working improvement to diffuse the innovation<br><br>Brief Description: what/ how (include above— limit 2 sentences)<br><br>Redesign the medical credentialing request process in order to reduce turnaround time and increase member access to medical providers through the improvement of communication and workflows between Provider Services and Credentialing Departments. | Objective 1: Reduce overall turnaround time by:<br><br>• Reducing time to notify Provider Services of outcome of Provider Credentialing<br>• Reducing amount of time for Credentialing to begin process once notified of need to credential provider.<br>• Reducing time it takes for Provider Services to notify Credentialing of new providers | A2 Eliminate Multiple Entry<br><br>B17 Use automation<br><br>H61 Use Constraints<br><br>H59 Use Reminders<br><br>B19 Do tasks in parallel<br><br>B20 Consider people as if in the same system.<br><br>B18 Smooth Workflow | 1. What is the current process and are standards being met for each step under the objective? (PDSA 1)<br>2. What are the standards in the P&P? (PDSA 1)<br>3. How does the current process support the objective of timely credentialing of providers? (PDSA 1)<br>4. How can the turnaround time be reduced? (PDSA 1 to determine TAT)<br>5. What are the Credentialing request sources for each department? (PDSA 1) |
| | Objective 2: Eliminate non-par providers and providers for whom credentialing is not required being sent to Credentialing. | B14 Minimize Handoffs<br><br>D27 Give people access to the information | 1. How does Credentialing receive non-par providers?<br>2. How can they be eliminated?<br><br>1. How can the **Credentialing request spreadsheet** be eliminated or minimized?<br>2. How much time is being spent tracking requests **Credentialing request spreadsheet.**<br>3. How can the time be reduced?<br>4. Does everyone have access to memos in QNXT?<br>5. What is the current level of employee satisfaction with regard to the current Credentialing workflow?<br>6. How can we use Call Tracking (contact mgt tool in QNXT) to improve communication? |
| Sponsor(s): Peter McGarry and Margaret Rowland, MD<br><br>Core team members: Ann Blume, Kim Thomas, Jane Brallstord Sharon Madara, Debra Sexton, Rebecca Whestine and Yedda Trawick | Objective 3: Streamline workflows between Credentialing and Provider Services to eliminate time and improve satisfaction.<br><br>• Reduce the number of hours by 50% on tracking credentialing requests.<br>• Increase employee satisfaction by 25% | B17 Use Automation<br><br>D27 Give people access to information<br><br>D34 Focus on Core Processes and Purpose (use system as designed) | |
| | Objective 4: Prevent Claims payment to un-credentialed providers at participating clinics. | | 1. How can we prevent claims from being paid prior to credentialing?<br>2. Is the system designed to be configured to automatically stop the claims?<br>3. What compliance requirements are impacted if we do this.? |

## FIGURE 12.10. FLOW DIAGRAM FOR CREDENTIALING REQUEST PROCESS.

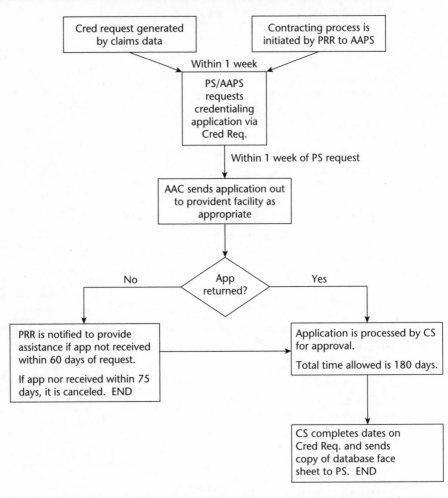

PS = Provider Services    CS = Credentialing Specialist    AAC = Credentialing Admin Asst.
AAPS = PS Admin Asst.     PRR = Provider Relations Rep

of weapons in security. Customers were doing research with the company's products that were packed in small quantities, called "prepack," but they often used competitors' products to scale up for industrial applications. The objective was to increase sales for these industrial applications. The manager of the product line believed they could differentiate their products on technical and manufacturing capabilities, customer service, and the breadth of products offered.

## FIGURE 12.11.  PDSA CYCLE NO. 4: TEST ELIMINATION OF TRACKING SPREADSHEET.

**Project Name**
Credentialing Process

**Date:**
November 15, 2007

**Cycle number:** 4

**Cycle Name and Brief Description**
Test eliminating Excel spreadsheet that is updated by two departments and is five feet wide.

**Objective(s) of This Cycle**
— Collect data
— Develop or modify a change
✓ Test a change
— Implement a change

**Plan: Identify the activity, predict the result, determine data collection**

*Questions*

1. What is the staff's confidence in the accuracy and efficiency of the current spreadsheet used to request provider credentialing?

2. How can efficiency be improved?

3. How can we eliminate the five-foot-wide spreadsheet?

4. What can we do about the providers that have new contracts?

*Predictions*

1. 50% of the staff (both Credentialing and Provider Services) will agree or strongly agree the current tool is accurate and efficient.

2. By eliminating the Excel spreadsheet that is being maintained and updated by six or seven staff simultaneously, the time per provider will be reduced by 25%.

3. By developing a daily report from both systems and using certain field information to identify physicians to include only those fields necessary.

4. Provider Services can mark them in the system as incomplete (temporary) in order to add the providers, which will flag them as noncredentialing and "incomplete" to users and for creating the new report.

**What data will be collected during this time?**

A survey of staff satisfaction will be sent out to measure staff satisfaction, to
all staff within both Credentialing and Provider Service Dept.

Ann and Kim will identify the fields needed by each department in order to develop the new report(s).

*(continued)*

## FIGURE 12.11. (*continued*)

| | |
|---|---|
| **Project Name** | **Date:** |
| Credentialing Process | November 15, 2007 |

*Assignments:*

Yedda will send out a survey to Provider Services and Credentialing departments to measure staff confidence and satisfaction with the current process of identifying and processing credentialing request. After the staff has been trained on the test version, the same survey will be repeated. Scale to be used:

Strongly agree (5), agree (4), neither agree nor disagree (3), disagree (2), strongly disagree (1)

Ann and Kim will identify the fields necessary for identifying and processing credentialing requests and submit IS request to Karen to develop a daily report, which we will test as a replacement for the spreadsheet.

(Revised: all Credentialing Specialists had been working the current Excel spreadsheet and we had planned on testing the new tool (report) in the same way. After discussing, the plan was changed to have Issa test; see Study part).

Ann will have Issa (new to the job and process) and Rebecca (expert) use the data collection form used in PDSA 2 to test whether the new tool (report) is more efficient than the current (Excel) tool. Issa and Rebecca will work the new report on separate days and track the number of providers per half hour.

Kim and Ann will train the staff on using the new report. Kim and Rebecca will audit the new report by comparing it to the spreadsheet.

### Do: Carry out the change or activity and collect data

*What actually happened? What went wrong? Observations?* Team members were surprised and relieved that spreadsheet was not needed. Karen created two types of reports: one for credentialing and one for use by Provider Services

### Study: Complete the data analysis, summarize what was learned, compare data with predictions

The report to Provider Services appeared to be very functional; no suggestions were made at this time.

**Question**: What is the staff's confidence in the accuracy and efficiency of the current tool (spreadsheet) used to request provider credentialing?

**Prediction**: 50% of the staff (both Credentialing and Provider Services) will **agree** or **strongly agree** the current tool is accurate and efficient.

**Result:** Prediction that 50% of staff feel like the current tool is accurate was too low. We learned that 88% *strongly* disagreed or disagreed that the tool was accurate, and 70% strongly disagreed or disagreed it was efficient! The same survey was sent to the exact same staff members and the results for accuracy are shown below. **100%** agreed or strongly agreed the new tool was efficient. *Note:* we did not ask them if it was more efficient than the old, just "the new communication tool used for requesting provider credentialing and updating QNXT is efficient."

**Before:**

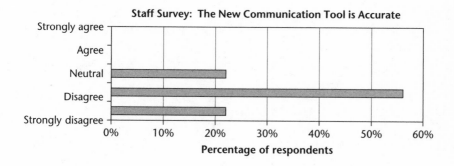

**Staff Survey: The New Communication Tool is Accurate**

**After:**

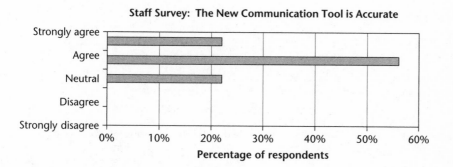

**Staff Survey: The New Communication Tool is Accurate**

*(continued)*

FIGURE 12.11. (*Continued*)

| **Project Name** | **Date:** |
|---|---|
| Credentialing Process | November 15, 2007 |

**Question**: How can staff efficiency be improved?

**Prediction**: By eliminating the Excel spreadsheet that is being maintained and updated by six or seven staff simultaneously. Staff is spending enormous amount of time sorting, updating the spreadsheet. It is difficult to work and filter.

**Results**: Before the change, the average time (total) for updating and maintaining the spreadsheet per provider was 21 minutes. The time for an expert is now 3 minutes per provider, and for the rookie it is 5 minutes (this is Issa's time and includes sending out applications) and, as a bonus, Provider Services is not performing dual entry!

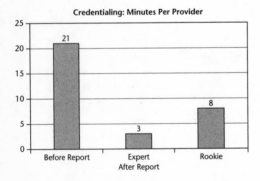

Credentialing: Minutes Per Provider

**Question:** How can we eliminate the five-foot-wide spreadsheet?

**Prediction**: By developing a daily report from both systems and using certain field information to identify physicians to include only those fields necessary.

**Result**: Report was developed and reviewed by users and tweaked with feedback. The report is now one single portrait 8-1/2" x 11" and can be run by end users.

**Question:** What can we do about the providers that have new contracts?

**Prediction**: Provider Services can mark them in the system as incomplete (temporary) in order to add the providers

**Result:** No need to test since this is a flag in the system (QNXT) and is static. Prediction is correct since this is just a check box in the system. This information will be given to Karen to use to query for incomplete or NEW providers needing to be identified as requesting credentialing. The plan was to have the credentialing requests (new report) be worked by all Credentialing Specialists during the testing. However, after reviewing the process and sources for requests, it was obvious that Issa, the administrative assistant who sends out applications, run the report and update the Credentialing database, which in turn allows the Credentialing Specialists to "Credential Providers" and streamlines the process. Staff will be cross-trained; however, Issa will work with Ann on testing and identifying any issues or new opportunities with the new process.

The new tool not only reduced the time per provider taken to communicate (log and research) physicians to be credentialed, but it has improved staff's confidence and work satisfaction.

### ACT: Determine next steps

What decisions were made from what was learned?

Testing the tool, the staff did *not* want to revert back to the current (former) tool. Karen will make the suggested changes to the reports.

New questions? Having mailing addresses for the clinics would be important to automate the process for Credentialing. How can the new report be used to generate mailing labels? But could merge into Excel for this purpose. The address listed on the report is from QNXT and reflects the physical address for the clinics. Credentialing will need a mailing address in order to automate this process. Can Karen help us with listing the address and automating the mailing labels?

### What will be the next cycle?

Sharon or Karen to generate a PDSA on getting mailing addresses from Providers at the time of contract.

## FIGURE 12.12. EFFECT OF CHANGES ON THE TIME SPENT PER CLAIM BY CREDENTIALING ADMINISTRATIVE ASSISTANT AND PROVIDER INFORMATION SPECIALIST.

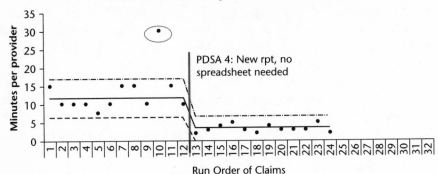

**Credentialing Specialist 1: Time to Research and Update Information Per Provider**

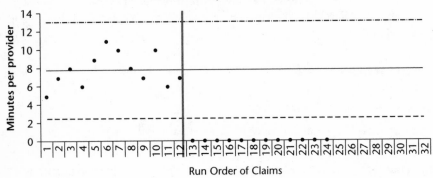

**Provider Services Admin Assistant: Time to Research and Update Information Per Provider**

To answer the question "What are we trying to accomplish?" the manager developed an aim for the improvement effort:

| Charter for Improving Sales at a Specialty Chemical Company | |
|---|---|
| General description | Grow sales in the specialized product line by 40 percent this year |
| Measures | Total dollars in sales for the product line |
| Guidance | Number of new customers<br>Monitor sales in other similar product lines<br>Use a list-offer-convert framework to improve sales processes<br>Explore larger industrial markets |
| Team | Product line manager, technical experts, and sales representatives |

The team used an initial PDSA Cycle to determine if the project was worth pursuing. The market for these specialized products is a small community of customers. The question was "Is there sufficient business that can be captured?"

## Cycle 1: Market Exploration

The objective of this cycle was to gain knowledge about the players in the market and the sales potential. Calls were made to customers of the company's other products to determine if they had applications for the specialty products. By scanning the market, the team learned significant money was available from National Institutes of Health and the Department of Homeland Security for R&D work and contract business for products in this product line. The quality of competitors' products and their pricing were also explored. The knowledge gained in this cycle resulted in the team making the decision to continue the project.

## Cycle 2: Developing the "Offer"

The objective of the cycle was to learn how the company could best meet the needs of customers. The team planned to track a qualitative measure of how potential customers reacted to key dimensions of the company's product line. The team put together a one-page marketing brochure explaining what their products had to "offer." Besides the available products, the brochure included information on:

Competitiveness of pricing
Superior purity of the products
Multiple packaging alternatives
Technical help and customization
Technology
Analytic capabilities

A technical expert on the team called a few companies that were customers of other prepack products. Customers were walked through the offer sheet. They reacted very positively when they understood more about the capabilities within the product line. Learning from the calls resulted in the team revising the offer sheet, to include:

- A master list of products and information on which of these products could be produced in bulk
- More on certain key quality characteristics
- A greater focus on proprietary technology owned by the company (this technology was very important to customers)

## Cycle 3: Developing the "List"

The objective of the cycle was to identify and document a list of potential customers. The goal was to have the number of customers increase over time. In addition to the information gained in cycles 1 and 2, a number of other sources were used to generate leads:

- Data mining the current sales list
- Relationships with other companies
- Companies receiving grant money
- Conversations with thought leaders in the industry
- Internet searches
- Networking with trade associations

The team was able to increase the number of customers on the list using these sources.

## Cycle 4: "Converting" Customers

The plan was to use the offer sheet and the list of potential customers to gain new customers. The improvement team believed the key to closing business is technical selling. The objective of the cycle was to test having technical experts call two potential customers on the list using the offer sheet. This resulted in one customer placing an order and the other expressing serious interest. The offer sheet proved to contain good talking points for the call, and no revisions were planned. The results reinforced the belief that technical nurturing is the key to building credibility to close deals and can differentiate the company from competitors. Two process issues did arise during the test:

1. The technical experts making the phone calls to qualify the customers are the constraint in the process.
2. The handoff to field sales representatives is clumsy and their follow-up is weak.

## Cycle 4a: Prequalification by Telesales

The objective of this cycle was to test having nontechnical persons (telesales) do the initial call to filter the list. From telesales making calls to a few customers, it was learned that telesales staff using the offer sheet can sufficiently filter the list into customers who are nos, yeses, and maybes.

After cycle 4a, the initial screening of customers was moved to telesales. However, even with this change, the technical experts still proved to be the bottleneck. Another cycle was run to test further prequalification by telesales.

## Cycle 4b: Further Prequalification by Telesales

A test was run to have telesales staff further qualify the maybes so the technical experts only follow up with yeses and close to a yes. This test proved successful in freeing additional time for technical experts to make calls with the greatest potential for sales.

## Cycle 5: Handoff to Field Sales Representatives

The objective of the cycle was to test a standard process to transfer customers from technical experts to field sales staff, who would then arrange the details of the sale and ongoing maintenance of the account. The process included a formal introduction (in-person or on a call) of the field sales representative to the customer by the technical expert. This happened after the customer was sufficiently qualified. To accommodate this change, the sales representative group was restructured to have clearly defined roles and responsibilities for handoffs from the technical experts and subsequent follow-up with customers. The technical experts and sales representatives were very satisfied with the new process, and customers were pleased with the immediate follow-up.

## Results

The commitment of the team to improve sales resulted in an increased number of customers through 2005 and 2006 (see Figure 12.13). This measure was officially presented only through mid-2006. Sales dollars increased more than 50 percent from 2004 to 2005 and were maintained through 2008 (2008 sales were projected on the basis of first-quarter 2008 sales; see Figure 12.14). The project team ended in 2007.

## Lessons Learned

- *Sales can be improved through a focused improvement effort.* A team was formed with an aim to improve sales in a specific product line by 40 percent within one year. The team included committed technical experts and sales representatives. The team used PDSA Cycles to gain knowledge about their customers and

## FIGURE 12.13.  CUMULATIVE NUMBER OF NEW CUSTOMERS.

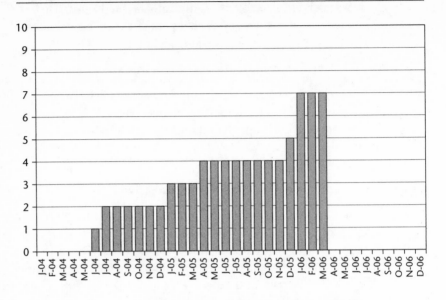

## FIGURE 12.14.  YEARLY WORLDWIDE SALES DOLLARS.

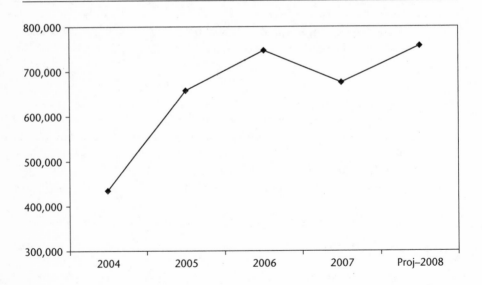

their competitors. They used tests of change to improve sales processes. They monitored the number of new customers and sales dollars, which showed significant improvement. When the project team ended in 2007, mechanisms were in place to hold the gains. (See Chapter Eight, on implementing a change.)

- *List-offer-convert can be used as a framework for improving sales.* The team used the framework to improve their sales processes. They created a list of potential customers, developed a one-page market piece explaining what their products had to offer. The team then used the offer sheet with the list of potential customers to gain new customers (convert). Because improvement in sales dollars often lags the initial improvement work, the list-offer-convert framework is an opportunity to track progress. The team monitored the number of customers added to the list, a qualitative assessment by customers of the offer, and the number of customers that were converted. The team predicted correctly that if these three process measures increased, then the outcome measure of sales dollars would also increase.

## Key Points from Chapter Twelve

- Chapter Two introduced the six skills necessary to support improvement. The case studies discussed in this chapter employed most if not all of the skills for each case. Here is a summary of the key points from the cases presented, arranged by the six skills.

  1. *Supporting change with data.* In each case, data were collected for each cycle to ensure that questions were answered relative to the predictions for the applicable PDSA Cycles. Data were also collected to ensure that the question, "How will we know that a change is an improvement?" was answered, displaying the use of outcome, process, and balancing measures in some of the cases.

  2. *Developing a change.* Various methods were used to develop changes. Critical thinking about the process and use of data was employed in most cases to develop changes.

  3. *Testing a change.* Each case study also involved cycles to test changes before implementation.

  4. *Implementing a change.* After testing the changes, degree of belief was such that changes were implemented, taking advantage of what was learned in testing relative to training of people, documenting standards, and use of measures for sustainability of the changes where applicable.

5. *Spreading improvements.* The pediatric intensive care unit (PICU) mortality case acted as an example of where a *change package* was adapted and spread to a new environment. The team was able to take changes from adult populations and tailor these changes to their circumstances. In addition, a summary is supplied to help others adopt and test the change package for caring for children.

6. *The human side of change.* The PICU was an excellent account of the impact on people in the system. The CareOregon case reinforced the importance of developing the group into a team (using the SDI instrument) before the team starts working together to develop, test, and implement changes. The drill case mentioned the impact on operators as new equipment was introduced.

• Deming has estimated that 94 percent of the problems and opportunities for improvement belong to the system. Because people are part of the system, we must simultaneously view them as part of an interdependent system and independent of that system. However, there are times when the more traditional disciplinary process must be followed to cause corrective action at the individual level or to remove the individual from the system. This is particularly important when the issue is related to safety. The case study on safety in a manufacturing plant is such an example.

## PART THREE

---

# IMPROVING VALUE AS A BUSINESS STRATEGY

---

The first two parts of the book explored key concepts for maximizing the results of the improvement efforts and the Model for Improvement, which is a framework for individuals and groups to gain and apply knowledge to the improvement of a variety of endeavors.

This third part of the book presents a guide for the executive or manager wishing to make value the underlying business strategy for the organization. Improving value is the theme and some approaches to thinking strategically about improvement are presented. Improvement efforts are integrated into a system of improvement.

Chapter Thirteen describes a system for improvement that any organization or organizational unit can develop and integrate into its management and leadership structure. Three types of organizational units are used to illustrate the principles and methods of this system for improvement.

Chapter Fourteen discusses the development of the internal capability to ensure that improvements can be developed, tested, and implemented. This includes development of employees in the knowledge and skills of improvement and the structure necessary to ensure that improvements will have the support to be integrated into the system.

CHAPTER THIRTEEN

# MAKING THE IMPROVEMENT OF VALUE A BUSINESS STRATEGY

In Parts One and Two of this book, we dealt with making improvements at the project level. The vehicle for improvement was often a temporary team that came together to work on the project. In Part Three, we consider the organization or its operating units within which improvement efforts are done. An operating unit might be a bank, a manufacturing plant, a hospital, a school, or the Department of Motor Vehicles. We also include operating units with just a few employees, such as a primary health care practice, a print shop, a travel agency. Any of these operating units could define the improvement of value as its underlying strategy. This part of the book should draw the attention of executives and managers.

Consider the example of the cleaning business in Chapter One. The owners of the business had successfully completed an improvement project to remove defects in their cleaning business, mostly through standardization of the cleaning process. The project was conducted mainly through finding some extra time here and there for meetings and follow-up. The experience led the owners to pursue a more organized approach to the improvement of value.

The sisters decided to focus their attention on a more general approach to improvement of the services provided by their company. To begin with, they formulated an overarching purpose for their improvement efforts: expansion of an aim that they had established for their initial project. They hoped that this would permit consistency, and communicate their intentions to their employees and customers. The original statement of their improvement aim was:

"In order to become the best cleaning service and grow our business, Can-Dew Cleaning Services will continuously work to improve our services. We will do this by working to match our cleaning services to the needs of our customers. Our focus will be on cleanliness and reliability. We want our customers to know that they can rely on our services."

They went on to state several goals for their business:

"Our customers will be satisfied with the cleanliness of their house or business
   when we finish a job, and
We will arrive on time, and
We will finish on time."

Because they intended to integrate improvement into their business, they expected results in financial measures such as sales and profits would be affected by their work. In addition to these financial measures, they began tracking two system-level measures:

Number of new customers per month
Retention of existing customers per quarter

Their theory was if they accomplished their goals related to serving customers, existing customers would retain them and they would attract new customers. If they did a good job matching their capacity to the growth in customers, their finances would improve. They were envisioning a chain reaction that started with improvement of service to customers.

The chain reaction illustrated in Figure 13.1 is one way of depicting the implications of improving value.

The specifics of the chain reaction in Figure 13.1 will change for organizations in government, health care, education, and private not-for-profit organizations. Figure 13.2 is an example of what the chain reaction might be for a government organization. A good learning exercise is to write this chain reaction using the situation and language relevant to your organization.

The decision to make the improvement of value a strategy for an organization usually rests on several assumptions:

- The organization has been successful with some initial improvement efforts and has learned why improvement is essential to the future of the organization.

## FIGURE 13.1. CHAIN REACTION FROM IMPROVING VALUE.

Improve the value of products and services
from the viewpoint of the customer

↓

Increase demand for the organization's products and services

↓

Improve financial performance

↓

Stay in business

↓

Provide jobs

## FIGURE 13.2. CHAIN REACTION FROM IMPROVING VALUE IN A GOVERNMENT ORGANIZATION.

Improve the value of products and services
from the viewpoint of the public

↓

Increase public satisfaction with government performance

↓

Increase public willingness to invest tax dollars in government functions

↓

Remain a viable government service and positive contributor to society

↓

Provide jobs

- Leaders are ready to invest in improvement because they have experienced the *chain reaction*—that is, focusing on improving value from the viewpoint of the customer leads to improved financial performance, at least in one operating unit.
- There is a desire to integrate improvement into the normal organizational process used for planning and setting strategic direction.

The sisters were beginning to imbed the improvement of value as a theme for their company. Their employees and customers now realized that change would be a constant focus, but the change always has a specific aim: improved value of their cleaning services. To be successful, the sisters will need to continue to adopt a more formal approach to their improvement efforts and expand them beyond their original three goals. They will need a system of improvement.

## Building the System of Improvement

One widely used system of improvement is built on five components:

1. Establishing constancy of purpose in the organization
2. Understanding the organization as a system
3. Designing and managing a system for gathering information for improvement
4. Conducting planning for improvement and integrating it with business planning
5. Managing and learning from a portfolio of improvement initiatives

These five activities are focused on aligning all of the improvement efforts in an organization so that the changes that are developed and implemented move the organization in a desired direction. The activities are very interdependent and have to be considered as a system. This approach protects against suboptimization from independently managed individual improvement efforts. Figure 13.3 is an adaptation of Deming's Production Viewed as a System, in which he depicted the integration of improvement with operations. The five activities are methods to bring this framework to life in an organization.

### Establishing Constancy of Purpose

Every person in management is faced with short-term pressures to run the business day-to-day, solve immediate problems, and ensure stable operations within a budget. Constancy of purpose refers to the long-term responsibilities of executives and managers. A first set of tasks to build constancy of purpose is to establish

## FIGURE 13.3. DEMING'S PRODUCTION VIEWED AS A SYSTEM.

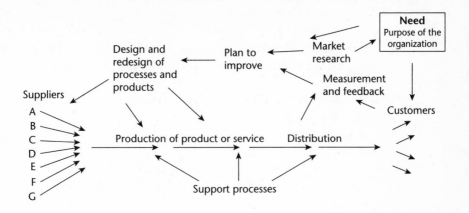

a statement of the purpose of the organization, communicate it, and measure progress toward it over the years. Table 13.1 contains the statement of purpose and some related measures for three organizations. One is a production facility that assembles cabinets within a company that is focused on the residential market. Another is a county government. The third is a not-for-profit organization

## TABLE 13.1. STATEMENTS OF PURPOSE AND ASSOCIATED MEASURES.

| Organization | Statement of Purpose | Measures |
|---|---|---|
| Cabinet assembly facility | The mission of our facility is to contribute to business results for the company by safely and efficiently assembling defect-free cabinets and shipping them on time to the customer. | Sales from new products<br>On-time deliveries<br>Refunds to customer<br>Direct labor efficiency<br>Injuries<br>Healthy community index |
| County government | Ensure that our county is a great place to live, raise a family, and operate a business through accountable and responsible county government. | Tax burden<br>Population growth<br>Business growth<br>Trend in homelessness in partnering cities |
| Off the Streets, a not-for-profit to end homelessness | We are solving homelessness through innovative programs that transform people, buildings, and communities. | Trend in homelessness in partnering cities<br>Savings of tax dollars from appropriate housing and services |

that addresses the issue of homelessness from a systems perspective; their services include developing or finding appropriate housing, securing supportive services, and developing job opportunities for their clients.

A useful statement of purpose for an organization can take a variety of formats. Some of the labels for the statement are mission, vision, values, and guiding principles. Here are some of the uses for a statement of purpose:

- To introduce and manage change in the organization
- To provide input to decisions at all levels of the organization
- To serve as a basis for feedback to those in the organization who behave in conflict with the purpose
- To offer input to strategic and business planning
- To communicate with customers, suppliers, potential employees, and the community
- To aid innovation, by reminding people of the need for the organization's products and services
- To communicate the need for cooperative interactions

Simply stating the purpose of the organization is not enough, however, to obtain constancy in the pursuit of the purpose. It is also necessary to promote an environment and a culture in which everyone in the organization can contribute to achieving the purpose. Although culture varies widely among industries and among organizations within the same industry, some elements of a culture to support constancy of purpose seem to be essential:

- *Long-term results focus.* The ultimate goal of the improvement efforts is to obtain sustainable results to foster the mission and sustain the business for the long run.
- *Desire for continual improvement.* Continual improvement of the experience of all involved with the organization, including customers (or other beneficiaries of products and services), employees, and suppliers.
- *Stewardship of resources.* Reduction of waste and its associated cost is a core value.
- *An environment of cooperation.* The attributes of systems make it obvious that without cooperation among members an organization will be severely limited in the types of improvements that can be accomplished. Achieving cooperation among people and organizational entities is one of the biggest contributions a leader can make to an organization's ability to improve. An environment of mutual respect and encouragement is a good start toward fostering cooperation. However, before people can cooperate they must know

the common purpose of the system in which they reside. Without knowledge of this common purpose, people will avoid or fail to consider decisions that lead to cooperative improvement of the system.

Each statement of purpose and measures in Table 13.1 gives an indication of a long-term results focus. For the assembly facility, the measure of sales of new products is an example. As the tastes and preferences of customers change, new styles and configurations for the cabinets will be needed to increase competitive position. These product changes require new capabilities and new production methods. These styling changes could be considered disruptions to efficient assembly or, as the measure indicates, vital to serving the needs of the business. The healthy community's index includes components related to health, quality of life of residents, education, and employment opportunities. Including this measure as part of the responsibility of county government sets a longer-term expectation for the services and responsibilities of government that span multiple election cycles. If the community as a whole had constancy of purpose, then in each election cycle two of the questions to the candidates would be "Is our community getting better as measured by the index and its components?" "How would you accelerate progress?" Many charitable organizations and individuals devote time and money to caring for individuals who are homeless—*the* problem of today. The measures of trends in the number of homeless individuals in a city or country are related to progress in solving the long-term systemic problems that cause individuals to live on the street.

Constancy of purpose calls for long-term efforts on the part of all who are involved with the organization and who are committed to accomplishing its purpose. Such dedication to years of effort requires that the experience of these individuals be constantly improving and that each has the opportunity to improve processes and systems under his or her control. Talented and dedicated people are in demand and can easily find other employment. Organizations with constancy of purpose would expect to have long-term relationships with customers and suppliers and low turnover among employees.

Constancy of purpose will require a flow of money from customers, investors, taxpayers, or philanthropic individuals and institutions over many years. Each source will expect that its investment, money, or time is not being wasted. The funders must be convinced that their money could not be put to better use elsewhere or invested for shorter-term returns. Thus, the reduction of waste and its associated costs is vital to constancy of purpose.

Cultural change takes time and demands that the beliefs of the individuals in an organization be changed. Although changing culture has not been a focus of this book, the methods for improvement that have been described can contribute to changing culture through changing structures (see Chapter Eleven for some of the elements of system structures), which requires changed work behaviors. Figure 13.4 illustrates the relationship among culture, individual attitudes, and behaviors in an organization.

For example, consider the case study in Chapter Twelve relating to safety in the cabinet assembly facility. Changes in the physical structure of the guards protecting operators from rotating shafts changed the unsafe behavior of machine operators, which contributed to a change in attitude of the operators toward safe operating policies. The change in attitude then contributed to fostering a culture of safety at the facility. Many large and small structural changes that are consistent with a desired culture are strong drivers of culture change toward constancy of purpose.

## Viewing the Organization as a System

In earlier chapters of this book, we focused on improving processes and progressed to more ambitious improvement aims associated with spreading improvement widely (see Chapter Nine) or changing larger or more complex systems (see Chapter Eleven). Flow diagrams, operating rules, and other methods were used to describe the processes or systems and make them visible. The second

**FIGURE 13.4. STRUCTURE, BEHAVIOR, ATTITUDES, AND CULTURE.**

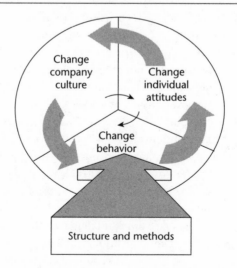

component of a system of improvement is to do the analogous task for an entire organization or operating unit: to help employees understand the organization as a system with a purpose and many interacting components. Some methods to assist with this task:

- Surface the interactions and connections that are necessary to accomplish improvement initiatives
- Broaden operations planning to include more parts of the organization
- Describe the organization using system maps or a linkage of processes
- Promote regular visits and other interactions between departments (see the first case study in Chapter Three, on improving the morning meeting)

Strategic improvement initiatives usually require many parts (divisions, departments, offices, and so on) in the organization to cooperate. An initiative gives concrete meaning to cooperative interactions to achieve an aim. Consider an initiative in a county government related to reducing pedestrian accidents. When the county executive began establishing the team, she realized that many departments would be needed to accomplish the aim: transportation, police, fire and rescue, public schools, permitting services. Each department had a parochial view of its function. However, this view was changed by considering what needed to be done to improve the safety of pedestrians.

Individual department managers can also foster a systems view in their employees by relating the department's work to the overall organization's initiatives. For example, county government had six long-term initiatives:

1. Affordable housing in an inclusive community
2. An effective and efficient transportation network
3. Children prepared to be contributing members of society
4. *Healthy and sustainable neighborhood communities*
5. *Safe streets and secure neighborhoods*
6. Strong, growing economy

The Fire and Rescue Department got together and discussed which initiatives they could make a contribution to. The initiatives in italics were the two they concluded they could influence through department improvement projects. The discussion itself promoted a new view of county services as a system for them.

Operations planning is a process that in its simplest description is matching capacity to predicted demand. This type of planning is routine in production facilities. One of the means to accomplish the efficiency goals in the cabinet assembly facility was to improve planning and scheduling of production among four operations that had to synchronize their work over a period of a week to meet daily shipments. Executives can promote systems thinking by broadening the boundaries within which this planning takes place.

Let's look at a common problem in health care. Emergency rooms (also called emergency departments) are notorious for being "overcrowded" and having long waits. Patients needing to be admitted to the hospital after being stabilized in the ER often find that a bed is not available for them, so they wait in the ER for hours or even overnight for a bed to be open. This of course ties up beds in the ER and causes longer waits. The easy answer is that the hospital or the ER needs more beds. Including all departments and medical specialties in operations planning reveals that part of the problem is how nonemergency surgeries (such as knee replacements) are scheduled. Traditionally the only aspect of the hospital that is scheduled for such a surgery is the operating room in which the surgery will take place. The surgeries are often bunched on two or three days in the middle of the week, putting stress on the hospital's capacity to accommodate the patients after surgery, causing beds that are needed for admissions to the hospital through the ER to be given to surgical patients, causing the ER beds to be used for holding patients to be admitted, causing longer waits in the ER, resulting in demands for more ER capacity. The problem is lack of system thinking and an absence of comprehensive operations planning, not lack of ER beds.

Another way to promote viewing the organization as a system is to develop and use systems diagrams or maps to describe the organization. One method to do this is a linkage of processes where the key work processes in the organization become the building blocks for constructing a view of the system. Appendix B describes this tool and includes a linkage of processes for a bank. The linkage is particularly effective in promoting a systems view when it is related to improvement initiatives. Which processes need to be improved to accomplish the initiative? Which departments are responsible for those processes? The linkage is also helpful for establishing internal customer-supplier relations. People can visualize who depends on their work and whose work they depend on. Managers can foster cooperative interactive by allowing time for these employees to visit one another's work places and discuss how they could work together.

For example, Off the Streets had a goal in a large but sprawling urban environment of reducing people living on the street by 50 percent in a two-year period. After viewing their work as a system, they realized that to accomplish their goal the processes of identifying and engaging these people as clients needed improvement. One change was to enlist the Parks Department and the Police Department and to give these departments an easy way to contact them twenty-four hours a day when they came across individuals or groups of people living on the streets. This greatly increased their opportunity to provide services to those in need of help.

To decide whether a system is moving closer to accomplishing its purpose, some measurement of the system should be done. Examples of such measures are return on investment, throughput, percentage of legal cases won, scores on standardized tests, and volume of sales. Given one measure of success, almost any group can be successful in the short run by improving that measure at the expense of other important measures; for example, profits can be increased in the short run by decreasing investment in research and development.

Improvement of a system results in the improvement of a family of measures. Some organizations call this approach a balanced scorecard or "whole system measures." The family of measures should serve as both indicators of present performance and predictors of how the system will perform in the future. These measures should relate to a variety of dimensions of the system, such as customers, employees, business and financial dimensions, operations, and outside environment. One way to develop a family of measures is to use the purpose statement as a guide. Examples of measures related to purpose were shown in Table 13.1. Leaders should review each part of the purpose statement and decide how it could be measured. In the beginning, it is best to identify a set of ten or fewer measures and establish a system for collecting the appropriate data for regular review. This set of measures can then be enhanced over time.

## Designing a System for Gathering, Analyzing, and Managing Information

A third component of a system of improvement relates to gathering and processing information. Most organizations have many systems in place to collect both qualitative information and quantitative data from customers, suppliers, employees, and other relevant stakeholders. This information is used for operations, problem solving, and developing ideas for improvement. If properly analyzed and summarized, it can also be used as an input to planning for improvement at various levels in the organization. One useful model for the component related to information has four parts:

1. Direction: determining what is to be collected and analyzed
2. Collection: obtaining the information from a variety of sources
3. Analyzing: extracting some opportunities and priorities for improvement
4. Dissemination: furnishing the conclusions and priorities in formats that are understandable to their consumers

These four components can be part of a periodic cycle that corresponds to various planning cycles in the organization.

This chapter began with a discussion of measures related to the purpose of the organization. Making sure those measures are up to date and accurate is perhaps the primary direction for information gathering. The three categories for improvement were discussed in Chapter Ten. In that chapter, the type of data that would be useful to identify defects, to uncover sources of waste, and to determine what might be attractive to customers was also discussed. Other directions for information gathering might include competitors' actions, strategic directions of customers, and new legislation or regulatory initiatives that could affect the business.

There is a vast supply of sources from which information can be collected. Frontline employees—those making the product or directly servicing the customer—see defects every day, and some of their work involves fixing them. Simple check sheets embedded in work ensures the information on type and frequency of defects is captured reliably. Routine interactions with customers are another underused source of information. Customers use phone calls to technical support or e-mails to ask questions about the product or service. Just a bit of planning for capturing the information in these interactions yields valuable information. One company realized that, because some of their products were used by their employees, these employees could become a ready source of "customer" information. Incident reports required by regulation of airline pilots, nurses, or managers when there is a near miss or when an employee or customer is injured are a source that comes with little extra work.

In the Internet age, open (or publicly available) sources are an increasingly efficient way of gathering information. One organization assigned to a carefully selected group of new managers two competitors each to monitor. The information available in open sources was incredible. The assignment was considered a development opportunity for the managers as well as an information collection assignment. Finally, scans by a capable team of observers to understand variation in performance and practice at different locations within the company are worth the investment of time and travel. There may be five cabinet assembly facilities with differing performance. The best have processes or a system related to this performance that could be adopted by other facilities. Some cities have superior ways of preventing homelessness. Some county governments are more efficient and effective than others. Some aspects of compiling the information from scans were covered in Chapter Nine, on spreading improvements.

A group of analysts must analyze the information and draw conclusions from it. These analysts may already be available in the marketing, finance, risk management, and quality control departments. A coordination function often is all that is needed to integrate the analyses that are already taking place.

Dissemination is the end of the cycle, but also a vehicle for learning and improving the information component. What did the consumers of the information find useful? What was acted on? How did the information affect planning and decision making? What was waste or overkill? What should the direction of the next cycle of information gathering be?

## Integrating Planning for Improvement with Business Planning

Executives running a business ceaselessly determine priorities to generate growth in revenues, control costs, allocate resources to operations, allocate capital to investments, and support profit margins in the face of market pressures. Most organizations have processes for strategic and business planning that create an opportunity to be proactive and make choices to set these priorities. Because of rapid changes in the environments in which many organizations operate, planning has become an increasingly important activity in companies, educational institutions, and government organizations.

If the comprehensive view of the improvement of value that was presented in Chapter Ten is integrated with business strategy and operations over a period of time, an organization has a competitive advantage that is very difficult to replicate. This integration is the fourth component of a system of improvement. The bridge between business planning and the improvement methods discussed in this book is the translation of strategy into a portfolio of improvement projects that support these initiatives. Strategic objectives, goals, and initiatives set the broad direction for improvement of the organization. Table 13.2 contains some examples of strategic initiatives.

These strategic initiatives or objectives are statements of what needs to be achieved by an organization to move it toward its purpose. They should be strategic in nature (long-run focused) and not tactical (short-term focused). They are *not* the specific actions required for improvement. Strategic objectives should reflect the information learned from the inputs to planning processes. The process to develop strategic objectives should include both divergence and convergence. Specific information must be analyzed and discussed, but the tone of the process should be holistic.

A group of improvement projects can be integrated and connected to the strategic initiatives in at least two ways: top-down or bottom-up.

1. The *top-down* approach starts with the strategic initiative and enumerates the issues that must be addressed. From this theory, a negotiation process is used to choose a group of projects.
2. A related but different, *bottom-up*, approach to selecting projects is to request nominations for projects related to a strategic initiative. These nominations

## TABLE 13.2. TRANSLATING STRATEGIC INITIATIVES TO IMPROVEMENT PROJECTS.

| Organization | Strategic Initiative | Bridge to Improvement |
|---|---|---|
| Cabinet business | Leverage assembly plants to better support the business growth and profitability | Each of five plants develops a set of projects for the year according to discussions with corporate executives and internal staff |
| County government | Safe streets and secure neighborhoods | County executive sets some areas of focus such as pedestrian safety for cross-departmental teams; county departments negotiate with the county executive the priorities for the year in this area of focus |
| Not-for-profit to end homelessness | Focus on ending homelessness rather than only serving those who are already homeless | Set up focused improvement efforts in defined geographic regions |

may be for new projects or for existing ones that need a boost in priority. The list under each strategic priority is then pared down and connected into a coherent whole.

Both of these approaches can be useful. The top-down approach emphasizes integration of efforts to focused goals. The bottom-up approach offers some assurance all strategic priorities are receiving attention. The approach also takes into account the many projects, perhaps uncoordinated, that are already under way. In practice, some combination of the two approaches may be best.

To illustrate the top-down, cascading approach, consider the cabinet business and its strategic initiative of leveraging the assembly operations to achieve business goals. Each of the five assembly plants was given the task to produce a driver diagram of the issues at the plant and the associated initiatives to address them. The vice president for operations and the five plant managers would then meet to discuss the initiatives and produce an overall improvement plan for assembly operations. Figure 13.5 contains the driver diagram from one of the plants.

A charter for each of the four areas for improvement was written and a team was formed. Each team then created a driver diagram at the next level of detail as a starting point for their efforts.

Figure 13.6 contains the driver diagram for the productivity team.

## FIGURE 13.5. DRIVER DIAGRAM FOR PERFORMANCE OF A CABINET ASSEMBLY PLANT.

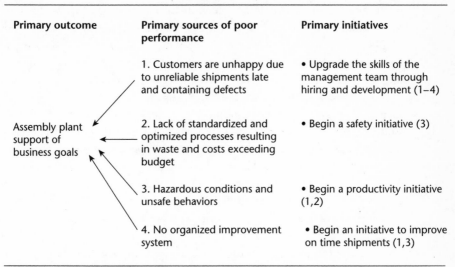

| Primary outcome | Primary sources of poor performance | Primary initiatives |
|---|---|---|
| | 1. Customers are unhappy due to unreliable shipments late and containing defects | • Upgrade the skills of the management team through hiring and development (1–4) |
| Assembly plant support of business goals | 2. Lack of standardized and optimized processes resulting in waste and costs exceeding budget | • Begin a safety initiative (3) |
| | 3. Hazardous conditions and unsafe behaviors | • Begin a productivity initiative (1,2) |
| | 4. No organized improvement system | • Begin an initiative to improve on time shipments (1,3) |

*Note:* Numbers in parentheses indicate the driver to be affected by the initiative

## FIGURE 13.6. DRIVER DIAGRAM FOR PRODUCTIVITY AT A CABINET ASSEMBLY PLANT.

| Primary outcome | Primary sources of poor performance | Primary changes |
|---|---|---|
| | 1. Poor matching of crew capacity to demand | • Develop, test, and implement a scheduling algorithm for crews (1) |
| Productivity (cabinets shipped)/ (total direct labor hrs) | 2. Waste associated with material handling, long cycle times, lack of synchronization | • Move to continuous flow through work flow and line configuration changes (2,3) |
| | 3. High defect rates resulting in inefficient rework | • Upgrade the maintenance function (4) |
| | 4. Equipment downtime | • Move responsibility for effective operation to the supervisor/lead level (2,3,4) |

*Note:* Number in parentheses indicate the driver to be affected by the change

Maintaining a systems view of the organization is important in developing a top-down portfolio of projects. The decisions on projects and allocation of improvement resources should be done after all the strategic objectives have been related to the structure of the system. Organizations that use a linkage of processes to describe their system can use the linkage to help with these decisions. Using the linkage, the planners identify the processes, products, and services that have an important impact on each strategic objective. New processes, products, and services that need to be designed are also considered. High-impact areas within the organization are identified if certain processes, products, or services are related to more than one strategic objective. After each strategic objective is related to each process and product, the "total" strategic impact of the process (or product) is determined by totaling the weightings for the strategic objective for each process, service, or product.

To illustrate the bottom-up approach, consider the county government. The county had invested heavily in developing an effective Internet site. The county had a vision of using the Internet to achieve the part of their mission about becoming a responsible and accountable county government. As a result of this vision numerous projects sprang up all over the departments in the county government. Many departments began using the Internet to announce new services. Residents were able to perform routine transactions online such as paying traffic tickets or applying for a building permit. Lots of good work was being done on using the Internet, but these efforts were not coordinated, so system-level results were unlikely and the overlap of effort was wasting resources. One of the county executive's staff was charged with rationalizing all these projects. She and a small team took an inventory of all the projects that were active or planned that involved the Internet. The list was long. Some projects were dropped, some were combined, and some were redefined.

The team decided on a portfolio of projects for the Internet Initiative. The portfolio was organized in four categories:

1. Content development
2. Search capability
3. Information for residents
4. Routine resident transactions

System-level measures for the large initiative included:

- County rank on third-party assessments of government Websites
- Total cost savings related to Website improvements
- Hits on the Websites overall and in specified areas
- Percentage of transactions being completed online

Each category was assigned a leader and a team to coordinate and sequence work in that category. Each team used one or more of the system-level measures as its primary measure. In some cases they enhanced the measures with more specific measures related to their category. An oversight team was established to coordinate efforts among categories.

## Managing and Learning from a Portfolio of Improvement Initiatives

Whatever method is used to choose the improvement projects, they must be managed as a portfolio, a group of complementary projects with a common goal (the strategic initiative). The individual projects must be managed to ensure their contribution to the whole. Decisions about conflicts and tradeoffs among the projects must also be made.

Consider for example the initiative to leverage the county's Website. Several key persons are needed to lead this effort. One is the initiative lead, the person who will integrate the projects in all the categories to obtain the expected results. Each category also requires a project leader. (Note: some persons may lead more than one project.) Organizations that are successful at execution take the process of deploying resources to the improvement projects in the portfolio very seriously. In the cabinet assembly plant, the production manager led the overall effort, and it was his primary improvement focus. Project leaders are often relieved of other duties to work full-time or at least a significant part of their time on the project. Sometimes the project leaders come from a staff dedicated to improvement. For example, in the cabinet assembly plant engineers lead the individual project teams (such as the team focusing on productivity improvement). Although this level of staffing may seem excessive or unaffordable, organizations that follow this approach recognize that the initiatives are large system projects demanding lots of time, are vital to the organization, and are expected to pay a substantial financial or strategic return (see further discussion in Chapter Fourteen).

The pace of these system-level projects is a deliberate choice ("how much, and by when"). An organization can choose to increase the pace without increasing resources significantly by focusing the leader's efforts. For example, consider a person leading two projects scheduled for one year and devoting 25 percent of his or her time to each. Each project takes one year to produce results. Consider another allocation of time: the same person allocates 50 percent of her time to a six-month project, finishes it, and goes on to a second project of six months' duration. The project leader has not increased her time allocation, but instead of producing results from two projects in an average of twelve months, she has produced results from the same two projects in an average of nine months. (The first project delivered results in six months and the second project in twelve months.) With a focused team leader, the other team members are made more efficient, so their time devoted to the project often does not need to be increased under this accelerated approach.

We recognize in some situations it may not be feasible to assign a leader to a project full-time, but allocating less than 40 percent of a person's time to a strategic initiative seems unwise given the stakes. Here are suggestions for aiding the proper allocation of resources to strategic initiatives:

- Do a thoughtful assessment of return on investment to reaffirm the importance of the project and build consensus for the allocation of time.
- Shorten the length of the project because of the increased allocation of time for the project leader.
- Be clear about what the person will stop doing to make time for the duties of project leader. Supply a means for assigning these duties to others if they are truly adding significant value to customers or the organization, or stopping or reducing them if they are not.
- Monitor the time spent on the project to prevent the erosion of the project leader's time and attention from the project.

Here is a structure for improvement projects of this scale:

- The team leader is responsible for the progress and pace.
- A day-to-day driver of the project is sometimes the team leader but often a staff person responsible for the logistics of the project.
- An executive sponsor keeps the team connected to organizational strategy, coordinates the efforts with other projects, and increases the chances of success.
- Technical experts advise in the subject matter.

Of course, for many organizations the issue is not how much of someone's time to allocate to a project. The issue is finding and developing people in the organization capable of integrating a portfolio of projects or leading one of those projects. We cover approaches to developing this capability in Chapter Fourteen.

In addition to allocating the time of the leader and team members, the allocation of other organizational resources to the portfolio of projects is a priority. These resources include:

- Capital for projects, such as information technology, construction, or new equipment
- Priority for requests to information technology services

- Priority for other support services such as finance or human resources
- Assignment of analysts or quality improvement specialists to assist the team

Well-developed executive review processes are essential for successful execution. These reviews should occur at least monthly with the executive sponsor of the project, and quarterly with an executive team that is responsible for execution of the strategic plan and the associated improvement initiatives. The best reviews seem to function as high-level problem-solving sessions, with an unwavering commitment to make the project and the team successful. The purposes of the review may be:

- To encourage and recognize the project teams
- To learn whether the project is on track, or is likely to fall short of the aim
- To develop action plans for getting projects back on track
- To decide whether the project should be modified in some way or stopped

A good executive review of improvement projects requires a good process for review, with these steps:

*Review of the context.* The project is nested in a portfolio of projects connected to a system-level goal or strategic initiative. Make this context clear, and use it as needed for the rest of the review.

*Efficient review of progress.* Many of the organizations emphasize the importance of good preparation of the "story" of the project. Elements of the story include the aim of the project, annotated time series for two or three important measures, the major system changes, and the degree of belief (high, medium, low) that the aim will be achieved. One can develop skills for communicating this information effectively by adapting techniques from abstracts for peer-reviewed articles, storyboards, sidebars in magazine articles, or illustrative graphics from newspaper articles. The SBAR (situation, background, assessment, and recommendation) format is associated with efficient and effective communication and can also serve as a template for the team's presentation. This review of progress should take between a quarter and a third of the time allotted for the overall review.

*Agreement on barriers and emerging issues.* If the project is not achieving the intended results, reach agreement on why:

- Lack of organizational will?
- Absence of strong enough ideas for improvement?
- Failure to execute changes?
- Unanticipated internal or external forces?

*Action plan.* During the discussion of barriers and issues, some solutions may surface and require action by one of the executives, or require a new approach that can be carried out by the team without executive action.

For example, the organization devoted to ending homelessness had an improvement initiative to reduce the population living on the streets by 50 percent in a sprawling urban area. To reach their goal, they needed to place at least three people a week into appropriate living arrangements and provide them with the needed services to treat mental and physical illnesses. During their monthly review, the team reported they were falling behind this rate and needed more people to achieve it. After some discussion of alternatives, two major changes to operations were agreed on for testing. The first was to split the team into two functions: outreach and benefits processing. The outreach team would focus solely on finding and building relationships with people living on the streets. The benefits processing team would make sure that those willing to be housed met criteria for city and state support and found living space for them. This increased productivity compared to the arrangement when both functions were done by one team. The second change was to enlist local hospitals to help find those living on the streets when they came to their emergency room and refer them to the outreach team. These two changes needed the guidance and support of the executive sponsor. The team would be responsible for the details of how the changes and the cooperation with the hospitals would occur in daily practice.

The review process is an ideal time to review the new knowledge that is emerging from the execution of the project. The executives and the team learn their way to new performance. Projects may have unexpected connections or reinforce each other in ways that were not anticipated. Effective review processes are a means of documenting and spreading this learning.

## Key Points from Chapter Thirteen

- It is typical that as organizations successfully execute projects to improve aspects of their business and its products and services, they gain confidence that improving value could set off a chain reaction: improve value of their products and services, increase demand, and sustain a viable business that produces jobs and opportunities for advancement.
- The confidence in the chain reaction motivates these organizations to build a formal system of improvement by which to execute improvement initiatives that support the mission or the organization and its strategic goals.

- A system of improvement described in this chapter includes five components:
  1. Establishing constancy of purpose in the organization
  2. Understanding the organization as a system
  3. Designing and managing a system for gathering information for improvement
  4. Conducting planning for improvement and integrating it with business planning
  5. Managing and learning from a portfolio of improvement initiatives

CHAPTER FOURTEEN

# DEVELOPING IMPROVEMENT CAPABILITY

Jim Edwards had just come from the morning executive meeting where he and several other executives sat through several presentations on various improvement efforts launched twelve weeks ago. Jim was reflecting on the impressive results. The five projects together had reduced costs by $1.2 million while actually improving service to customers. In addition, the employees who participated in the improvement efforts were enthusiastic and showed much pride in their accomplishment. Jim and his executive team had begun establishing a system of improvement to integrate their improvement work with their business strategy. The questions Jim and his team faced now were: How do we build up our internal capability to execute on key improvements that have been identified? What skills do people need? What is an effective way to develop those skills?

Jim is at the crossroads and considering making the investment to develop a more extensive internal improvement capability. He realized that he was relying on too small a group of people to lead the improvement initiatives. The decision to expand the pool of people with strong improvement capabilities usually results from realizing that improvement will be constrained by the amount of time that is invested in improvement and the skills of the people leading the improvement initiatives. We discussed the time investment in Chapter Thirteen. These are the topics discussed in this chapter:

- Developing improvement capability in the workforce
- Organization to support the focus on improvement
- Other capability development:
  - Database and data analysis capabilities
  - Capabilities to integrate knowledge into the system

An organization sets the context for development of improvement capability by setting and reinforcing the expectations for everyone within the organization with regard to their responsibility for improvement.

In general, everyone in the organization should be expected to:

- Search out challenging opportunities to change, grow, innovate, and improve products and services for customers
- Experiment, take risks, and learn from the accompanying mistakes to better satisfy customers and stakeholders
- Achieve small wins that promote consistent progress and build commitments
- Develop one's own skills and abilities to aid the organization's efforts at identifying, developing, testing, and implementing improvements
- Look for opportunities to collaborate and share learning throughout the organization

Table 14.1 contains more specific expectations for individuals at different levels in the organization. All have a role to play in developing improvement capability,

## TABLE 14.1. EXPECTATIONS FOR EXECUTIVES, MANAGERS, FIRST-LINE SUPERVISION, AND EMPLOYEES.

| Role | Expectations |
|---|---|
| Executives | • *Create* a system of improvement and integrate it with the business |
| | • *Build* collaboration by promoting cooperative goals and fostering trust between all stakeholders in the system |
| | • *Invest* time and other resources in improving products and processes and developing people to lead these efforts |
| Managers | • *Connect* the roles of people to the role of the department and purpose of the organization |
| | • *Lead* cross-functional improvement teams |
| | • *Develop* supervisors to lead process improvement in their areas |
| First-line supervision | • *Remove* defects and waste from processes of daily work |

- *Participate* in improvement teams that contribute to the larger aims of the department or organization
- *Help* people execute on the requirements of the job with the aim of delighting the internal and external customer

| | |
|---|---|
| Front-line employees | • *Engage* in improvement of daily work by suggesting and testing changes |
| | • *Participate* in improvement teams that contribute to the larger aims of the department |
| | • *Execute* on the requirements of the job, with the aim of delighting the internal and external customer |

but midlevel managers are particularly important. Executives often enlist them to lead cross-functional teams to improve large systems, so they must develop the skills to do so effectively. They also have a key role to play in developing those in their department. Midlevel managers can be very effective and efficient at developing people who work with them by having a system for improvement as described in Chapter Thirteen and using it to manage the department. In this way, their employees are exposed to improvement thinking and methods every day. They become accustomed to looking for new ideas, testing changes, and measuring results. This training, of course, can be supplemented by classroom-style training.

## Developing Improvement Capability in the Workforce

Reflecting on the joy in learning and contributing that Jim witnessed from the early improvement efforts, he was most interested in ensuring that the leaders in the organization at all levels had access to proper development. One of his friends, Orville Joseph, a CEO and owner of his own company, counseled Jim to ensure that his people learn the science of improvement. Orville was emphatic that once they understood and were able to apply the science of improvement the effort to improve would become sustainable. Jim still had questions: Who should be developed? What methods for development are effective? What skills and personality attributes should the leaders of improvement possess?

Who should be developed? Here is a list to get us started:

- Executives
- Managers
- Supervisors and frontline staff
- Internal improvement advisors

The plan for development of improvement capability should answer these questions:

- Who are the persons, line management, or workforce, in your organization capable of reliably producing results from improvement initiatives?
- Who could be part of that group with further development of their capabilities?
- How can we combine the actual job assignment with opportunities for improvement such that development happens in the course of the day?
- Does the organization view this person as a future leader in the organization? (Though it is desirable to have people with improvement skills, many organizations have realized that future leaders in the organization should understand these theories, methods, and tools.)

Table 14.2 lays out the capabilities of supervisors and lead operators at the cabinet assembly plant. For planning purposes, their capabilities were rated 1, 2, or 3 depending on whether their capability was below, meeting, or exceeding expectations. The plant had five major areas, each run by a supervisor who was assisted by two or three lead operators. The table indicates that Pat's area had the strongest improvement capability, followed by Susan's and Jorge's areas. Tommy's area was acceptable. Bill's had unacceptably low capability. The plant manager questioned whether Bill was in the right job. He did a good job running operations day to day, but for the more dynamic competitive environment that they were currently facing he was ill-equipped. He certainly could not develop his three leads, who all needed to develop their improvement capability. He and Bill were having ongoing discussions about whether Bill should switch jobs within the company or undergo an ambitious effort to upgrade his skills.

A more straightforward development plan was emerging for the area run by Tommy. He was a new supervisor with potential to be a strong leader of improvement. His leads also had some need for further development. If the skills in Tommy's area could be enhanced, then each area in the plant except Bill's would have strong improvement capabilities. This would allow some very ambitious goals to be set in the next business planning cycle. The improvement plan included some one-on-one coaching. Susan, a strong improver, did some coaching with Tommy about leading projects in his area. She also helped him develop LaShon. LaShon was a highly capable lead who needed a bit more process orientation. He was too quick to blame operators for defects and other system problems. In addition, LaShon was made a member of the safety team led by one of the plant engineers, another capable improver.

### TABLE 14.2. ASSESSMENT OF THE CAPABILITIES FOR IMPROVEMENT OF SUPERVISORS AND LEADS.

| Supervisor | Capability | Lead | Capability |
|---|---|---|---|
| Jorge | 3 | Jim | 1 |
| | | Kathy | 3 |
| Susan | 3 | Carlos | 3 |
| | | Mary | 2 |
| Tommy | 2 | Arminda | 2 |
| | | Greg | 2 |
| | | LaShon | 2 |
| Pat | 3 | Luca | 3 |
| | | Darrel | 3 |
| | | Judy | 2 |
| Bill | 1 | Eric | 1 |
| | | Foster | 1 |
| | | Billy | 2 |

This type of analysis and planning is helpful in setting a development plan for the organization. The Human Resources Department can be a terrific resource to help create the plan.

Let's look more specifically at the development activities that are appropriate for executives, managers, supervisors, frontline staff, and internal improvement advisors. We begin with the development of executives, considering four stages:

Stage 1: Discovery
Stage 2: Learning
Stage 3: Implementation
Stage 4: External promotion to others

***Stage 1: Discovery*** During the *discovery* stage the executive should have the opportunity to listen to other leaders who have successfully integrated improvement with their business strategy. The discussion allows the executives to see the possibilities and gauge their own ability to actually lead the organization in making improvements.

In addition to learning from other executives, the executive should seek out quality data for his or her own circumstances:

- How well are we serving customers?
- What is the failure rate?

- What is the death rate in our hospital?
- How much rework goes on in the organization?
- What are our warranty costs per unit sold?

As the executive begins to see the data regularly, this creates the need and desire to learn more. This usually contributes to the will to start considering changes for the organization.

***Stage 2: Learning*** Learning can take place in many ways for the executive. Of course, there are many workshops and consultants who can share knowledge. There are also many other avenues that may be as useful for learning. Here are some ideas:

- One on one: working with another executive, coach, or consultant.
- Self-development: executives are usually very good at researching new ideas and self-education.
- Find out who the executives admire and respect, and connect them.
- External courses offered at universities or societies.
- Personally lead an improvement team.
- Integrate measurement into their work and job description.
- Site visits with respected organizations.
- Internal review of projects within the organization.
- Lead internal company diagnosis of defects, warranty claims, or opportunities to delight customers.
- Give a speech or a lead a short seminar on improvement and its role in the company.
- Align mission and vision with improvement.

***Stage 3: Implementation*** Implementation is where theory and practice meet. All of the learning and synthesis of the various improvement ideas, methods, and tools are to be acted on. Building the system for improvement discussed in Chapter Thirteen is part of the development in this phase. It is here that the executive will tailor what has been learned to the unique circumstances of the organization. It is here also that the additional learning will take place as action is taken on what is being learned. The learning can be enhanced by reflecting on this experience with an external peer, a consultant, and members of the executive team.

***Stage 4: External Promotion to Others*** Once the efforts to improve have been successful, the organization will usually receive requests from others to visit and learn from them. This presents the executive team with the experience of promoting their development, which will foster more learning as they prepare for these visits and answer questions. Companies that win the Malcolm Baldrige National Quality Award are expected to share their experience and learning.

## Development of Advanced Skills for Improvement

People with advanced skills for improvement are a valuable asset to any organization. However, skilled midlevel managers are particularly vital to the overall development of capability in the workforce. This group is the essential foundation. The prerequisites for further development would be mastery of the application of methods in Chapters One through Five in this book. The next level of development builds capability to apply methods in Chapters Six through Twelve.

Vehicles for development of these skills in midlevel leaders include:

- Leading a project with help from a capable colleague or improvement advisor
- Leading an improvement workshop for those reporting to you
- Rotating into the central improvement group
- Training other managers by helping them get results related to the business or the mission
- Writing an article for the company magazine or trade journal about improvement

In addition to these opportunities, these potential leaders could avail themselves of education and training in a more traditional fashion. These opportunities would include:

- Self-study
- E-learning modules
- Attending seminars and conferences
- Joining an internal interest group or study groups (for example: safety)

To identify candidates for this level of intensive development consider people with these traits:

- *Curiosity.* To achieve results at the system level requires system-level change. No easy answers are available. A successful leader of large-scale execution must be open to finding and translating ideas both from within outside the organization.
- *Capability to move between conceptual thinking and execution.* Integrating a portfolio of improvement projects and learning about what changes are producing system-level results requires conceptual thinking skills. It also takes disciplined project management skills. Leaders who are effective at execution have both.

- *Quantitative and related computer skills.* Effective improvement almost always requires measurement. The measurement and learning challenge increases as the size and ambition of the portfolio of projects increase.
- *Ability to work well with all levels of the workforce and professional disciplines.* To achieve system-level results requires contributions from all levels of the organization and also requires cooperation among them.
- *The confidence to link with senior executives.* Senior executives play a vital role in ensuring that the overall strategic improvement aims are achieved. Leaders will require cooperative interaction with executives as peers to effectively execute projects that achieve system-level results.
- *Ability to be a good communicator.* When the organization sets system-level aims and makes fundamental changes to accomplish them, people in the organization will want to know, "What are we going to do?" and "Why are we doing it?" One successful executive said he was not confident that his message was understood until he communicated the message "eight times, eight ways."

In considering the list of attributes for those who would be successful leading projects, many people observe that it would also apply to good leaders for the business or organization. Forward-thinking organizations have used the development process for improvement leaders as a first step to ensure that the future leaders of the organization have these skills and capabilities.

Education: *those activities that are designed to improve the overall competence of the employee in a specified direction and beyond the job now held.* Training: *those activities that are designed to improve performance in the job the employee is presently doing. The purpose of training is to either introduce a new behavior or modify the existing behaviors so that a particular and specified kind of behavior results.*

Besides training in methods and their application, this group of people would profit from some education in addition to skills training.

Education in the science of improvement covered in Chapter Four could commence in parallel with training in methods without an expectation of immediate results that could directly be attributed to the education. Education is conducted with the intention that a more proficient manager or employee will emerge in the future.

## Organizationwide Capability for Improvement

Making improvements requires people at all levels of the organization to develop, test, and implement changes. They will need capability in the basics of improvement, material covered in Chapters One through Five. Topics for training include:

- Training in the use of a methodology to improve
- Training in the use of the improvement tools
- Training and education in group dynamics and interpersonal skills
- Training on how to conduct effective meetings, including roles and responsibilities of the team participants

Some organizations have fallen into the trap of doing more training than improvement. The thought is that since we are training people, improvement is taking place. Some organizations have even encouraged this misallocation of resources by measuring how many people have been trained and then using this measure to identify those managers "who support the improvement effort." Training can become an "activity trap."

How do we avoid this activity trap? First, avoid any type of mass training that is not connected to specific improvement aims and follow-up coaching. Adults are motivated to learn when they perceive a need to gain knowledge and believe that training will satisfy this need. Second, training should be effective. Bruce Joyce and Beverly Showers, of the University of Oregon, have explored various training modes and their effectiveness. These typical training modes were compared with the expected results of knowledge, skill, and application. Table 14.3 combines the conclusions of their study with the authors' experience of working with adult learners

To develop improvement capability through training implies that the training includes making improvements. Participants should be members of an ongoing project team, or one that will be formed shortly after the training is completed.

## TABLE 14.3. EFFECTIVENESS OF VARIOUS TRAINING MODES.

| Training Mode | Understanding of Material (Knowledge) | Ability to Demonstrate New Tools and Concepts (Skill) | Ability to Apply to New Situations (Application) |
|---|---|---|---|
| Lecture, information transfer | 80% | 10% | 0% |
| Demonstration, modeling | 100% | 30% | 0% |
| Practice, exercises | 100% | 70% | 20% |
| Exercises in application area | 100% | 90% | 50% |
| Coaching and review | 100% | 100% | 80% |

Consider the example of a skilled manager promoted to vice president of an operating unit that was responsible for transfer and scale-up of products from research and development to full production. She had four managers reporting to her. She immediately began establishing a culture of improvement in the department by establishing some department measures related to meeting schedules and problem-free transfer of products to production. Each of the four managers was required to have two improvement projects in his or her area. She used a workshop run by a central process improvement group to build the managers' skills. For two managers, the workshop was a review, and for the other two it was new material. After the workshop she coached each manager individually on how to set up a project with aims and measures, and suggested some change concepts that might apply to the project.

Every two weeks, she held a one-hour meeting with the managers and their supervisors. The standard agenda was:

• Discuss general company issues
• Review action items from the previous meetings
• Review department measures
• Make one or two presentations on the improvement projects led by the managers
• Give a short news brief from each area

In between meetings, she coached the managers on their projects. After about three months, three of the managers could run their projects without much guidance from her. One needed some extra support from her and a member of the central process improvement group. The managers began applying the same approach to developing their supervisors. Development of people in her department was integrated into her daily work and had a predictable rhythm to it. She used the training workshop as an aid to accomplish her development goals for the department but did not rely entirely on it.

At the end of this chapter, the reader will note three sample topical agendas. The agendas address these workshops:

1. Getting Started on Improvement Efforts (two-day agenda)
2. Sponsor Role in Identifying and Managing Improvement Projects (one day)
3. Development of Internal Improvement Advisors (five sessions, eighteen days)

## Organization to Support the Focus on Improvement

Before many individuals and teams begin participating in improvement, the management of the organization must prepare the organization for its participation. Listed below are three frequently asked questions that leaders pose as they begin the task of organizing to sustain the organization's approach to improvement. The answers to these questions depend on the current management style and the complexity of the organization.

### How do we organize to make continuous improvement part of our daily work?

From the collective experience of the authors, the preferred organization for improvement is the current management structure. The effort to integrate improvement into the normal organizational plans, goals, and strategies should begin as soon as possible. Improvement should be connected to real work for the organization. If improvement is viewed as an extra assignment or something in "addition to our normal work," the improvement projects will probably be delayed or not happen at all.

### What sort of additional structure do we need to ensure that our improvement efforts receive the guidance and sponsorship necessary for proper execution?

Although the preferred organization for improvement uses the current management structure, many organizations find the need to create additional structure in the beginning of the process. Some examples of this type of structure:

- Improvement management positions
- Facilitator positions (called improvement advisors or "black belts")
- Special teams or committees
- Steering committees or improvement councils

The amount of structure required depends on the strength of the leadership, the complexity of the organization, and its size. Figure 14.1 describes this conceptual relationship. The chart is a depiction of the general experience from several organizations that have been applying quality improvement as a business strategy.

Many larger organizations require additional structure in the early phases of improvement. As top management integrates the improvement effort with that of the business, there is less and less need for additional structure. Sometimes a need for "some" structure remains, even with excellent top management leadership, for coordination of efforts.

For smaller, less complex organizations, the need for additional structure is usually slight because line management can manage the activities early in the process.

Some organizations have gone as far as creating additional organizational structures specifically to manage the improvement process. A risk of this separate structure

## FIGURE 14.1. NEED FOR ADDITIONAL STRUCTURE OR POSITIONS FOR IMPROVEMENT.

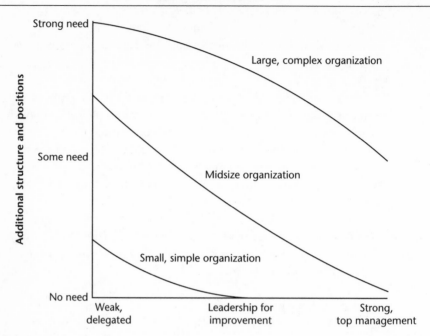

is that it can cause a result opposite from what was intended. Rather than making quality a focus for the business, it is now viewed as a committee activity. Instead of a cultural change in the "work organization," management time and effort are now dedicated to defining a set of norms for the "new" organization. These norms can be difficult to transfer into the work organization.

### Do we need additional people? If so, what types of positions will be needed?

Almost every organization that has begun an improvement process started with some type of added positions:

*   *Quality managers.* This would include the creation of management positions to coordinate the improvement effort and provide consultation and advice to management. Examples: vice president of quality, manager of quality improvement, quality coordinator, and director of quality. Sometimes the improvement effort is assigned to the position currently responsible for conformance, analysis, and reporting: the quality control and quality assurance function. Often, these positions are differentiated from the classic quality control and assurance departments.
*   *Internal advisors.* These advisors or facilitators normally fill the role of change agent and internal consultant to managers and teams. They are usually skilled

in working with teams, improvement tools, and philosophy. This position may be either full-time or part-time. In recent years, people who fill this role have sometimes been called black belts or improvement advisors.

- *Quality technology staff.* Many times these positions already exist in the quality control or quality assurance organization. The staff has experience and is generally skilled at using the improvement tools for problem solving, analysis, and reporting.
- *Improvement teams.* These are described in a variety of ways: quality circles, interdepartment teams, intradepartment teams, natural work groups, process improvement teams, diagnostic arm. Teams are generally used to involve people in improvement efforts.
- *Quality council (sponsors and champions).* The council usually consists of the senior management team plus some quality specialists. This group is responsible for leading the improvement effort.
- *Steering committees.* The typical steering committee is usually a group of managers who furnish coordination, guidance, and review of the improvement efforts. There are two basic approaches to creating committees:

  1. Use the current management structure
  2. Select managers from various levels and parts of the organization to serve in temporary roles

Organizations have used a mix of these various positions and groups to create a "structured" approach to improvement. As their process matures, many of these companies turn over more responsibility for improvement to line managers and away from auxiliary organizations.

# Development of Other Capabilities

People involved in improvement need access to data and information that enables them to create and bring knowledge to bear on circumstances in their work situations. In this section we discuss:

- Database and data analysis capabilities needed
- Capabilities to integrate knowledge into the system

## Database and Data Analysis Capabilities

Throughout the book, we have emphasized the collection and analysis of data for learning about processes, developing changes, and knowing whether a change is an improvement. In local improvement work, the necessary data can often by gathered in the course of daily work by using simple check sheets or hand-drawn charts.

However, as the scope of improvement grows from processes to larger systems to the entire organization, the collection of useful data becomes more scattered in various sites. Sometimes the data that are needed for large system improvement are not available. However, it is more common that the data are available in a database somewhere, but perhaps not conveniently available in the right form for use by the improvement team or manager. The database and the reports from it may have been designed and used for operating purposes but not for improvement. Enhancing the information technology applications to include convenient access to data for improvement is a component of building organizational capability. For example, in Chapter Ten one of the measures that was suggested under the category of eliminating quality problems was the number of products returned because they were damaged during shipment. No doubt any organization of reasonable size keeps track electronically of the shipments that were returned and generates electronically a replacement order to be used by operations to send the new shipment. It is less likely that these data are routinely aggregated and plotted electronically in a run chart or a control chart for use in reducing this defect.

Three principles for building database capability for improvement are described here.

*Design databases and reports from them to facilitate improvement of systems in addition to their primary use in operations.* It takes some forethought during the design or upgrade of an information system to decide what data might be useful for improvement. This is usually more efficient than requesting changes once the system has been designed or the upgrade is completed. For example, a teaching hospital (a hospital that is affiliated with a medical school) was implementing an electronic medical record, or EMR, to replace its traditional paper charts. Each department in the hospital decided what data on patient outcomes would be important to them (such as infections related to surgery for the orthopedics department) for improving performance or for doing research. These outcomes were added to the requirements for implementing the EMR.

*Make the information conveniently available to all who need it, including customers.* Information technology facilitates the connection of people in the system. The first priority is often to connect people inside the company to each other to facilitate efficiency of operations. Using the information system to connect the customer with operations can be an innovative improvement. For example, when one orders a product that is shipped by national distributors, it is possible to track progress of the shipment over the distributor's Website. Companies that use the distributors to ship their product can give the customer a link to the shipper's Website so that tracking the shipment is a seamless handoff of the customer from the company to the distributor.

*Electronically generate run charts and other formats that are useful for improvement.* Time series displays and tools for analysis that are described in this book may not be part of the standard reporting format of the information system. Building this capability into the information system prevents the wasteful practice of exporting data to a different system for analysis. Of course some tasks may require more sophisticated statistical analysis and customized statistical programs, but many of the routine analyses and displays can be done by general information systems.

## Capabilities to Diffuse Knowledge in the System

Organizations have increasingly come to understand the power of knowledge to make their organizations more effective and profitable. Within Hewlett Packard, the former CEO, Lew Platt, is often remembered for a quote relative to capturing and sharing knowledge:

> An intensive study of an effort to make a Hewlett Packard (HP) manufacturing unit more effective reported: "By interviewing thirteen such stakeholders from other departments, including procurement, process generation, engineering, and finance, design team members discovered that communication between departments was poor, thus limiting the degree to which they learned from each other.... Opportunities to share innovative process technologies or other sources of competitive advantage were being overlooked." The problems associated with transferring knowledge within HP have led Lew Platt, the CEO, to lament, "I wish we knew what we know at HP."

In Chapter Nine we discussed spreading improvements through a social system. In some cases connections between members of the system were made temporarily for a specific project. To build capability for knowledge transfer and spread of innovation, organizations have used a variety of methods to make social systems more permanent, even though the members of the group might not be in the same location or even on the same continent. Some of the methods:

- Periodic meetings by phone, video, or in person among people in the same function but divergent locations. If time is included in the agenda for the exchange of ideas for improvement, the meetings become a knowledge exchange rather than just an information exchange. In Chapter Nine, on spread, the meeting of the fabricators of kitchen counter tops was an example of routine knowledge exchange.
- Using a standard set of measures for quality and costs in different locations. If the organization has a culture of learning, then the side effects that result from

making comparative data transparent can be mitigated. The comparisons can then be used to begin inquiries among locations about variation in performance and its causes. These discussions are a method for learning at a deep level about the structures, operating rules, and processes in various locations and their effect on performance. A famous example in health care concerns a group of heart surgeons in New England who standardized their measures and then visited each other's hospitals to observe surgeries and discuss differences in performance. The results included a substantial decrease in deaths during or shortly after surgery.

- Multidisciplinary events that aid cross-fertilization between departments. These events might be quarterly or yearly meetings of top management, or they might be monthly meetings of several teams involved in a strategic initiative. For example, each year a large community college held an Innovation Fair at the end of the academic year. Administrative and academic departments submitted ideas and improvements in administrative processes, logistics, teaching, or curriculum design that they had implemented during the year. It became an event that celebrated the end of the year and attracted many people on campus. Through the event, knowledge developed in one department was spread to others.

- Make knowledge gained through testing changes readily accessible. In this book, we have used tools such as linkage of processes to make the system visible to those working in it. We have also used tools such as driver diagrams to make explicit the current theory about how to improve the system. If these tools are used as "living documents" containing the latest knowledge concerning a system and its performance, then they become an effective and efficient method of exchanging knowledge about complex topics.

## Key Points from Chapter Fourteen

- Integration of improvement as part of a business strategy requires substantial capability in the workforce. Development of this capability can proceed along parallel paths. The development of executives progresses through four phases: awareness, learning, implementation, and external promotion. Another path is the development of midlevel leaders of improvement, especially managers. These people are the building blocks on which the rest of the workforce can be developed. Methods for development of these leaders include a mix of practical experience with leading improvements mentored by an expert as well as attending seminars and conferences. The broader workforce is best developed by working on improvement in daily work guided by a skilled midlevel leader.

Mass training of the workforce unconnected to real improvement in daily work should be avoided.

- The most desirable structure for fostering improvement is the current management structure. At times it may be useful to have an auxiliary management structure such as a quality council, but one should be cautious about such structures adding bureaucracy rather than capability.
- The increasing importance of organizationwide information systems is another opportunity to build capability for improvement. These systems should be configured to produce data and graphs for use in improvement work. Finally, the capability to diffuse knowledge effectively in the organization builds on the methods discussed in Chapter Nine. Social systems that were used to spread specific changes as part of an improvement initiative can be strengthened so that spread of knowledge becomes a routine part of managing the organization.

# Sample Agendas for Getting Started, Sponsors, and Improvement Advisors

## Getting Started on Improvement Efforts (Two-Day Agenda)

### Day One

*Review from E-Learning and Prework*

- Review profound knowledge
- Team selection criteria
- Roles and responsibilities
- Team charters

*Introduce Model for Improvement*

- Use of tree or driver diagrams to focus and scope the project
- PDSA Cycles (review)
- Using quick multiple cycles to learn

*Workshop*

- Review draft charter for project
- Generate questions to answer
- Make predictions

*Understanding People Skills Workshop: Team Exercise*

- Decision making
- Discussion and dialogue
- Ladder of inference
- Trust and relationship model

*Workshop*

- Relationship awareness theory and conflict resolution in teams
- Develop team norms

*Assignment*

- Plan initial PDSA Cycles using identified grouping of questions

## Day Two: Testing Changes

Workshop: Testing to Learn Quickly

*Type of Changes*

- First- and second-order change
- Change categories
- Change concepts

*Workshop*

- Identify change concepts that apply to the project
- Develop specific changes to test
- Develop questions and predictions
- Update multiple cycle summary

*Use of Data for Improvement*

- Interpreting measures
- Special causes

*Workshop*

- Review charter measures
- Types of measures
- Develop measures for PDSA Cycles
- Document on multiple cycle summary

*Workshop*

- Identify all PDSA Cycles for testing
- Plan test cycles

*Assignment*

- Reference: e-learning courses 3–5
- Run assigned cycles

## Sponsor Role in Identifying and Managing Improvement Projects

### *(One Day) Agenda Review/Session Purpose*
*Review of Preparation Material*

- Improvement Guide
  - o Profound Knowledge
  - o Model for Improvement
  - o Building a System for Leaders
- Tame vs. Wicked Problems

*Project Selection*

- Sources of Improvement Projects
- Examples of Good/Poor Projects

*Workshop:*

- Connect Organizational Strategy to Needed Improvement Projects
  - o From formal organizational plans
  - o Goals and objectives (Driver Diagrams)

*Aligning Improvement Targets – Creating Improvement Charters*

- Improvement Categories – Align with Driver Diagram
- The Model for Improvement
- Write Improvement Charters

*Measurement: Ensure that Selected Charters will Accomplish Organizational Measures*

- Three Types of  Measures
- Ensure Portfolio of Projects with accomplish Organizational Goals and Objectives
- Update charters to reflect necessary measures and alignment

*Establish Resources for the Project and Define Necessary Roles*

- Team Selection
- Review Team Roles
  - o Sponsor Role
  - o Team Leader Role
  - o Individual Team Member Role
- Meeting & Reporting Frequency

*Workshop:*

- Estimate the potential financial/customer impact to the Organization
- Use the Evaluation Form and rate your Improvement Charter
- Revise your Improvement Charter based on the Evaluation results

*Assessing Improvement Progress*

- Team Progress Report Format
- Rating Improvement Plan Progress
- Assess Team Progress Examples.

*Managing Improvements*

- Integrating Improvement Reports into Existing Meetings
- Ensuring Results are Integrated into the Organizational System
- Recognizing Individual and Team Project Results

*Summary/Next Steps/Adjourn*

# Development of Internal Improvement Advisors: Topical Agenda

## Five Sessions (Eighteen Days)

### Session One: Getting Started (Four Days)
- Orientation to Improvement Advisor Workshop
- Review improvement charters
- Improvement advisor knowledge base
  - Psychology
  - Systems
  - Understanding variation
  - Theory of knowledge
- The Model for Improvement: Three fundamental questions
- The PDSA Cycle for learning and improvement cycle (card deck exercise)
- Relate improvement efforts to change, categories, concepts
  - First- and second-order change
  - Categories of improvement
  - Change concepts
- People Skills: relationship awareness theory
- Change management for improvement advisors
- Use of data
- Measures
  - Outcome, process, and balancing measures
  - Intensive and extensive measures
  - Identify data types for BB project
- Tools for gathering and organizing information
- Developing changes; critical thinking, creativity, automation, and change concepts
- Change concepts; application of concepts related to Lean
- Testing changes
- Plan for initial PDSA Cycles to be completed between sessions I and II

### Session Two: Systems Thinking and Analytic Methods to Understand Variation (Four Days)
- Systems thinking simulation
- Quality as a business strategy
  - Connecting improvement project to the organizational plan
  - Role of the improvement advisor
- Review documentation of first PDSA Cycles (selected)
- Introduction to variation (demonstrate bean machine)

- Tools for understanding variation (run charts, frequency plots, Pareto chart)
- Control charts
- Rational subgrouping
- Calculating capability from a stable process
  - CP, Cpk, Ppk Indices
- Selection of control chart workshop
- Capability and Six Sigma
- Visual display of data (other types of graphs)
- Project planning: PDSA Cycles during the next month

### Session Three: Creativity (Three Days)
- Creativity
- Six Hats
- Timing and sequences
- Lateral Thinking: Introduction
- Alternatives
- Focus
- Random entry
- Provocation, movement
- Harvesting and treatment
- Discussion of plans for projects

### Session Four: Design of Experiments (Four Days)
- Project reports (eight-minute presentation, five-minute discussion per improvement advisor
- Design of experiments overview (simulation)
- Application of data types, stability, and capability to improvement advisor projects
- Measurement processes
- Evaluating measurement processes (simulation application)
- Application to IA projects
- Planned experimentation (theory and one-factor experiments)
- Application to IA project team cycle 3
- One factor with background variables
- Review project PE planning form
- Multifactor experiments ($2^k$ factorial designs)
- Screening studies (fractional factorial designs)
- PE in product development (QFD overview)
- Other types of experiments
- Improvement advisor technical consulting

### Session Five: Enumerative and Analytic Studies in Statistics (Three Days)

- Enumerative vs. analytic studies
  - W. Edwards Deming's ideas on enumerative and analytic studies
- Using statistics to summarize data
- Standard distributions used to model data
- Statistical tests and drawing inferences; understanding the limitations of significance testing
- T-test, one mean; Is average delivery time within plus or minus fifteen minutes?
  - T-test, difference between two means
  - T-test, paired t-test
  - F-test
- Case study assignment: using enumerative and analytic methods
- Analysis of variance (ANOVA)
  - One-way (one factor, chemical process, three response variables)
  - Two-way
  - Fixed-effect ANOVA
- Nested factors
- Model building (GLM)
- Regression and correlation
- Coefficient of determination
- Regression analysis
- Multiple regression
- Review of enumerative methods and project applications

# APPENDIXES

# A RESOURCE GUIDE TO CHANGE CONCEPTS

Not all changes lead to improvement, but all improvement requires change. The ability to develop, test, and implement changes is essential for any individual, group, or organization that wants to continuously improve. But what kinds of changes will lead to improvement? Usually, a unique, specific change is required to obtain improvement for a specific set of circumstances. Thus there are many kinds of changes. These specific changes, however, are developed from a limited number of change concepts.

A *concept* is a general, abstract notion (approach, thought, belief, or perception) carried out through a more specific idea. A *change concept* is a general notion or approach to change found to be useful in developing specific ideas for changes that lead to improvement. Creatively combining these change concepts with specific subject matter knowledge can result in specific changes that have good system properties and do not require trade-offs between costs and quality.

This appendix enumerates seventy-two change concepts. The use of change concepts was introduced in Chapter Six, "Developing a Change." They are examined more specifically in several of the other chapters. Many of the change concepts can be derived by applications of W. Edwards Deming's System of Profound Knowledge, introduced in Chapter Four. Others have been collected over time by this book's authors. Several of the concepts are included in other approaches to improvement, such as Total Quality Management, Reliability, Safety, Six-Sigma, and Lean.

Regardless of the origin of the concepts, it is their usefulness to improvement that makes them valuable. This appendix organizes these ideas in one place for ease in reference and use. A complete list of the seventy-two change concepts is given here. How should they be used for any specific improvement effort? The next section offers some guidance.

## How to Use Change Concepts

The change concepts in this appendix are not specific enough to be applied directly to making improvements. Rather, the concept must be considered within the context of a specific situation and then turned into an idea. The idea needs to be specific enough to describe how the change can be tested and implemented in the specific situation. In describing the change concepts, we have tried to be consistent in the specificity or "degree of generality" of the concepts. Sometimes a new idea you have at first seems to be a new change concept. But often, with further thinking, you can see that the idea is an application of one of the more general concepts.

Some of the change concepts appear to offer conflicting advice for developing changes. Change concept 4, Reduce Controls on the System, and concept 51, Standardization (Create a Formal Process), are an example. The important consideration is the context in which the change concept is being considered. Standardization is appropriate for high-leverage processes, but it may be overkill for processes that are not leverage points for costs, capacity, or quality. In using a change concept to develop specific ideas for a change, understanding and knowledge of the particular circumstances will always be the determining factor concerning the appropriateness of the concept.

1. Eliminate things that are not used
2. Eliminate multiple entry
3. Reduce or eliminate overkill
4. Reduce controls on the system
5. Recycle or reuse
6. Use substitution
7. Reduce classifications
8. Remove intermediaries
9. Match the amount to the need
10. Use sampling
11. Change targets or set points
12. Synchronize
13. Schedule into multiple processes
14. Minimize handoffs
15. Move steps in the process close together
16. Find and remove bottlenecks
17. Use automation
18. Smooth workflow
19. Do tasks in parallel
20. Consider people as in the same system
21. Use multiple processing units
22. Adjust to peak demand
23. Match inventory to predicted demand
24. Use pull systems
25. Reduce choice of features
26. Reduce multiple brands of the same item
27. Give people access to information
28. Use proper measurements
29. Take care of basics
30. Reduce demotivating aspects of the pay system
31. Conduct training
32. Implement cross-training
33. Invest more resources in improvement
34. Focus on core process and purpose
35. Share risks
36. Emphasize natural and logical consequences
37. Develop alliances and cooperative relationships
38. Listen to customers
39. Coach the customer to use a product/service
40. Focus on the outcome to a customer
41. Use a coordinator
42. Reach agreement on expectations
43. Outsource for "free"
44. Optimize level of inspection
45. Work with suppliers
46. Reduce setup or startup time
47. Set up timing to use discounts
48. Optimize maintenance
49. Extend specialist's time
50. Reduce wait time
51. Standardization (create a formal process)
52. Stop tampering
53. Develop operation definitions
54. Improve predictions
55. Develop contingency plans
56. Sort product into grades
57. Desensitize
58. Exploit variation
59. Use reminders
60. Use differentiation
61. Use constraints
62. Use affordances
63. Mass customize
64. Offer product/service anytime
65. Offer product/service anyplace
66. Emphasize intangibles
67. Influence or take advantage of fashion trends
68. Reduce the number of components
69. Disguise defects or problems
70. Differentiate product using quality dimensions
71. Change the order of process steps
72. Manage uncertainty, not tasks

We make no claim to have included all of the useful change concepts that exist. (Note: we have added numbers 71 and 72 to the original list found in the first edition of this book.) As you use this appendix, try to develop more concepts. One way to discover concepts is to study the improvements recently made in your organization:

1. What was the specific change that was made?
2. What was the idea used for the change?
3. Where (who) did the idea come from?
4. Which of the change concepts could generate that idea?
5. Can the idea be generalized for other situations?
6. Would a new concept be useful to describe this idea for change?

The primary purpose of this appendix is to help individuals and teams who are trying to answer the question, "What change can we make that will lead to improvement?" The change concepts can provoke a new idea for an individual or team. A team leader can choose one of the concepts and then the team can explore some ideas for possible applications of this change concept to the situation of interest. The list of ideas should be recorded. After the generation of ideas is complete, a discussion and critique of the list can be done. Any of the ideas that show promise can be further enhanced by the team to obtain a specific idea for a change.

How do you select a particular change concept to be the focus of a session to generate ideas? The aim of the improvement effort will suggest some direction. Here are four ways that have been found useful:

- Choose a change concept that someone on the team thinks might contain some ideas that would be useful to the aim of the improvement effort.
- Choose change concepts not previously considered by the team.
- Randomly choose a change concept from the list of seventy-two. More creative ideas can be expected to come from a session because people might get further away from their usual thought processes.
- Select one from Table A.1, Applications of Change Concepts, using the category that best matches the aim of your improvement effort.

Table A.1 is laid out in a *what*, *where*, and *how* format. What are we trying to accomplish (for example, eliminate waste)? Where are we going to do it (design a process or system, or redesign)? How do we get the ideas for change from the list of change concepts? The list is divided into the three categories of improvement presented in Chapter Ten of the book, plus an additional category focused on managing people:

## TABLE A.1. APPLICATIONS OF CHANGE CONCEPTS.

| *WHERE:*<br>*WHAT: . . .* | *Design or redesign process or system* | *Design or redesign product or service* |
|---|---|---|
| **Eliminate Quality Problems (Category 1)** | | |
| Address customer problems | 38. Listen to customers<br>42. Reach agreement on expectations | 38. Listen to customers<br>39. Coach the customer to use a product/service<br>50. Reduce wait time |
| Meet customer expectations | 40. Focus on the outcome to a customer<br>44. Optimize level of inspection | 41. Use a coordinator<br>42. Reach agreement on expectations<br>57. Desensitize<br>58. Exploit variation |
| Eliminate mistakes | 59. Use reminders<br>60. Use differentiation<br>61. Use constraints<br>62. Use affordances | 59. Use reminders<br>60. Use differentiation<br>61. Use constraints<br>62. Use affordances |
| Manage variation | 51. Standardization (create a formal process)<br>52. Stop tampering<br>53. Develop operational definitions<br>54. Improve predictions<br>55. Develop contingency plans<br>56. Sort product into grades<br>57. Desensitize<br>58. Exploit variation<br>72. Manage uncertainty, not task | 9. Match the amount to the need<br>22. Adjust to peak demand<br>55. Develop contingency plans<br>56. Sort product into grades<br>57. Desensitize<br>58. Exploit variation<br>72. Manage uncertainty, not task |
| **Expanding Customer Expectations to Increase Demand (Category 3)** | | |
| Delight customers | 37. Develop alliances and cooperative relationships | 34. Focus on core processes and purpose<br>43. Outsource for "free"<br>63. Mass customization<br>64. Offer product/service anytime<br>65. Offer product/service anyplace<br>66. Emphasize intangibles<br>67. Influence or take advantage of fashion trends<br>70. Differentiate product using quality dimensions |
| **Manage People (Category 4)** | | |
| Change the work environment | 4. Reduce controls on the system<br>20. Consider people as in the same system | |

(continued)

## TABLE A.1. (*continued*)

| WHERE: | Design or redesign process or system | Design or redesign product or service |
|---|---|---|
| WHAT: . . . | | |

### Manage People (Category 4) (cont.)

27. Give people access to information
28. Use proper measurements
29. Take care of basics
30. Reduce demotivating aspects of the pay system
31. Conduct training
32. Implement cross-training
33. Invest more resources in improvement
34. Focus on core processes and purpose
35. Share risks
36. Emphasize natural and logical consequences
37. Develop alliances and cooperative relationships
49. Extend specialist's time

### Reduce Costs While Maintaining or Improving Quality (Category 2)

**Eliminate waste**

| |
|---|
| 1. Eliminate things that are not used |
| 2. Eliminate multiple entry |
| 3. Reduce or eliminate overkill |
| 4. Reduce controls on the system |
| 5. Recycle or reuse |
| 6. Use substitution (value engineering) |
| 7. Reduce classifications |
| 8. Remove intermediaries |
| 9. Match the amount to the need |
| 10. Use sampling |
| 11. Change targets or setpoints |
| 23. Match inventory to predicted demand |
| 48. Optimize maintenance |
| 50. Reduce wait time |

3. Reduce or eliminate overkill
5. Recycle or reuse
6. Use substitution
7. Reduce classifications
25. Reduce choices of features
50. Reduce wait time

**Improve work flow**

2. Synchronize
13. Schedule into multiple processes
14. Minimize handoffs
15. Move steps in the process close together
16. Find and remove bottlenecks

12. Synchronization
13. Schedule into multiple processes
18. Smooth workflow
19. Do tasks in parallel
21. Use multiple processing units
22. Adjust to peak demand

|  | | |
| --- | --- | --- |
| | 17. Use automation | |
| | 18. Smooth workflow | |
| | 19. Do tasks in parallel | |
| | 20. Consider people as in the same system | |
| | 21. Use multiple processing units | |
| | 22. Adjust to peak demand | |
| | 41. Use a coordinator | |
| | 46. Reduce setup or startup time | |
| | 48. Optimize maintenance | |
| | 71. Change the order of process steps | |
| Decrease cycle time | 4. Reduce controls on the system | 19. Do tasks in parallel |
| | 19. Do tasks in parallel | 23. Match inventory to predicted demand |
| | 23. Match inventory to predicted demand | |
| | 24. Use pull systems | |
| | 46. Reduce setup or startup time | |
| Reducing costs | 43. Outsource for "free" | 7. Reduce classifications |
| | 44. Optimize level of inspection | 25. Reduce choices of features |
| | 45. Work with suppliers | 26. Reduce multiple brands of same item |
| | 47. Set up timing to use discounts | 68. Reduce the number of component parts |
| | | 69. Disguise defects or problems |

Category 1: Eliminate quality problems

Category 2: Reduce costs while maintaining or improving quality

Category 3: Expand customer expectations by offering products and services that customers perceive as unusually high in value

Category 4: Manage people

Selection of the specific change concept can be done by starting in any one of the four categories.

# The Change Concepts

In this section, each change concept is discussed in numerical order (from Table A.1). The category for improvement is included along with a short description of the concept and one or two applications of improvements to process, system, product, or service.

# 1. Eliminate Things That Are Not Used

*(Reducing costs while maintaining or improving quality)* Constant change in organizations results in less demand for specific resources and activities that were once important to the business. Unnecessary activities and unused resources can be identified through surveys, audits, data collection, and analysis of records. The next step is to take the obvious actions to remove the unused elements from the system.

*Design or redesign process or system. A manufacturing company conducted an audit of the tools, equipment, and supplies in the organization. They found that almost one-half of these items were no longer useful. They sold, recycled, or scrapped the unnecessary tools and supplies. Not only did this reduce inventory costs but the actions freed up space and allowed better arrangement of stored materials.*

*Design or redesign process or system. A service organization conducted an audit of all the meetings and reports that occurred in the organization. For each meeting and report they answered these questions: When was this meeting or report initiated? How does this meeting or report help our external customers? Are there other compelling reasons to conduct this meeting or produce this report? From analysis of the data from this audit, one-third of the meetings and 20 percent of the reports were eliminated.*

*Design or redesign process or system. The financial department spent about 700 worker-hours each quarter collecting data from the organization and updating the financial forecast for the year. At one time, these updates were used by managers in decision making and planning. But about three years ago, the managers began to rely on analysis of historical data to develop and update their forecasts. The quarterly input collected from the finance group had not been used for the past two years. After this realization, the financial manager eliminated the quarterly updates and dedicated the resources to analysis of pricing and other business decisions.*

# 2. Eliminate Multiple Entry

*(Reducing costs while maintaining or improving quality)* In some situations, information is recorded in a log or entered into a database more than one time, creating no added value. This is also called data redundancy. Changing the process to require only one entry can lead to improvement in productivity and quality (by reducing discrepancies). Recent technology developments (such as optical scanners) make it possible to enter data directly from sight or by voice. Once data are recorded, there should be no reason to reenter the same information at a latter time.

*Design or redesign process or system. Currently the production and accounting departments enter the same data in two computer systems. A common database (with entry only at original source) was established; both departments use this database for their analysis and reports. Staff were then reassigned to value-added activities.*

*Design or redesign process or system. A law firm created central files so that everyone could access data and written documents. This eliminated the need for the development and maintenance of individual files in each lawyer's office.*

## 3. Reduce or Eliminate Overkill

*(Reducing costs while maintaining or improving quality)* In many organizations, a common reaction to a special problem is to add more resources to the process, product, or service so the problem will not recur if the special situation arises again. Although this can be effective in solving quality problems, the result is overkill, with higher costs and lower productivity every time the process is run, the service is conducted, or the product is produced. Changing the standard to the appropriate amount of resources for the normal situation (minimum) will reduce waste. Use additional resources only when the situation requires it.

*Design or redesign process or system. A hospital explored opportunities to reduce waste. First they eliminated overuse of technologies such as MRI and ultrasound by placing them outside the normal treatment process. Then they eliminated automatic daily lab tests for patients in the hospital and multiple tests that add no new information. They were able to reduce blood assays required for a particular situation from twenty-three to five. The principle they began to focus on was to reduce the sampling and testing frequency for any process that is working as it is supposed to.*

*Design or redesign process or system. A production services company required two days to heat-treat steel parts because a thirty-six-hour processing requirement had been the practice for the past twenty-three years. The company's engineers designed a series of experiments and learned that processing times of twelve to twenty hours were enough to meet customers needs (except for a few situations that represented less than 1 percent of their business). By specifying target times to meet needs of the various products, the company more than doubled its capacity and offered one-day turnaround to most customers.*

## 4. Reduce Controls on the System

*(Reducing costs while maintaining or improving quality, or managing people)* Individuals and organizations use various types of controls to make sure a process or system does not stray too far from standards, requirements, or accepted practices. Though useful for protection of the organization, these controls can increase costs, reduce productivity, and potentially stifle improvement. Typical forms of controls are a layered management structure, approval signatures, standardized forms, and reports. A regular review of all of the organization's control procedures by everyone working in the system can result in identifying opportunities to reduce controls on the system without putting the organization at risk.

*Design or redesign process or system. The travel department reviewed its control requirements. It was currently requiring receipts for all charges before reimbursement. This resulted in many call-backs and delays in payment. They changed the procedure to not require receipts for charges less than $25. This eliminated about one-half of the delays in reimbursement.*

*Design or redesign process or system. An organization did a thorough review of existing forms, reports, meetings, and procedures and identified things done primarily for control purposes. Staff then decided what minimum levels of control were required and redesigned the activities and reports to meet these minimum levels. They found that many of the midlevel management functions were focused on control activities.*

## 5. Recycle or Reuse

*(Reducing costs while maintaining or improving quality)* Once a product is created and used for its intended purpose, it is natural to discard it and the by-products created by its use. But if other uses can be found for the discarded product or by-products, the cost to produce the product can be spread out over its use and reuse. As environmental issues concerning disposal of materials become more critical, organizations will be reassessing the costs associated with throwing away materials. Many times, recycling is found to be a cost-effective alternative. Design engineers in most manufacturing companies are learning how to "do green design" and "design for disassembly."

In developing new products, design the products as components or modules with a plan for reuse. Computer programs can be developed from a set of modules of computer code that perform specific tasks such as sorting data, plotting data, etc. Scaffolding at a construction site can be designed for easy disassembly for reuse at the next site. The ease of *destruction* of a product is becoming just as important as ease of construction.

*Design or redesign process or system. A manufacturing organization had a significant monthly cost from waste water. They studied all of their processes that generated waste water. From this analysis, they were able to make changes in operating practices to generate 12 percent less waste water and reuse 20 percent of the waste water in other processes.*

*Design or redesign product or service. A camera manufacturing company designed a camera in the late 1980s that could be thrown away after a roll of film was taken. Hundreds of thousands of these cameras ended up in landfills. The company engineers redesigned the camera for disassembly and component reuse; they converted the disposable camera to a recyclable camera. Eighty-seven percent of the camera (by weight) is now reused or recycled. This redesigned product became the company's fastest-growing and most profitable product.*

## 6. Use Substitution

*(Reducing costs while maintaining or improving quality)* Waste can often be reduced by replacing some aspect of the product or process with a better alternative. One type of substitution is to include lower-cost components, materials, or methods that do not affect the performance of the process, service, or product (this is sometimes called value engineering). Another type of substitution is to switch to another process with fewer steps, less manual effort, and so on.

*Design or redesign product or service.* *Timber prices doubled in the last ten years, adding as much as $5,000 to the cost of a typical house. Environmental issues make the prospect of higher lumber prices more likely in the future. What are the alternatives to wood in framing a house? The housing industry is looking at steel. Steel has many advantages (against fire, warping, rotting, termites, and so on), but only since the recent price increases in lumber has it become an attractive alternative for building a house. The biggest drawback is unfamiliarity with using steel. Recently, a housing industry survey showed that one-third of builders planned to try using steel in the home building process.*

*Design or redesign process or system.* *Changes in precious metal prices were increasing the catalyst costs of a commodity chemical manufacturer. They developed alternative formulations that could be substituted for their catalysts as prices in the metals fluctuated.*

## 7. Reduce Classifications to Remove Complexity

*(Reducing costs while maintaining or improving quality)* Classifications are often developed to differentiate elements of a system or to group items with common characteristics. But these classifications can lead to complexity in a system that increases costs or decreases quality. Reduce classifications if the complexity caused from the classifications is worse than the benefit gained.

*Design or redesign product or service.* *A commodity chemical company developed sixty-eight grades to try differentiating its products from its competitors and help market the product to new customers. These "special grades" did not result in premium pricing. But the grades required complex production schemes, excessive inventory, and late deliveries (about 15 percent). A joint production and marketing team studied the grade slate and recommended that they produce and sell twelve grades that would meet the needs of all except one of their existing customers. For that customer, they offered to produce a product at a premium price. Manufacturing productivity increased, inventory costs decreased, and late deliveries were reduced to fewer than 2 percent of shipments.*

*Design or redesign product or service.* *A concert hall sold twelve classifications of tickets, each for a different price. Anytime someone attempted to purchase tickets, a lengthy explanation of the classifications was required. Regular customers complained that the ticket type they wished to purchase was never available. The theater developed three classifications, resulting in less hassle and fewer customer complaints.*

## 8. Remove Intermediaries

***(Reducing costs while maintaining or improving quality)*** Intermediaries such as distributors, handlers, agents, and carriers are currently part of many production and service systems. Consider eliminating these activities by linking production directly with the consumer. Some intermediaries add value to a process because of their specialized skills and knowledge. But many times, eliminating these services can increase productivity without reducing value to the customer.

   ***Design or redesign process or system.*** *A manufacturer of floor coverings sold its products through a network of independent dealer-installers. Consumers buying the flooring experienced high markup and a waiting time of a month or more. When large home center chains developed as a place where do-it-your-selfers bought home improvement products, the manufacturer established relationships directly with these retail centers to sell its products. The manufacturer provided displays for the flooring products, trained the salespeople, and managed the inventory for the home centers. Sales of the products have increased dramatically by selling directly to retail market.*

   ***Design or redesign product or service.*** *A popular restaurant chain established an in-house credit system for regular customers rather than rely on credit card companies or banks. The savings in credit fees more than offset the increased costs of billing and collections.*

   ***Design or redesign process or system.*** *For a number of years, a chemical plant focused on standardizing equipment and supplies purchased from industrial distributors. Through this standardization, they were currently buying from one or two supplier items such as valves, fitting, pumps, seals, pipe, and so on. Because of their knowledge of the suppliers, they did not need the level of expertise formally required of their distributors. They consolidated all of their nonstandard purchases with one industrial supplier and began purchasing directly from the supplier for the standard items. They were able to reduce their total equipment and supply purchasing costs by 5 percent. By working directly with the supplier, they were also able to get better service and get one key supplier involved with a joint improvement effort.*

## 9. Match the Amount to the Need

***(Reducing costs while maintaining or improving quality, or eliminating quality problems)*** By studying patterns of use by customers, one can adjust products and services to match the amount required for a particular situation. This reduces waste and carryover inventory.

   ***Design or redesign product or service.*** *Medical supplies come in standard packages of six units. Physicians want to give a week's supply (seven units), so they are forced to give two packs of six. Five of the units often ended up being wasted. After study of this* *application and other uses of the supplies, the manufacturer developed three standard package sizes: four, seven, and ten units.*

    ***Design or redesign process or system.*** *A recreational facility reserved tennis courts in blocks of one hour. Study of playing patterns found that most groups wanted to play for seventy-five to ninety minutes. Groups would typically reserve the courts for two hours, but for the last thirty to forty-five minutes the court was often not used. They changed the reservation system to schedule in blocks of one-half hour. This reduced the wasted court time and allowed more players to use the facility.*

## 10. Use Sampling

    *(Reducing costs while maintaining or improving quality)* Reviews, checks, and measurements are made for a variety of reasons. Can these reasons be satisfied without checking or testing everything? Many times, standard 100 percent inspection and testing results in waste of resources and time. Formal sampling procedures are available that can often provide information as good as or even better than 100 percent checking does.

    ***Design or redesign process or system.*** *The infection control group in a hospital estimated the infection rate in the hospital by following up on every positive culture to see if it was an infection. They then used the concept of sampling to change this process. They began to take a sample of twenty positive cultures each day and estimate the infection rate from the samples.*

    ***Design or redesign process or system.*** *Insurance companies have a requirement of prehospital screening of all patients by an insurance company before allowing admission to a hospital. After review of the costs and quality hassles that resulted from this screening, they began to sample patients and determine reasons for inappropriate hospitalization. On the basis of the information from this sample, they made monthly recommendations to improve the process for admitting patients.*

## 11. Change Targets or Setpoints

    *(Reducing costs while maintaining or improving quality)* Sometimes problems go on for years because some piece of equipment is not designed or set up properly. Make sure process settings are at desirable levels. Investigate places where waste is created, and consider adjustments to targets or set points to reduce the waste.

    ***Design or redesign process or system.*** *The machine operator found that about 10 percent of the parts he was cutting had excessive burrs and required a rework step in the process. After talking to some of the engineers about the causes of burrs, he adjusted the coolant and speed settings on the saw he operated. Burrs were reduced to fewer than 2 percent of the parts.*

*Design or redesign process or system.* *The custodian noticed that the white paper recycle boxes in one of the copier rooms filled up almost every day. In the other similar rooms, the boxes were usually not full after a week. After the custodian mentioned this to his friend Robert, one of the managers on that floor, an investigation was done. Robert found that almost everyone who made copies would throw away the first two or three copies, adjust the machine, and redo these copies. A few individuals would immediately adjust the machine before starting to copy. After talking to some of the users, Robert found that the default setting on the copier was not making the copies dark enough. He adjusted the light-dark setting on the copier to a default value more appropriate for most copies. The problem of wasted paper (and waste of people's time) went away.*

## 12. Synchronization

*(Reducing costs while maintaining or improving quality)* Products and services are produced by processes. Are the various stages or steps in the process arranged and prioritized to obtain quality outcomes at low costs? These stages operate at different times and speeds, resulting in an operation that is not smooth. Much time can be spent waiting for another stage. By focusing on the flow of the product (or customer) through the process, all of the stages can be brought into harmony. Changes developed from this concept include the use of just-in-time inventory practices, linking parallel activities during the process and developing timing of events to match the predicted flow of the process.

*Design or redesign product or service.* *The final closing on real estate transactions usually involve buyers, sellers, agents, brokers, bankers, title companies, and lawyers. "Closing day" is usually very stressful for the buyer and seller. One real estate company formed a team with a title company and financing organization to take the hassle out of the closing. They studied typical flows of activities that led up to the closing and developed a standard synchronized system to bring all of the required activities and information together for the closing. By cooperating to support this standard process, they were able to take the stress out of closing day.*

*Design or redesign process or system.* *When a commercial airplane arrives at the gate, the ground crew assists in the docking and preparation for unloading. Some airlines wait until a plane has arrived before discharging the ground crew to assist. This results in frustrated passengers standing in the aisles after a long trip, waiting for the door to open. One airline synchronized the ground crew so that they could open the door immediately when the plane touched the gate. This resulted in a noticeable difference to passengers in waiting time.*

## 13. Schedule into Multiple Processes

*(Reducing costs while maintaining or improving quality)* A system can be redesigned to include multiple versions of the same process focused on the specific requirements of the situation. Rather than a "one-size fits all" large process,

multiple versions of the process are available, each tuned to the needs of customers or users. Priorities can be established to allocate and schedule the inputs to maximize the performance of the system. The specific processes can then be greatly simplified because they address only a limited range of input requirements. This change concept should be considered only if the requirements, cycle times, and so on differ significantly.

*Design or redesign product or service. An airline in a large airport required twenty check-in stations during peak hours. They developed multiple processes for passengers with differing needs: baggage check-in only, buying tickets, checking in for the next flight to leave, and another for members of the airline's frequent flyer club. This system improved the flow of passengers through the check-in system.*

*Design or redesign process or system. An improvement team focused on increasing efficiency and effectiveness in the emergency department. They improved the triage system to better prioritize medical urgency. Patients could then be directed to the appropriate team and location to handle their care.*

## 14. Minimize Handoffs

*(Reducing costs while maintaining or improving quality)* Many systems require that elements (a customer, a form, a product) be transferred to multiple people, offices, or work stations to complete the processing or service. The handoff from one stage to the next can increase time and costs and cause quality problems. The workflow can be rearranged to minimize any handoff in the process. Redesign the process so that any worker is only involved one time in an iteration of a process. Making changes in organization structure or position descriptions is one type of change that can be used to minimize handoffs. For example, we can reduce layers of management that require multiple reviews, meetings, and approvals. We can expand clerical jobs to include scheduling, staffing, planning, and analysis. Or we can cross-train workers to handle many functions rather than be specialists in one specific function.

*Design or redesign process or system. An automotive service organization had trouble with completing work by the promised time. Cars were backed up on the lot waiting for the next technician to do their specialty. Over a two-year period, the technicians were cross-trained in the ten most-demanded services. Now, a car can be repaired with one pass in the service center at one station rather than shuttling it in and out of the service center. Cycle time for repairs decreased by one-half.*

*Design or redesign process or system. A hospital redesigned patient transfer processes to minimize handoffs of patients. Some patients can now be admitted directly to the intensive care unit after surgery rather than to a postanesthesia care unit and then to ICU. These and similar changes to other transfer processes resulted in higher patient satisfaction with services and lower costs for the hospital.*

## 15. Move Steps in the Process Close Together

*(Reducing costs while maintaining or improving quality)* The physical location of people and facilities can affect processing time and cause communication problems. If we move the physical location of adjacent steps in a process close together, work can be directly passed from one step to the next. This eliminates the need for communication systems (such as mail) and physical transports (such as vehicles, pipelines, and conveyor belts).

The result of moving steps closer together can be lower capital and maintenance costs, reduced inventory (especially work in process), and more frequent improvement (from better communication). If it is not possible to physically move steps in a process together, electronic hookups should be considered. For some processes, computer networks with common file structures can have an effect similar to physically moving the steps together.

***Design or redesign process or system.*** *Social services, such as drug abuse counseling, teen pregnancy prevention, Medicaid registration, public health clinics, and unemployment services, were spread throughout a large city in separate buildings. The customers of these services were often the same people, or from the same family. The services were reorganized into centers that provided a range of services. This allowed the city to cut costs of these programs through reduction of overlap and shared administrative support and equipment. It also gave the customers more convenient access to the services.*

***Design or redesign process or system.*** *A company that sold its products by catalogue moved the order takers and those who shipped the product into the same area; previously they were on different floors. This eliminated the time it took to walk up and down stairs when there was a need to exchange information or check on an order. It also facilitated a smoother flow of orders through the entire system.*

## 16. Find and Remove Bottlenecks

*(Reducing costs while maintaining or improving quality)* A bottleneck or constraint is anything that restricts the throughput of a system. A constraint within an organization would be any resource where the demand for that resource is greater than its available capacity. To increase the throughput in a system, the constraints must be identified, exploited if possible, and removed if necessary. Bottlenecks occur in many parts of our lives: exiting a concert hall, rush-hour traffic, channeling through the telephone receptionist, or funneling past the cashier in a cafeteria line. You can usually find bottlenecks by looking at where people are waiting or where work is piling up.

***Design or redesign process or system.*** *The Department of Motor Vehicles required everyone to go through a series of steps to renew a driver's license: complete form, take eye* *test, have picture taken, pay fee, and pick up new license. Citizens regularly complained about having to wait in long lines. Rather than hire additional workers, the department manager began collecting data on the length of the line at each station. She redesigned the process at the step with the longest line to reduce the time required. She then focused on other steps as they became the chronic bottleneck. She also established two floater employees to assist at the particular bottleneck on a given day.*

*Design or redesign process or system. The company's reports were not getting to customers in the time period promised. The manager of the unit looked around to see where the work was piling up. He found that word processing was the bottleneck. He spent time with the people in word processing and discovered more than one-half of their time was spent in updating and reworking reports. He was able to remove the bottleneck by redistributing responsibilities for updating the reports. The timeliness of the reports improved.*

## 17. Use Automation

*(Reducing costs while maintaining or improving quality)* The flow of many processes can be improved by the intelligent use of automation. Consider automation to improve the workflow for any process to reduce costs, shorten cycle times, eliminate human slips, cut repetitive manual tasks, and provide measurement.

*Design or redesign process or system. A hospital developed a system to automate the completion of many forms required by the various departments in the hospital, by the customer, and by the insurance companies. They recorded patient records electronically and then were able to generate completed forms for transfer to the interested parties.*

*Design or redesign process or system. A potato chip manufacturer had a reputation with customers of no discolored chips in the product. Because some discoloration was fundamental to the process, inspection was required. Manual inspection was expensive and imperfect, and the job was boring. The company developed optical inspection equipment that could be put on the production line to find and remove defective potato chips. This use of automation decreased costs, increased the quality of this product to customers, and improved staff satisfaction.*

## 18. Smooth Work Flow

*(Reducing costs while maintaining or improving quality)* Changes in demand often cause workflow to fluctuate widely at various times of the year, month, week, or day. Rather than try staffing to handle the peak demands, steps can often be taken to better distribute the demand. This results in a smooth workflow rather than recurring peaks and valleys.

*Design or redesign product or service. People complained that they had a long wait to get a safety inspection at a gas station. A study of the system found that safety inspections have a rush period during the last week of each month (when the sticker expires). Rather than add capacity (license additional stations), the state government changed the regulations to allow an increased charge at end of month with a lesser charge during the first three weeks of the month. Each gas station could then use the fee structure to balance the inspection work demand during the month.*

**Design or redesign process or system.** *A landscaping company's busiest time was in the spring. Workers could not keep up with requested work during that time. They studied the type of work they did throughout the year, identifying a number of activities (trimming of trees, fertilizing, soil preparation, preparing beds, and supporting indoor plants) that could be done in other time periods. They developed packages of services that would spread this work throughout the year. They were able to increase their capacity without adding new resources.*

## 19. Do Tasks in Parallel

*(Reducing costs while maintaining or improving quality)* Many systems are designed so that tasks are done in series or a linear sequence; the second task is not begun until the first task is completed. This is especially true when different groups in the organization are involved in the steps of a process. Sometimes improvements in time and costs can be gained from designing the system to do some or all tasks in parallel. For example, the work on step 5 can begin as soon as step 1 is complete rather than waiting until steps 2, 3, and 4 are done.

**Design or redesign product or service.** *Customers complained about having to wait while their invoice and other paperwork was prepared. The service organization redesigned its system to begin processing the paperwork while the service was being conducted. As soon as the service technician completed the work, a release was entered in the computer system and preparation of the invoice and other paperwork was begun. The paperwork was usually ready when the customer arrived at checkout.*

**Design or redesign product or service.** *A restaurant developed its business concept around fast service of high-quality food. They designed the system to take the customers' order before they were seated. Then work on seating, drinks, and meal preparation could all begin in parallel. By the time the customers were seated and served drinks, the meal was well on its way to being prepared.*

## 20. Consider People in the Same System

*(Reducing costs while maintaining or improving quality, or managing people)* People in systems are usually working toward differing purposes, all trying to optimize their own system. Taking actions that help people think of themselves as part of the same system can give them a common purpose and constitute a basis for optimizing the larger system.

**Design or redesign process or system.** *A company had trouble with on-time deliveries from suppliers. After discussions and data sharing with the key suppliers, staff realized that their irregular ordering patterns made planning very difficult for the suppliers. They began to* *share their production forecasts with the suppliers so they could develop plans compatible with the manufacturing company. They tested this with five key suppliers for one year and saw a dramatic reduction in late deliveries.*

  **Design or redesign process or system.** *A clinic and the nearby hospital had different identification systems for physicians. This resulted in duplicating work and numerous coding errors. At the encouragement of the doctors, they worked together to develop a common ID system. This decreased costs, reduced error corrections, and helped communication.*

## 21. Use Multiple Processing Units

*(Reducing costs while maintaining or improving quality)* To gain flexibility in controlling the workflow, try to have multiple work stations, machines, processing lines, fillers, and so forth in a system. This makes it possible to run smaller lots, serve special customers, minimize the impact of maintenance and downtime, and add flexibility to staffing. With multiple units, the primary product or service can be handled on one line to maximize efficiency and minimize set-up time. The less frequent products and services can be handled by the other units.

  **Design or redesign process or system.** *After studying alternative designs, a soup processing plant decided to build three smaller filler lines rather than one large one. This gave them more flexibility in filling a variety of soups on any day by reducing clean-up and setup time between changeovers.*

  **Design or redesign process or system.** *A print shop wanted to offer faster turnaround services to maintain and attract customers. Employees redesigned their facility using five smaller copiers rather than two large copiers. They generated faster turnaround for 92 percent of their jobs with the new system.*

## 22. Adjust to Peak Demand

*(Reducing costs while maintaining or improving quality, or eliminating quality problems)* Sometimes it is not possible to balance the demands on a system. In these cases, rather than keep a fixed amount of resources (materials, workers, and so on), historical data can be used to predict peak demands. Then methods to temporarily meet the demand can be implemented.

  **Design or redesign process or system.** *The hospital staff could not keep up with the demand for drawing blood samples from patients. Rather than just add staff, they studied the demand for taking blood samples. The data showed a peak demand from 6:00 to 8:00 a.m. every day. This peak created a backlog that was not cleared up until the afternoon. They established part-time positions for people to draw blood each morning. This eliminated the backlog.*

  **Design or redesign product or service.** *A new restaurant expected peak demand periods during the lunch and dinner hours of the day. The owners designed their service jobs* *around these peak periods and hired people who were comfortable working just during these hours. Most of the service positions would work from 11:00 to 2:00 and from 5:00 to 10:00 each day. This system of work hours eliminated potential problems from the peak demand periods. They had a backlog of job applicants of college students and others who could benefit from the hours.*

## 23. Match Inventory to Predicted Demand

***(Reducing costs while maintaining or improving quality)*** Inventory of all types is a possible source of waste in organizations. Inventory requires capital investment, storage space, and people to handle and keep track of it. In manufacturing organizations, inventory includes raw material waiting to be processed, in-process inventory, and finished good inventory. For service organizations, the number of skilled workers available is often the key inventory issue. Extra inventory can result in higher costs with no improvement in performance for an organization. An understanding of where inventory piles up in the system is the first step in finding opportunities for improvement. The use of inventory pull systems such as just-in-time is one philosophy of operating an organization to minimize the waste from inventory.

One approach to minimizing the costs associated with inventory is to use historical data to predict the demand. Use these predictions to replenish inventory economically (lead times, order quantities, and so on). This is often the best approach to optimizing inventory if there are long production times involved in the process.

***Design or redesign process or system.*** *An automotive dealership used the judgment of the sales staff to decide what styles of cars to order every week. Many times cars were not sold within ninety days after they were available, and cars with particular colors and features that the customer requested were not available. The company studied historical demands for each type and style of car. From this analysis, they developed a model to predict the demand for the next ninety days. They then used this model to guide order decisions. After six months of using the new model, they were able to cut inventory costs and do fewer dealer trades for other cars.*

***Design or redesign process or system.*** *An office supply warehouse had inventory problems because of long lead times on specialty items. Over the years, inventory costs had steadily increased because purchasing would automatically increase lead time or order in larger quantities whenever a shortage occurred. An effort was made to study historical order patterns for the twelve product lines with the highest inventory costs. They found some seasonal patterns as well as a number of special purchases in the historical data. After adjusting the data for these special orders, they developed predictions of monthly orders for each product line. Orders were placed on the basis of these predictions. These changes resulted in reduced inventory costs and fewer shortages during the next year. A plan was made to extend this process to fifty more product lines.*

## 24. Use Pull Systems

*(Reducing costs while maintaining or improving quality)* In a "pull" system of production, work is done at a particular step in the process only if the next step in the process is demanding the work. Enough product is ordered or made to replenish what was just used. This is in contrast to most traditional "push" systems where work is done so long as inputs are available. A pull system is designed to match production quantities with a downstream need. This often results in lower inventories than a schedule-based production system. Pull systems are most beneficial in processes with short cycle times and high yields. Some features of effective pull systems are small lot sizes and container quantities, fast setup times, and minimal rework and scrap.

Concepts 23 and 24 seem to offer two conflicting approaches to optimizing inventory. Matching inventory to predicted demand is most appropriate if cycle times for production or assembly are long. In these situations, it is not acceptable to wait until an order is received to begin production. The use of pull systems is more appropriate when production times are short. These two concepts might be combined to develop an optimum inventory strategy.

*Design or redesign process or system. A company introduced a system of manufacturing based on the idea that plants manufacture products as customers order them. Suppliers deliver the required components directly to the assembly line. This reduces the need to stock these component parts, and because product is shipped as ordered there is no need for a large inventory of finished goods. Using this approach, the company reduced its inventories by more than 50 percent. By saving interest payments on supplies, the company has also increased its cash flow.*

*Design or redesign process or system. The staffing of nurses in a hospital can be studied as an inventory problem. Each floor wants to maintain a staff of nurses available to meet routine and emergency needs twenty-four hours per day. Because of the variety of skills required, overstaffing is often the result. One hospital cross-trained (change concept 32) its nurses to be able to work in all areas of the hospital. They then created a hospital pool of nurses on each shift. A floor would staff to meet routine needs according to patient census. Additional help for new patients and emergencies was obtained from the nursing pool. This pull-system approach resulted in a 15 percent reduction in nursing costs.*

## 25. Reduce Choices of Features

*(Reducing costs while maintaining or improving quality)* Many features are added to products and services to accommodate desires and wants of diverse customers and markets. Each feature makes sense in the context of a particular customer at a particular time. But taken as a whole, these features can have tremendous

impact on inventory costs. A review of current demand for each feature and consideration of grouping the features can allow a reduction in inventory without loss of customer satisfaction.

***Design or redesign product or service.*** *A sandwich wagon took prepackaged sandwiches to job sites and sold them to workers for lunch. They had to stock a large number of sandwiches to maintain a supply of all of the varieties customers requested, so they usually threw away about 15 percent of their stock every day. From high, consistent demand, they changed the distribution process to minimize the number of varieties offered. One-half of the sandwiches were prepared as before. The other half did not have condiments and extras (cheese, tomatoes, peppers, and the like) on the sandwich. A table at the end of the lunch wagon contained these extras so that customers could customize their sandwich as desired. After two weeks with the new system, inventory waste was reduced to about 3 percent, with no change in sales.*

***Design or redesign product or service.*** *A manufacturer of personal computers wanted to improve both delivery time and inventory costs for their dealers. They also wanted to maintain the high level of customer satisfaction they had obtained by offering customers the features they wanted. They studied the last six months' demand for features on all of their models. From this analysis, they were able to design a standard model that could accommodate about 80 percent of all orders without an increase in costs; they eliminated a few of the features that were rarely ordered. They asked their dealers to stock only these standard models. Then they designed their assembly system to offer two-day delivery on the expected 20 percent custom orders. These changes resulted in reduced inventory costs and reduced delivery times for about 80 percent of their sales.*

## 26. Reduce Multiple Brands of the Same Items

***(Reducing costs while maintaining or improving quality)*** If an organization uses more than one brand of any particular item, inventory costs will usually be higher than necessary because a backup supply of each brand must be kept. Consider ways to reduce the number of brands while still providing the required service. This concept is applicable to manufacturing, wholesalers, and retail establishments.

***Design or redesign product or service.*** *A grocery store stocks eight brands of bread. In reviewing their customer feedback, "product out of stock" was one of the biggest complaints. Because of the large number of brands, they could afford to stock only a minimum of inventory for each brand. A quality improvement team surveyed customers and studied buying patterns for bread over the next three months. They then reduced the brands offered to three and developed inventory levels for the three brands that would make the chance of a stockout very small. Total inventory shrank; customer complaints about stockouts for bread were greatly reduced. A few customers were disappointed in losing their favorite brand, but they were offered an explanation and coupons for the brands of bread now stocked.*

*__Design or redesign process or system.__ A chemical plant uses seven brands of pump seals in its plant. They had to maintain inventories of every size for every brand. An engineering group studied the specification process and standardized with two brands of pump seals. As maintenance was done, modifications were made, and the old seals were replaced with the appropriate one of the two selected brands. After two years, all the pump seals in the plant were of one of the two types. Inventory cost for pump seals was reduced by about two-thirds.*

## 27. Give People Access to Information

**(Managing people)** Changes to the environments in which we work, study, and live can often leverage improvements in performance. Production of products and services takes place in some type of work environment. As we try to improve quality, reduce costs, or increase value of these products and services, technical changes are developed, tested, and implemented. But many of these technical changes do not lead to improvement because the work environment is not ready to accept or support the changes. Changing the work environment itself can be a high-leverage opportunity for making other changes more effective.

One way to change the work environment is to give people access to information. Many organizations carefully control the information available to various groups of employees. Making available to employees information (such as sales) relevant to their job allows them to suggest changes, make good decisions, and take action that leads to improvements.

*__Design or redesign process or system.__ A company had schedulers working in all of its manufacturing units. The scheduler used production measures and the customer order database to modify the manufacturing plan real-time to make sure shipments were made on time. The company decided to make these data available to all production personnel and, after training, give them more responsibility for scheduling. Computer terminals at all job stations were modified to allow access to real-time information on production and orders. For the first three months, there were some problems with delayed orders, but after that performance returned to the previous level. Most schedulers were reassigned to other jobs.*

*__Design or redesign process or system.__ A service organization was disappointed in initial efforts to get employees involved in its quality improvement efforts. Many of the employee groups were working on projects that were not strategically important to the company. When this issue was raised, the managers found out that the employees did not understand the strategic issues in the company. The company began distributing a summary of their strategic and business plans each year to all employees. Quarterly updates in the plan were discussed in the employee newsletter. Employees were asked to get involved with improvement efforts in their area related to these plans. Within six months, the results from quality improvement efforts throughout the company began to positively influence key performance measures.*

## 28. Use Proper Measurements

*(Managing people)* Measurement plays an important role in focusing people on particular aspects of the business. In many organizations, the things that are measured are considered important while the things not measured are deemed unimportant. Wrong measures motivate people to do the wrong things. Developing appropriate measures, making better use of existing measures, and improving measurement systems can lead to improvement throughout the organization.

*Design or redesign process or system.* *A hospital had a cesarean section rate of greater than 40 percent. All previous efforts by the administration to reduce this level had not been successful. The head nurse in the hospital began to display the C-section rate, by doctor, in the doctors' lounge every month. Within six months, the rate went down to near the national average of 25 percent.*

*Design or redesign process or system.* *A company measured inventories on the last day of every quarter. They began holding operating managers accountable for inventories above targets. Reported inventories immediately went down, but other performance measures indicated problems. Investigations found that massive changes were being made during the last week to redistribute the inventory where it would be difficult to measure. The measurement system was changed to an average daily inventory. This eliminated the end of the quarter-disruptive activities.*

## 29. Take Care of Basics

*(Managing people)* There are certain fundamentals that must be done to make any organization successful. Sometimes it is useful to take a fresh look at these basics to see that the organization is still on track. If there are fundamental problems in the business, changes in other areas may not lead to improvements. Concepts such as orderliness, cleanliness, discipline, and managing costs and prices are examples of fundamentals in any organization. Also, if people's basic needs are not being met, we cannot expect to make meaningful improvements in other areas. The Five-S movement, which is the beginning for quality control in Japanese workshops, gets its name from the Japanese words for straighten up, put things in order, clean up, personal cleanliness, and discipline.

*Design or redesign process or system.* *A quality improvement team was established to reduce errors in assembly. From their interviews with assemblers and technicians, they found that noise from equipment and radios was thought to be the number one cause of errors. The team developed a rearrangement of the floor space that would separate workers who like to listen to the radio from those who did not. Barriers were established around equipment to minimize noise, and an isolated area for equipment repairs was set up. After implementing these changes, the assembly errors dropped by 40 percent.*

*Design or redesign process or system.* *A leasing company found the changes they had been making were not improving their competitive position. They had an outside group review all of their contracts and leases to see that they were charging and receiving fair amounts. They found the rents they had been collecting for the past two years were 30 percent under market value. After making significant changes to develop rates consistent with the market, the company's financial performance became very healthy. The focus then returned to improving the operation of the business.*

## 30. Reduce Demotivating Aspects of the Pay System

*(Managing people)* Pay is rarely a positive motivator in an organization, but it can cause confusion and become a demotivator. Some pay systems can encourage competition between employees rather than cooperation. Another result of some pay systems is the reluctance to take risks or make changes. Review the organization's system for pay to ensure that the current system does not cause problems in the organization. Change the pay system to support behavior that will lead to improvement.

*Design or redesign process or system.* *An automotive service organization was trying to reduce cycle times for activities that required customers to wait. A number of changes were developed and tested that indicated improvements in cycle time. But when these changes were implemented, no improvements resulted. An investigation indicated that the improvements in cycle times of these processes actually decreased the workers' pay. The company changed the pay system so that it did not discourage workers from making the cycle time improvements. They immediately started seeing improvements in their cycle time measures.*

*Design or redesign process or system.* *The organization's performance appraisal system was used to give merit pay increases. Employees and supervisors were constantly complaining about the inequities in the system. The company changed the pay system to one based on specific job skills and market rates. Everyone who performed successfully in a particular job received the same pay. They then changed their appraisal system to a supervisor-worker dialogue on how to improve the organization. Pay and appraisal were no longer issues in the organization.*

## 31. Conduct Training

*(Managing people)* Training is basic to quality performance and the ability to make changes for improvement. Changes will not be effective if people have not received the basic training required to do a job. Training should include *why* as well as *what* and *how*.

*Design or redesign process or system.* *Every spring a new lawn and facilities maintenance crew would damage and destroy equipment and landscaping when they began mowing. The maintenance manager developed a half-day training sessions for all new employees on how to use the equipment. The training also covered safety issues and the types of problems that had occurred in the past.*

*Design or redesign process or system.* *A supplier to the automotive industry trained all its employees in the basics of quality improvement and statistical process control. The training included the use of tools such as flow diagrams, control charts, and basic planned experimentation. They then built these concepts into the operation of the manufacturing facility. Workers were held accountable for conducting experiments and making suggestions for improvement, as well as production numbers. After everyone became experienced with the new way of operating, product quality became more predictable and improvements became a normal occurrence in the company.*

## 32. Implement Cross-Training

*(Managing people)* Cross-training allows people in an organization to do multiple jobs. Such training facilitates flexibility and change. The investment required for the "extra" training will pay off in productivity, quality, and cycle times.

*Design or redesign process or system.* *A home builder was interested in offering to build a house in significantly less time than the current industry practices. Right now, subcontractors are hired to build each part of a house (framing, plumbing, roofing, electrical, and so on). Each subcontractor tries to optimize the work and often damages work of the other contractors. The home builder changed his approach to one based on self-managed work teams whose members were all trained to build the whole house. Each member of the team had a specialty (according to prior training and experience) but was cross-trained for all jobs. The first homes built with the teams did not show much improvement. But after they learned to work as a team, they were able to reduce the time to build a home.*

*Design or redesign process or system.* *An oil production company in Canada was looking for ways to reduce costs. Their oil fields were spread throughout the country. Maintenance salaries were the biggest expense, notably for electricians, mechanics, and hydraulic specialists. A study of their work showed that about 83 percent of their time was spent in traveling from one well site to the next. Two or three workers with differing specialties were often required for a maintenance work order. They developed a two-year program to cross-train all of the maintenance personnel in all of the maintenance functions. Through cross-training, only one person needs to go to each well site; specialists can still be called in when needed. Three years after implementing cross-training, maintenance costs were down by 40 percent.*

## 33. Invest More Resources in Improvement

*(Managing people)* In some organizations, people spend more than a full-time job getting their required tasks completed and fighting the fires created in their

work. The only changes made are reactions to problems or changes mandated from outside the organization. Management should start investing time in developing, testing, and implementing changes that will lead to improvements. Some methods to focus resources on improvement are substituting improvement for non-value-added work, use of full-time "SWAT" teams assigned to a process or outcome, assignment of positions in research and development to process improvement, use of industrial engineers in service industries, and use of relief operators, temporaries, or overtime hours.

*Design or redesign process or system.* *A manager in a retail operation was aware of many problems that needed to be fixed in how the operation ran. Employees barely had time to complete their basic work and handle the problems that cropped up, so he could not ask them to spend time developing and making improvements. He decided to hire temporary workers to free experienced workers from routine and support tasks that did not interact with customers. He established quality improvement teams to invest the workers' freed-up time. These teams were able to develop and implement changes that eliminated many of the recurring problems in the stores. With fewer problems, employees were able to assume all of their previous duties and still have more than 5 percent of their time to invest in making improvements.*

*Design or redesign process or system.* *The president of a distribution company was frustrated in the progress his company was making in integrating ongoing improvements into their business. The management team developed a plan for each manager to ask his or her internal customers why they needed the current reports, meetings, and reviews. Next they met and eliminated the activities that did not directly support the purpose of the organization or were not viewed as high-priority by the customers. They were able to free up about 12 percent of the management's team time requirements. They invested this time in activities to integrate continuous improvement into their business activities. Three years later, this company was recognized as one of the top distributors in the industry.*

## 34. Focus on Core Processes and Purpose

**(Managing people, or expanding customer expectations to increase demand)** Why are we doing all of the activities that go on in the organization? Which are the activities directly related to the purpose of the organization (the core processes)? Core processes can also be characterized as those activities providing value directly to external customers. To reduce costs, consider reductions in activities that are not part of the core processes.

*Design or redesign process or system.* *A service company needed to reduce overhead costs to stay competitive in routine work areas. Each department manager asked everyone to review his or her work by asking the question, "How does this activity add value to our external customer?" To answer the question, they surveyed the group that received the work, continuing until the connection was made to an external customer. Each department manager developed a list of activities for which there is no positive answer and worked to phase out those activities.*

*Design or redesign product or service. An airline company was involved in making travel arrangements, including hotels, ground transportation, food service, and entertainment. At one time, this was considered an important and profitable part of their business, but over the years they changed to a low-cost, no frills airline. They cost of keeping up to date on hotel, rental cars, and so forth was greater than the revenue received from making travel arrangements. They ran some tests to see if eliminating this service would affect their core business. After finding no effect, they eliminated this noncore activity.*

## 35. Share Risks

**(Managing people)** Many people become more interested in the performance of an organization once they can clearly see how their future is tied to long-term performance. Developing systems that allow all employees to share in the risks of the organization can lead to an increased interest in performance by all. Some plans to share risks and gains are profit sharing, gain sharing, bonuses, and pay for knowledge. Care must be taken with programs of this type. Companies can undermine workers' job satisfaction and creativity by placing too much emphasis on extrinsic motivation from incentives. Systems must be carefully designed to keep everyone focused on the purpose of the organization and not just the potential short-term gains.

*Design or redesign process or system. A construction company had trouble convincing potential clients to consider new, unproven technologies and methods in their engineering and construction work. To obtain new business, they offered a sharing of risks and rewards with their clients. They agreed to accept half of the downside costs of failures in return for a percentage of savings from the successes. With this offer to share risks and gains, they were able to get commitment for new business that met their revenue requirements and created win-win situations for them and their clients.*

*Design or redesign process or system. A service company with a cyclical business wanted to reduce costs when business was down without laying off workers. The employees agreed to tie 25 percent of their current compensation to the company's net earnings each quarter. Their pay would depend on quarterly performance relative to the previous year's average quarterly revenue. When business was good, they received more than the previous salary. During a nine-month recession period when the company was not making money, they received significantly less pay than previously. The employees became much more interested in the business and markets in which they worked.*

## 36. Emphasize Natural and Logical Consequences

**(Managing people, or expanding customer expectations to increase demand)** An alternative approach to traditional reward-and-punishment systems in organizations is to focus on "natural and logical consequences." Natural consequences follow from the natural order of the physical world (not eating leads to hunger). Logical consequences follow from the reality of the business or social world (if you are late for a meeting, you will not have a chance to offer input on some of the issues). The idea of natural and logical consequences is to get everyone to be responsible for her or his own behavior rather than try to use power, judge others, and force submission. Instead of demanding conformance, the use of natural and logical consequences permits choice.

*Design or redesign process or system.* *Joe was having problems with drivers arriving at the terminal late in the morning. He had to repeat announcements a number of times and shift delivery assignments whenever drivers arrived late. He would regularly complain to certain drivers about showing up late, but this did not help the problem. Joe decided to quit complaining and reworking the load assignments, and instead emphasize the logical consequences of the drivers' late arrival. He made it clear that beginning next week, any driver who did not arrive in time for the 6:00 a.m. meeting would not receive any delivery assignment that day and would therefore not be paid for deliveries. After a few weeks (during which some drivers had to work overtime to cover loads missed), the late arrivals were eliminated.*

*Design or redesign product or service.* *Car manufacturers in Europe have begun to design their products to facilitate eventual recycle of materials. A concept proposed by some environmental advocates is that a producer of any product is also responsible for its ultimate disposal. When the consumer is finished with a product, it is returned to the producer. The producer can then reuse or recycle the product. This will require producers to consider recycle decisions in the design of products and packaging.*

## 37. Develop Alliances and Cooperative Relationships

***(Managing people, or expanding customer expectations to increase demand)***
During recent years, many industries have gone through a period of consolidation, acquisition, and merger. The result is often fewer and larger organizations with not much effort given to integrating the pieces into an overall system. Therefore, the industry's customers do not experience an increase in value. Various types of alliances, based on the principle of cooperation to optimize the interactions between the parts of the system, offer a better approach for integration of organizations.

*Design or redesign process or system.* *In the health care industry, many organizations came under common ownership through mergers and acquisitions. Some of the organizations formed alliances, with an objective to create a truly integrated health care system. These organizations first developed a statement of their common purpose. They then set out to optimize the interactions among the various parts of the system by predicting demand for services, smoothing the work flow between parts, and coordinating services from the customer perspective.*

*Design or redesign process or system.* *The demand for school services in a community decreased significantly as the population became older. The public and private schools in the community were competing for students. The result of the competitive efforts was increasing costs for all of the schools. This resulted in higher tuitions, losses, and higher tax rates. The chamber of commerce formed an alliance of all the schools in the community, one based on cooperation rather than competition. The alliance developed a purpose of optimizing the interactions between the various schools toward educating the children in the community. During the next five years, the community transitioned to a smaller system with lower costs and improved measures of learning of its students.*

## 38. Listen to Customers

*(Eliminating quality problems)* To benefit from improvements in quality of products and services, the customer must recognize and appreciate the improvements. Many problems in organizations occur because the producer does not understand the important aspects of the customer's needs, or customers are not clear about their expectations from suppliers. The interface between producer-provider and the customers is an opportunity to learn and develop changes that will lead to improvement.

It is easy to get caught up in the internal functioning of our organization and forget about why we are here: to serve our customers. Invest time regularly in processes that "listen to the customers." Sometimes it is important to figure out how to communicate with customers further down the supply chain, or even the final consumer of the product or service. Talk to customers about their experiences in using your products. Learn about improvement opportunities.

*Design or redesign product or service.* *After spending time with patients (the consumer), a medical supply company found that needles packaged with a drug they sold caused pain to the patients. The patients were buying their own needles and throwing away the ones in the package. The hospitals and clinics that the company supplied had never given them this feedback.*

*Design or redesign process or system.* *The owner of a hardware supply company wanted to differentiate his company from competitors on the basis of customer service. He developed a system to get his sales managers involved in learning from the customers. Once a quarter, each sales manager would identify her five largest accounts. She would follow an order from each of these customers from call-in to delivery at the customer site. The sales representative would talk to someone at the customer site while the delivery was being unloaded and listen for opportunities to make it easier to use the products he was receiving. This practice established his organization as the premier supplier in his market.*

## 39. Coach Customers to Use Product/Service

*(Eliminating quality problems)* Customers have quality problems that increase their costs because they do not understand all the intricacies of a product or service. Increase the value of your products and services by developing ways to coach customers and consumers on how to use them.

*Design or redesign product or service. A hospital had an aim to reduce readmissions. When staff studied the patients being readmitted, they found that many were not able to follow their discharge instructions. The units agreed they would schedule time on the day of discharge to more thoroughly review the instruction with patients and their families. Initial tests were focused on learning how to make the process for reviewing the instructions more efficient so staff would not be overburdened.*

*Design or redesign product or service. A supplier of expensive laboratory equipment was able to differentiate its products by assigning a technician to work in a laboratory that purchased the equipment. The technician would coach the laboratory personnel for one day a week for the first three months after purchase.*

## 40. Focus on the Outcome to a Customer

*(Eliminating quality problems)* Make the outcome (product or service) produced by your organization the focus of all activities. First, clearly understand the outcomes that customers expect from your organization. Then let the question that will focus improvement in any particular work activity be, "How does this activity support the outcome to the customer?" Make activity improvements in quality, costs, efficiencies, cycle times, and the like that contribute to the outcome. Organize people, departments, and processes in a way that best serves the customer, paying particular attention to the producer-customer interface.

*Design or redesign process or system. A health services organization was overwhelmed with the technological advances in the industry. They had spent more than $6 million during the last two years on new medical equipment. Their costs were higher, but there was no evidence in improvement of the quality of services. They decided to focus the decisions to purchase new types of equipment on the outcome of their services: diagnosis and treatment of patients. They began to buy new equipment only if they could conduct tests that would show how the equipment improved their medical diagnoses or the treatment of the patient. They found that their purchase of new equipment declined during the next year, but the equipment purchased was being used by all of the staff.*

*Design or redesign process or system. The approach of "outcome-based education" is premised on what students should do or be able to do. This approach offers a process that allows school districts to clarify what all stakeholders in the community want as a result of schooling for their students. Then personnel, facilities, equipment, and budgets are organized to accomplish the desired results. The school district managers hold themselves accountable to achieve these outcomes. A number of school districts throughout the United States have used this approach and achieved higher student scores on standardized tests, lower dropout rates, and advanced placement in schools at the next level.*

## 41. Use a Coordinator

***(Eliminating quality problems, or reducing costs while maintaining or improving quality)*** A coordinator's primary job is to manage the producer-customer linkages. For example, an expediter is someone who focuses on ensuring adequate supplies of materials and equipment or coordinates the flow of materials in an organization. For critical processes, someone coordinating the flow of materials, tools, parts, and processed goods can help prevent problems and downtime. A coordinator can also be used to work with customers to furnish extra services. One example of a coordinator is a "case manager" acting as a buffer between a complex process and the customer. The case manager must have the authority to get things done if the customer's needs are not being met.

**Design or redesign product or service.** *A trucking company wanted to differentiate its delivery and hauling services by offering additional value to customers who used these services. Management developed a position at each delivery terminal to focus on minimizing the impact problems had on the customer. Some of the services and activities were calling truckers to find out the status of a delivery, sending help or calling the customer when a delivery was going to be late, and suggesting tips for customers to make it easier to use their services day to day. Customers began to depend on this service and were willing to pay a premium on their deliveries.*

**Design or redesign process or system.** *To manage patient flow, a hospital created a position of "flow coordinator." This person would look for and expedite situations where the handoffs between departments in the hospital are not smooth.*

## 42. Reach Agreement on Expectations

***(Eliminating quality problems)*** Many times customer dissatisfaction occurs because the customer does not feel he or she has received the products or services expected. At times, advertising, special promotions, and promises by the sales group do not match what they receive. These marketing processes should be coordinated with capabilities. Establish clear expectations before the product is produced or the service is delivered to the customer.

**Design or redesign product or service.** *A help line company advertised "friendly service" but had no hiring, development, or training process to deliver such service. After numerous customers questioned their friendly service, they learned not to advertise until they had a system that could really deliver it.*

*Design or redesign process or system.* *A study by a quality improvement team in a construction company found that fewer than 15 percent of their jobs were completed within the original schedule. They tried to handle customer complaints by showing the customer that most of the delays were in areas beyond their control (weather, financing, customer changes). Customers still responded negatively in satisfaction surveys. The team recommended that a written schedule showing the key stages of construction be used to determine how long each stage normally took. This schedule was reviewed with the customer prior to signing a contract. The customer was notified about the cause of any significant delays immediately when they occurred. These changes in clarifying expectations resulted in better management of job schedules and an increase in customer satisfaction ratings.*

## 43. Outsource for "Free"

*(Reducing costs while maintaining or improving quality, or managing people, or expanding customer expectations to increase demand)* Sometimes it is possible to get suppliers to perform additional functions with little or no increase in the price to the customer. A task that is a major inconvenience or cost for the customer can be performed inexpensively and efficiently by the supplier. The supplier might be willing to do this task for free to secure ongoing business with the customer.

*Design or redesign process or system.* *A distribution company offered to order and stock supplies for a chemical plant's warehouse. The chemical company could eliminate six full-time positions currently used to stock the supplies delivered by the distributor. By performing the stocking, the distributor could obtain better lead times for deliveries and learn about other supply needs of the customer. The savings in inventory more than offset the labor costs incurred by the distributor. After six months of performing this service, the distributor made a series of recommendations on layout and ordering patterns that further reduced the chemical company's cost of materials.*

*Design or redesign process or system.* *Through observation of customers, a computer distributor found the biggest hassle with the purchase of a new computer was loading all the desired software on the system. They began advertising that they would load all standard commercial software "for free" at the time the computer was ordered. The company developed agreements with software suppliers to purchase the software at a discount.*

## 44. Optimize Level of Inspection

*(Eliminating quality problems, or reducing costs while maintaining or improving quality)* What level of inspection is appropriate for a process? All products will eventually receive some type of inspection (possibly by the user). Options for inspection at a given place in the supply chain are no inspection, 100 percent inspection, or reduction or increase in the current level of inspection. A study of the level of

inspection can potentially lead to changes that raise quality of outcomes to the customers or decrease costs.

*Design or redesign process or system.* *W. Edwards Deming developed a method to base an economic decision on the amount of inspection that should be done at various stages of manufacturing and assembly. A manufacturing company used this economic analysis to decide on the best place to do 100 percent inspection for each product type. They were able to decrease defects going to their customers and also decrease their total cost of inspection.*

*Design or redesign process or system.* *A chemical producer had a series of expensive settlements that were due to contaminated products. One of the potential sources of contamination was the rail car the product was loaded into. They started doing railroad car inspections prior to loading and kept records on how often they found problems during these inspections. After one year, they shared these data with their customers and decided to eliminate the inspections. By conducting the inspections and sharing the data, they were able to develop fair and cost-effective practices for both parties.*

## 45. Work with Suppliers

*(Reducing costs while maintaining or improving quality)* Inputs or raw materials have an impact on the costs and quality of performance of a process, product, or service. Working with suppliers to use their technical knowledge can sometimes reduce the cost of using the product or service. Sometimes your suppliers even have ideas on how to make improvements that will delight your customers.

*Design or redesign process or system.* *A food company requires its suppliers of processing equipment to participate on improvement teams focused on customizing their equipment. The suppliers assisted the company in designing planned experiments to improve the performance of various types of processing equipment. In one series of studies, they were able to practically eliminate bone chips from a processed meat product.*

*Design or redesign process or system.* *A large oil company asked the liquid storage tank supplier how they could reduce the total cost of tank construction and maintenance. On the basis of their recommendations, the supplier took over the inspection responsibility for the constructed products. This reduced the number of previously redundant inspections and has cut typical project costs by 2 percent.*

## 46. Reduce Setup or Startup Time

*(Reducing costs while maintaining or improving quality)* An organization can gain a competitive advantage by reducing the time to develop new products, waiting time for services, lead time for orders and deliveries, and cycle time for all functions in the organization. Many organizations spend much of the overall production time starting up or waiting.

Time can be lost and costs increased in getting ready to produce a product or service. Setup time can often be cut in half just by getting organized for the setup. The ability to minimize setup or startup time allows the organization to maintain a lower level of inventory and get more productivity out of its assets. One approach to reducing setup time incorporates four steps:

1. Define the activities that can be completed before the startup begins (external activities)
2. Do all the external work ahead of time
3. Convert as many activities as possible currently being carried out during the startup (internal activities) to external activities
4. Improve the processes to reduce the time to accomplish the internal activities

*Design or redesign process or system. A consulting organization received inquiries about services from all over the world. Consultants in the organization communicate with the potential clients over the phone and then write a letter describing the conversation and actions to be taken later. After a period of time, someone noted that this resulted in several "standard" types of letters. These letters were reviewed and three types of letters were developed into a template the consultant could use for 90 percent of the inquiry types. This reduced the need to set up a new letter of response for each inquiry. It also enabled the consultant to spend a little more time in making sure the letter addressed the particular concerns of the potential client. Overall, the amount of time crafting letters declined, more timely responses to potential clients resulted, and more useful communication was produced.*

*Design or redesign process or system. When patients come out of bypass surgery in a hospital, they need to be immediately placed on a monitor. This is a very risky time period for a patient. The first step in hooking up the monitor is to remove the intravenous lines put in during surgery. To reduce this setup time, assistants in the recovery room began removing the lines before sending the patient to be placed on the monitor. This change in the process reduced the setup time during this risky period by one-third.*

## 47. Set up Timing to Use Discounts

*(Reducing costs while maintaining or improving quality)* The planning and timing of many activities can be coordinated to take advantage of available savings and discounts. Designing a process to do so can save money and reduce operating costs. An organization must have a system in place to take advantage of such opportunities. For example, using discounts offered by suppliers for paying bills within ten days of the invoice date requires a system that can process an invoice and cut a check within the discount period. The opportunity to apply this concept requires a flexible process and knowledge of the opportunity to take advantage of the timing.

*Design or redesign process or system. Airlines set their rates to take advantage of the traveler who cannot plan ahead. Business people often end up paying two to four times the ticket price of someone who has a Saturday night stayover and who purchased the ticket in advance. One company decided to turn this situation into a possible perk for their employees. They offered employees who were willing to travel early or stay over through Saturday two-thirds of the saving in ticket price. This saving could be applied to hotel, restaurant, and entertainment during their weekend stay where they were working. The company did save some money, and many employees were delighted to take advantage of this perk.*

*Design or redesign process or system. Large groups in an organization or industry can be set up to take advantage of volume discounts. Thirty pharmacies in a hospital system coordinated their purchase of drugs. Together they were large enough to negotiate directly with the drug manufacturers for timing and volume discounts. This coordination of purchases reduced their costs by 15 percent.*

## 48. Optimize Maintenance

*(Reducing costs while maintaining or improving quality)* Time is lost and quality often deteriorates when production and service equipment breaks down. A preventive maintenance strategy attempts to keep people and machines in good performance condition instead of waiting until there is a breakdown or failure to take action. Through proper design and the study of historical data, an efficient maintenance program can be designed to keep equipment in production with a minimum of downtime for maintenance. Learning to observe and listen to equipment before it breaks down is also an important component of any plan to optimize maintenance.

*Design or redesign process or system. A large corporation wanted to decrease costs for medical insurance. Leadership structured the medical package to encourage employees to invest in prevention of health care problems through regular check-ups and eliminating behaviors potentially detrimental to their health. The company offered regular education in their newsletters about health tips and healthy eating habits. After focusing on these preventive health maintenance methods for two years, staff saw health care costs decline and started receiving discounts in their insurance premiums.*

*Design or redesign process or system. A power plant could not afford to have one of its large turbines break. The plant was designed with extra capacity to keep one turbine off-line at any time for maintenance. This strategy worked until demand increased beyond planned capacity. To reduce off-line time for maintenance, they developed vibration monitoring equipment to "listen" to the turbines. Measurements were plotted out and studied to decide when to perform preventive maintenance on a turbine. Using this strategy to optimize maintenance, they reduced down-time of the "extra" turbine and were able to meet the greater capacity demands.*

## 49. Extend Specialists Time

*(Managing people)* Organizations employ specialists who have specific skills or knowledge. But not all of their work duties use these skills or knowledge. Try to remove assignments and job requirements that do not employ the specialists' skills. Find ways to let the specialist have a broader impact on the organization, especially if the specialist is a constraint to throughput in the organization. The availability of video and information technology offers opportunities to extend specialists' time.

*Design or redesign process or system. The principal of a school wanted the teachers to spend more of their time developing new teaching methods. They negotiated with the local university to furnish more "practice teachers" to the school. The practice teachers were assigned routine teaching assignments to free up the experienced teachers to work on curriculum development.*

*Design or redesign process or system. In rural communities, there is always a shortage of medical specialists. It is not practical to have specialists available for all possible medical conditions in a sparsely populated area. One hospital system has used information technology to extend the availability of all its medical specialists to assist primary care doctors in these communities. The results of X-rays, EKGs, and other tests are transferred electronically to the specialist. The specialist reviews the test results and then communicates back to the primary care physician.*

## 50. Reduce Wait Time

*(Reducing costs while maintaining or improving quality, or eliminating quality problems)* Nobody likes to wait. Reduction in wait time can lead to improvements in many types of services. Ideas for change that can reduce the time customers have to wait are especially useful. This applies not only to the time to perform a service for the customer but also to the time it takes the customer to use or maintain a product.

*Design or redesign product or service. A chemical supplies manufacturer studied customer systems to find how to differentiate its products from others. Wait time from order to receipt was the most important measure of quality to work on. Management changed inventory practices, contracted with an overnight delivery company, and began offering overnight delivery on about 90 percent of their chemicals (with about a 20 percent increase in price). This change differentiated the products from their competitors and helped them increase sales because many customers gladly paid the 20 percent premium to not have to wait.*

*Design or redesign product or service. Rental car companies changed their systems for regular customers to have a car ready without waiting in line or signing any forms. At first this differentiated the services of a few of the major companies, but now it has become a customer expectation.*

## 51. Standardization (Create a Formal Process)

*(Eliminating quality problems)* The use of standards, or standardization, has a negative and bureaucratic connotation for many people. But an appropriate amount of standardization can be a foundation on which improvement in quality and costs is built. Standardization is one of the primary methods to reduce variation in a system. The use of standardization, or creating a more formal process, should be considered for the parts of a system that have a big effect on the outcomes (leverage points).

*Design or redesign process or system.* *A hospital's records showed much variation among patients in recovery time from knee operations. The average costs for this particular operation were higher than for other health systems. Staff worked with a team of doctors and therapists to develop a standard process for patients who have a knee joint replaced. After implementing the standard process, recovery times became more consistent, and the hospital's costs were in line with those of other systems.*

*Design or redesign process or system.* *In the United States, school curricula vary from district to district and from state to state. This variation causes problems when students transfer to other districts. In Japan, the elementary school curricula have been standardized throughout the country. This allows teachers to focus their energies on teaching technique rather than content. When students transfer to a new school, there are no gaps or duplication.*

## 52. Stop Tampering (Use Statistical Process Control)

*(Eliminating quality problems)* Tampering is defined as interfering so as to weaken or change for the worse. In many situations, changes are made on the basis of the last result observed or measured. These changes often actually increase the variation in a process or product. The methods of statistical process control, drawn from the concepts of common and special causes, can be used to decide when it is appropriate to make changes based on recent results. Adjustments to a stable process stemming from the previous result will usually make performance worse. But when special causes are present, adjustments can be useful.

*Design or redesign process or system.* *An engineering company demanded a written report for any project whose estimated cost was not within plus or minus 10 percent of the actual cost of the project. Explanations were written for eight projects during a one-year period. When a review of these reports was done at the end of the year, only one of the reports was found to contain information useful for future projects. The others were just reiteration of the events that transpired during the project. The company changed its focus to study common aspects of all projects and do special investigations only if there were indications a project was affected by special causes.*

*Design or redesign process or system.* *Laboratory procedures required a certain gauge be recalibrated to standard after every inspection. The laboratory manager found the gauge variation was reduced if it was recalibrated only when the difference from standard was outside control limits established for the value (actual minus standard). She changed the procedure to reflect this new learning.*

## 53. Develop Operational Definitions

*(Eliminating quality problems)* Reduction of variation can begin with understanding of concepts commonly used in transacting business. The meaning of a concept is ultimately found in how that concept is applied. Simple concepts such as on-time, clean, noisy, secure, and so on need operational definitions in order to reduce variation in communications and measurement. An operational definition usually has two parts: (1) a measurement procedure, and (2) criteria for judgment.

*Design or redesign process or system.* *An automotive service dealership found that "noise not fixed" was one of the biggest reasons customers brought their cars back complaining they were not fixed. The company developed a check sheet with operational definitions of such words as* whine, click, hum, knock, hiss, *and* growl. *The use of these definitions by customers, service advisors, and technicians helped focus on the specific problem and reduced the number of comebacks (cars that returned to be fixed again).*

*Design or redesign process or system.* *A trucking company and a major chemical producer needed a common definition of* on-time. *The supplier and customer agreed the delivery would be considered on-time if it arrived at the receiving dock no more than fifteen minutes earlier or later than scheduled, using the time clock at the dock. All parties were then able to collect consistent data and focus on improvements in timeliness.*

## 54. Improve Predictions

*(Eliminating quality problems)* Plans, forecasts, and budgets are based on predictions. For many situations, predictions are built from the ground up each time a prediction is required, and historical data are not used. The study of variation from past predictions can lead to alternative ways to improve the predictions. There are a number of useful approaches to develop predictions:

- Use simple averages of historical data.
- Anticipate special causes (airlines change cutoffs for loads when a large group books a flight).
- Use leading indicators (as with housing starts to predict demand for flooring material).

- Develop time series models to take advantage of point-to-point correlation (autocorrelation) in historical data.
- Make real-time updates of predictions as new information becomes available.
- Use research when results cannot be seen for a long time (for example, with a school curriculum).

*Design or redesign process or system.* A company that distributed heating oil found itself responding to many panic calls from customers whose furnaces stopped running because they had run out of oil. The company designed a new service that allowed them to deliver oil periodically (the frequency was established using predictions developed from both weather patterns and historical data on customer's use) without the customer having to call.

*Design or redesign process or system.* An important task for bulk chemical companies is the management of their rail fleet. They want to always have cars available when a shipment is due, but they also want to minimize the number of cars in the fleet. One company developed a simulation model based on historical data to predict the number of cars required in the fleet in order to meet shipment demands. The model considered variation in customer orders, fleet maintenance issues, and variation in transit. The model was run annually to make decisions on purchasing or releasing cars. It was also run quarterly with updated data to make decisions on short-term leasing of cars.

## 55. Develop Contingency Plans

*(Eliminating quality problems)* Variation in our everyday life often creates problems. Reducing the variation might eventually eliminate the problems, but how do we survive today? One way is to prepare backup plans, or contingencies, to deal with the unexpected problems due to variation. Whenever variation is from a special cause that can be identified, then contingency plans can be ready.

*Design or redesign process or system.* The staff of the doctor's office knew that waiting time to see the doctor was very important to their patients. They continually worked to develop a schedule that would minimize wait time and allow the doctor to see all patients. But if the doctor was called to the emergency room at the hospital, people would have a long wait. The office developed a contingency plan for times when the doctor was called out to the emergency room. The receptionist would immediately notify all patients in the waiting room and offer to reschedule. She then would call the patients scheduled to come in for the next appointments and offer to reschedule, or she would let them wait at home until she called back. The patients were very appreciative of this plan.

*Design or redesign product or service.* Why do people lose their car keys? There is usually a lengthy explanation of the special circumstances. But losing your car keys or locking the key in the car can be traumatic. One automotive manufacturer provides a "credit card *key" to be carried in the wallet or purse in case you lock yourself out of the car. This is a backup and offers some peace of mind. It also conveys a message that the company has your well-being in mind, which is the focus of their marketing strategy.*

## 56. Sort Product into Grades

**(Eliminating quality problems)** Creative ways can be developed to take advantage of naturally occurring variation in products. Sorting the product or service into grades can be designed to minimize the variation within a grade and maximize the variation between grades. They can then be marketed to differing customer needs.

**Design or redesign product or service.** *Food products have natural patterns of variation determined by growing and weather conditions. Because this variation will not go away, the U. S. Department of Agriculture develops grades according to variation in quality characteristics of a product. The grades are sold for different end uses; for example, USDA grades of poultry and beef allow consumers to buy the quality of meat they need for baking, frying, or grilling.*

**Design or redesign process or system.** *A company manufacturing cardboard drums had problems in the appearance (color, grain, texture) of the drum. No economical solutions were found to eliminate the appearance problem, primarily due to raw material variability. This appearance was important to some customers but did not matter to others. The company established a grading scheme and sorted the drums into grade A (no appearance problems), grade B (standard), and grade C (appearance problems). They charged a premium price for grade A to offset the discount offered for grade C. Customers were able to get the quality of drum that met their needs.*

## 57. Desensitize

**(Eliminating quality problems)** It is impossible to control some types of variation: between students in a class, the ways customers try to use products, the physical condition of patients who enter the hospital, and so on. We minimize the impact on the outcome (education, health) by desensitizing or opting for nonreaction to the variation. Focus on desensitizing the effect of variation rather than reducing it. Examples of this concept include desensitizing the customer to variation in a product or service, desensitizing a process to variation of incoming parts, and desensitizing a product to variation from the perspective of diverse users.

**Design or redesign product or service.** *Disney uses flowers, music, and Disney characters throughout the theme parks to create an environment that is clean and pleasant and communicates a "good day" to the theme park customer. On normal days, everyone is pleased with the environment. On days in which the lines are long, this environment acts to desensitize the customer to the longer waiting time. They hum "zip-a-dee-doo-dah" and watch their children play with Disney characters as they wait in line.*

***Design or redesign process or system.*** *A chemical company decided to dif-*
*ferentiate its batch products from competitors by minimizing batch-to-batch variation. Over a*
*two-year period, they eliminated many of the sources of variation. The current biggest contributor*
*to variation is the ambient weather (temperature, humidity, barometric pressure) while a batch*
*is being produced. Because they could not eliminate this source of variation, they ran a series of*
*experiments to find operating conditions that minimized the impact of weather changes on the*
*process. These experiments led to an additional 30 percent reduction in the variation of the key*
*quality characteristics of the product.*

## 58. Exploit Variation

*(Eliminating quality problems)* Sometimes it is not obvious how variation can
be reduced or its effect minimized. Rather than just accepting or "dealing with"
the variation, we can think of ways to exploit it—that is, turn the variation into a
positive method to differentiate our products or services.

    ***Design or redesign product or service.*** *A tennis camp has learned to differ-*
*entiate its services by exploiting variation in how people learn. It is well known that people have*
*preferred learning styles. Some people learning by reading and study, Some by listening, others by*
*watching, and still others by doing. Previously, the camp's solution for dealing with this was to*
*offer a variety of teaching styles to all students so eventually they get to experience their preferred*
*style. A few seasons ago, staff changed their approach to exploit this variation and thus differenti-*
*ate the services of their camp. At the beginning of a visit to the camp, each athlete was given a*
*series of tests designed to identify preferred learning style. They were then organized into groups*
*and the instruction for each group was designed to optimize the use of the preferred learning style.*
*This approach has led to delighted customers of the tennis camp.*

    ***Design or redesign process or system.*** *Diversity in the workplace is a major*
*issue. Diversity among people is a form of variation that can be exploited. An organization*
*that produced consumer products found its products were not often purchased by women and*
*numerous ethnic groups. The company began to emphasize diversity in hiring and development*
*of product design engineers. The design of the products received inputs from engineers with a*
*greater range of backgrounds. The result was new products that were acceptable in a much*
*broader market.*

## 59. Use Reminders

*(Eliminating quality problems)* Eliminating mistakes is an important activity in
reducing quality problems. Mistakes (also called errors or slips) occur when our
actions do not agree with our intentions even though we are capable of carrying
out the task. We often have to act quickly in a given situation or are required
to accomplish a number of tasks sequentially, or even simultaneously. Making

these slips is part of being human. Although these mistakes are the result of human actions, they occur because of the interaction of people with a system. We can reduce mistakes by redesigning the system to reduce the likelihood of people in the system making mistakes. This type of system design or redesign is called mistake or error proofing. We can mistake-proof by using technology (adding equipment to automate repetitive tasks), by using methods to make it more difficult to do something wrong, or by integrating these methods with technology.

The first change concept in eliminating mistakes is to use reminders. The related change concepts of "use differentiation," "use constraints," and "use affordances" follow.

Mistakes are frequently caused by forgetting to do something. Reminders are aids for remembering. They can come in many forms. A reminder can be a written notice, e-mail, phone call, checklist of things to accomplish, alarm such as on a clock, standard form, or the documented steps to follow for a process. Reminders are simple to develop but probably the least effective way to mistake-proof. Although they do make information available in the external world, reminders can still be overlooked or ignored; a standard process can be documented but people may nevertheless choose not to refer to the flow diagram or other documentation.

**Design or redesign process or system.** *A number of people were missing or arriving late for their dental appointments. This caused disruption in the schedule of the dentist, which had an effect on other patients. The dentist asked the receptionist to call and remind patients the day before their appointment. This resulted in a reduction in the number of late arrivals and cancellations.*

**Design or redesign process or system.** *Laboratory experiments determined that a critical characteristic of a final product was affected by the temperature at a particular stage in the chemical process. If the temperature was above or below a certain level at this stage, the quality of the final product was affected. Because the operators were so busy, they sometimes forgot to check the temperature readout and make the appropriate adjustment. Therefore, they decided to install an alarm that would signal to them when the temperature was outside the acceptable range.*

## 60. Use Differentiation

*(Eliminating quality problems)* Mistakes can occur when we are dealing with things that look similar. We may copy a wrong number or grab a wrong part because of its similarity or close proximity to other numbers or parts. Mistakes can also occur when actions are similar. We may end up in the wrong place or use a piece of equipment in the wrong way because the right directions or procedures

are similar to others we might have used in another situation (we wind up driving to work on Sunday morning instead of to the bakery). Our mind at times will associate the required things and actions with similar but inappropriate ones. Familiarity that results from experience can actually increase the chance of committing mistakes of association. To reduce mistakes, steps should be taken to break patterns. This can be done in such ways as color coding, sizing, using different symbols, or separating similar things.

*Design or redesign process or system. An eight digit number (for example, 31469518) was used by an order processing group to identify a specific product. Each pair of digits represented a specific bit of information that was necessary for inventory and shipping purposes. Mistakes were so frequent in these numbers that 100 percent inspection was used. Even then, not all of the mistakes were found and corrected. The group suggested that numbers and letters (e.g. 31DF95AH) be alternated in pairs. This made it easier for them to distinguish the different columns and reduced the number of mistakes.*

*Design or redesign process or system. A mail order company offered different types of clothing, each in a number of sizes, styles, and colors. The orders were picked and shipped from one central area. The numbering of an item followed a rational approach: similar items had similar numbers. This resulted in gloves being in one section, socks in another, and so forth. The people who filled the orders often made mistakes by picking the wrong type of glove or the wrong type of sock from the many kinds that were available in each section. Mistakes were greatly reduced when random stock numbers were used and similar types of clothing were no longer in close proximity.*

## 61. Use Constraints

***(Eliminating quality problems)*** A constraint restricts the performance of certain actions. A door that blocks passage into an unsafe area is a constraint. Constraints are an important method for mistake-proofing because they can limit the actions that result in mistakes. They make information available not just in the external world but within the product or system itself. To be effective, constraints should be visible and easy to understand. Constraints can be built into a process so that accidental stopping or an unwanted action that will result in a mistake can be prevented. Constraints can also be used to make sure the steps performed in a process or in using a product are accomplished in the correct sequence.

*Design or redesign product or service. Many customers of a bank were leaving their card behind after using the automated teller machine (ATM). At this bank, if a person was making a withdrawal from the ATM, money would come out first and then the card. The result was that once people had received their money, they often forgot to wait for their card. The bank changed the procedure so that the money would come out only after the card was removed.*

*Design or redesign process or system.* *The operators of a certain machine were experiencing some hand injuries. To reduce the injuries, dual palm buttons were installed to operate the machine. This kept both of the operator's hands busy and out of the way of the machine. Hand injuries were reduced by 37 percent during the next year.*

## 62. Use Affordances

*(Eliminating quality problems)* An affordance provides insight, without the need for explanation, into how a task should be done or how something should be used. In contrast to a constraint, which limits the actions possible, an affordance offers visual (or other sensory) prompting for the actions that should be performed. Once we see the fixtures on a door, we should be able to determine whether it opens in, opens out, or slides. There should not be a need to refer to labels or to use trial and error. If a process or product can be designed to lead the user to perform the correct actions, fewer mistakes will occur.

*Design or redesign process or system.* *An organization started a recycling program in the cafeteria, to separate cans, bottles, plastic utensils, and paper plates and cups. Bins were used to collect the items, and each one was identified by a sign. At the end of the day, the workers in the cafeteria still had to spend more than an hour separating the items placed in the wrong bin. They decided to put a top on each bin with an opening in the shape of the appropriate item to be recycled. After this change, the workers in the cafeteria spent little or no time separating misplaced items.*

*Design or redesign product or service.* *When visitors to a hotel entered their room, they were met with a horizontal array of eight switches controlling the lights in various areas of the room. Guests would get very frustrated trying to figure out which switch affected which lights. To make it easier, the hotel arranged the switches on a diagram of the room. This diagram was visible as soon as the door to the room was opened.*

## 63. Mass Customization

*(Managing people, or expanding customer expectations to increase demand)* Most consumers of products and services would agree that quality increases as the product or service is customized for unique circumstances. Most would also expect to pay more or wait longer for these customized offerings than for a mass-produced version. "Mass customization" means combining the uniqueness of customized products with the efficiency of mass production.

New technology may contribute to the ability to mass customize; genetically engineered drugs are an example. A key method of mass customization is differentiating the product or service at the last moment, perhaps even done by the customer himself. Learning to design and use modules is another way to apply this concept. Mass customization can be done after building knowledge to predict the most likely choices of customers or to understand the causes of desired outcomes. For example, knowledge of which fertilizer will work best under certain conditions can lead to a product or service customized for particular customers.

**Design or redesign product or service.** *A telephone company developed more than two hundred options for local telephone service. Rather than offer all of these potential options to any one customer, they analyzed historical use and then sent each customer a customized letter identifying the services that would actually save this customer money. The letter also offered some new services that analysis indicated might interest the customer.*

**Design or redesign product or service.** *A publishing company serving the college market found a way to customize textbooks to the course being taught. Rather than have authors write a complete textbook, they commissioned specific modules. The professors were then given the opportunity to choose from a number of modules to assemble the text for the course. Besides the increase in quality from customization, this approach reduced the cost and time of publishing subsequent additions.*

## 64. Offer the Product or Service Anytime

**(Managing people, or expanding customer expectations to increase demand)** Many products and services are available only at certain times. A movie will be shown at 7:00 p.m. and 9:30 p.m. The Motor Vehicle Bureau is open from nine to five. The doctor's office hours are one to five Monday through Friday. The bank is open from nine to three. Your new car will be available in two weeks. These constraints almost always detract from the quality of the product or service. How can they be removed? In some cases a technology breakthrough (such as the ATM) is needed. In others, prediction plays an important role, as in predicting what type of cars customers will order. However, in many situations the constraint is created because it is more convenient for the provider of the service than for the customer. Would most people prefer the bank to be opened from 9:00 A.M. to 3:00 P.M. or from 3:00 P.M. to 9:00 P.M.?

Offering the product or service anytime is different from just reducing wait time. To achieve this goal often takes a totally new conceptualization of the product or service. For this reason, "anytime" is an important concept for changing the expectations of customers.

**Design or redesign product or service.** *An HMO and a private specialty physician practice cooperated to design a system that allowed patients to see a specialist as soon as the health problem was recognized. Previously, patients who needed to see the specialist had a two-week wait. By analyzing the historical rates of referral from the HMO to the specialty practice, they were able to predict the number of appointments needed each week. The specialty practice reserved an appropriate amount of appointments, allowing the HMO's members almost daily access to them.*

*Design or redesign product or service.* *A law firm received frequent complaints from clients that they could not contact their lawyer when they needed to. The firm realized that access to information anytime, not access to the lawyer, was the issue. A system of digital pagers, confidential computer bulletin boards, and knowledgeable backups for each attorney was designed and the quality problem was eliminated.*

## 65. Offer the Product or Service Anyplace

*(Managing people, or expanding customer expectations to increase demand)* An important dimension of quality for most products and services is convenience. To make a product or service more convenient, free it from constraints of space; make it available anyplace. For products, the constraint of space is often related to the size of the product. Making a product smaller or lighter, without adversely affecting any of its other attributes, almost always improves the quality of the product. Miniaturization is often the result of technology breakthroughs. However, technology is not the only means by which to obtain the "anyplace" attribute. Anytime the customer must come to the provider's place of business or facility to obtain the service, there is an opportunity to change expectations by making the product available in the *customer's* space instead.

*Design or redesign product or service.* *A county education system was interested in offering a diverse curriculum delivered by teachers with special knowledge. The ten high schools in the county were electronically hooked together to allow classes such as Chinese and highly advanced mathematics to be offered to the thirty or so students in the county high schools who desired them. The students remained in their home school and participated in the class through a computer connected to a common Website.*

*Design or redesign product or service.* *A company that specialized in the repair of glass such as car windshields and windows wanted to grow the business. The current system required the customer to come to them. This was the norm in the industry. They equipped several vans to repair windows and windshields anyplace the customer needed them. Customers were not even required to be present. They simply had to tell the company what needed to be repaired and where it was located. This resulted not only in more business but also in higher profits; customers were willing to pay more for the service, and the increased price more than offset the increased cost of providing it.*

## 66. Emphasize Intangibles

*(Managing people, or expanding customer expectations to increase demand)* When we talk about the tangible aspects of a product or service, we are referring to the aspects readily perceived, especially by the sense of touch. Tangible aspects are associated with mass or matter (the shape of a table;

the roominess of the interior of an airplane). Although services have matter associated with them, as with equipment, they are usually less tangible than products.

Opportunities for improvement can be found by embellishing the product with intangible aspects. Two ways to accomplish this are supplying information (electronically or otherwise) or developing product-customer relationships.

***Design or redesign product or service.*** *One of the negative experiences, or intangibles, of being in the hospital is loss of privacy. One cause of sensing this is the variety of strangers who come to take a temperature, draw blood, bring food, and move the patient from place to place. A hospital reorganized services so most of the people needed to satisfy the patient's needs were resident on the unit. Teams of nurses and other workers were assigned to specific patients. This enabled them to establish a better working relationship with the patients. The result was a reduction in the number of people who came into a patient's room and a substantial increase in satisfaction with the experience of care as measured by interviews.*

***Design or redesign product or service.*** *A local hardware store found itself competing with a new facility that was part of a national chain, whose economies of scale allowed it to charge low prices. To keep customers, the local store focused on the intangible of "advice." First the staff developed education programs at night and slow times during work, to increase the knowledge level of their employees about home repair. They also changed hiring processes to make knowledge of home repair an important criterion. The tangible hardware could be bought at either store, but the intangible advice was available only at the local store. Initial worries that customers would buy their products at the new store but get advice from the local one disappeared during a test of the new service.*

## 67. Influence or Take Advantage of Fashion Trends

***(Managing people, or expanding customer expectations to increase demand)*** The word *fashion* evokes images of French dress designers presenting their new collections of expensive women's clothes in Paris. However, for many products such as everyday clothes, automobiles, furniture, dishes, and floor coverings, quality is defined as much by aesthetics as utility. The utility of the product is often assumed, and aesthetics are what can change the customer's expectations.

Trends in public opinion have an aspect of fashion to them and as such are also a source of ideas for new or redesigned products. Health, safety, and security concerns may dominate public discourse. The economic environment will influence whether people prefer luxury or frugality in products they buy.

***Design or redesign product or service.*** *A food products manufacturer predicted trends in consumer preferences by keeping up to date with the latest medical research relating* *to nutrition. By keeping up with the research as it was being done, the company was able to design products consistent with the findings and the resulting public opinion.*

**Design or redesign product or service.** *An automotive manufacturer found that colors and styles that customers wanted in automobiles could be predicted by the popular colors and styles for less-expensive consumer items that were purchased in the previous year. By keeping track of these fashion trends in other consumer items, they were able to offer aesthetics in their cars that were at the leading edge of the trends.*

## 68. Reduce the Number of Components

*(Reducing costs while maintaining or improving quality)* Reducing handoffs was one of the change concepts for simplifying a process. Similarly, reducing the number of component parts is a way to simplify a product. Benefits accrue to the manufacturer, the customer, and those repairing or maintaining the product. In this context, *components* can mean parts, ingredients, or multiple types of the same item.

Reduction of components can be achieved in a number of ways. One is through design of the product so that one component performs the functions previously performed by more than one. Another method is to standardize the size, shape, or brand of similar components. A third method is to package components into modules.

**Design or redesign product or service.** *A company that sold propane gas–fired barbecue grills received complaints from customers about how difficult it was to assemble the grills. The company redesigned the product so that it could be shipped in six modules arranged for each component to be produced by one supplier to promote efficiency of assembly. Assembly time for the customer was reduced substantially, and complaints dropped 90 percent.*

**Design or redesign product or service.** *A pharmaceutical manufacturer realized that people were often using more than one of their products at the same time because they had more than one ailment. This necessitated multiple purchases and some "bookkeeping" to take the correct pills at the correct time. From interviews with doctors, pharmacists, and patients, they determined some of the most frequent combinations of drugs taken. They then developed pills that contained the multiple medications. This was particularly helpful for the elderly, who often had trouble keeping track of the multiple medications they needed.*

## 69. Disguise Defects and Problems

*(Reducing costs while maintaining or improving quality)* "Buy the darker color; it will hide the dirt." One can easily imagine this bit of advice being given to a couple with two young children who are purchasing a rug for their living

room. The darker color will hide the defect (the dirt) although not remove it. The couple could try to remove the defect by not allowing the children in the living room, but this change would cause more problems than it solves.

In some instances, especially in the short run, it may be better to hide the defect in the product or service than to remove it. The longer-term strategy remains removing the defect. Also included in this category are actions taken to make the defect more palatable to the customer. This change concept does *not* include false advertising, in which claims about the product are made that are not true. Also excluded are defects that are hidden at the time of sale only to emerge in later use of the product.

***Design or redesign product or service.*** *A manufacturer of vinyl floor tiles was testing a new flat white pattern. The pattern was very attractive to customers who wanted the look of a ceramic tile floor but at a cheaper price. This was the first time this type of pattern had been produced. During manufacturing tests it was discovered that small black specks were evident in some of the tiles. The flat white surface of the tiles made them particularly conspicuous. This was not a problem for the other patterns and colors they made. Rather than install an expensive air filtration system in the plant, the designers added some small points of black to the pattern itself, which essentially camouflaged specks of dirt.*

***Design or redesign product or service.*** *To compensate for people who do not show up for their flights, airlines frequently book more passengers for a plane than there are seats available. Every once in a while, more people show up for the flight than can fit in the plane. The airlines give the available seats to passengers on a first-come, first-served basis. Those who are not able to get on the flight are furious. One airline changed its approach and asked for volunteers to take the next available flight to the destination. In addition the volunteers would get a coupon redeemable for a free flight anywhere in the country at some later date. This virtually eliminated complaints about overbooking of flights and allowed the airline to continue a cost-effective policy of overbooking.*

## 70. Differentiate Product Using Quality Dimensions

***(Expanding customer expectations to increase demand)*** We improve quality as we improve the match between products and services and the need they are designed to satisfy. The degree of matching is determined by the customer's definition of *quality*. Customer research can aid understanding of how customers define it and how this definition differs among customer groups. Two completely different products can be considered high-quality as contrasting dimensions of quality are considered important for the two products. To compete on quality, an organization must determine what dimensions are important to the group of customers (segment of the market) on which the organization is focusing.

*Design or redesign product or service.* *A manufacturer of electronic equipment focused its business strategy on service. The company was close to the industry average on most of the other dimensions of quality but number one on service. It maintained about a 12 percent market share and was consistently more profitable than competitors.*

*Design or redesign product or service.* *An overnight package delivery company learned that "personal interface" was an important dimension of quality to many customers as well as the employees. Though many of their current procedures emphasized on-time delivery, productivity, and efficiency in their drivers' interaction with customers, they changed internal procedures to allot each driver a half-hour per day to spend time strengthening ties with customers in the interface moments. The revenue increases obtained from this change are many times the cost of the drivers' time.*

## 71. Change the Order of Process Steps

*(Reducing costs while maintaining or improving quality)* One way to improve flow, increase customer satisfaction (in service processes), and reduce waste is to document each step in the current process (possibly with a flow diagram) and then rearrange the order in which the steps are done to better serve the goals of the process. This concept is especially useful if there are multiple exit points in the process. For example, if someone comes to a facility to donate blood, it would be optimal for all parties to identify someone who is not qualified to donate at that time as soon as possible. It would waste resources, irritate potential donors, and cause backups if a donor was processed through a number of the steps in the process before learning she cannot donate at this time (see a donor example in Chapter Six). The change in order of steps could require a physical rearrangement of equipment, a change in job duties for some employees, or a change in instructions to customers.

*Design or redesign process or system.* *An assembly process had five stations. The first inspection of the parts was done as part of step 3 to take advantage of equipment available at that step. An investigation of rejected parts found the biggest cause of rejection was problems with the characteristics of a part provided by supplier. Parts were being returned to the supplier after disassembly of the rejected parts in the inspection department. The organization was bearing the cost of performing steps 1 and 2 as well as the cost of disassembly. The process was redesigned by moving the inspection of parts for supplier characteristics to follow step 1. After balancing the flow in the redesigned process, a significant cost savings was obtained.*

*Design or redesign process or system.* *A Web-based service organization analyzed the activities of potential customers who visited their Website but did not complete registration. They analyzed the steps in the process where a potential customer would abort the registration process and found two elements near the end of the process where more than half of the customers stopped the process. The order of the registration steps was changed so that the two elements were included in the beginning of the process. A simple Save function was added so a customer who did not have the information could obtain it and then easily pick up on the registration process without having to reenter information. The result was an increase of greater than 10 percent in registrations the month after this redesign.*

## 72. Manage Uncertainty, Not Tasks

*(Eliminating quality problems)* Methods and tools for project management methods typically focus on (1) completing tasks within a specified time line and (2) the interdependencies among those tasks. Many improvement projects face major uncertainties from lack of the knowledge necessary to make decisions on what the tasks are or how to complete them. These uncertainties must be managed first, with much of the resources devoted to reducing them as well as project reviews focusing on the progress of the learning necessary to reduce these uncertainties.

*Design or redesign product or service. A software company decided to develop a new application that would have a large market with little or no competing current software. Knowing this program would be a challenge, the product development team met weekly to identify and reduce the uncertainties in the project. They formed small teams to work on a number of areas associated with the uncertainties. Also, they assembled weekly prototypes of the program even though they knew it would not be very functional in the early stages. With more effort in the early stages, they would not be a costly change in direction—something that has plagued them in all previous programs. Their product development time was cut in half and the software was the most successful launch ever. They documented all their learning around the uncertainties and adopted this change concept and practice for all future software development work.*

# APPENDIX B

---

# TOOLS AND METHODS TO SUPPORT IMPROVEMENT

---

The Model for Improvement, with its three questions and the PDSA Cycle for learning and improvement, constitutes the framework and roadmap for accomplishing improvements of processes, products, and systems. In many improvement efforts, this is all that is required to guide the development, testing, implementation, and spread of ideas for change. But sometimes, teams get stuck looking for an idea or trying to understand the problems in the current process. Over the past eighty years, the quality improvement profession has developed, adopted, and adapted methods and tools to assist with the improvement process. Today, the science of improvement has a set of methods and tools that should be available for use on improvement projects when applicable. The most common methods and tools are briefly described in this appendix.

The purpose of this appendix is to document the set of tools and methods typically included in the "science of improvement." Some of these tools and methods have been referenced in previous parts of this book. Because information on all the tools and methods is readily available in other publications and on many Internet sites, we have not included how to construct or use the tools and methods here. Rather, we have focused on documenting a complete set of tools and how they connect to the Model for Improvement. Please see the Notes section of this book for references or conduct an internet search if you plan to use any of these tools or methods.

When thinking about these methods and tools, it is important to keep a perspective on the improvement initiative. The objective should always be to make an improvement, not to use tools. If a project's charter can be accomplished without the use of any of the tools, then we would encourage the reader to maintain the focus on making the improvements. The tools and methods exist to lend additional insight whenever questions exist, next steps are not obvious, or potential solutions are not available.

At the end of this appendix are some forms to support the use of the Model for Improvement as well.

Tables B.1 and B.2 summarize the methods and tools for improvement. As used here, a "method" is a broad procedure or approach to accomplishing something following a specific plan and set of tools. A "tool" is a technique, object, or device for completing a specific task. So the Model for Improvement described in this book is a method to organize and manage the thinking in an improvement project. Tools such as the charter, run charts to display measures, check sheets to collect data, and flow diagrams to understand how a process works are examples that might be used with the Model for Improvement on a particular project.

Two tables follow that organize tools and methods for improvement into these six categories:

1. Viewing systems and processes
2. Gathering information
3. Organizing information
4. Understanding variation
5. Understanding relationships
6. Managing projects

The categories are based on broad objectives for using the method or tool. A brief description of each method and tool follows Tables B.1 and B.2.

## Methods and Tools for Viewing Systems and Processes

An important diagnostic strategy for improvement projects focused on improving a process or system is to understand how the current process (or system) works. An important method to accomplish this is *process mapping*. There are a number of tools associated with this method.

A *flow diagram* is one of the basic tools for improvement that gives a visual picture of a process being studied. The flow diagram (often called a flowchart) is

**TABLE B.1. OVERVIEW OF *METHODS* FOR IMPROVEMENT.**

| Category | Method | Page | Typical Use of Method |
|---|---|---|---|
| Viewing systems and processes | Process mapping | p. 414 | Various approaches (flow diagrams, value stream mapping, Supplier-Inputs-Process-Outputs-Customers (SIPOC) Diagrams etc.) to make the activities and performance of a process or system visible. |
| | Dynamic simulation | p. 417 | Map relationships with mathematical equations and then simulate performance. |
| Gathering information | Surveys | p. 417 | Obtain information from people. |
| | Benchmarking | p. 418 | Obtain information on performance and approaches from other organizations. |
| | Creativity methods | p. 418 | Develop new ideas and fresh thinking. |
| Organizing information | Quality function deployment (QFD) | p. 423 | Communicate customer needs and requirements through the design and production processes. |
| | Failure mode and effects analysis (FMEA) | p. 423 | Used by process and product designers to identify and address potential failures |
| | Problem solving | p. 426 | A collection of concepts and tools (is-or-is-not, five *whys*, stratification) to address the special case of improvement where a problem has been identified |
| Understanding variation | Statistical process control | p. 433 | A philosophy and a set of methods for improvement with its foundation in the theory of variation. SPC incorporates the concepts of an analytic study, process thinking, prevention, stratification, stability, capability, and prediction. |
| | Measurement system analysis | p. 434 | Procedures to understand the impact of bias and precision of the measurement process on variation in data |
| | Statistical methods | p. 434 | Graphical and numerical procedures to help understand, quantify, and communicate patterns of variation in data |
| Understanding relationships | Planned experimentation | p. 440 | Design studies to evaluate cause-and-effect relationships and test changes. |
| Project management | Model for Improvement | p. 442 | A framework or roadmap for an improvement project |
| | PDSA Cycle | p. 443 | Method for organizing learning, testing, and implementing during an improvement project |

## TABLE B.2. OVERVIEW OF *TOOLS* FOR IMPROVEMENT.

| Category | Tool | Page | Typical Use of Tool |
|---|---|---|---|
| Viewing systems and processes | Flow diagrams | p. 414 | Develop a picture of a process. Communicate and standardize processes. Includes value stream mapping spaghetti diagrams, etc. |
| | Causal loop diagrams | p. 415 | Identify reinforcing and balancing processes |
| | Linkage of processes | p. 416 | Develop a picture of a system composed of processes linked together |
| Gathering information | Form for collecting data | p. 418 | Plan and organize a data collection effort |
| | Operational Definitions | p. 419 | Provide communicable meaning to a concept by specifying how the concept will be applied within a particular set of circumstances |
| Organizing information | Affinity diagram | p. 427 | Organize and summarize qualitative information |
| | Force field analysis | p. 427 | Summarize forces supporting and hindering change. |
| | Cause-and-effect diagram | p. 429 | Collect and organize current knowledge about potential causes of problems or variation. |
| | Driver diagram | p. 429 | Display the theory for improvement in an improvement project. |
| | Matrix diagram | p. 430 | Arrange information to understand relationships and make decisions. |
| | Tree diagram | p. 430 | Visualize the structure of a problem, plan, or any other opportunity of interest. |
| | Interrelationship diagram | p. 432 | Identify and communicate logical and sequential connections between components of a problem. |
| | Radar chart | p. 432 | Evaluate alternatives or compare against targets with three or more variables or characteristics. |
| Understanding variation | Run chart | p. 435 | Study variation in data over time; understand the impact of changes on measures. |
| | Frequency plot | p. 436 | Understand location, spread, shape, and patterns of data. |
| | Pareto chart | p. 436 | Focus on areas of improvement with greatest impact. |
| | Shewhart control chart | p. 438 | Distinguish between special and common causes of variation. |

| | Other graphs | p. 439 | Variety of graphs used to display data for learning. |
|---|---|---|---|
| Understanding relationships | Scatterplot | p. 441 | Analyze the associations or relationship between two variables; test for possible cause-and-effect. |
| | Two-way table | p. 441 | Understand cause-and-effect for qualitative variables |
| Project management | Gantt chart | p. 443 | Organization of the project tasks over time with key milestones identified |
| | PERT chart | p. 443 | Display the sequential relationships of the project tasks and determine the critical path |
| | Work breakdown structure | p. 444 | Develop a hierarchical relationship between the tasks on a project |
| | A3 diagram | p. 444 | One-page format for summarizing improvement projects |

a graphic representation of a series of activities that define a process. There are several types of flow diagram that can be useful in an improvement effort:

- Top-down flow diagram
- Matrix or group (also known as "swim-lane" flow diagram)
- Complexity diagram (separating basic process functions from activities due to waste, work flow, or poor quality)
- Value stream mapping (see description below)

The flow diagram displayed in Figure B.1 is typical of the types used in quality improvement projects. The flow diagram is used with the Model for improvement in a number of ways:

- Defining the scope of an improvement effort (What are we trying to accomplish?)
- Serving as a date collection form (How will we know that a change is an improvement?)
- Identifying obvious changes that can be made (What changes can we make that will result in improvement?)
  - Understand the context in which a change will be made
  - Furnish a tool for logical thinking about the current process
  - Define the vision for a new process

# FIGURE B.1. FLOW DIAGRAM FOR THE "RETURN PARTS" PROCESS.

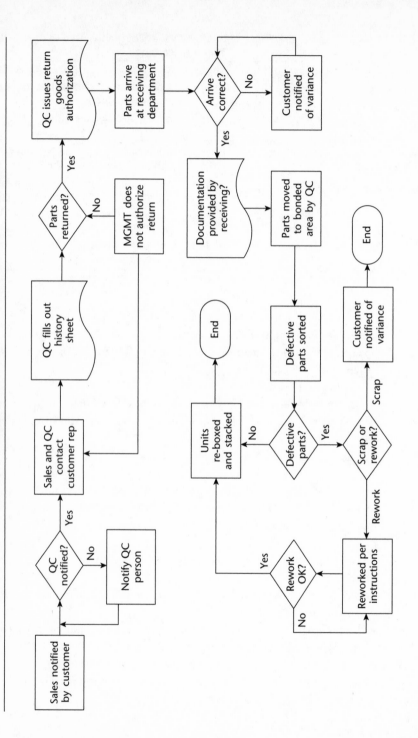

*Value stream mapping (VSM)* is a specific type of flow diagram recommend for lean improvement projects. The VSM approach shows not only process flows but also information flow that signals and controls the material flows. This visual representation identifies the value-adding steps in a process and assists in finding the non-value-adding steps or waste. A timeline is displayed at the bottom of the process map, showing the processing time for each operation and the transfer delays between operations. The timeline is used to identify the value-adding steps, as well as wasted time.

A *causal loop diagram* is a type of flow diagram that focuses on identifying reinforcing and balancing processes in a system. These diagrams consist of arrows connecting variables (things that change over time) in a way that shows how one variable affects another. A causal loop diagram is a tool for communicating our understanding of the dynamic aspects of a process or system. Multiple causal loops can be linked together to develop a diagram of a particular issue in a complex system. Figure B.2 is an example of a causal loop diagram.

A flow diagram is a very useful tool for data collection. For example, a *spaghetti diagram* (see Figure B.5) is constructed by following the path of someone working in the process to better understand workflow.

A *linkage of processes* extends the flow diagram to a system. The linkage of processes is a tool to develop a view of a system composed of processes linked together to accomplish a common purpose. This view helps people understand the interdependencies in a system. Figure B.3 shows linkage of processes for a banking organization (a "system for banking"). In viewing a system, one can think of processes as the building blocks of the system.

## FIGURE B.2.  EXAMPLE OF CAUSAL LOOP DIAGRAM.

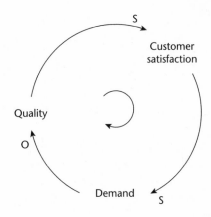

# FIGURE B.3. LINKAGE OF PROCESSES FOR A BANKING ORGANIZATION.

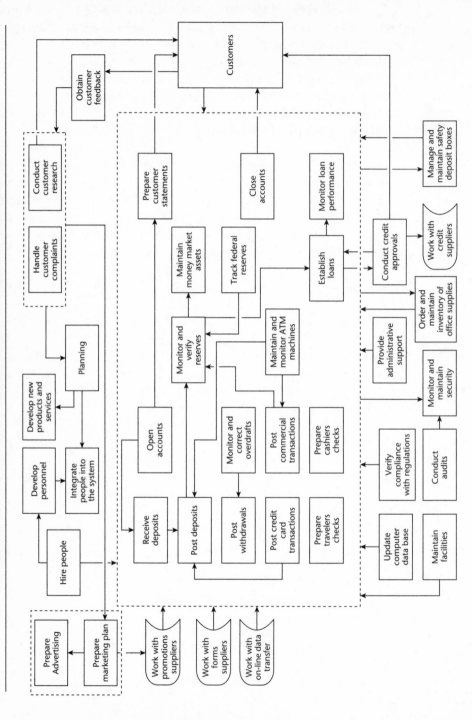

*Dynamic simulation* is a method to map relationships in a process with mathematical equations and then simulate performance of the process. Computer simulations allow one to predict the performance of a system or explore changes to system. The computer model can include mathematical relationships as well as actual data results.

## Methods and Tools for Gathering Information

A *survey* is a method of collecting information directly from people about their feelings, motivations, plans, beliefs, experiences, and backgrounds. Standard surveys often generate the data to answer, "How will we know that a change is an improvement?" Various types of surveys are used as a data collection process to answer questions posed in the planning phase of a PDSA cycle. There are several types of more formal surveys that can obtain both qualitative and quantitative data:

- Written surveys
- Personal interviews
- Group interviews
- Observation
- Trading places

Here is a useful guide for planning a survey for a PDSA Cycle:

1. Clarify the purpose of the survey relative to the PDSA Cycle objective.
2. Consider why a survey is the best method for obtaining the desired information.
3. What questions are to be answered by the survey?
4. Decide on the type of survey (written, phone, interview).
5. Select the survey's design, content, writing questions, and testing out the form.
6. Decide who should participate and when (will sampling be used?).
7. Will there be follow-up surveys?
8. Attend to survey administration (for example, collecting survey forms, conducting interviews).
9. Analyze, interpret, and report results.
10. Act (if appropriate) on the survey results.

Figure B.4 shows an example of a form that can be used as a written survey or personal interview. The survey includes both qualitative information (ideas for improvement) and quantitative information (satisfaction rating to be used as project measure).

*Benchmarking* is a name given to the various approaches used to obtain information on performance and approaches from other organizations. See Chapter Six for a discussion of using benchmarking to develop ideas for change.

*Creativity methods* include tools and approaches to develop new ideas on the basis of different thinking (see Chapter Six for discussion of using creativity to answer, What change can we make that will result in improvement?) Specific creativity tools can be used in both problem-solving activities and generation of fundamental change in products (services) and processes. Producing new perceptions, ideas, and concepts is very often a necessity to develop changes that improve the system beyond historical levels. Table B.3 lists some of the specific creativity tools useful in improvement activities.

A *form for collecting data* is a useful tool in many PDSA Cycles to plan and organize the data collection effort needed to answer the questions posed in the cycle. A specific form is designed for collecting data to:

- Answer specific questions posed in the planning phase of the improvement cycle
- Make the recording of observations easy, efficient, and accurate
- Facilitate data analysis during the study phase of the improvement cycle

### FIGURE B.4. SURVEY FOR BANK IMPROVEMENT TEAM, PDSA CYCLE 7.

*Thank you for doing business at our branch today. Please help us improve our service to you by completing this survey:*

List three ways we can improve our service to you:

1.

2.

3.

Please rate your experience with our services today (circle one)

Poor             Fair             Good             Very Good             Excellent

Other suggestions:

## TABLE B.3. SOME CREATIVITY TOOLS.

| Tool | Some Uses of the Tool with Model for Improvement in Developing Changes |
|---|---|
| Creative focus | To define the focus and changing focuses of the thinking. To seek alternative framing or level of abstraction of the thinking processes. |
| Challenge | To challenge traditional thinking, existing thinking, and the thinking taking place during a creative thinking session. Also to challenge the surroundings of the thinking: assumptions, boundaries, essential factors, avoidance factors, etc. |
| Alternatives | To find other ways of doing things and of satisfying a defined fixed point. Can be operated at levels ranging from the broad to the detailed. |
| Concept fan | An elaborated tool for defining different ways of doing things by going through concepts. Useful in achievement thinking. |
| Concept extraction | Deliberate attention to concepts. Seeking to extract and crystallize concepts. Pulling back from ideas to the concept level. Useful in all areas that are driven by concepts. |
| Escape provocation | Useful in all areas where challenge is helpful. Escape provocation turns the challenge into a provocation. Useful for looking at current thinking on a subject or process. |
| Stepping-stone provocations | Generally used to try to get radical changes in the whole system or approach. The methods are called reversal, distortion, exaggeration, and wishful thinking. The wishful thinking method has a special use in generating ideas from a "clean sheet of paper" situation. |
| Random entry | Used to generate fresh ideas on any occasion. Helps to get going in "greenfield" situations or when ideas have run out. Seeks additional and different ideas when there are already some ideas on the table. |

There are two basic types of forms for collecting data: check sheets and recording forms. Use check sheets when specific values of the data are defined and planned for prior to collection. If values are not defined before collecting data, use recording forms. Table B.4 shows a check sheet that is a simple tally of problems with a copier machine. The check sheet itemizes the types of defects prior to collecting the data. The last row of the form allows open comments (recording form).

A flow diagram or a process layout picture can also be used as a data collection form. For example, a spaghetti diagram is developed by observing the flow in a process and drawing lines on the flow diagram to represent the flow (see example in Figure B.5).

An *operational definition* puts communicable meaning to a concept by specifying how the concept will be applied within a particular set of circumstances. Once collection of data begins and the data to be recorded are identified, questions may

## TABLE B.4.  EXAMPLE OF CHECK SHEET TO TALLY PROBLEMS.

| Problem | Occurrences | | | | |
|---|---|---|---|---|---|
| | Monday | Tuesday | Wednesday | Thursday | Friday |
| Out of paper | | | | | |
| Out of toner | | | | | |
| Copies too light | | | | | |
| Sorter not working | | | | | |
| Document feeder | | | | | |
| Transparency feed | | | | | |
| **Other:** | | | | | |
| Copier just stopped | | | | | |
| Panel won't clear | | | | | |
| No power to copier | | | | | |
| Please record other comments and suggestions here | | | | | |

arise where an operational definition is lacking. For example, a team is planning a PDSA Cycle to collect data concerning late deliveries. The questions surface: "What do we mean by on-time delivery? If a delivery is scheduled for 8:00 A.M., is it late at 8:01 A.M.? Whose watch should be used to measure the time?" The team agrees to the operational definition that *on-time* means a margin of plus or minus fifteen minutes of the scheduled delivery according to the clock at the plant. Now that on-time is operationally defined, the collection of data can begin.

*Data on personal experience:* Data based on personal experiences plays a key role in many improvement efforts. Most people think of data as numbers that result from measurement of such factors as time, cost, and length—elements of the physical world. The idea of data is often associated with the physical sciences. Documentation, however, can take the form of activities recorded on videotape or in a photograph; ideas and feelings written in a diary; and words, letters, or numbers written on paper or in an electronic file. People engaged in improvement efforts should also be interested in data about personal experience.

Data on personal experience can be obtained indirectly by recording observations (written or visual) or by counting the frequency of certain behaviors. Some

# FIGURE B.5. SPAGHETTI DIAGRAM VERSION OF A DATA COLLECTION FORM.

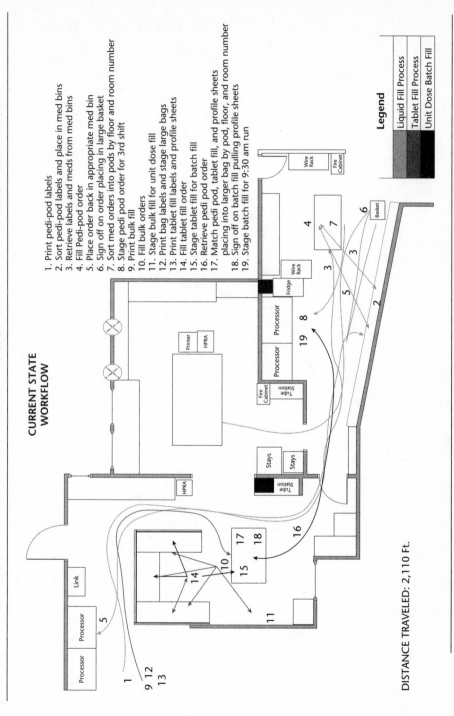

## CURRENT STATE WORKFLOW

1. Print pedi-pod labels
2. Sort pedi-pod labels and place in med bins
3. Retrieve labels and meds from med bins
4. Fill Pedi-pod order
5. Place order back in appropriate med bin
6. Sign off on order placing in large basket
7. Sort med orders into pods by floor and room number
8. Stage pedi pod order for 3rd shift
9. Print bulk fill
10. Fill bulk orders
11. Stage bulk fill for unit dose fill
12. Print bag labels and stage large bags
13. Print tablet fill labels and profile sheets
14. Fill tablet fill order
15. Stage tablet fill for batch fill
16. Retrieve pedi pod order
17. Match pedi pod, tablet fill, and profile sheets placing into larger bag by pod, floor, and room number
18. Sign off on batch fill pulling profile sheets
19. Stage batch fill for 9:30 am run

### Legend

Liquid Fill Process
Tablet Fill Process
Unit Dose Batch Fill

**DISTANCE TRAVELED: 2,110 Ft.**

*Source:* from prescription fill process developed by Carl Donisi and Jason Combs at Cincinnati Children's Medical Center.

examples of observations of behavior that could be recorded and analyzed are absenteeism, volunteering answers in a seminar, searching for a salesperson in a store, people paying attention to a product displayed in a store, volunteering for a task, and committing an unsafe act. These observations can be quantified by using classifications or counts of the observed behavior during a fixed period of observation.

Data about personal experience can be obtained more directly by asking people about their feelings or to record their feelings at specified or random times. Ranking or rating scales can be used to obtain data on personal experience. Figure B.6 shows three such rating scales. Here are some examples of questions and statements that could be used with the scales:

*Examples of Questions Used with the Poor-Excellent Scale*

- How would you rate your health in the last four weeks?
- How would you rate the courtesy shown to you during your stay at this hotel?
- How would you rate the landscaping around this building?
- How would you rate the relationship you have with our project manager?

*Examples of Questions Used with the Worse-Better Scale*

- How would you rate your overall health now compared to four weeks ago?
- How would you rate the new process for taking orders compared to the old one?
- How would you rate the appearance of floor tile A compared to tile B?
- How would you rate the new sick-leave policy versus the old one?

## FIGURE B.6. SIMPLE SCALES FOR TURNING PERSONAL EXPERIENCE INTO DATA.

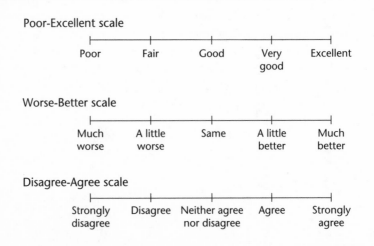

*Examples of Questions Used with the Agree-Disagree Scale*

- Our attorneys exhibit the highest integrity.
- Our instructions for assembly of the bookcase are easy to follow.
- It is easy to find what you are looking for in our catalogue.
- Conscientious efforts were made to relieve your anxiety during your stay in the hospital.

The response to the question can be put anywhere on the scale. It need not be limited to the five discrete labels. In some cases it may be appropriate to insert another label titled "Don't know." The scales are provided to establish a basic level of measurement for almost any application. Theresa could use some questions along with the scales to learn about her staff's experiences with the new computers and software.

The use of the scales also affords the opportunity to collect additional information helpful in our efforts to make improvements. As people respond to questions, we can ask

- For examples and evidence that support their answer
- Suggestions for improvement that can help answer the question, "What changes can we make that will result in improvement?"

# Methods and Tools for Organizing Information

*Quality function deployment (QFD)* is as a method for organizing knowledge on relationships between measures (quality characteristics) of a product, service, or process and factors that affect their performance. In the context of the Model for Improvement, it is an effective way to help answer the second and third questions: "How will we know that a change is an improvement?" and "What changes can we make that will result in improvement?" When used in the framework of the Model for Improvement and supplemented with other tools such as planned experimentation, QFD is a useful approach to manage and document the design of products and processes. The QFD method incorporates matrix diagrams, interrelationship diagrams, and other tools described in this section. Figure B.7 shows an example of a completed QFD analysis.

*Failure mode and effects analysis (FMEA)* is a systematic, proactive method of identifying and preventing product and process problems before they occur. FMEA uses a standardized approach to analysis that includes review of function, failure modes, failure causes, and failure consequences. In an improvement project, the method is used as part of designing a process and product to identify and address potential failures. Figure B.8 shows a part of a completed FMEA for a chemotherapy process.

# FIGURE B.7. EXAMPLE OF COMPLETED QFD DIAGRAM.

Quality Function Deployment Worksheet

Customer: End State Chemical
Customer Needs: Intermediates for cosmetics and

- ☐ Product ____
- ☐ Service ____
- ☑ Process Carbizene
- ☐ Design ☑ Re-design

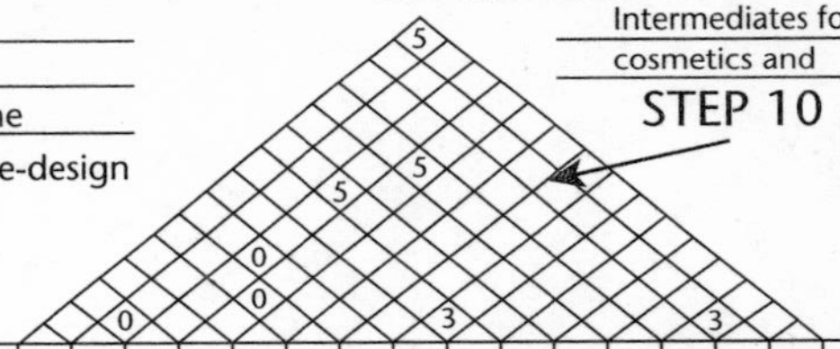

**STEP 10**

**FACTORS**

**QUALITY CHARACTERISTICS**

| Customer | Measurable | Importance | Prod. Tower OH Flow | Catalyst Supplier | Reaction Temp | Amount of Chem.A | Operator Training | Mixing Direction | Reaction Order | Mixing Speed | Mixing Time | Reaction Time | Amount of Catalyst | Amount Chemical B | Prod. Tower stm Rate | Prod. Tower stm Pressure | Prod. Tower Temp. | Cust. Satisfaction: US | Cust. Satisfaction: X |
|---|---|---|---|---|---|---|---|---|---|---|---|---|---|---|---|---|---|---|---|
| Good Carbizene | High Yield | 5 | 5 | 1 | 3 | 5 | 1 | 0 | 3 | 3 | 5 | 5 | 5 | 5 | 3 | 3 | 3 | 3 | 1 |
|  | Low Var. | 5 | 5 | 1 | 3 | 5 | 1 | 0 | 1 | 0 | 3 | 3 | 1 | 5 | 0 | 3 | 3 | 3 | 3 |
| Good Color | Low Score | 3 | 5 | 0 | 5 | 5 | 1 | 0 | 1 | 5 | 5 | 5 | 0 | 3 | 5 | 3 | 0 | 5 | 1 |
|  | Low Var. | 3 | 3 | 0 | 3 | 3 | 1 | 1 | 3 | 3 | 3 | 3 | 0 | 1 | 3 | 3 | 5 | 3 | 3 |
| No Foreign Made | Low Count | 3 | 5 | 5 | 0 | 0 | 3 | 0 | 3 | 0 | 0 | 5 | 5 | 5 | 0 | 0 | 0 | 5 | 1 |
|  | Low Var. | 5 | 3 | 5 | 0 | 0 | 0 | 0 |  | 0 | 0 | 5 | 3 | 5 | 5 | 0 | 0 | 2 | 3 |
| No Damnitol | Low Conc. | 4 | 5 | 0 | 3 | 0 | 1 | 0 | 0 | 0 | 0 | 5 | 1 | 3 | 3 | 3 | 3 | 5 | 3 |
|  | Low Var. |  | 5 | 0 | 0 | 0 | 1 | 0 | 0 | 0 | 0 | 5 | 3 | 5 | 3 | 3 | 3 | 3 | 3 |
| No Endene | Low Conc. | 1 | 0 | 0 | 3 | 1 | 1 | 1 | 5 | 3 | 5 | 1 | 3 | 3 | 3 | 3 | 3 | 1 | 5 |
|  | Low Var. | 2 | 1 | 0 | 3 | 1 | 1 | 1 | 5 | 5 | 3 | 3 | 1 | 1 | 1 | 3 | 1 | 1 | 5 |
| **Factor Target Value** | | | 300 lbs/hr | Wright-A | 260 F. | 1600 lbs. | complete | clockwise | A then B | 200 RPM | 20 min. | 120 min. | 80 lbs. | 1500 lbs. | 1500 lbs. | 22 PSI | 185 F | | |
| **Leverage Values – Import.** | | | 146 | 50 | 95 | 77 | 19 | 6 | 47 | 52 | 75 | 86 | 67 | 107 | 90 | 81 | 48 | | |
| **Leverage Values – Sat.** | | | 120 | 41 | 82 | 63 | 16 | 6 | 33 | 51 | 66 | 72 | 49 | 87 | 87 | 73 | 36 | | |

QC Targets

— STEP 12 —
— STEP 11 —

Importance Rating: 1 = least important.....5 = most important
Customer Satisfaction: 1 = very satisfied.....5 = very dissatisfied
Strength of Relationship: 0 = none, 1 = weak, 3 = moderate, 5 = strong, blank = unknown

1. Focus on "product," "service," or "process."

2. List all relevant customers.

3. List quality characteristics (QC) expressed in the customers' own words.

4. Assign a rating of relative importance (customers' view) to each QC.

5. For a redesign, enter a rating that indicates the customer's current satisfaction with each QC.

6. Enter a similar rating for an important alternative product or service available to the customer.

7. List all the important factors believed to have influence on the list of QCs.

8. Using the matrix format inside the main body of the "house," enter a rating in each QC/factor location that expresses the strength of the relationship between that factor and QC.

9. In each factor column in the third row from the bottom of the worksheet, enter the current target value for that factor.

10. Use the matrix in the "roof" of the house, except now enter numbers to represent strength of relationship for any pairs of factors thought to be related.

11. Determine the leverage of each factor on all the QCs weighted by importance to the customer.

12. Determine the leverage of each factor on all the QCs, weighted by current level of customer satisfaction.

*Note:* **steps 10, 11, and 12 on the QFD diagram are from the steps to complete a QFD.**

# FIGURE B.8. PARTIAL FMEA FOR CHEMOTHERAPY PROCESS.

| Steps in the Process | Failure Mode | Failure Causes | Failure Effects | Likelihood of Occurrence (1–10) | Likelihood of Detection (1–10) | Severity (1–10) | Risk Priority Number (RPN) | Comments |
|---|---|---|---|---|---|---|---|---|
| MD Order | Incorrect drug is ordered | Mental slip; handwriting issue, misreading protocol; lack of knowledge; protocol printed incorrectly Database for protocols | Potentially fatal outcome | 1 | 8 | 10 | 80 | Will require long-term commitment to maintain database and careful attention to complying with policies |
| | Incorrect dose is ordered | Calculation error; misreading protocol, incorrect patient data (weight, height, WBC, creatinine), BSA calculated incorrectly, handwriting issue; patient data not available; mental slip; protocol printed incorrectly. | Potentially fatal outcome | 2 | 1 | 10 | 20 | Having database available to MDs may assist with this element; will require careful attention to complying with policies |

*Source:* from FMEA tool at www.IHI.org.

## FIGURE B.9. EXAMPLE OF IS-OR-NOT-IS ANALYSIS.

|  | Is (the problem occurs) | Is Not (the problem does not occur) |
|---|---|---|
| Where? Physical or geographical location | Samples after the tower process | Samples before the tower process |
| When? Time of day, month, year; relationship to other events | During the summer months the last two years | October through March; all times prior to 2006 |
| Who? Groups, individuals, organizations | Feedstock from supplier B, C, E, and F; all shifts in plant | Feedstock from suppliers A and D |
| What Kind? Category, type, other stratification variables | Regular-grade product; high feed rates | Premium-grade product; low feed rates |
| How Much? Extent, degree, duration | More discoloration on hot days; more when running feedstock B; more during last two months | Less discoloration on cool days; less discoloration with feedstocks E and F |

*Problem solving* is the name used to describe a collection of concepts and tools designed to address the special case of improvement where a particular problem has been identified. Because problem solving is just a special category of improvement, all of the methods and tools presented in this appendix can be used to aid problem solving. In particular, a Pareto analysis is one of the most powerful methods of solving problems. Two additional tools have been found useful in problem solving efforts: an *is-or-is-not analysis* and a *pro-and-con analysis*.

The is-or-is-not analysis offers a useful way to summarize current knowledge about a problem and get started on investigations to make this knowledge more complete. The pro-and-con analysis is a format for moving a group to problem resolution; it favors a win-win solution for all parties involved. Both tools are helpful in answering the question, "What changes can we make that will result in improvement?"

Is-or-is-not analysis is a tool used to understand the differences in the situation where the problem is occurring and where the problem is not occurring. It is a special application of the matrix diagram for problem solving. The questions *where, when, who, what kind,* and *how much* are used to better understand the problem. Figure B.9 shows an example of an is-or-is-not analysis.

A pro-and-con analysis can be used to select a potential approach to solving the problem from different alternatives. For each alterative approach, collect information on the advantages and positive impacts (the pros) and the disadvantages, negative impacts, and side-effects (the cons). The pro's and con's can

## FIGURE B.10. EXAMPLE OF PRO-AND-CON ANALYSIS FOR PROBLEM SOLVING.

| Expected impact on: | Alternative A | | Alternative B | |
|---|---|---|---|---|
| | Pros | Cons | Pro | Cons |
| Customers | Continued supply of product to meet demand | Risk of losing supply in long run | Improved image of products they are buying | Possible price increases in future |
| Suppliers | Predictable demand in near future | Less business in short run | Possibly more business | Increased competition from new suppliers |
| Employees | Job security for employees with high seniority | Layoffs of employees with low seniority | Possible new opportunities for promotion | Risk of more layoffs in future |
| Stockholders | Stability of investment | Less long-term growth potential | Growth potential of investment | Lower returns in short run |
| Community | Maintain viable business | Unemployment increases | New companies doing business in community | Increases in water pollution |

be grouped in various ways (customer, supplier, worker, investor; immediate, short-range, long-term; etc.). The information can then be organized in a matrix diagram to compare the alternatives. Figure B.10 shows an example of a pro-and-con analysis of a problem with a product.

An *affinity diagram* is a method to summarize qualitative data. The purpose of the diagram is to categorize or group together available items that have some relationship or association (affinity). In PDSA Cycles that collect qualitative data from customer surveys, employee surveys, and benchmark data about competitors, complaints, suggestions, and ideas, the affinity diagram has proven useful. It is a good tool to analyze the output from a brainstorming session to develop changes. The tool is also useful to summarize input from stakeholders in conducting planning for improvement. Figure B.11 presents an example of an affinity diagram.

A *force field analysis* is a useful tool for uncovering both restraining and driving forces for a change. It is useful when planning PDSA Cycles to implement changes. The tool will help to organize the change effort and may uncover restraining or driving forces that those planning the changes were unaware of. Figure B.12 shows a completed force field analysis.

A *cause-and-effect diagram* (also known as a fishbone diagram or Ishikawa diagram) is used to collect and organize current knowledge about potential causes of problems or variation. The diagram is a useful tool in a PDSA Cycle for

## FIGURE B.11. AFFINITY DIAGRAM FOR INPUT TO PLANNING PROCESS.

| *Management Issues* | *Product Issues* | *Customer Issues* |
|---|---|---|
| Each manager is doing the next-level job | Products routinely miss the market window | Customer complaints about product consistency |
| Managers are task-oriented | Increase in unprofitable products | Customer complaints about product consistency |
| Employee grievances have increased 14% | Change over from one product campaign to another is difficult and time-consuming | Product variability causes downtime of equipment & maintenance PM time increase |
| Turnover rate is high at 23% | Costs associated with product introduction are typically 30% over estimates | Customer inspection results do not match our documented results |
| Decision-making process is cumbersome | | |
| Globalization of market requires managers that appreciate other cultures | | |

## FIGURE B.12. EXAMPLE OF A FORCE FIELD ANALYSIS.

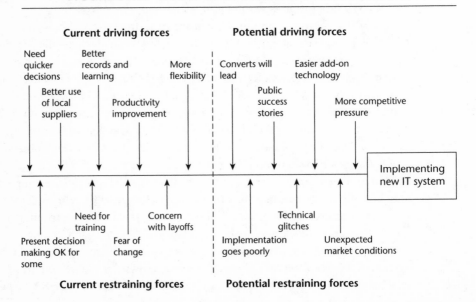

## FIGURE B.13.  EXAMPLE OF A CAUSE-AND-EFFECT DIAGRAM FOR COLOR IN A CHEMICAL PROCESS.

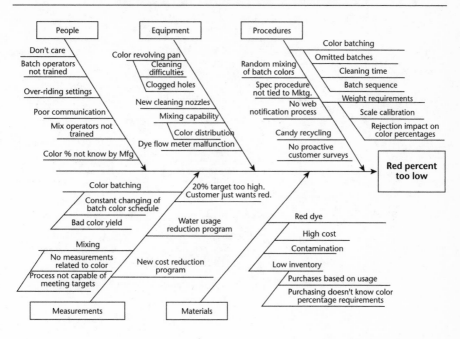

developing changes for discovering, organizing, and summarizing a group's knowledge about causes contributing to variation or to a problem. Figure B.13 is an example of a cause-and-effect diagram.

A *driver diagram* is another approach to describing our theories of improvement. In an improvement project, a driver diagram is a tool to help organize our theories and ideas in an improvement effort as we answer, "What change can we make that will result in improvement?"

The initial driver diagram for an improvement project might lay out the descriptive theory of improved outcomes that can then be tested and enhanced to develop a predictive theory. The driver diagram should be updated throughout an improvement effort and used to track progress in theory building. Figure B.14 presents a driver diagram for improving clinic access and reducing wait times. Other examples of this diagram are in Chapters Six, Eleven, and Twelve.

A *matrix diagram* is a tool used to arrange and display information to help the user understand important relationships and make decisions. The diagram (see Figure B.15 for an example) displays the relationship between two groupings (such as steps in a process and departments that accomplish that step, customer needs and features offered with your service, vendors and selection criteria, and so on).

## FIGURE B.14. EXAMPLE OF A DRIVER DIAGRAM FOR AN ACCESS IMPROVEMENT PROJECT.

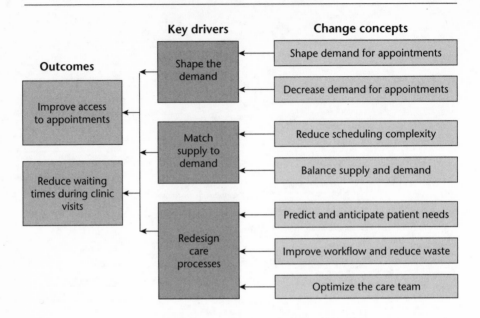

## FIGURE B.15. DECISION MATRIX FOR COMPUTER TO SUPPORT CHANGE.

| | | | Criteria | | | | |
|---|---|---|---|---|---|---|---|
| Computer Type | Disk size | Memory size | Processing speed | Features | Standard software | Costs | Total Score |
| Brand A | 1 | 2 | 4 | 3.5 | 1 | 2.5 | 14 |
| Brand B | 4 | 4 | 3 | 3.5 | 3 | 2.5 | 20 |
| Brand C | 2 | 1 | 1 | 1 | 2 | 4 | 11 |
| Brand D | 3 | 3 | 2 | 2 | 4 | 1 | 15 |

Scores are rankings of the four computer types: 1 = worst of the four on this criterion. 4 = best of the four on this criteria (use average ranking for items).

This tool is useful in decision making (picking a change to test) and for summarizing data from a PDSA Cycle. The diagram is a key part of the QFD method.

A *tree diagram* (also called a systematic diagram) is a tool used to visualize the structure of a problem or a plan or any other opportunity of interest. The diagram, which can resemble the branches on a tree when completed, helps you

## FIGURE B.16. EXAMPLE OF TREE DIAGRAM TO ORGANIZE AN IMPROVEMENT PROJECT.

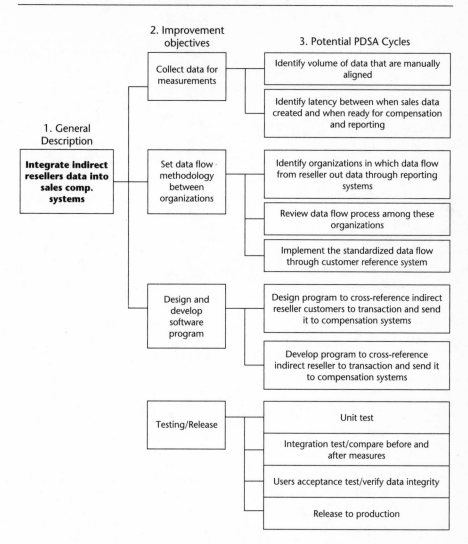

think systematically about each aspect of the situation. Figure B.16 shows a tree diagram. A tree can be developed horizontally or vertically on the page.

A tree diagram can be used in all phases of an improvement project. In answering, "What are we trying to accomplish?" the tool can be used to break the project down into subobjectives. A tree diagram can be useful when planning an implementation PDSA Cycle for implementation to break down a complex implementation plan into more manageable pieces. Tree diagrams can also be

## FIGURE B.17. EXAMPLE OF AN INTERRELATIONSHIP DIAGRAM FOR COMMUNITY ISSUES.

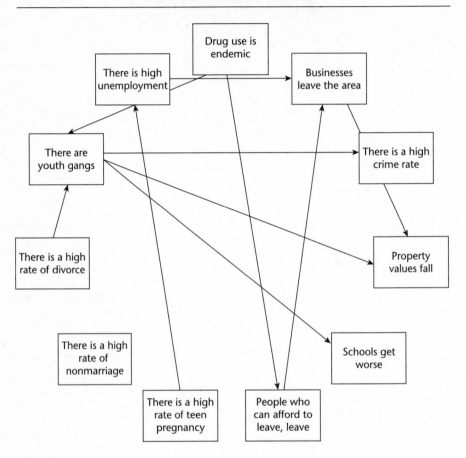

used in planning for improvement to display approaches, tactics, and methods for systematically achieving objectives and goals.

An *interrelationship diagram* identifies and communicates logical and sequential connections between components of a problem. As an analysis tool, it can also be used to identify the cause-and-effect relationships among issues. The analysis helps a team distinguish between issues that serve as drivers and those that are outcomes. The tool is used to study complex problems when it is difficult to identify the interrelationships between the concepts and it is unclear if the issue is the problem or the solution. Figure B.17 shows an example of this tool.

A *radar chart* (also called a spider chart or star chart) displays multiple quantitative variables on axes from the same starting point. Used to present the measures

## FIGURE B.18.  EXAMPLE OF RADAR CHART.

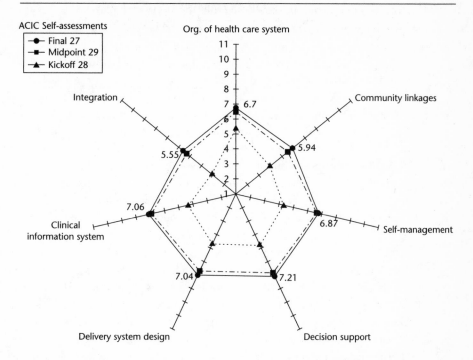

in an improvement project, the chart will graphically show areas of relative strength and relative weakness, as well as depicting general overall performance. The chart can be used to evaluate alternatives or compare against targets with three or more variables. The radar chart will graphically show areas of relative strength and relative weakness, as well as depicting general overall performance. An example is in Figure B.18.

## Methods and Tools for Understanding Variation

*Statistical process control (SPC)* is a philosophy, a strategy, and a set of methods for ongoing improvement of processes and systems to yield better outcomes. SPC is data-based and has its foundation in the theory of variation (differentiating between common and special causes of variation in data). SPC tools can be used to evaluate current process performance, search for ideas for improvement, tell if our changes have yielded evidence of improvement, and track implementation efforts to track sustainability of our improvement. SPC includes a focus on processes, stratification, rational subgrouping, and methods to predict future performance of processes such as stability and capability analysis. SPC incorporates measurement, data collection methods, and planned experimentation. Graphical tools such as Shewhart charts, run charts, frequency plots, Pareto analysis, scatter diagrams, and flow diagrams are key parts of SPC.

The methods of *measurement system analysis* are tools and procedures to understand the impact of bias and precision of the measurement process on the variation in data. Once measures have been selected for an improvement project, some method must be used to obtain data of these measures. Understanding and improving the quality of the process for measurement plays an important role in the improvement of processes and products. The selected measures constitute "windows" through which we are able to observe the performance of a process or the quality of a product. If those windows do not offer a predictable, consistent view, intelligent decisions about actions to be taken cannot be made.

There is a close tie between measurement and operational definitions (discussed earlier). An important component of an operational definition is the statement of the measurement process used. In studying systems for measurement, it is useful to think of the "process" of measurement. Measurement systems consist of standard units of measure (meters for length, hours for time, early or late minutes, hours or days for time, as well), and procedures for producing values in terms of these units of measure. The procedures may include physical instruments or may be subjective determinations made by people using one or more of the senses. Three important characteristics in studying measurement processes are accuracy, precision, and bias. Calibration is a critical component of the measurement process. The bias of the measurement is controlled by the calibration procedures.

There are a variety of *statistical methods* used in quality improvement projects. They include both graphical and numerical procedures to help understand, quantify, and communicate patterns of variation in data collected in PDSA Cycles. Some of these tools and methods are:

- Summary statistics: use mean, mode, median, and other summary statistics to summarize data sets
- Correlation analysis: quantify associations among measures
- Regression analysis: develop a linear model to describe relationships between outcome measures and one or more process variables
- Data transformations: use square root, logarithm, and other data transformations to make data symmetric to facilitate other analyses
- Capability analysis: predict future performance of a process measure on the basis of control chart analysis
- Variance component analysis: describe the contribution to variation from various process factors (separating measurement variation from process variation is an example of this analysis)

- Reliability analysis: predict failure rates of products over time
- Power calculations: select the sample size required to determine effects of factors of interest
- Time series analysis: methods to model data over time with seasonal and other factors causing correlation in the data

These quantitative statistical methods should always be used in conjunction with graphical tools that allow one to see the analysis being done.

A *run chart* is a graphical display of data plotted in some type of order. The run chart is also called a trend chart or a time series chart. The chart is easy to construct and simple to interpret. The simplicity makes it one of the most important methods for communicating and understanding variation. Numerous examples of run charts are used in this book. Three important uses of the run chart in improvement activities:

- Display key project measures over time to make progress visible
- Determine if changes result in improvement
- Determine if gains are held after a change has been implemented

Figure B.19 is an example of a run chart for a key measure on a laboratory improvement project. Changes made by the improvement team are annotated on the chart.

## FIGURE B.19. EXAMPLE OF RUN CHART.

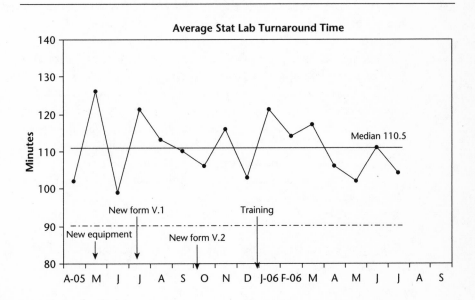

There are four rules useful with run charts to determine if a change has led to improvement:

*Rule one: shift.* Six or more consecutive points either all above or all below the median. Values that fall on the median neither add to nor break a shift. Skip values that fall on the median and continue counting.

*Rule two: trend.* Five or more consecutive points all going up or all going down. If the value of two or more successive points is the same, ignore one of the points when counting; like values do not make or break a trend.

*Rule three: number of runs.* A nonrandom pattern is signaled by too few or too many runs, or crossings of the median line. A run is a series of points in a row on one side of the median. Some points fall right on the median, which makes it hard to decide which run these points belong to. An easy way to determine the number of runs is to count the number of times the line connecting the data points crosses the median and add one.

*Rule four: astronomical point.* This rule aids in detecting unusually large or small numbers. An astronomical data point is one that is:

- An obviously, even blatantly, different value
- Something that anyone studying the chart would agree that is unusual
- Cause for caution: every data set will have a highest and a lowest data point. This does not mean the high and low are astronomical.

*Frequency plots* are used to understand location, spread, shape, and patterns of data. The histogram is widely used as a tool to help one understand variability and would be used in the Study step of a PDSA Cycle. Figure B.20 is an example of a frequency plot.

A *Pareto chart* is useful to focus a project on the areas of improvement with greatest potential impact. A Pareto chart for qualitative data is the equivalent of the frequency plot for a continuous measure. It is most useful to help focus improvement efforts and is a manifestation of the 80–20 rule (80 percent of problems are due to 20 percent of the reasons for them). Figure B.21 is an example of a Pareto chart. The classifications could be any qualitative categories (type of defect, reasons for warranty claims, medical codes, and so on).

A *Shewhart control chart* is a method to distinguish between special and common causes of variation:

*Common causes:* those causes inherent in the system (process or product) over time, affecting everyone working in the system, and affecting all outcomes of the system

## FIGURE B.20. EXAMPLE OF FREQUENCY PLOT OF PROCESS TIME.

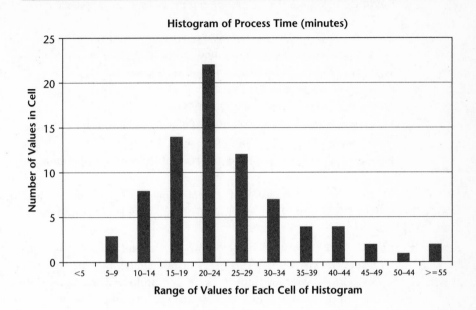

## FIGURE B.21. PARETO CHART.

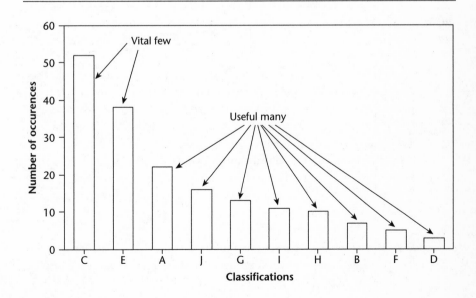

*Special causes:* those causes that are not part of the system (process or product) all the time or do not affect everyone but arise because of specific circumstances

The Shewhart chart (or control chart) is an extension of a run chart used to distinguish between variation in a measure of quality due to common causes and variation due to special causes. The construction of a control chart typically involves:

- Plotting the data or some summary of the data in a run order (time is the most common order)
- Determining some measure of the central tendency of the data (such as the average)
- Determining some measure of the common cause variation of the data
- Calculating a centerline, upper control limit, and lower control limit

Figure B.22 presents a typical Shewhart chart for variance from budget.

The control chart provides a basis for taking action to improve a process. A process is considered to be stable if there is a random distribution of the plotted points within the control limits. For a stable process, action should be directed at identifying the important causes of variation common to all of the points. If the distribution (or pattern) of points is not random, the process is considered to be

### FIGURE B.22. EXAMPLE OF A TYPICAL SHEWHART CHART.

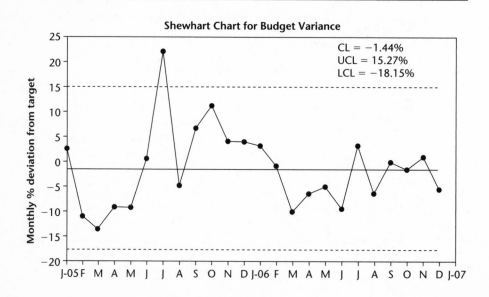

unstable and action should be taken to learn about the special causes of variation. There are a number of types of Shewhart control charts, according to the type of data that has been collected. Formulae to calculate control limits have been developed for each type. Thus there are Shewhart charts for the three common types of data:

1. Classification data: p chart or np chart
2. Count data: c chart or u chart
3. Continuous data: I chart (or X chart), Xbar chart (with R chart or S chart)

There are a variety of *other graphs* useful for communicating and learning from data, useful during the Study step in a PDSA Cycle where data collection is a key part of the cycle. Good data analysis begins with clarifying what question is being asked of the data. Are we trying to predict future performance, determine the extent of a problem, find out where we should focus our efforts, or determine a relationship? The question we want to answer guides us not only to the appropriate data but also to what type of data display is appropriate. There are five basic types of data display:

1. Plots showing data over time (run chart, Shewhart control chart, line graph)
2. Plots showing the distribution (shape and spread) of data (Pareto chart, histogram, dot plot, stem-and-leaf plot, box plot, pie chart)
3. Plots showing the relationship between characteristics (scatter plot, response plot)
4. Plots showing location of data (maps, as in Figure B.23; physical layout)
5. Plots showing results for multiple measures (radar chart or spider diagram, as in Figure B.18; Chernoff faces)

Of the many ways to analyze data, visual displays afford a particularly useful form of analysis. As we are constructing visual displays, we should consider that graphs useful for leaning, communication, and improvement should:

- Make it possible to quickly learn form a large amount of data
- Show all the data
- Separate sources of variation
- Emphasize comparisons and relationships (use stratification)
- Minimize text, markings, colors, and the like that are not directly related to the data
- Label axis and data to permit enough explanation to allow self-interpretation
- Avoid fancy embellishments such as huge splashy fonts, art deco backgrounds, or 3-D displays unless the data are three-dimensional

## FIGURE B.23. PLOT SHOWING LOCATION OF DATA.

### Number of Applications by Country

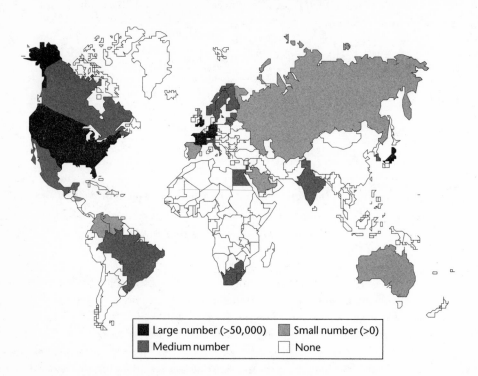

Large number (>50,000)  Small number (>0)
Medium number  None

# Methods and Tools for Understanding Relationships

*Planned experimentation* is a collection of approaches and methods to help increase the rate of learning about improvements to systems, processes, and products. The methods of planned experimentation are appropriate for understanding the important causes of variation in a process and evaluating changes to the process. The concepts and tools of planned experimentation are very useful when designing PDSA test cycles. These concepts are incorporated in Chapter Seven, on testing changes.

One of the most common patterns used in experiments to improve processes is called a factorial design. In a factorial design, tests are arranged in a pattern such that multiple factors are studied with each test. Factorial designs can be used to understand the interactions or synergistic effects of the factors. Here is an example of such a factorial design.

**Two-Factor Factorial Planned Experiment to Improve Advertising**

| Response Variable (number of mail orders placed during the month following the ad) | Factors Levels of Factors |
| --- | --- |
| 1. Size of ad | One-half page, full page |
| 2. Approach to ad | Direct, indirect |
| Background Variables | Control of Background Variable |
| Magazine | Study two extreme markets, Magazines A and B |

**Factorial Design Matrix.**

|  | **One-Half Page Ad** | **Full-Page Ad** |
| --- | --- | --- |
| Direct approach | Magazine A (October) | Magazine A (January) |
|  | Magazine B (November) | Magazine B (February) |
| Indirect approach | Magazine A (April) | Magazine A (July) |
|  | Magazine B (May) | Magazine B (August) |

Graphical tools (run charts, geometric displays, dot diagrams, response plots) are available to analyze and display the results of a planned experiment.

A *scatterplot* is a graphical tool used to examine the association between two measures. The variables plotted may be outcome or process measures or potential causal variables. It is one of the most powerful visual tools for learning about relationships and associations between pairs of process variables. When PDSA cycles are conducted to learn about variables that might affect the project measures, scatterplots should be prepared to display the data collected. Scatterplots allow us to see unusual patterns; data affected by special causes, and interesting clustering of data points (see the example in Figure B.24). The graph can also be used to show how changes in process measures are affecting outcome measures.

A *two-way table* is a tabular representation of the relationship between pairs of variables. The purpose of the two-way table is the same as with the scatter plot: to study relationships. Scatterplots display the relationship graphically, and the two-way table illustrates the relationship numerically. A two-way table is a versatile tool that is often an interim step in developing other graphical methods (scatter plots or response plots) and incorporating stratification into the other types of charts. Figure B.25 shows a typical two-way table.

The construction and interpretation of the two-way table depends on the type of data collected: count data or continuous data. The tables for count data are also called contingency tables. Two-way tables for continuous data are often used to develop responses plots (also called interaction plots) of data (tool for planned experimentation).

## FIGURE B.24. EXAMPLE OF SCATTERPLOT.

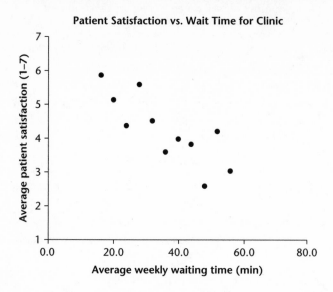

Patient Satisfaction vs. Wait Time for Clinic

## FIGURE B.25. A TWO-WAY TABLE TO EVALUATE EFFECT OF SALES BROCHURE.

|  |  | Sales | | |
|---|---|---|---|---|
|  |  | Made sale | No sale | |
| Strategy | Brochure | 60 | 20 | 80 |
|  | No brochure | 180 | 60 | 240 |
|  |  | 240 | 80 | 320 |

*Note:* table indicates sales made and not made, with and without use of brochure.

## Methods and Tools for Project Management

The Model for Improvement is a framework or roadmap to organize the work of an improvement project. The model has been featured throughout this book. Other improvement project frameworks are discussed in Appendix C. The Plan, Do, Study, Act (PDSA) Cycle is a method for organizing learning, testing, and implementing during an improvement project. The PDSA Cycle has also been featured throughout this book.

A *Gantt chart* is a tool to display the schedule for a project. It is used to plan, coordinate, and monitor project tasks over time. The chart was originally developed by Henry L. Gantt, an engineer and social scientist, as a horizontal bar chart for production control in 1917. Gantt charts can be created on graph paper, or more complex automated versions can be created using spreadsheet or project management software.

The Gantt chart is constructed with a horizontal axis representing the time line of the improvement project and the vertical axis listing the tasks associated with the project (PDSA Cycle could be used to describe each task). Horizontal lines or bars represent the order, timing, and expected completion for each task or cycle. Various methods can be used to indicate deadlines, milestones, completed tasks, and so on. Form B.2 at the end of this appendix is an example of a form that can be used to develop a Gantt chart for an improvement project.

A *PERT chart* is a project management tool that displays the sequential relationships of project tasks and determines the critical path to complete the project. The PERT chart is sometimes preferred over the Gantt chart because it illustrates interdependencies among the tasks. PERT stands for Program Evaluation Review Technique and was developed by the U.S. Navy in the 1950s to manage submarine projects. The tool is sometimes called the *critical path method* (CPM).

A PERT chart presents a graphic illustration of a project as a network diagram consisting of symbols that represent key tasks or components of the project. The symbols are linked by labeled arrows representing the tasks in the project. The direction of the arrows on the lines indicates the sequence of tasks. Figure B.26 shows a generic example of a PERT chart. Information on predicted time required, resources, budget, staff, and so forth are often included in the boxes on the chart.

## FIGURE B.26. EXAMPLE OF A PERT CHART FOR AN IMPROVEMENT PROJECT.

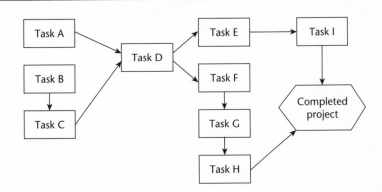

## TABLE B.5. FORMAT FOR A3 REPORT.

| Title: [Name of Project with Brief Description of What A3 Is About] | |
| --- | --- |
| Current<br>condition | Target<br>condition |
| Root cause<br>(5 whys) | Countermeasure<br>and action plan |
| Follow-up: plan including measures and time for review | |

A *work breakdown structure* (WBS) is an application of the tree diagram used to help in planning, organizing, and completing a project. The WBS was developed by the U.S. Defense Department in the 1970s and used in military standards. Examples of the use of WBS for improvement projects are described in Chapter Eleven.

An *A3 report* is a one-page format for summarizing an improvement project. Table B.5 shows the general form of an A3 report. It was so named by Toyota because it is written on an A3-sized paper (metric equivalent of 11" x 17"). Toyota has developed several kinds of A3 reports for different applications. The report flows from top to bottom on the left-hand side, and then top to bottom on the right-hand side:

- Current condition
- Target condition
- Causes
- Solutions and Action Plans

## Standard Format for an Improvement Team Charter

### General Description

#### Charter Description (Defines What Broadly)

- Provides an initial orientation toward the activities of the individual or team, that is, design of a new process, improvement of an existing process, and so on.

#### Reason for the Effort (Defines Why)

- States why the effort is important
- How will this improvement benefit the organization?
- What is the potential downside of this effort for the organization?
- What data and analysis support the choice?

### Expected Results

#### Expected Outcomes (Defines What Specifically, Not How)

- Lists anticipated outcomes or success criteria; you should be able to evaluate or measure the outcomes
- Are other measures needed to guard against suboptimization?

#### Measurements

- Defines what measures will be affected by this improvement
- Guides progress of work on charter
- What measures can be used to evaluate the progress of this improvement effort?

### Boundaries

#### Initial Activities

- Provides initial focus for the team or individual's work, for example, doing a process map of current reality

#### Limitations

- States project constraints, such as resources, as well as what the individual or team should not address

#### Time Frame

- States how often and for how long the team will meet
- Target dates for completion of major phases
- How often will the sponsor be updated on the team's progress?

### Participation

#### Team Membership

- Includes all members and the rationale for their inclusion on the team

#### Sponsorship

- Identifies the person or guidance team providing resources to work on the charter

# Form B.1: General PDSA Project Planning Form

| PDSA Cycle # <br> | Description (Change) and Objective of the Cycle (Learn, Test, Implement ) | Responsibility | Month 1 | Month 2 | Month 3 | Month 4 |
|---|---|---|---|---|---|---|
| | | | | | | |
| | | | | | | |
| | | | | | | |
| | | | | | | |
| | | | | | | |
| | | | | | | |
| | | | | | | |
| | | | | | | |
| | | | | | | |
| | | | | | | |

# Form B.2: Model for Improvement Cycle No.

Date _____

   Change or idea evaluated _____

   Objective for this PDSA Cycle: _____

   _____

   What question(s) do we want to answer with this PDSA Cycle?

*Plan* Plan to answer questions (test the change or evaluate the idea): What, Who, When, Where?

   Plan for collection of data needed to answer questions: What, Who, When, Where?

   Predictions (for each question listed, what will happen if plan is carried out? Discuss theories.)

*Do* Carry out the plan; document problems and unexpected observations; collect data and begin analysis.

*Study* Complete analysis of data. What were the answers to the questions in the plan (compare to predictions)? Summarize what was learned.

*Act* What changes are to be made? Plan for the next cycle.

# Form B.3: PDSA Cycle Form with Checklist Format

**Date:**                    **Team:**                                        **Cycle #:**

**Plan**

---

**Objective of this cycle:**

☐ Collect data

☐ Develop a change (or modify a change from a previous change)

☐ Test a change

☐ Implement a change

Describe:

---

∞  *What additional knowledge is necessary to take action?*

---

**Questions to be answered from the data obtained in this cycle:**

1.
2.
3.
4.

**Predictions:**

1.
2.
3.
4.

∞  *Are historical data available to answer these questions?* ☐ Yes ☐ No

∞  *Does the team agree on the predictions?*

☐ Yes for question(s):                    ☐ No for question(s):

---

**Develop a plan to answer the questions (who, what, where, when):**
1.
2.
3.
4.

---

The plan considered these methods:
☐ Data collection forms
☐ Pareto diagrams
☐ Control charts
☐ Frequency plots
☐ Planned experimentation
☐ Survey methods
☐ Simulation and modeling
☐ Scatter diagrams
☐ Run charts
☐ Engineering analysis
∞  Did you assign responsibilities for collection and analysis of the data? ☐ Yes ☐ No
∞  Is training needed? ☐ Yes ☐ No
∞  Is the plan consistent with the charter? ☐ Yes ☐ No
∞  Can the plan be carried out on a small scale? ☐ Yes ☐ No
∞  Have you considered people outside the team who will be affected by this plan?
   ☐ Yes ☐ No

## Do

**Observations in carrying out the plan:**

∞   *Things observed that were not part of the plan.*
∞   *Things that went wrong during the data collection.*

  ☐ *Used a Control Chart*                    ☐ *Identified special causes as data were collected.*

## Study

**Analysis of data:**

**Compare the analysis of the data to the current knowledge:**

∞   *Do the results of the cycle agree with predictions made in the planning phase?*

  ☐ Yes ☐ No

∞   *Under what conditions could the conclusions from this cycle be different?*

∞   *What are the implications of the unplanned observations and problems during the collection of data?*

∞   *Do the data help answer the questions posed in the plan?* ☐ Yes ☐ No

**Summarize the new knowledge gained in this cycle:**

☐ *Flowcharts reflect what was learned.*
☐ *Cause-and-effect diagrams reflect what was learned.*
☐ *What was learned can be applied in another area. Comments:*

**Act**

**What changes are to be made to the process?**

**List other organizations and people that will be affected by the changes:**

☐ *The cause system is sufficiently understood.*
☐ *An appropriate action or change has been developed or selected.*
☐ *The changes have been tested on a small scale.*
☐ *Change responsibilities for implementation and evaluation completed.*
☐ *Actions or changes will improve performance in the future.*
☐ *Completed an analysis of forces in the organization that will help or hinder the changes*

**Objective of next cycle:**
☐ Collect data
☐ Develop a change (or modify a change from a previous change)
☐ Test a change
☐ Implement a change

**Description:**

# APPENDIX C

## THE MODEL FOR IMPROVEMENT AND OTHER ROADMAPS

How do you make improvements? Historically people have used a trial-and-error approach to improving all aspects of their life. Typically an idea for an improvement (a change) comes to us. These ideas are often reactions to problems or difficulties that we all face in life and in our work, so we make a change and then see if the situation improves. Sometimes we also check to see if anyone complains, or if something else stops working because of the change that we made. Because of its sporadic track record on real, sustainable improvement, this natural trial-and-error approach has often been criticized as "jumping to solutions" without sufficient study.

As a response to this criticism, some improvement specialists have turned to extensive study of the problem before a change or trial is attempted. Sometimes this approach leads to a better track record on making sustained improvements, but more often it can lead to an unnecessary delay in making obvious changes—or worse, never actually making changes. The person with the problem gets bogged down in the study, "paralysis by analysis" sets in, or other problems begin to take priority. Also, the search for the "perfect change" sometimes contributes to this paralysis (see mention of the utopia syndrome, in Chapter Six). How do we balance the need to do something with the desire to be sure we know what we are doing before we take any action?

This book has presented the Model for Improvement, which attempts to strike that balance. The model is a framework for developing, testing, implementing, and spreading changes that result in improvement. It can be applied to the improvement of processes, products, and services in any organization, as well as improving aspects of one's personal endeavors. The model attempts to balance the desire and rewards from taking action with the wisdom of careful study before taking action.

## Fundamental Questions for Improvement

The Model for Improvement is based on three fundamental questions—What are we trying to accomplish? How will we know that a change is an improvement? What changes can we make that will result in improvement?—and a "cycle" for learning and improvement. Variants of this improvement cycle have been called the Shewhart Cycle, Deming Cycle, and PDSA Cycle. The cycle promotes a trial-and-learning approach to improvement efforts, with encouragement to test an idea rather than do extensive analysis. The cycle is used for learning, to develop changes, test changes, and implement changes.

Figure C.1 diagrams the basic form of the Model for Improvement.

### FIGURE C.1. MODEL FOR IMPROVEMENT.

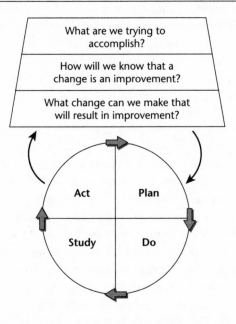

Why are we promoting the use of this particular approach to improvement? Our experience with the Model for Improvement since its development in the 1980s shows that it:

- Is useful as a roadmap for small, simple projects as well as large-system projects
- Is useful for both process and product improvement
- Can be used for the design of new processes and products
- Is applicable to all types of organizations
- Is applicable to all groups and levels in an organization
- Facilitates the use of teamwork to make improvements
- Provides a framework for the application of improvement tools and methods
- Encourages planning to be based on theory
- Emphasizes and encourages the iterative learning process
- Allows project plans to adapt as learning occurs
- Offers a simple way to empower people in the organization to take action

Experts in complexity science have been critical of quality improvement frameworks that follow a linear sequence of steps to accomplish a project. Complexity science suggests that inconsistent outcomes may result from an implicit assumption of linear, mechanistic relationships between cause and effect in implementing organizational interventions. Studies of innovation have shown that discovery, learning, and intervention cannot be reduced to a linear model. Instead, researchers suggest the "innovation journey is a nonlinear cycle of divergent and convergent activities that may repeat over time."

Complex, adaptive systems, which describe organizations in which we apply improvement methods, are characterized by individuals who can learn, interconnect, self-organize, and co-evolve with their environment in nonlinear and dynamic ways. A step-by-step framework associated with many improvement roadmaps may not support this way of thinking.

In contrast, a complex systems approach would suggest that each environment is unique, and that outcomes of interventions may be greatly affected by situational differences. Some of the frameworks (such as the QC story) make it clear that the sequence of steps implied in the framework is not the way that most improvement projects are actually done. Rather, the steps are used to describe the completed project in a uniform way that everyone can understand.

The Model for Improvement encourages the nonlinear learning and adaptation suggested by complexity science. By encouraging early testing of ideas in the specific environment of interest, the model allows the intervention to gradually be modified and then optimized to the uniqueness of the system where implementation is taking place.

---

# Alternative Roadmaps for Improvement Projects

Many authors and experienced improvers have recognized the importance of an organization having a consistent framework for conducting their improvement initiatives. This consistent, structured approach affords a common language and allows improvement teams to be formed from different departments and groups in the organization. As well as accomplishing a specific improvement, participants following the structure become better improvers.

In addition to the Model for Improvement, there are a number of other frameworks or roadmaps that have been used to guide improvement projects. These frameworks are briefly described in this appendix:

- Juran's Universal Sequence for Quality Improvement
- Six-Sigma DMAIC
- Six-Sigma DFSS
- Seven-step problem-solving model
- FOCUS-PDCA
- The 8-D Model
- The QC Story
- Lean improvement

## Juran's Universal Sequence for Quality Improvement

On the basis of his years of experience in quality improvement projects, Joseph Juran observed that improvement in a variety of contexts and environments was carried out following a "universal sequence of events":

1. Identify a problem—something wrong with a product, service, or process that has an impact on the performance of the organization
2. Establish an improvement project
3. Measure and analyze the current process to establish knowledge of baseline performance

*Diagnostic Journey (from Symptom to Cause)*

4. Analyze the symptoms
5. Generate theories as to the causes of the symptoms

6. Test the theories
7. Establish the causes

*Remedial Journey (from Cause to Remedy)*

8. Develop remedies
9. Test and prove the remedies in operations
10. Deal with resistance to change
11. Establish controls to hold the gains

This universal sequence has been the basis for many of the other frameworks presented here. The sequence puts emphasis on understanding how the current process or product performs and identifies causes of the problem (that is, the diagnostic journey) before beginning to think of remedies.

## Six-Sigma DMAIC

DMAIC (define-measure-analyze-improve-control) is a basic component of the Six Sigma methodology. Six Sigma was developed in Motorola in the late 1980s and built on TQM (total quality management) programs with a focus on reducing variation. The Six Sigma methodology has evolved into a number of distinct versions. For example, one version is called "Lean Six Sigma" to incorporate the ideas of lean improvement (see later discussion).

There are many versions of the five steps of the Six Sigma DMAIC roadmap for improving existing processes. These are typical definitions of the five steps:

1. **D**efine process improvement goals that are consistent with customer demands and the organization's strategy.
2. **M**easure the current process (defect focus) and develop baseline for future comparison.
3. **A**nalyze to verify relationship and cause and effect of factors. Attempt to identify all factors that could be relevant.
4. **I**mprove or optimize the process on the basis of the analysis. Transition to standard processes.
5. **C**ontrol to ensure that any variances are corrected before they result in defects.

In many published descriptions of the DMAIC framework, the *measure* and *analyze* steps do not emphasize Shewhart's theory of common and special causes.

Various tools and methods are associated with each step of DMAIC. For example, the *define* step typically includes:

- Establish a sound project foundation
  - Ensure leadership and team are aligned
  - Form improvement team
  - Develop a problem statement and a business case
- Scope document
  - Set goals (deliverables, timeframe, budget)
  - Keep team on target (scope creep)
- Process documentation
  - Suppliers-inputs-process-outcomes-customers (SIPOC) diagrams
  - Stakeholder analysis
  - Process maps and value stream maps
- Voice of the customer
  - Establish or validate customer needs
  - Internal and external customers
  - Interviews, surveys

Similar guidance for tools and methods are associated with each of the other four steps.

## Six-Sigma DFSS

The DFSS roadmap stands for "Design for Six Sigma." There are many versions of DFSS in the literature and application, with steps defined differently. DFSS was developed for improvement projects directed at design or redesign of a product or service. One popular DFSS methodology is called DMADV, which has parallels to DMAIC. The five steps of DMADV are defined as:

1. **D**efine the project goals and customer (internal and external) requirements.
2. **M**easure and determine customer needs and specifications; benchmark competitors and industry.
3. **A**nalyze the process options to meet the customer needs.
4. **D**esign the process to meet the customer needs.
5. **V**erify the design performance and capability to meet customer needs.

Other DFSS approaches have been described to emphasize various steps in the process or product design steps:

- DMADOV: define, measure, analyze, design, optimize, and verify
- DMCDOV: define, measure, characterize, design, optimize, and verify
- DCOV: define, characterize, optimize, and verify
- DCCDI: define, customer, concept, design, and implement
- DMEDI: define, measure, explore, develop, and implement
- DMADIC: define, measure, analyze, design, implement, and control

The particular version of DFSS is designed to align with an author or organization's product design process. All of the DFSS versions connect to these improvement tools and methods:

- Quality function deployment
- Failure modes and effects analysis
- Benchmarking
- Design of experiments
- Simulation
- Statistical optimization
- Mistake proofing

## Seven-Step Method Problem-Solving Model

The "Seven-Step Method," also called the "Seven-Step Problem-Solving Model" and "Seven-Step Practical Problem Solving," is a disciplined framework for completing an improvement project and a useful framework for documenting the project. This model was promoted to go beyond plan-do-check-act cycles to provide:

- A framework with which we can visualize progress through a project
- Check steps that allow us to see that we are not trying to proceed too quickly through part of the improvement process without having gained sufficient understanding
- A means of documenting a project

This model is directed primarily at eliminating quality problems, as opposed to the design or redesign of products or processes. Here are typical descriptions of the seven steps in the model:

*Step 1: Define Project Purpose and Scope*

- Focus on strategically important problems
- Choose an appropriate project team and team leader

- Clarify the project mission
- Determine how much progress can be expected
- Formulate a framework and execution plan for the project

*Step 2: Current Situation*

- Understand the present process
- Determine customer needs and expectations
- Flowchart the process
- Collect data to identify the real problem
- Standardize the process, if necessary

*Step 3: Cause Analysis*

- Dig down for the root causes of the problem
- Identify the major potential causes
- Verify them with data, if possible

*Step 4: Solutions*

- Choose between alternative solutions
- Keep solutions simple
- Identify barriers to implementing solutions
- Plan and make necessary changes (use plan-do-check-act)

*Step 5: Results*

- Evaluate the solutions
- Collect data, to compare before and after improvement
- Compare results with what we expected

*Step 6: Standardization*

- Standardize the new process
- Document the changes made
- Error-proof the process

*Step 7: Future Plans*

- Review what has been learned from this project
- Decide whether to continue with this project, or
- Close project and move on to a more pressing project

Toyota's "Practical Problem-Solving Process" is a similar model with seven steps:

1. Initial problem perception
2. Clarify the problem
3. Locate area or point of cause
4. Five whys, investigation of root cause
5. Countermeasure
6. Evaluate
7. Standardize

## FOCUS-PDCA

FOCUS-PDCA is another framework developed in the late 1980s as a way to better use PDCA (plan-do-check-act) on improvement projects. The framework is designed for both problem solving and process improvement. The steps of the framework follow from the name:

**F**ind a process to improve
**O**rganize a team that knows the process
**C**larify the current knowledge of the process
**U**nderstand the causes of process variation
**S**elect the process improvement
**P**lan improvement, data collection (key quality characteristics and other)
**D**o improvement, data collection, data analysis
**C**heck data for process improvement, customer outcome, lessons learned
**A**ct to hold the gain, reconsider owner, and continue improvement

## The 8D Problem-Solving Methodology

The 8D problem-solving methodology (8D = eight disciplines) was developed in Ford Motor Company in the mid-1980s to be used by their suppliers to improve the resolution of problems. It appears in a variety of forms used to define eight disciplines. Sometimes it is defined as a nine-step problem-solving process:

D0: preparing for 8D
D1: assembling the team
D2: describing the problem
D3: developing interim containment actions
D4: defining the root cause
D5: choosing permanent corrective actions

D6: implementing permanent corrective actions
D7: preventative actions
D8: recognition of the team

Other applications of the 8D methodology describe a problem resolution framework (to address part supplier problems):

- Part and lot information
- Description of concern
- Containment
- Root cause
- Corrective actions
- Verification of containment and corrective actions
- Action to prevent recurrence
- Congratulate the team

Because the 8D model is designed to solve specific problems that arise, more emphasis is placed on containing the problem (discipline 3) than in most other frameworks. The idea is to implement intermediate actions that will protect the customer from the problem until permanent solution can be developed and implemented. This roadmap also makes recognition of the improvement team for their effort an explicit part of the framework.

## The QC Story

The QC Story (or quality improvement story) was developed in Japan by the Union of Japanese Scientist and Engineers (JUSE) Research Committee. It has been used extensively by QC Circles to document their journey on improvement projects. Having a common structure and language helps people working on a project tell their "story" to management and other parties interested in their project. There are seven steps to "telling the QC story":

1. Situation: identify the problem or opportunity for improvement (plan and problem definition)
   - State history
   - State priority and impact
   - Relate to strategy, customers, and employees
   - Define theme for improvement project
   - Organize improvement project team
   - Create improvement project plan

2. Observation and data: understand the situation
   - Understand current circumstances
   - Collect and display data
   - Establish improvement targets
3. Analysis: find out the main causes
   - Establish hypotheses for causes
   - Test hypotheses
   - Decide on improvements
4. Action: eliminate the causes
   - Plan execution of improvements
   - Execute improvements
5. Study: confirm the effectiveness of the action
   - Verify improvement results
6. Standardization: permanently eliminate the causes
   - Establish control methods
   - Update appropriate standards
   - Implement education and training
   - Establish inspections
7. Conclusion: review activities and plan for future work
   - Review activities
   - Plan next steps
   - What other problems did we identify during this work?

Promoters of this framework emphasize that the seven steps in the QC story do not necessarily describe the specific order in which the problem was solved. Because problem solving usually requires a great deal of iteration, during the project it is often necessary to go back to a previous step as new data are found and analyses permit additional insight. However, when it comes time to report on what was done, the seven-step format is the basis for telling the story in a way that makes it comprehensible to all levels of management, suppliers, and customers.

## Lean Improvement

Lean Improvement has been defined as "a systematic approach to identifying and eliminating waste (non-value-added activities) through continuous improvement by flowing the product at the pull of the customer in pursuit of perfection." Lean approaches have been adapted from the Toyota Production System (TPS). There is not a specific roadmap for a lean project.

The lean improvement approach is based on five principles:

1. Defining *value* from the customer perspective
2. Identifying *value streams,* the activities required to provide the customer with a product or service
3. Making the value added steps *flow* smoothly
4. The *customers "pull"* the products and services when needed
5. Everyone is pursuing *perfection*

Some key definitions are:

- Value: what the customer is willing to pay for; an activity that changes form, fit, or function
- Nonvalue add: no added value from customers' definition, but must be done under the present conditions (e.g., walking over to the printer, putting together binders)
- Waste: what the customer is unwilling to pay us to do

A lean approach focuses on continuously reducing waste in operations and in product and services and continuously enhancing the value proposition to customers. Some organizations have called their approach to quality improvement "lean six sigma" to incorporate the ideas from both of these improvement strategies. The Six Sigma DMAIC model (described earlier) is then adopted as a framework for improvement projects.

The concepts of lean thinking are incorporated into the Model for Improvement in answering the fundamental question, "What change can we make that will lead to improvement?" Many of the change concepts from Appendix A are associated with lean improvement methods. Change concepts 1 through 11 and 23 are about ways to eliminate waste, and concepts 12 through 23 focus on ways to improve workflow. Other change concepts often associated with lean improvement are 24, 46, 48, 50, 51, and 71 (see Appendix A for descriptions of these concepts).

## Summary

It is widely recognized that organizations benefit by having a consistent framework or roadmap for conducting their improvement initiatives. The Model for Improvement is the framework used throughout this book. A number of other improvement models or frameworks are also available in the improvement literature.

# Notes

## Chapter One

p. 16    Definition of *improvement* was influenced by Ademir J. Petenate, UNICAMP, Campinas, SP, Brazil. The authors have borrowed from his work.

p. 23    The ideas of a fundamental approach to improvement, the structure of the three questions, and the PDSA Cycle were derived mainly from the work of Deming, Shewhart, and Lewis:

Deming, W. E. *The New Economics for Industry, Government, Education.* Cambridge: Massachusetts Institute of Technology, Center for Advanced Engineering Study, 1993.

Lewis, C. I. *Mind and the World Order.* New York: Dover, 1929.

Shewhart, W. A. *Economic Control of Quality of Manufactured Product.* Milwaukee, Wis.: American Society for Quality Control, 1980. (Originally published 1931.)

Shewhart, W. A. *Statistical Method from the Viewpoint of Quality Control* (edited by W. E. Deming). Washington, D.C.: Graduate School, Department of Agriculture, 1939.

## Chapter Two

All the skills introduced in Chapter Two are explored in more detail later in the book. The endnotes associated with those later chapters will therefore be more thorough. However, particular influences in Chapter Two need to be mentioned here:

p. 32    Definition of *data*: Hubbard, H. *How to Measure Anything: Finding the Value of Intangibles in Business.* New York: Wiley, 2007.

p. 32     Understanding variation: Shewhart, W. A. 1980. *Economic Control of Quality of Manufactured Product*. Milwaukee, Wis.: American Society for Quality Control, 1980. (Originally published 1931.)

           Shewhart, W. A. 1939. *Statistical Method from the Viewpoint of Quality Control* (edited by W. E. Deming). Washington, D.C.: Graduate School, Department of Agriculture, 1939.

p. 37     Creative thinking: de Bono, E. *Six Thinking Hats*. New York: Little, Brown, and ICCT, 1986.

p. 45     Stages of change: Prochaska J., Norcross J., and DiClemente, C. *Changing for Good*. New York: Morrow, 1994.

           Attributes of an idea: Rogers, E. *Diffusion of Innovations*, 4th ed. New York: Free Press, 1995.

# Chapter Three

p. 60     The example of improving the teaching of biology is based on the work of LaVonne Batalden at Volunteer State Community College.

p. 66     This case study is based on work led by Kevin Little of Informing Ecological Design, LLC, at Hitch Elementary School, a public school on the north side of Chicago. The teachers leading the work at Hitch School are Carolyn Smarz and Phyllis Kuziel-Perri. Carol Timms of Educational Dividends in Champaign, Illinois, organized the lesson plans and seeded the idea of the energy patrols.

# Chapter Four

p. 76     System of profound knowledge: Deming, W. E. *The New Economics*, 2nd ed. Cambridge: Center for Advanced Educational Services, Massachusetts Institute of Technology, 1994.

p. 77     Key ideas from systems theory:

           The boundary of a system: Deming, 1994.

           Temporal effects and dynamic complexity: Senge, P. M. *The Fifth Discipline*. New York: Doubleday/Currency, 1990.

           Theory of constraints: Goldratt, Eliyahu, and Cox, Jeff. *The Goal*. New York: North River Press, 1986.

           First- and second-order change: Watzlawick, P., Weakland, J., and Fisch R. *Change: Principles of Problem Formation and Problem Resolution*. New York: Norton, 1974.

p. 79     The theory of variation is founded on the work of Walter Shewhart: *Economic Control of Quality of Manufactured Product*. New York: Van Nostrand, 1931. (Reprinted by the American Society for Quality Control, 1980.)

           A practical reference on variation is Nolan, T. and Provost, L., "Understanding Variation." *Quality Progress*, May 1990.

p. 82    Figure 4.4 is adapted from Box, G., Hunter, W., and Hunter, J. S. *Statistics for Experimenters*. New York: Wiley, 1978.

p. 82    For further study of enumerative and analytic studies, see Deming, W. E. *Sample Design in Business Research*. New York: Wiley; and Deming, W. E. "On Probability as a Basis for Action." *American Statistician*, 1960, *29*(4), 146–152.

p. 83    The idea of operational definitions is credited to Percy Bridgman, *The Logic of Modern Physics*. New York: Macmillan, 1927.

p. 84    Contributions from psychology and change management:

Differences in people and behavior driven by motivation: *Relationship Awareness Theory*, 9th ed., Elias H. Porter. Personal Strengths Publishing, 1996.

Basis of attribution theory was developed by Edward E. Jones and Keith Davis; the term *attribution error* was developed by Lee Ross, 1977; Jones, E. E. & Harris, V. A. "The Attribution of Attitudes." *Journal of Experimental Social Psychology*, 1967, 3, 1–24.

Ross, L. "The Intuitive Psychologist and His Shortcomings: Distortions in the Attribution Process." In L. Berkowitz (ed.), *Advances in Experimental Social Psychology* (vol. 10, pp. 173–220). New York: Academic Press.

Intrinsic and extrinsic motivation: Herzberg, Frederick. *The Motivation to Work*. New York: Wiley, 1959.

Herzberg, F. I. "One More Time: How Do You Motivate Employees?" *Harvard Business Review*, Sept//Oct. 1987, *65*(5), 109–120.

Dynamic administration: *The Collected Papers of Mary Parker Follett*, Henry C. Metcalf and L. Urwick (eds.). New York: Harper, 1940.

Five attributes of an innovation to facilitate adoption: Rogers, E. *Diffusion of Innovations*, 4th ed. New York: Free Press, 1995.

p. 85    Some recommended readings on the four parts of profound knowledge are included in the bibliography section on the Website www.apiweb.org.

# Chapter Five

p. 92    For a discussion on the use of numerical goals, see Deming, W. E. *The New Economics*, 2nd ed. Cambridge: Center for Advanced Educational Services, Massachusetts Institute of Technology, 1994.

p. 97    The PDSA Cycle, also referred to as the Shewhart Cycle, was popularized by W. Edwards Deming.

Deming, W. E. 1994. *The New Economics*, 2nd ed. Cambridge: Center for Advanced Educational Services, Massachusetts Institute of Technology, 1994.

Shewhart, W. A. 1931. *Economic Control of Quality of Manufactured Product*. New York: Van Nostrand (reprinted by the American Society for Quality Control, 1980).

p. 107   For methods to construct good visual displays, see Tufte, E. *The Visual Display of Quantitative Information*. Cheshire, Conn.: Graphics Press, 1983.

p. 107   A good reference for methods to build effective teams is Scholtes, P. *The Team Handbook*. Madison, Wis.: Joiner and Associates, 1988.

# Chapter Six

p. 110   Both the idea of "more of the same" changes and the utopia syndrome come from the book *Change: Principles of Problem Formation and Problem Resolution* by P. Watzlawick, J. Weakland, and R. Fisch. New York: Norton, 1974.

p. 111   The structure of reactive and fundamental changes is also based on concepts of first- and second-order change from Watzlawick, P., et al. cited above.

p. 114   The idea of small changes leading to big improvements is an important system principle called leverage, which is introduced in Chapter Four. This concept is discussed in *The Fifth Discipline*, Peter Senge, New York: Doubleday, 1990, pp. 63–65.

p. 116   Theory building is introduced in Chapter Four in the section "Building Knowledge." A more detailed discussion of theory building can be found in "Practice and Malpractice in Business Research," Paul R. Carlile, Boston University, and Clayton M. Christensen, Harvard Business School, version 6 of a draft paper, Jan. 2005.

p. 118   Fred's mistakes in developing the theory for late shipments illustrate a common learning bias called the "confirmation trap." See *Psychology of Judgment*, Scott Plous, New York: McGraw-Hill, 1993, for a discussion of this and other learning biases.

p. 122   The case study approach is discussed in *Making Social Science Matter*, Bent Flyvbjerg, Cambridge University Press, Cambridge, U.K., 2001, Chapter 6, on the "Power of Example."

p. 123   Many of the ideas in this section come from Camp, Robert. *Benchmarking: The Search for Industry Best Practices That Lead to Superior Performance*. Milwaukee, Wis.: ASQ Quality Press, 1989.

p. 125   See the National Institute for Standards and Testing (http://baldrige.nist.gov) for more information on the obligations of Baldrige Award winners.

p. 125   The example of the transportation company is taken from Henkoff, R. "Smartest and Dumbest Managerial Moves of 1994." *Fortune*, Jan. 16, 1995, p. 94.

p. 127   For further discussion of generating changes based on the theory of common and special causes, see Nolan, T. W., and Provost, L. P. "Understanding Variation." *Quality Progress*, May 1990, pp. 70–78.

p. 130   Edward de Bono's ideas on creative thinking are the basis of our approach to innovation and methods of creativity. See de Bono, E. *Serious Creativity*. New York: HarperCollins, 1992. For a discussion of integrating creative methods in quality improvement efforts, see "Creativity and Improvement: A Vital Link," by Lloyd P. Provost and R. M. Sproul, *Quality Progress*, ASQC, Aug. 1996, pp. 101–107.

p. 131   The importance of concepts in developing ideas for change became clear to us as we applied Edward de Bono's creativity tools in our work. See "The Importance of Concepts in Creativity and Improvement." L. P. Provost and Gerald J. Langley. *Quality Progress*, ASQC, Mar. 1998, pp. 31–38.

p. 133   For more on "lean methods," see *The Machine That Changed the World*, J. Womack, D. Jones, D. Roos, New York: Rawson Associates, 1990; or *Lean Thinking: Banish Waste and Create Wealth in Your Corporation*, revised and updated, James P. Womack and Daniel T. Jones, eds. New York: Free Press, 2003.

p. 133    For more on Six Sigma programs, see *Six Sigma for Green Belts and Champions: Foundations, DMAIC, Tools, Cases, and Certification,* Howard S. Gitlow and David M. Levine, Upper Saddle River, N.J.: Prentice-Hall, 2004.

p. 136    To learn more about TRIZ, visit www.triz-journal.com; or see *And Suddenly the Inventor Appeared,* Altshuller, Genrich, translated by Lev Shulyak, Worcester, Mass.: Technical Innovation Center, 1994.

# Chapter Seven

p. 141    The concept of degree of belief is from Shewhart, W. A. *Statistical Method from the Viewpoint of Quality Control.* Washington: Department of Agriculture, 1939. Degree of belief is one of three components of knowledge (along with data of experience and prediction).

p. 149    This example in Figures 7.3 and 7.4 is taken from Moen, R. D., Nolan, T. W., and Provost, L P. *Quality Improvement Through Planned Experimentation,* 2nd ed. Chapter 2. New York: McGraw-Hill, 1999.

p. 153    For further study, see:
          Box, G., Hunter, W., and Hunter, J. S. *Statistics for Experimenters Design, Innovation, and Discovery,* 2nd ed., Chapter 5. New York: Wiley, 2005.
          Moen, R. D., Nolan, T. W., and Provost, L P. *Quality Improvement Through Planned Experimentation,* 2nd ed. New York: McGraw-Hill, 1999. The reference covers the designs discussed in this chapter in more detail as well as block designs, fractional factorial designs, nested designs, and designs for special situations, including interchangeable parts and formulations or mixtures.

p. 156    Speroff, T., and O'Connor, G. "Study Designs for PDSA Quality Improvement Research." *Quality Management in Health Care,* Jan.–Mar. 2004, *13*(1), 17–32.
          This reference presents several time series designs using one or more baselines (AB, AABB, AAAB, ABBB). These are derived from Campbell, D. and Stanley, J. *Experimental and Quasi-Experimental Designs for Research,* Boston: Houghton Mifflin, 1963.

p. 158    The four tools for experimentation (replication, planned grouping, study designs, randomization) were developed by R. A. Fisher. *Design of Experiments.* New York: Hafner, 1935. (8th ed. published in 1966.)

p. 162    This design is called the randomized clinical trial (RCT) in the medical research community. For example, see Lachin, J. M., Matts, J. P., and Wei, L. J. "Randomization in Clinical Trials: Conclusions and Recommendations." *Controlled Clinical Trials,* 1988, 9(4), 365–374.

p. 167    Moen, R. D., Nolan, T. W., and Provost, L. P. Quality Improvement Through Planned Experimentation, 2nd ed. New York: McGraw-Hill, 1999. Besides the run order plot and interaction plot, this reference adds a dot diagram and a geometric figure or other display of paired comparison.

# Chapter Eight

p. 185   The authors wish to recognize the contribution of Jane Norman for work on the checklist for implementation displayed in Figure 8.1.

p. 186   More information on how individuals react to change can be found in these two sources:

Myers, D. G. *Social Psychology* (3rd ed.). New York: McGraw-Hill, 1990.

Kreitner, R., and Kinicki, A. *Organizational Behavior* (2nd ed.). Homewood, Ill: Irwin, 1978.

p. 187   Weisbord (1987) noted that for every technical change in a system, there are usually social and economic changes as well.

p. 189   The role of leaders in communicating the need for change was adapted from Pfeffer, Sutton. *Hard Facts, Dangerous Half-Truths & Total Nonsense.* Boston: Harvard Business, 2006.

p. 191   The zoo story is taken from Priest, G. "Zoo Story." *Inc.,* Oct. 1994, pp. 27–28.

# Chapter Nine

p. 196   Definition of diffusion: Rogers, E. *Diffusion of Innovations,* 4th ed. New York City: Free Press, 1995.

p. 197   Social learning theory: Bandura, A. *Social Foundations of Thought and Action.* Upper Saddle River, N.J.: Prentice Hall, 1986.

p. 197   Social marketing: Kotler, P., and Roberto, E. *Social Marketing: Strategies for Changing Public Behavior.* New York: Free Press, 1989.

p. 197   Theory of Self-Change: Prochaska, J., Norcross, J., and DiClemente, C. *Changing for Good.* New York: Morrow, 1994.

p. 197   Spread projects:

Meteer, J., et al. "Global Improvement Initiatives." *Multinational Business Review,* Spring 2004, 12, 111–120.

Massoud, R., et al. *A Framework for Spread: From Local Improvement to System-Wide Change.* IHI Innovation Series White Paper. Cambridge, Mass.: Institute for Healthcare Improvement, 2006. (www.ihi.org)

Nolan K., et al. "Using a Framework for Spread: The Case of Patient Access in the Veterans Health Administration." *Joint Commission Journal on Quality and Patient Safety,* 2005, *31,* 339–347.

Nolan, K., and Schall, M. (eds.). *Spreading Improvement Across Your Healthcare Organization.* Joint Commission Resources, 2007.

p. 200   Attributes of an innovation: Rogers, E. *Diffusion of Innovations.*

p. 202   The case study on reducing returns to job sites because of damage to the customer's site was adapted from the work of Jeff Bangs of Topwright in Madison, Wis.

p. 202    The central line and other bundles are contained on the Institute for Healthcare Improvement's Website (www.ihi.org).

p. 206    Communication methods: Fraser, S. *Accelerating the Spread of Good Practice*. West Sussex, U.K.: Kingsham Press, 2002.

p. 207    Educational outreach: Avorn, J., and Soumerai, S. "Improving Drug Therapy Decisions Through Educational Outreach." *New England Journal of Medicine*, 1983, *308*, 1457–1463.

p. 207    Communities of practice: Wegner, E., McDermott, R., and Snyder W. *Cultivating Communities of Practice*. Boston: Harvard Business School Press, 2002.

p. 207    The collaborative method: Wilson, T., Berwick, D. M., and Cleary, P. D. "What Do Collaborative Improvement Projects Do?" Experience from Seven Countries." *Joint Commission Journal on Quality and Patient Safety*, 2003, 29, 85–93.

p. 208    Opinion leaders:

Lomas, J., et al. "Opinion Leaders vs. Audit and Feedback to Implement Practice Guidelines: Delivery After Previous Cesarean Section." *JAMA*, 1991, *265*, 2202–2207.

Soumerai, S. et al.: "Effect of Local Medical Opinion Leaders on Quality Care for Acute Myocardial Infarction: A Randomized Controlled Trial." *JAMA*, 1998, *279*, 1358–1363.

p. 210    Adopter categories: Rogers, E. *Diffusion of Innovations*.

p. 210    Diffusion curve: Bass, F. "A New Product Growth Model for Consumer Durables." *Management Science*, 1969, *13*, 215–227.

p. 212    Transition issues: Cool, K., Dierickx, I., and Szulanski, G. "Diffusion of Innovations Within Organizations: Electronic Switching in the Bell System, 1971–1982." *Organization Science*, 1997, *8*, 543–559.

p. 213    Knowledge management: Brown, J., and Duguid, P. "How to Capture Knowledge Without Killing It." *Harvard Business Review*, 2000, *78*, 73–80.

# Chapter Ten

p. 218    The three categories of improvement were adapted both from discussions with Noriaki Kano and from N. Kano, "Quality in the Year 2000: Downsize Through Reengineering and Up Size Through Attractive Quality Creation." Paper presented at American Society for Quality Control Conference, Las Vegas, Nevada, May 24, 1994.

p. 222    Technical Assistance Research Programs Institute (TARP) for the United States Office of Consumer Affairs. *Consumer Complaint Handling in America: An Update Study*. Arlington, Va.: TARP, 1986. TARP can be reached at (703) 524–1456. This study is an update of the original study conducted in 1979.

p. 223    Based on a system developed and used at the Supelco a facility of the SigmaAldrich Corporation.

p. 231    Kano has called this category Attractive Quality Creation.

p. 232    Feigenbaum, A. V. *Total Quality Control: Engineering and Management*. New York: McGraw-Hill, 1961. Feigenbaum discussed the different characteristics that form the composite concept of quality. The original list of dimensions of quality was proposed by David Garvin in an article entitled "Competing on the Eight Dimensions of Quality," *Harvard Business Review*, Nov. 1987, pp. 101–109. The list of fifteen dimensions is based on the work of Garvin and others.

p. 234    Kaplan, R. S., and Norton, D. P. "The Balanced Scorecard: Measures That Drive Performance," *Harvard Business Review*, Jan.–Feb. 1992, pp. 71–80.

p. 234    Reichheld, F. "The One Number You Need to Grow," *Harvard Business Review*, Dec. 2003.

# Chapter Eleven

p. 237    The authors are grateful to many individuals who contributed to our understanding of methods for improving large systems. Conversations with Jim Meteer, Phil Hansen, Larry Hummel, and Kevin Krosley were particularly helpful.

p. 238    For study of disruptive innovation, see Christensen, C. M., and Raynor, M. E. *The Innovator's Solution*. Boston: Harvard Business School Press, 2003.

p. 239    Kotter, J. S. *Leading Change*. Boston: Harvard Business Press, 1996.

p. 241    These questions were a result of an R&D project sponsored by the Institute for Healthcare Improvement in 2008.

p. 243    For further study of structures, see Galbraith, J., *Designing Organizations; An Executive Guide to Strategy, Structure, and Process*, San Francisco: Jossey-Bass, 2002; and Thompson, Fred, "Management Control and the Pentagon: The Strategy-Structure Mismatch," *Public Administration Review*, 1991, *51*(1), 52–66.

p. 247    Goldratt, E. *The Theory of Constraints*. Croton-on-Hudson, N.Y.: North River Press, 1990.

p. 250    Simon, H. A. *Administrative Behavior: A Study of Decision-Making Processes in Administrative Organizations*, 2nd ed. New York: Macmillan, 1957.

p. 250    Snowden, D. J., and Boone, M. E. *A Leader's Framework for Decision Making*. Harvard Business Review, 2007.

p. 251    http://www.dartmouthatlas.com.

p. 254    Boynton, R. S. *The New New Journalism*. New York: Vintage Books, 2005.

p. 254    Schrage, M. *Serious Play*. Boston: Harvard Business School Press, 2000.

p. 257    Discussions with Dr. Roger Resar were particularly helpful in formulating the concepts in this section.

# Chapter Twelve

p. 269    The authors wish to thank Bruce Boles for his knowledge and work in creating the no-fault-found case study.

p. 269   The planned experiment form is taken from Moen, R. D., Nolan, T. W., and Provost, L P. *Quality Improvement Through Planned Experimentation*, 2nd ed. New York: McGraw-Hill, 1999.

p. 273   The software used for this example is called Study-it and was developed by Jim Imboden of Virtual Chaos. This software is included in the book by Moen, Nolan, and Provost (1999) just cited.

p. 276   The authors wish to thank Dave Hearn for sharing the results of the drill experiment performed at his plant in Beaumont, Texas.

p. 290   The authors wish to thank Cincinnati Children's Hospital Medical Center for sharing their work on the Pediatric Intensive Care Unit (PICU) case study. This project won the Child Health Corporation of America 5th Annual RACE for Results completion in 2008. These were the key members of the improvement team:

Richard J. Brilli, M.D., medical director, PICU; Stefanie Newman, assistant vice president, Critical Care Administration; Derek Wheeler, M.D., associate medical director, PICU; Terry Palmisano, R.N., senior clinical director, PICU; Brandy Seger, RT, respiratory therapist; Mary Jo Giaconne, R.N., outcomes coordinator; Rosie Gibson, R.N., clinical nurse specialist; William Kent, senior vice president, Care Delivery (Cabinet Champion); Sarah Myers, MPH; Melinda Corcoran; Lloyd Friend; Jennifer Russell, MHSA, quality improvement consultants; Arthur Wheeler, data analyst; Nancy Hutchinson, R.N., infection control, senior executive. Contact Uma Kotagal, vice president, quality and transformation.

p. 291   *Relationship awareness theory*, 9th ed., Elias H. Porter, Personal Strengths Publishing, 1996. Also Strength Deployment Inventory (SDI) is a method to use Porter's theory. Contact Personal Strengths at http://personalstrengths.com.

p. 292   The authors wish to thank CareOregon for contributing their learning on the credentialing process. Sponsor: Peter McGarry; coach: Yedda Trawick; team leader: Kim Thomas; core team members: Rebecca Whetstine. Ann Blume. Jane Brail.

p. 305   *Out of the Crisis*, W. E. Deming. Cambridge, Mass.: MIT Press, 1986 (p. 315).

# Chapter Thirteen

p. 310   The chain reaction from improving value is adapted from Figure 1 in Deming, W. E. *Out of the Crisis*. Cambridge: Center for Advanced Engineering Study, Massachusetts Institute of Technology, 1986.

p. 310   The chain reaction for a government organization was suggested to us by A. Keith Smith.

p. 312   The information in the section "Building a System of Improvement" is based on material developed over the past twenty years by Associates in Process Improvement (API). The book *Quality as a Business Strategy* (Austin, Tex.: API, 1998) describes the philosophy and methods for making improvement the focus of an organization's business strategy. The elements of the strategy evolved from Deming's "Production as System," first presented by him in 1950. In the API system, five activities are led by the leaders of the organization to provide the structure to begin working on making quality a business strategy. These activities center around the purpose of the organization, viewing the organization as a system, obtaining information to improve, planning, and managing improvement. The five activities formed a system for the leaders of an organization to focus their learning, planning, and management of improvement.

The authors' experience with quality as a business strategy has been that it accelerates the pace at which organizations improve, and it reduces the chance that improvement will be a short-lived experience. The structure of the strategy, centered around the five activities, permits enough guidance to begin the process of building improvement into the fabric of the organization.

p. 312   Figure 13.3 is a modification of Deming's "Production Viewed as a System," from Deming, W. E., *Out of the Crisis.* Cambridge: Center for Advanced Engineering Study, Massachusetts Institute of Technology, 1986, p. 4.

p. 314   Deming, *Out of the Crisis.* For more on creating an environment conducive to improvement, see Chapter Fourteen in this volume.

p. 320   This has been referred to as the intelligence cycle. Search Wikipedia for more information about how national and military intelligence is gathered.

p. 322   Those familiar with the Japanese approach to strategic improvement will recognize this approach to setting priorities as Hoshin planning and the negotiation referred to as "catch ball."

p. 328   For more on the SBAR communication approach, see www.ihi.org/IHI/Topics/ PatientSafety/SafetyGeneral/Tools.


# Chapter Fourteen

p. 335   Many of the ideas related to development options came out of a meeting of the Global Quality Futures Workshop, GQFW, in Tokyo in September 2005.

p. 335   Noriaki Kano, a participant in the GQFW, suggested these four phases.

p. 338   Knowles, Malcolm. *The Adult Learner: A Neglected Species,* 4th. ed. Houston: Gulf, pp. 114–115.

p. 339   Joyce, Bruce R., and Showers, Beverly. *Student Achievement Through Staff Development: Fundamentals of School Renewal,* 2nd ed. White Plains, N.Y.: Longman, 1995.

p. 344   For study in this area, see *Quality by Design: A Clinical Microsystems Approach,* edited by Eugene C. Nelson, Paul B. Batalden, and Marjorie Godfrey. San Francisco: Jossey-Bass, 2007. Methods for building what is termed a "rich information environment" are discussed on pages 185–187.

p. 345   Pfeffer, Jeffrey, and Sutton, Robert I. *The Knowing-Doing Gap: How Smart Companies Turn Knowledge into Action.* Boston: Harvard Business School Publishing, 2000.

# Appendix A

The information in this resource guide came from hundreds of sources collected by the authors over the last twenty-five years. Many of the examples came from experiences with clients the authors have helped with improvement efforts. Many came from other sources, including newspapers, magazine articles, and stories told to the authors by friends and colleagues. Many of the change concepts have been presented individually in books and published papers on quality, marketing, industrial engineering, and social psychology. The importance of using concepts to get ideas for change came from Edward de Bono's work.

p. 358 Here are some references that have been useful in the research on the seventy-two change concepts presented in this resource guide.

Ackoff, Russell, L. *Creating the Corporate Future.* New York: Wiley, 1981.

Argyris, C., and Schön, D. *Organizational Learning: A Theory of Action Perspective.* Reading, Mass: Addison Wesley, 1978.

Bazerman, M. A. *Judgment in Managerial Decision Making.* New York: Wiley, 1990.

Davis, S. M. *Future Perfect.* Reading, Mass: Addison-Wesley, 1987.

de Bono, E. *Serious Creativity.* New York: HarperCollins, 1992.

de Bono, E. *Sur/Petition.* New York: HarperCollins, 1992.

Deming, W. E. *Out of the Crisis.* Cambridge: Center for Advanced Engineering Study, MIT, 1986.

Deming, W. E. *The New Economics*, 2nd ed. Cambridge: Center for Advanced Educational Services, MIT, 1994.

Goldratt, E., and Cox, J. *The Goal.* New York: North River Press, 1986.

Hall, R. W. *Attaining Manufacturing Excellence.* Irwin, Ill.: Dow Jones, 1987.

Imai, M. *Kaizen: The Keys to Japan's Competitive Success.* New York: Random House, 1986.

Joiner, B. *Fourth Generation Management.* New York: McGraw-Hill, 1994.

Juran, J. (ed.). *Quality Control Handbook* (3rd ed.). New York: McGraw-Hill, 1979.

Myers, D. G. *Social Psychology.* New York: McGraw-Hill, 1990.

Senge, P. M. *The Fifth Discipline.* New York: Doubleday/Currency, 1990.

Shewhart, W. *Economic Control of Quality of Manufactured Product.* New York: Van Nostrand (reprinted by the American Society for Quality Control, 1980).

Lewis, C. I. *An Analysis of Knowledge and Valuation.* Chicago: Open Court, 1946.

p. 408 Change concept 72: This change concept has its origin from practices by Toyota engineers. It was observed by a few engineers at General Motors who worked on joint projects with Toyota and researchers from University of Michigan who have been studying Toyota for more than twenty years. But because of Toyota's unique history and evolution (the Toyoda family, Japanese culture, and the decades of effective companywide learning), nobody was able to describe in a comprehensive way why the Toyota system is superior. They could see a whole gamut of Toyota methods for product development (simultaneous engineering, front-loaded product development process, leveled process flow, rigorous standardization of design, process, and engineering skills).

The book on product development at Toyota by Michael Kennedy, *Product Development for the Lean Enterprise,* from Oaklea Press, 2003, describes why Toyota's product development is four times more productive. Here are some of the quotes from this book that support change concept 72 (manage uncertainty, not tasks):

Chief engineer reviews status through prototypes and analysis, not completed tasks (p. 101).

Lots of prototyping and testing primarily to gain "live" knowledge required for decision making (p. 102).

At Toyota, all individuals are expected to learn what works and what doesn't. They don't have procedures on how to do things. They have documentation on actual design results, which everyone has access to and is expected to use (p. 104).

In a task-based environment (as opposed to Toyota being knowledge-based), traditional administrative project management is characterized by the counting of tasks completed as the primary focus of project reviews and a basic *measure of progress* (pp. 149–150).

# Appendix B

p. 409   Most of these tools and methods are described in detail (using these first five categories) in *The Improvement Handbook: Model, Methods, and Tools for Improvement,* Associates in Process Improvement, Austin, Tex., 2005. Other general references for the tools and methods are:

*Guide to Quality Control,* Kaoru Ishikawa, Asian Productivity Organization, 1982.

*Juran's Quality Handbook,* 5th ed., Joseph M. Juran and A. Blanton Godfrey (eds.). New York: McGraw-Hill, 1999.

*The Quality Toolbox,* 2nd ed., Nancy R. Tague, ASQ Quality Press, 2004.

p. 417   *How to Conduct Surveys,* Arlene Fink and Jacqueline Kosscoff, Newbury Park, Calif.: Sage, 1985, is a very practical book for specifics on designing and conducting surveys p. 477.

p. 419   Edward de Bono's ideas on creative thinking are the basis of our approach to innovation and methods of creativity. See de Bono, E. *Serious Creativity.* New York: HarperCollins, 1992. For a discussion of integrating creative methods in quality improvement efforts, see "Creativity and Improvement: A Vital Link," by Lloyd P. Provost and R. M. Sproul, *Quality Progress,* ASQC, Aug. 1996, pp. 101–107.

p. 436   *Process Quality Control,* Ellis Ott, New York: McGraw-Hill, 1975, has more information on run charts and rules for interpreting run charts.

p. 436   "Tables for Testing Randomness of Grouping in a Sequence of Alternatives," F. S. Swed and C. Eisenhart, *Annals of Mathematical Statistics,* 1943, *14,* pp. 66 and 87, Tables II and III.

p. 439   *The Visual Display of Quantitative Information,* Edward Tufte, Cheshire, Conn.: Graphics Press, 1998, has much more on developing excellent graphs.

p. 440    The methods of planned experimentation (or experimental design) are described in:
          *Quality Improvement Through Planned Experimentation,* Ronald Moen, Thomas Nolan, and
              Lloyd Provost, New York: McGraw-Hill, 2nd ed., 1999.
          *Experimental and Quasi-Experimental Designs for Research,* Donald Campbell and Julian
              Stanley, Boston: Houghton Mifflin, 1963.
p. 444    *The Toyota Way,* Jeffrey K. Liker, New York: McGraw-Hill, 2004, has a good description
              and example of the A3 report to summarize an improvement project.

# Appendix C

p. 455    The idea that improvement efforts do not follow a linear sequence is discussed in
          *Wicked Problems and Social Complexity,* Jeff Conklin, 2001–2003, CogNexus Institute,
              http://cognexus.org.
p. 456    Juran's universal sequence for quality improvement is discussed in Juran's *Quality
          Handbook,* 5th ed., J. Juran and A. B. Godfrey (eds.). New York: McGraw-Hill, 1999.
p. 457    The Six Sigma DMAIC framework is available many places. On the Web, www
              .isixsigma.com has presentations and discussions of this project framework. Other
              references are:
          Six Sigma for Green Belts and Champions: Foundations, DMAIC, Tools, Cases, and
              Certification, Howard S. Gitlow and David M. Levine, Upper Saddle River, N.J.:
              Prentice-Hall, 2004.
          "Use DMAIC to Make Improvement Part of 'The Way We Work.'" Quality Progress,
              Ronald D. Snee, Sept. 2007, pp. 52–54.
p. 458    "Design for 6-Sigma Demystified," Phong Vu and Kempton Smith, *Quality Digest,* 2005.
p. 458    The various Six-Sigma DFSS frameworks are discussed in *Design for Six Sigma,* Greg
              Brue, New York: McGraw-Hill Professional, 2003.
p. 459    The seven-step problem-solving model is described further in *The Problem-Solving
          Memory Jogger: Seven Steps to Improved Processes.* Salem, N.H.: GOAL/QPC, 2000.
p. 461    The FOCUS-PDCA framework is described in *Mentoring Strategic Change in Health Care:
          An Action Guide,* Chip Caldwell, 1995 ASQ, Milwaukee, 1995.
p. 461    The 8-D model is described in "Team Oriented Problem Solving," Eileen J. Beachell,
              Ford Motor Company, Detroit, 1987.
p. 462    Various forms of the Japanese quality story are described in these references:
          *Management at Work,* Mary Walton. New York: Putman, 1990.
          *Statistical Methods for Quality Improvement,* Kume, Hitoshi (trans. by John Loftus). Tokyo:
              Association for Overseas Technical Scholarship. ISBN 4–906224–34–2. Chapter
              10, 1985.
          *TQC Solutions: The 14-Step Process,* JUSE Problem Solving Research Group, Education
              Applications, Portland, Ore.: Productivity Press.
p. 463    This definition and other aspects of lean improvement are described in *Lean Thinking,*
              James P. Womack and Daniel T. Jones, New York: Simon & Schuster, 1996.

# Index